D1282853

ARISTOTLE ON COMEDY

Towards a reconstruction of *Poetics* II

ARISTOTLE

ON COMEDY

Towards a reconstruction of *Poetics* II

Richard Janko

University of California Press
Berkeley and Los Angeles

First published in 1984 by
University of California Press
Berkeley and Los Angeles

Library of Congress Cataloging in Publication Data

Janko, Richard, 1955-
  Aristotle on comedy.

  Bibliography: p.
  Includes index.
  1. Comedy.   2. Tractatus Coislinianus.   3. Aristotle –
Authorship.   I. Aristotle.   Poetics.   II. Title.
PN1924.J36   1984   808.2′523   84-2460
ISBN 0-520-05303-6

Typeset and Printed in Great Britain

Contents

μόνον γελᾷ τῶν ζῴων ἄνθρωπος

Aristotle

'Truth can only be found by the exclusion of untruth.'

A. Conan Doyle

'Books are not made to be believed, but to be subjected to enquiry.'

William of Baskerville

Acknowledgements

This book began to form in my mind when I was given the opportunity to lecture on Aristotle's *Poetics* at the University of St Andrews; when one evening the diligent undergraduates had borrowed all modern texts of the work, I was obliged to use von Christ's Teubner, wherein I first encountered the Tractatus Coislinianus. It is therefore to them, even if indirectly, that I owe the most, but I must also thank them and their counterparts at Cambridge for listening to my ideas and making me develop them further. My College, by electing me to a Research Fellowship in Classics, has given me the precious gift of time, time not only to round off a previous work but to complete this also. For providing a forum at which the central hypothesis could be subjected to expert scrutiny and criticism, I am most grateful to the organisers of the London seminars on Aristotle's *Rhetoric* and *Poetics*, Mr Myles Burnyeat and Prof. Richard Sorabji, and to all those who contributed to the discussion after my paper in January 1982, and indeed to the other seminars of the series.

The following have rendered me kind assistance, in conversation or correspondence, with regard to particular topics or sections of the work: Mr J. Barnes, Mr M.F. Burnyeat, Dr R.D. Dawe, Mr H.J. Easterling, Mrs P.E. Easterling, Prof. A. Gotthelf, Prof. R. Kassel, Dr A.J. Kenny, Dr Theodore Redpath, Prof. F. Rosenthal, Mr Leo Salingar, Dr R.W. Sharples and Dr Fritz Zimmermann. For reading large parts of the MS at various stages of illegibility and revision, and making comments that have contributed to the shape of the whole, as well as to individual sections, I am especially indebted to Prof. E.S. Belfiore, Prof. C.O. Brink, Dr C. Carey, Dr P.F. Hammond, Dr R.W. Jordan, Prof. G.S. Kirk, Mr D.A. Russell and Prof. F.H. Sandbach; it is from cautious and thorough critiques by the last two scholars in particular that the work has benefitted most of all. I would not wish it thought, in a matter so controversial, that the scholars just mentioned necessarily agree with my views either in detail or in essentials, and responsibility for them remains entirely mine.

Aristotle wrote with pen and ink on papyrus; this book about him has passed through an electric typewriter, a computer and a laser. I am most grateful to Mr Colin Haycraft for undertaking to publish a book so venturesome by so novel a method, at a time when technological innovation is hindering rather than helping the production of scholarly books which scholars can afford: the appearance of this one shows, I hope, a way forward by which proper standards — and reasonable prices — can be maintained, but it is certainly a laborious way for the author. For typing the MS I thank Valerie and Ed Piercy, and for substantial help with the computer typesetting and at every stage in the preparation of a difficult text I thank Dr John Dawson and the staff of the Literary and Linguistic Computing Centre, Cambridge, especially Yeshe Zangmo, and Mr Ian Marriott of Oxford University Computing Service. The Plates are reproduced by kind permission of the Bibliothèque Nationale, Paris and of the Biblioteca Nazionale Marciana, Venice.

Trinity College, Cambridge   R. J.
21 May 1982

Nos patriae finis et dulcia linquimus arva.

I wish to acknowledge a generous grant from the Columbia University Council for Research in the Humanities, which enabled me to return to Cambridge in May 1983 to complete the revision and production of this work. I also wish to thank Martin Secker and Warburg Ltd. and Harcourt Brace Jovanovich Inc. for permission to quote from *The Name of the Rose* by Umberto Eco, which came to my attention only after this book had attained its final form.

For help with final editing at OUCS I wish to thank Dr Ruth Glynn.

PART I

Introduction: the anonymous 'Treatise on Comedy'

Compared with W. von Christ's Teubner text of 1878, the 1965 Oxford text of the *Poetics* by R. Kassel reveals a great diminution in the material presented as the fragments of the lost Book II, in which Aristotle discussed comedy. This is due to Kassel's total omission of a document normally known by the name *Tractatus Coislinianus* after the Parisian codex (no. 120 in the de Coislin collection) from which Cramer first brought it to light in 1839.[1] This untitled and anonymous document has been variously hailed as the key to Aristotle's views on comedy and denounced as a sorry Byzantine fabrication. The prevailing view is rather negative: of those who have considered the matter at all, most have followed the authority of scholarship that is now somewhat dated, rather than looked at the matter afresh. But views of the *Poetics* itself are changing, and the time is thus ripe for a reopening of the debate on the Tractatus. Debate is to be expected, since I shall argue not only that the latter throws light both on controversial and on accepted views of the *Poetics*, but also that it is considerably closer to Aristotle than is usually thought.

1. The 'Tractatus Coislinianus'

In 1839 J.A. Cramer introduced the Treatise as follows:

'The words are, I believe, those of a commentator on Aristotle's treatise on the Art of Poetry, and are all the more noteworthy because the writer seems to have had a fuller text than that which has reached us, especially in the "analysis of humour".'[2]

In 1853 Jacob Bernays published his *Ergänzung zu Aristoteles' Poetik*, building on Cramer's remarks; this was to prove fundamental to the scholarly view of the Tractatus.[3] While arguing strongly that parts of it, especially the analysis of humour referred to by Cramer, do derive from Aristotle, he suggested that the rest was the product of an ignorant and yet pedantic and persistent compiler who used the *Poetics*, *Rhetoric* and *Nicomachean Ethics* to reconstruct the lost Book II. His essay was reprinted in *Zwei Abhandlungen über die aristotelische Theorie des Drama* (1880), and, in accord with the intellectual climate of the time, its more negative conclusions attracted much support. Kaibel summed up the view of many when he wrote that Bernays tried to prove Cramer's suggestion, 'with the result, however, that he showed that no small amount of extraneous and silly material is jumbled together with what is truly Aristotelian'.[4] Against the consensus,[5] only Baumgart in 1887 saw fit to protest: he pointed out that the sections condemned by Bernays were those which seemed to contradict his influential theory of catharsis.[6]

Apart from Baumgart's critique, various individual points in Bernays' indictment have been overturned by scholars who accept the whole, for example J. Kayser in 1906.[7] Meanwhile, others were adopting a different and fruitful line of approach, that of investigating the applicability of the section Περὶ τοῦ γελοίου to comedy, both Aristophanic and later. Arndt, Rutherford and Starkie[8] all concluded that this portion is genuinely Aristotelian, and a valuable analysis of the laughable; they refrained from passing judgement on the rest of the document.

Another possibility to be considered was that the Tractatus reflected the doctrines of Theophrastus rather than of Aristotle. In 1922 Rostagni initiated a line of research that was to reveal something of Theophrastean literary theory and its differences from Aristotle's, but his followers Plebe (1952) and especially Dosi (1960) have tended to underestimate these differences in their hunt for evidence.[9]

In 1922 Lane Cooper's book *An Aristotelian Theory of Comedy* also appeared. The exact title is to be noted; Cooper did not set out precisely to reconstruct what Aristotle thought, although he surveyed the evidence of Aristotle's acknowledged writings. On the Tractate he began by making some criticisms of the Bernaysian orthodoxy, but then refrains from pressing the attack:

'But I make no point of defending the Tractate on the ground that any large share of it is original. In it the hand of an unskilful adapter may have levied upon an earlier, more ample source, or more than one source . . . Parts of it may not ultimately derive from Aristotle; others may show an unintelligent use of the *Poetics*, or else a badly mangled tradition. But if in others there is a combination of materials from the *Poetics*, *Rhetoric* and *Ethics*, the adaptation has been made with skill. When all possible objections have been urged against the fragment, there remain certain elements in it that, we may contend, preserve, if not an original Aristotelian, at all events an early Peripatetic, tradition'

(op. cit. 13). He continues by defending parts of it, especially the analysis of humour, against which section the destructive critics have had least to say, and remarks on their generalising power. But Cooper avoids committing himself to the authenticity of the Tractate, and instead reconstructs an Aristotelian theory of comedy by translating the extant *Poetics* into comic terms, a speculative and hazardous as well as stimulating venture. In a lengthy appendix (227—286) he amplifies the Tractatus with copious illustration and discussion, producing more arguments against Bernays; however, desirous of writing a book intelligible to the Greekless reader, he employs translations throughout, and any defence of the Tractatus' authenticity must begin with its Greek text. One suspects that it was this desire, rather than any lack of conviction, that prevented him from trying to vindicate the Tractate as Aristotelian; he did, after all, devote sixty pages to it.

Subsequently, the Tractatus has been largely ignored. Writers on ancient literary criticism, such as D'Alton,[10] Atkins,[11] Duckworth,[12] Plebe,[13] Grube,[14] Fuhrmann[15] and Russell[16] still continue to follow Bernays; Cantarella[17] rejects both the Tractatus and the idea of a second book; scholars of the *Poetics* are either non-committal, like Else,[18] as negative as Bywater, like Kassel, or entirely silent, like D.W. Lucas or Gallavotti.[19] So too writers on comedy, such as Feibleman,[20] Swabey,[21] or Gurewich.[22]

Despite the extent of the discussion, there is no shortage of
questions which remain to be properly formulated and investiga-
ted. Both the external and the internal evidence for the Tractate's
date and origin require fresh scrutiny. Is it a compilation, an
epitome or an epitome of a compilation? How does it relate to some
passages in the *Prolegomena to Comedy* that seem very similar? Are
these fuller passages Byzantine re-expansions of the Tractatus, as is
the standard view, or do they represent extracts from its more
complete source? Regarding its date, is it a purely Byzantine
concoction, or is it indeed Peripatetic, or does it represent some
mixture of the two? If Peripatetic, is it connected with the studies of
the first century before Christ associated with Andronicus of
Rhodes, as has been suggested? Or with Theophrastus? Or with
Aristotle himself, and in particular with *Poetics* II?

Then there are literary questions. What exactly does it say about
comedy? Indeed, with what kind of comedy is it concerned? Is
what it says sensible? Or original? Does it provide a useful analysis
of the comedy it describes? Is this analysis of any lasting value for
comedy in all the Protean disguises she has assumed since Classical
Greece?

Hae nugae seria ducunt.

2. The Manuscripts

It is usual in an edition with commentary to delay the technical
details of how the text reached us. Here, as the work is unfamiliar,
it is better to give its sources first, especially as they may throw
light on its origin, and supply a text and translation, before
discussing the nature of the Treatise on Comedy and what can be
learnt from it. I shall employ this title to denote the whole
constituted by the *Tractatus Coislinianus* and other sources here to be
delineated and compared, although sometimes during the commentary I may refer to it by the more convenient name of the
Tractate, as the MS Coislinianus is after all the paramount source.

2.1 MS Parisinus Coislinianus 120 (C)

The sole source of the *Tractatus Coislinianus* is MS no. 120 in the de Coislin Collection of the Bibliothèque Nationale in Paris. It is assigned by R. Devreesse[23] and other authorities[24] to the early tenth century. Little is known of its history before 1643, when it was sent to Séguier from Cyprus by Father Athanasios Rhetor, whose signature it bears; but it once belonged to the monastery of the Great Lavra on Mount Athos, *c.* 1218. The parchment measures 300 × 206 mm., with 263 folios and 31 lines to the page.

The MS consists of two parts, in very similar if not identical hands — good clear early minuscule, written *above* the ruled lines, and closely comparable to that of such datable MSS as Vaticanus Graecus 1, 90 and 204.[25]

(i) The first contains patristic extracts (fol. 1 — 229v.; 114 missing). A date is supplied by a list of patriarchs of Constantinople, ending with Nicolas for the second time, A.D. 911 — 925 (fol. 228v.). The last folio (229) breaks off in a list of Roman Emperors with Pertinax, and is badly worn, which suggests that it once concluded a separate volume.

(ii) The second part comprises Aristotelian extracts, summaries and commentaries (fol. 230 — 261, including 246a), in the following order:

(a)   An abstract of part of Porphyry's 'Introduction to Aristotle's Categories' (*Isagoge*). This is untitled and opens in mid-sentence (fol. 230r. — 231r.).[26]

(b)   Extracts from David the Philosopher's commentary on Porphyry's *Isagoge*, again untitled (fol. 231r. — 238r.).[27]

(c)   Another commentary on Porphyry's *Isagoge* by one Theodore, entitled Σύντομα ἀπὸ φωνῆς Θεοδώρου ἢ εἰσαγωγή· τὸ δὲ ἐπίσταλμα 'Ιωάννου (fol. 238r. — 240v.).[28]

(d)   An abstract of syllogisms and logical schemata from Aristotle's *Analytica Priora* I 4 — 5, untitled:[29] inserted into the first schema (fol. 241r., 247r. — 248v.) is the following item:

(e) (Pseudo-) Andronicus Peripateticus, *On the emotions* I—II (fol. 241v.—247r.), entitled Ἀνδρονίκου Περιπατητικοῦ περὶ παθῶν.[30]

(d) After the first schema, and before the rest of the abstract from the *Analytica Priora* I 4—5 (fol. 249v.—252r.), we find:

(f) An abstract on comedy, the *Tractatus Coislinianus*, anonymous, untitled,[31] fol. 248v.—249v.

(d) The rest of the abstract from the *Prior Analytics*, as stated above.

(b) More extracts from David's commentary on Porphyry, again untitled (fol. 252v.—261v.).[32]

This portion of the MS reflects the philosophical learning of the sixth century. It is the work of one hand, and corrections in a second are very sparse indeed; none occur in the Tractatus. Not only is this MS, or its exemplar, damaged at both ends, but the pieces are copied in an order which indicated to Devreesse that the exemplar was badly jumbled. The jumble seems to be due to the sequence of folios and quires in the exemplar, but it is difficult to unravel precisely what has happened. At least we can argue that if the epitome was made when C was written, there is no reason why the scribe should not have waited and copied it without interrupting his work. It is much better to suppose that our knowledge of the Tractatus results from a loose leaf or leaves, whether from the codex of Aristotelian abstracts from which the remainder was copied, or, less likely, from elsewhere, which was reinserted in the wrong place, and copied mechanically in the erroneous order.

The scribe has been somewhat careless.[33] Accentual errors and incorrect breathings abound: punctuation is erratic. The content of the Treatise was clearly unfamiliar, and its terminology is badly corrupted. Vowel-confusions are common: *Tract.* X ὕλη for εἴδη, XI σύστασην for -ιν, XVII 3 χορικόν for -ῶν, XVIII μεμηγμένη for μεμιγμένη. Letters are omitted: μιμητ<ικ>ή II, ὁμωνυμί<αν> V 1. Words are lost: οὐ III, τὰ VI 8, οὐκ XVI (?). There are changes in grammatical agreement: note in IV γελοίου, τελείου, and the certain error ἑκάστου for ἑκάστῳ; also my emendation αὐτῶν for αὐτοῦ in XIV. Other errors are ἐπαγγελτικόν for ἀπ- in II, παραινοῦσα for περαίνουσα III, δυναστου for δυνατοῦ VI 4, προσαπα for πρόσωπα VI 6, φαυλοτητα for φαυλότατα VI 8 (mediated by haplography in μέγιστα <τὰ> φαυλότατα), χυρικόν for χορικόν XVII.

I have noted only one error partially due to uncial letter-forms, namely ὕλη in X for εἴδη. It is interesting that in this word the scribe used capitals as if suddenly aware that it is a heading, which suggests that he was copying an exemplar entirely in capitals (inf. on X); but note also that the error προσαπα (VI 6) may be owed to confusion of minuscule ω with α. Thus it is not clear whether MS C is the first transcription of the material it contains into minuscule, from an exemplar three or more centuries old. Despite his superficial carelessness, however, its anonymous scribe is honest and deserving of much gratitude.

An unexplained feature is the scribe's irregular application of a large sigma, for σημείωσαι ('n.b.'), and/or a dash (*paragraphus*) to many of the sections.[34]

The form of the Tractatus, with its schematic representation and family trees, is unfamiliar. The précis is what we expect: the précis is common, not only of philosophical but also of literary treatises, e.g. that on tragedy ascribed to Michael Psellus of the eleventh century (cf. inf. on XVII): but the diagrammatic form of the schemata is known in a number of epitomes of Aristotelian logical works in late MSS,[35] and also in Stephanus' Commentary on the *Rhetoric*, I 9 (1366a27), II 21 (1394a27−b7), al.,[36] where the parts of πίστις and γνώμη are given in stemmatic format. The alternatives are:

(a) that the Tractate originated in the sixth century or thereabouts, in accord with the sixth-century origin of most of the material in the latter part of MS C. But by the same token one might argue that the nearby treatise of 'Andronicus Rhodius' shows that it was made in the late Republic or early Empire. Yet interest in Aristophanes was increasing in the fourth and fifth centuries A.D., as we know from quotations and papyrus finds.[37]

(b) that it originated in the ninth century, when Photius was compiling his epitomes, or early tenth. Little interest seems to have been taken in Greek poetry by Photius or Arethas,[38] and the revival of its study came in the second quarter of the tenth century. However, this is not relevant, since the Tractatus was transmitted in a philosophical rather than a literary context. But sound evidence proves that it was transmitted in epitomised format (and

was therefore not made by the scribe of C), notably the lateral
displacement of subheadings in section I,[39] and the reversals of
headings in VI 1 − 2 caused by the recopying of a marginal
insertion sideways on.[40] The probably majuscule error διδόμενον for
ᾀδόμενον[41] in **d** (below) suggests that an epitome of XVII existed in
majuscule; although it cannot be conclusively proved that such an
epitome was also ancestral to the Tractate as a whole, it is an
economical hypothesis that it was. No text of this kind would have
been created much after A.D. 600, when interest in such questions,
and copying too, reached a very low ebb indeed, so the archetypal
epitome is likely to go back to late antiquity at least: a sixth
century origin does seem the most probable.

2.2 Extracts in the Prolegomena to Aristophanes

Two portions of the Treatise are also found in other versions of the
same material — the analysis of the laughable (Tractate V − VI)
and the quantitative parts of comedy (XVII).[42] These are preserved primarily amongst introductory matter in MSS of Aristophanes.

(i) The analysis of the laughable

A more complete version of portions of this survives in more than
one source. It does not correspond exactly to MS C, and lacks the
last seven kinds of 'laughter from things', but clearly derives from
the same origin.[43] The sources are:

(a) The anonymous *Prolegomenon to Comedy* VI Koster (entitled
simply ἄλλως περὶ κωμῳδίας: siglum, **a**). This fragment first occurs
in Venetus Marcianus 474 (V), dating from the eleventh or twelfth
centuries, and then in other MSS of Aristophanes. Koster in his
Introduction discusses the tradition at length; his conclusions are
widely accepted. The reader is referred to his work for accounts of
the individual MSS. The main recensions are those of V and E's
family η (for sigla, cf. inf. p.20f.), from which Triclinius made two
distinct recensions: in that based on V (siglum Ps) he also used
another tradition, represented by $N^1ΘM$ (which I call μ), and a
third as well, which survives in U. The stemma resulting from

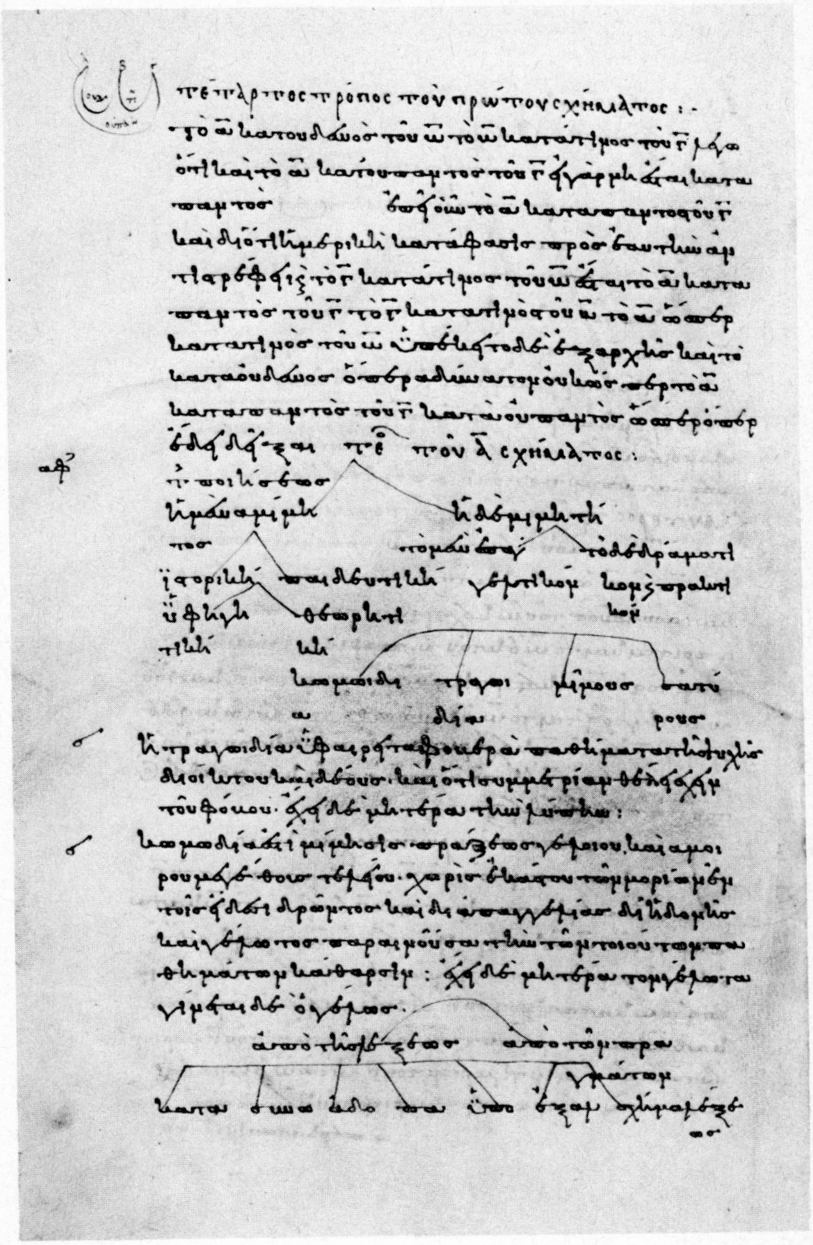

Plate 1. MS Parisinus Coislinianus 120 (C), fol. 248v.:
Tractatus I—V. (Photo. Bibl. Nat., Paris)

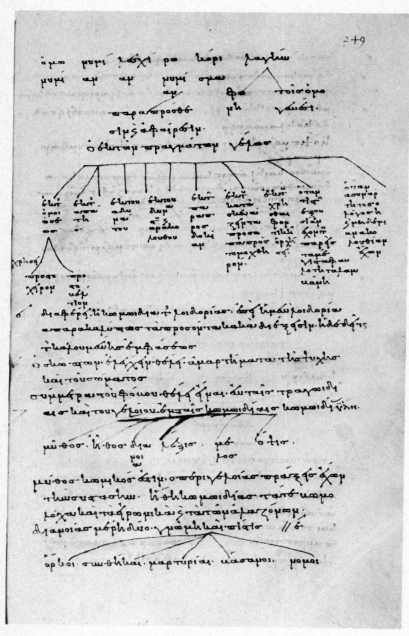

Plate 2. MS Parisinus Coislinianus 120 (C), fol. 249r.:
Tractatus V — XIII. (Photo. Bibl. Nat., Paris)

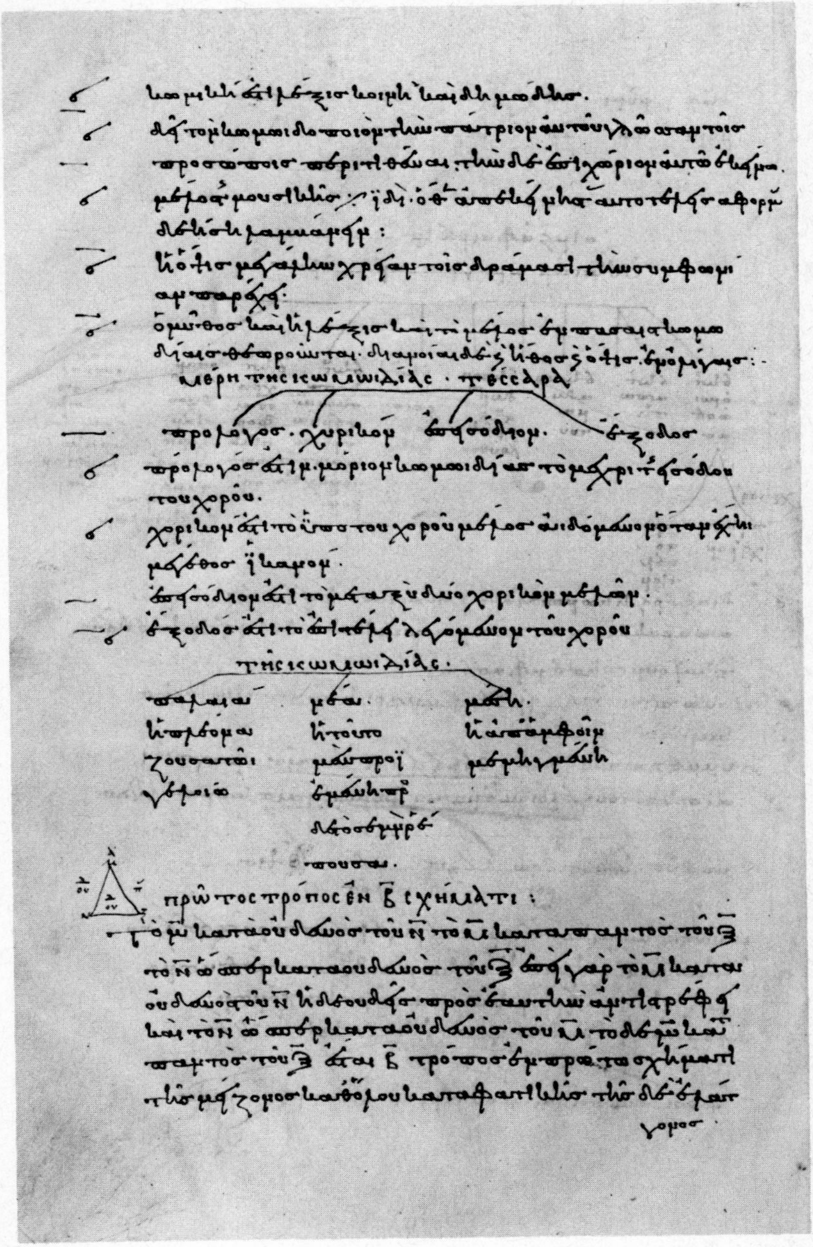

Plate 3. MS Parisinus Coislinianus 120 (C), fol. 249v.:
Tractatus XIV—XVIII. (Photo. Bibl. Nat., Paris)

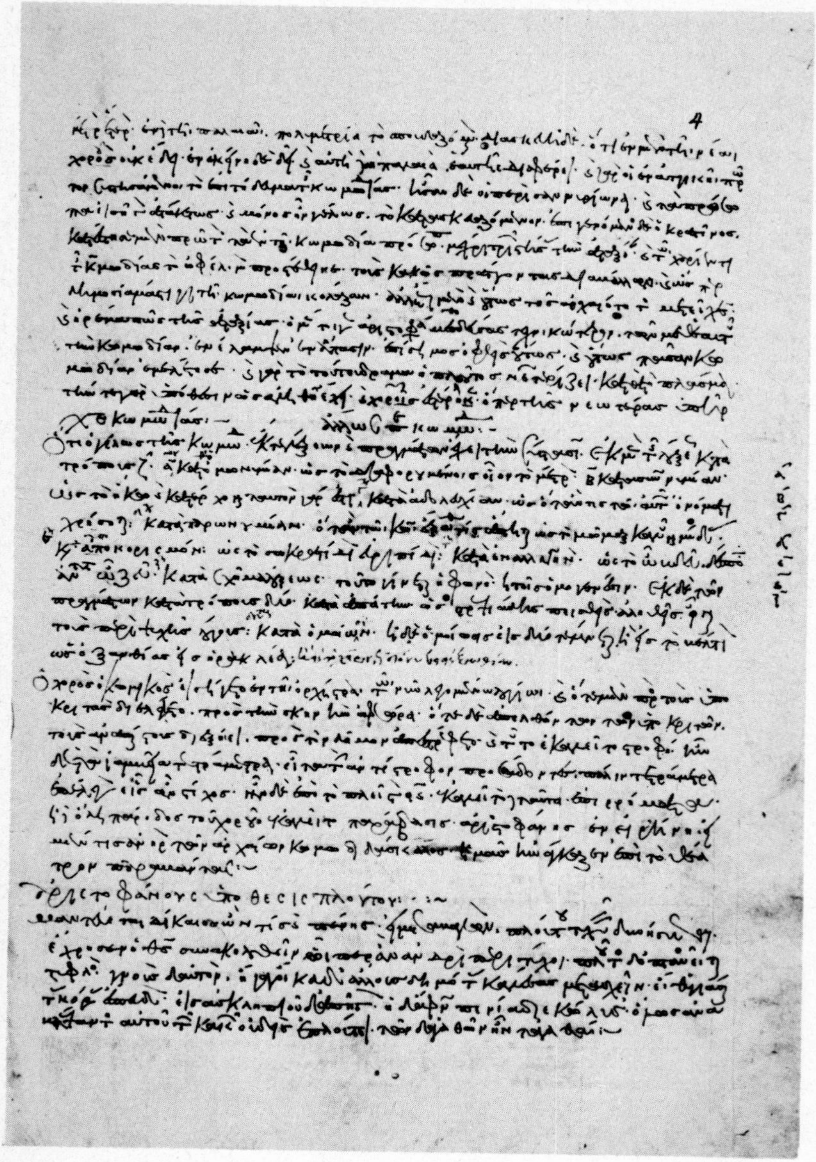

Plate 4. MS Venetus Marcianus 474 (V), fol. 4r.:
Prolegomenon VI. (Photo. Bibl. Naz. Marc., Venice)

Koster's arguments looks something like this (Tr^2 is reconstructed from its descendants, with Laur eliminated as a copy of Vat;[44] the date of V is controversial, but it certainly need not postdate Tzetzes[45]):

date
(approx.)

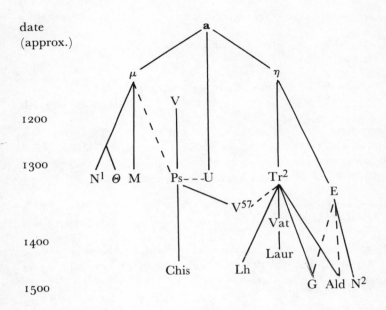

The archetype was perhaps in minuscule: note its errors μώμαξ for βώμαξ, ψυχῆς for ψύλλης (*Tract.* V 4a, VI 1).

(b) The anonymous Prolegomenon XIb Koster, the 'Anonymus Crameri' (siglum: **b**), first occurs in Parisinus 2821 (Reg) of the fourteenth century, which Koster[46] has shown is the archetype for other copies. It occurs in two families, **r** and **m**; the latter contains only worthless conjectures and easy improvements.

b is a compilation with scholarly pretensions from various sources.[47] An extract from the scholia to Dionysius Thrax (XVIIIa 1 – 39 Koster) precedes others resembling XVIIIb4, b1 Koster, mixed with parts of *Prolegomenon* IV: *Prolegomena* V and VI conclude the work. Koster has shown that **b** contains readings from both Triclinian recensions (Koster's numeration):

IV 18 κωμῳδία μAld, κωμῳδοί PsV⁵⁷Chis   XIb 38 κωμῳδοί **b**
V 19 πράττοντας VEUV⁵⁷Tr²GAld, πράσσ- PsChis:
                                      XIb 68 πράσσ- **r**
VI 6 ὅταν cett., ὡς ὅταν PsChisG   XIb 72 ὡς ὅταν **b**
VI 12 Ἡρακλέα cett., Ἡρακλῆν PsChis   XIb 79 Ἡρακλῆν **r**

These reveal an affinity with the first recension; one reading betrays the second:

V 18 προστέθεικε VEUPsV⁵⁷Chis, προσέθηκε Tr²:
                                      XIb 69 προσέθηκε **b**

Agreements with other MSS as well as with Triclinius' first recension at *Prol.* VI 2 διαφορουμένοις, 3 om. δὲ, 8 ἐναλλαγήν, and with others besides Tr² at V 20 οὗτος, VI 6 μώμαξ, are no proof of independence of Triclinius. Similarly trivial are:

VI 1 ὅτι ὁ cett., ὁ δὲ M   XIb 67 ὁ δὲ **b**
VI 6 τις cett., τι EᵃᶜN²G   XIb 73 τι **b**

The latter is an easy and false correction, the former a consequence of running the Prolegomena together. The special features distinguishing **b** from **a** are these:

VI 2 τῆς λέξεως **a**:   XIb 68 τῶν λέξεων **b** (a new error)
VI 3 οἷον τὸ μέτρον **a** (an example of homonymy):
                       XIb 69 σημαίνει γὰρ τό τε διαφόροις οὖσι
                       καὶ τὸ ἐπικερδέσι **b** (an elucidation of
                       διαφορουμένοις)
VI 5 χρήσηται cett., -σηται ex ? Ps, -σεται ΘV⁵⁷Chis (s.v.l.):
                       XIb 72 χρήσαιτο **b** (an error, correcting -σεται?)
VI 6 ἅπτηται cett., καθάπτηται Chis:
                       XIb 73 καθηται superscr. τά Reg,
                       κατάθηται cett., (an error, deriving from
                       καθ[άπτ]ηται?)

The major change is the omission of the difficult words οἷον τὸ μέτρον in favour of a lucid gloss on διαφορουμένοις: the others are worthless. In view of all we have seen, it seems unlikely that this change has any authority, and Koster is right to argue that this is true of this section of the Anonymus Crameri as a whole.

(c) John Tzetzes' *Iambi on comedy* (XXIb Koster: siglum, Tz) 68—81, composed in the twelfth century, incorporate part of *Prolegomenon* V and most of *Prolegomenon* VI. These are curtailed: V 4—11 corresponds to 69—75 in the poem, but the rest is omitted, except that πλάσμα at V 25 is picked up by Tzetzes in line 76, and V 26 χορῶν ἐστέρηται is perhaps picked up by χορῶν ἀποτρέχει at line 75. There is also an echo of the end of *Prolegomenon* IV, on laughter as the σκοπός of comedy, in τὸ τοῦ σκοποῦ at 76. Similarly, from *Prolegomenon* VI, Tzetzes mentions verbal laughter alone in terms of specific sub-types, although πλάσμα is an unhelpful garbling of the πράγματα of the *Prolegomenon*. In both cases Tzetzes simply does not trouble to complete the versification of all the items, unless he was using a more condensed version than has come down to us. Now in the types of humour he supplies two items absent from all versions of the *Prolegomenon* — parody and catachresis (metaphor). At first one is naturally inclined with Koster to suspect Tzetzean misremembering and misinterpretation of paronymy and σχῆμα λέξεως respectively. But in fact parody and metaphor are sorely desired in an Aristotelian analysis of laughter, as references in Aristotle indicate; I can show that some words in **a** and C, otherwise obscure, make sense if they once belonged to metaphor; and the loss of two main headings will explain difficulties over paronymy and its parts. But more on this later: for the present it suffices to say that, were these items not in Tzetzes, we would have supplied them: Tzetzes himself could not have made such a supplement. The loss of these items in a lacuna affecting both the Tractate and **a** is inescapable. Further evidence that Tzetzes had access to lost material is his statement that content and diction aim to introduce ἡδονὴν κωμῳδίαις | καὶ τὸν γέλωτα (77f.): **a** refers to γέλως alone. Now this phrase occurs in the scholia to Dionysius Thrax (XVIIIb4 Koster), which Tzetzes uses elsewhere but not otherwise in this poem; it also occurs in Tractate IV, just preceding the section covered by **a**. He *could* have drawn on the scholia solely for this phrase, but it seems even less likely when we add his equally apposite use of the word ἐσχηματισμένον at 79 (inf. p.163) and the similarities to Tractatus VII in his prose Prolegomenon XIaI (inf. p.207). There are now hints that he knew something like Tractatus IV, V and VII.

If he is quoting correctly, we expect him to be drawing on a source different from **a**; yet he renders *Prolegomena* V and VI in sequence, just as we find them in two branches of **a**, namely V and η. After excerpting VI he proceeds to Xb on scolia; the order VI, Xb is limited in our tradition to μ, which lacks *Prolegomenon* V entirely. Either he used more than one MS, or he had one much fuller than any that survives. Since both C and **a** have the lacuna, Tzetzes' material must derive, albeit indirectly, from a different branch of the tradition. In the stemma below (p.18) I postulate two streams of transmission from the archetype Ω, one lacunose, Λ, the other more complete, Ξ; the branch of **a** affected by Ξ is labelled ξ.

The excerption of **a** presumably occurred at the time when the scholia to Aristophanes were being compiled from different sources, in particular from separate *hypomnemata* or commentaries; the use of different sources is confirmed by the term ἄλλως in its title, as often in the scholia. There are two possible dates for this compilation — late antiquity, or the ninth century as urged by Zuntz.[48] The prior epoch seems more likely than formerly, in view of recent evidence, even if the process continued later.[49] Bernays suggested that **a** is a Byzantine re-expansion of the Tractate's headings: the 'compiler' explained some of the terms and supplied examples drawn from Aristophanes, then a very popular writer. This is *a priori* unlikely, and ruled out by the two or more otherwise unknown comic fragments among the examples; we now know that the present selection of Aristophanes' eleven plays was already made *de facto* by the fourth century A.D., as Athenaeus is the last writer to quote from the whole range of his plays, and papyrus discoveries confirm.[50] Far from being expanded, **a** is compressed and summarised, as will become evident. This material was used, like the scholia, with some liberty by copyists; normally only simple paraphrase is added, while abbreviation occurs at will, and there is no reason to think that any expansion has occurred in **a**.

That Tzetzes should have had access to a version of **a** superior to ours accords with his knowledge of a manuscript or manuscripts of Aristophanes now lost to us, as evidenced by his own scholia.[51]

(ii) *The parts of comedy*

Chapter XVII of the Tractate reappears in more than one source. Unfortunately all but one are purely secondary, and even that provides no new information save on the history of the text.

(a) *Prolegomenon* Xd Koster (siglum: **d**) is found among matter prefatory to Aristophanes in V, G, E and the Aldine, and also in Rs, an idiosyncratic MS of the early fourteenth century.[52] G probably descends from V, the Aldine from E, and Rs stands alone (so Koster).

d is a very brief extract, opening with the question 'how many are the parts of comedy?' It is untitled, anonymous and less detailed than the Tractate, from which it could be an apograph, but for the likelihood that it derives not from a minuscule MS like C but from one in majuscule, since it has the frequent majuscule error διδόμενον for ᾀδόμενον in C.[53] **d** also appends the comment that it has been stated how many parts of the parabasis there are, and that the parabasis belongs to the choral part of comedy. However, this is far less significant than at first appears, since these parts are given in another nameless and brief paragraph, *Prolegomenon* Xa Koster, which in all MSS except Rs precedes **d**. This is simply a reference back to another extract drawn from a different source; the collector of excerpts is providing us with a convenient cross-reference, nothing more.

Thus **d** presents a condensed version of the material in C, drawn from a common ancestor (τ), an epitome. That the Tractate was copied in epitomised state at least once is clear from C's dislocations of subheadings (sup. p.8).

The question-and-answer format of **d** does not help us to date it. Designed for the school-room, this format (ἐρωτηματαπόκρισις) is already current in the Roman Empire, and incipient in Dionysius Thrax.[54] It is used on an especially large scale in an anonymous treatise on rhetoric, *Prolegomenon Sylloge* 6B Rabe, e.g. p.61.13 πόσα εἴδη τῆς ῥητορικῆς; γ' . . . This is definitely a reworking for school use of the more standard introductions elsewhere in Rabe, and **d** may be of like origin.

(b) In Tzetzes' *Iambi on Comedy* and his prose *Prolegomenon to Comedy* I (XIaI Koster) we find passages similar to Tractate XVII and to **d**, but always closer to the latter than to the former, e.g. in omitting the qualification of size for a choral song. Moreover, the *Iambi* are closer than is the prose essay.[55]

The order in which Tzetzes' *Iambi* draw on the pre-existing *Prolegomena* is Xd, VII, Xa; V, VI, Xb. His own *Prolegomenon* XIaI has extracts from the following *Prolegomena*: Schol. Dion. Thr. XVIIIa: Xd, VII, Xa. Note the consistent order Xd, VII, Xa. The order Xd, Xa (but without VII) is limited to Rs in the tradition; whether or not the change is due to Tzetzes, the sequence is certainly more logical. Tzetzes' source had a lacuna in the first and second parts of the parabasis, just as does Xa in all our MSS; the scholard's efforts to tidy up the grammar, in both his verse and his prose versions, have left the anomaly that only the first and third parts are enumerated, while the second is not. His relation to **d** is similar: in place of its corrupt definition of the choral element, χορικὸν τὸ τοῦ χοροῦ διδόμενον μέλος, his *Prolegomenon* XIaI 108 Koster offers correct grammar but an absurd meaning — ἡ δὲ ἅμα τῇ εἰσόδῳ τοῦ χοροῦ λεγομένη ῥῆσις μέλος καλεῖται χοροῦ (the *Iambi* offer τὸ τοῦ χοροῦ μέλος δὲ δεύτερον λέγω, which betrays nothing). Tzetzes is trying to improve the text. Other divagations in the prose *Prolegomenon* are probably his own also. He avoids the adjective χορικός, replacing it in the definition with μέλος χοροῦ, and, in discussing the episode, with χορός, which is not to be emended away. The choral song is defined as the ῥῆσις λεγομένη upon the chorus' entry; similarly the episode is the λόγος between choral μέλη and ῥήσεις, and the exodos is the ῥῆσις spoken by the chorus at the end. The emphasis on speech at the expense of song marks a deliberate restatement.

There are fewer divagations in the *Iambi*, which were written earlier.[56] These are so close to **d** that they are clearly taken therefrom. The verses omit any reference to ῥῆσις as well as the preliminary list of four parts, and supply ordinal numerals, exactly as does **d**. They have at most no more authority for **d** than one of its subordinate manuscripts, and, as in fact they add nothing to our knowledge, can be disregarded. It is hard to tell from what kind of MS Tzetzes knew **d**, but he has none of the absurd errors of Rs, while sharing an easy error with VRsG:

Xa 2 ἀψῖδος EAld, ἀψίδος VRsG:

Tzetzes XXIb 36, XIaI 126 ἀψίδος
There is no reason to suppose that his prose *Prolegomenon* here reflects any other source than the verse *Iambi*: Tzetzes merely recast his own juvenilia into prose, without, as was so often his misfortune, having his source to hand. The prose *Prolegomenon* can be discounted as an independent source for **d**.

However, although Tzetzes has been cut down to size, we are not yet finished with him. In all direct sources for **d** including Tzetzes' *Iambi*, and in those for *Prolegomenon* Xa on the parts of the parabasis, there is no indication of origin or authorship: but in *Prolegomenon* XIaII 53 − 5 Tzetzes names Euclides, Crates and Dionysius as sources for the parts of comedy, as well as for those of the parabasis. Included also in this ascription is a section of *Prolegomenon* VII, excerpted at XIaI 119ff. At 137 he complains that ἐπίρρημα is used in several different senses, without realising that *Prolegomena* VII and Xa are of different origins. He specifically refers to this passage in a scholium to Aristophanes' *Plutus* 253, and names the sources as Dionysius of Halicarnassus, Euclides and Crates: they are οἱ διδάξαντες περὶ κωμῳδίας. As usual, he vehemently disagrees with them. Thus this trio are, in his view, the authors of *Prolegomena* Xd, VII and Xa. But these Three Wise Men did not restrict themselves to comedy: Tzetzes attacks them in a colourful stream of abuse for the (absurd) view that Euripides' *Orestes* and *Alcestis* and Sophocles' *Electra* are satyr-plays (*Prol.* XIaI 151, II 58; the idea is found in the second hypothesis to the *Alcestis*, where the *Orestes* is compared). But all these references are in his later writings. In the *Iambi* Euclides and company survive unmentioned (although 'their' material is used) until the poem on Tragedy (XXIc Koster), where Euclides often and Crates once only are named.[57] A prose fragment of the source for the views of 'Euclides' on tragedy is known (Cramer, *Anecd. Par.* I 19f.): reading it, one suspects that it derives from the Roman Empire (v. p.239f.). Who exactly Euclides was, is mysterious: whether it was the same man who discussed *Iliad* A 5 according to the BT scholia is unknowable. Even his existence is doubted by Koster,[58] who thinks him a fiction intended to bolster Tzetzes' authority, comparing other passages in Tzetzes and a similar procedure in Eustathius. Certainly Dionysius of Halicarnassus and Crates[59] make infinitesimal sense as a pair, and one is at first inclined to suspect that

they were merely seized upon as appropriate names, just as the
treatise *On the Sublime* is ascribed to Dionysius *or* Longinus in two of
its three MS rubrics: it is by neither, and solely from the foggy
union of two such non-authors did the ludicrous centaur 'Dionysius
Longinus' come to birth. Another example is the ascription of a
paragraph on comedy to an Andronicus, which is in fact a pseudepigraph by Palaeocappa.[60] But if we are charitable to Tzetzes, as
merits his amiable buffoonery, it still appears suspicious that he sees
fit to refer to Euclides and Crates in the poem on tragedy only (line
147), while his criticism of the ideas on comedy, which he later
ascribes to Euclides, is very restrained; only in the poem on tragedy
does he increase his vociferocity. Moreover, if Euclides composed
the elaborate division of tragedy into ten parts, one would expect
him to have done a better job on comedy to match. Thus I believe
that the name Euclides ought genuinely to attach only to the
analysis of tragedy, and that he was originally not connected with
comedy at all: but this scholiast on tragedy has been stretched by
Tzetzes in his sloppy later work to embrace the anonymous writers
of *Prolegomena to Comedy* too. Koster was right to think Euclides an
irrelevance. The presence of Crates and Dionysius is most readily
explained if Euclides quoted them, as Gudeman suggested.[61]

(c) The third possible source is *Prolegomenon* XIc Koster (the
'Anonymus Crameri II'), of which the author's MS still exists: it is
Estensis a.U.9.22, fifteenth century (M[9]). The same man created
recension **m** of *Prolegomenon* XIb, also in M[9]. Koster[62] proved from
shared errors that he was dependent on MS Amb of Tzetzes' prose
Prolegomena. He adds some new details, however, which deserve
examination in case they are the result of contamination with a
better source. First, he states that the parts of comedy are given
'according to Dionysius and Crates and Euclides'. Koster[63] says
that the Anonymous has anticipated this reference, which belongs
only to the parts of the parabasis in Tzetzes. At XIaI 111 Tzetzes
does introduce them as the authorities for these parts only, when he
has already dilated on the parts of comedy as a whole; but in fact
the compiler is right, because at XIaII 53−5 Tzetzes ascribes *both*
sections to this trio. The alteration demands no knowledge apart
from that of both Tzetzes' *Prolegomena*, knowledge which the
compiler certainly possessed. Second, he fills the lacuna of the first
and second parts of the parabasis; and correctly (XIc 66 Koster).

His supplement is in the margin of the autograph MS M^9: his knowledge of the *kommation* clearly derives from scholarly sources outside the *Prolegomena* to comedy, most probably Hephaestion, *Poem.* 9.2, and does not require us to postulate access to a fuller source in which the lacuna was absent. Thus we can disregard XIc entirely, since it has no independent value for **d**.

(iii) *Conclusions*

(a) Chapters V—VI 2 of the Tractate survive in a fuller version **a** (*Prolegomenon* VI Koster) excerpted along with the scholia to Aristophanes. This exists in four lines, μ, U, η and V. Triclinian recensions of **a** were used to compile *Prolegomenon* XIb in the fourteenth century; this almost certainly has no independent authority. Like C, **a** has a lacuna, which shows that they share a source (Λ).

(b) Tzetzes' *Iambi on Comedy*, largely based on *Prolegomena* to Aristophanes, nonetheless contain matter lost in **a** and C, unless he is simply garbling. Knowledge of Tractate IV and VII can also be argued in his work, and in this case he must draw from a branch of the *Prolegomena* at least partly independent of **a** and C ($\varXi$, ξ).

(c) Chapter XVII of the Tractate recurs in a condensed version **d** (*Prolegomenon* Xd Koster). **d** cannot derive from C however, as it contains an error likely to have originated in majuscule: a common source is required, a majuscule epitome. **d**'s sources are V, Rs and E: Tzetzes' *Iambi* contribute nothing of interest. From these derive his prose *Prolegomena* XIaI—II: the latter, and the anonymous *Prolegomenon* XIc, are secondary. Tzetzes seems to have been the first to connect **d**, and other writing on comedy, with 'Euclides', a writer on tragedy: the connexion is first made in his unreliable prose works.

Two areas of doubt remain:

(i) Whether the sources of **d** and C, and C and **a**, each successively less abbreviated than the preceding, are one or two (as shown in the stemma, Λ *and* τ); if one, the more economical hypothesis, τ can be expunged as equal to Λ.

(ii) The exact status of Ω. The text we shall print as that of Ω only deserves the name where we have several sources, as in Chapter V. Even here we can scarcely penetrate back beyond Λ: Ω

could have been as heavily abbreviated as *Λ* seen in **a**, or fuller, as I believe, noting how **a**, C and **d** are each more brief.

With these provisos, we have the stemma given below. The relative placing of stages prior to MS V is doubtful: **a** may have come into existence before **d**, after, or at the same time, for example. The letters are so placed for ease of presentation only; but the lines of descent are fixed.

cent.

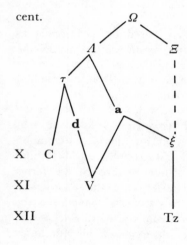

archetype, I — XVIII

hyparchetypes (*Λ* lacunose in V)

epitome (majuscule?), I — XVIII

extract (minuscule?), V — VI 2
extract from epitome, XVII
more complete extract, IV — V, VII?
MS of epitome, I — XVIII

earliest MS of **a**, **d**

Tzetzes, *Iambi on Comedy*, IV, V (VII)

PART II

Text and translation

The text is drawn from the following sources:

(1) The Tractatus Coislinianus, C: sections I — XVIII
(2) Prolegomenon to Comedy VI Koster, **a**: sections V — VI 2
(3) Prolegomenon to Comedy XIb Koster, **b**: sections V — VI 2
(4) Prolegomenon to Comedy Xd Koster, **d**: section XVII
(5) John Tzetzes, *Iambi de Comoedia* XXIb Koster, Tz: section V.

The sigla are as far as possible Koster's (p. xl): I have made a few changes to avoid confusion. For ease of presentation I have altered the excerptor's stemmatic format, of which paragraphs I — II may serve as an example: see the Plates. Only *loci similes* important for establishing the text, and a few others, are given: many more will be found in the commentary. I have omitted the misreadings of C's editors before Kaibel; their errors were even more frequent than is apparent from Koster's apparatus. Roman numerals for the sections, with appended Arabic numerals for subsections, replace the Arabic numerals of the original editors: their divisions are often too large to be useful in discussing the text, but are given in round brackets. The new divisions also correspond more closely, I believe, to the structure of the underlying work.

I have tried to give the text as far back as it can be reconstructed from the above sources at any given point. It should be kept in mind that the archetype may never have looked precisely like this, but was almost certainly fuller. Using other sources soon to be assembled, I could have pressed the reconstruction further, beyond the series of extracts that Ω represents, but this would have begged too many important questions to be raised later. However, I must apologise if I have occasionally relied on conclusions not yet argued in establishing the text that follows. From this text I hope it will be agreed that C, **a**, **d** and Tzetzes do indeed have a common source, Ω. What Ω itself represents, and how accurately, will be mooted below.

SIGLA

a = Prolegomenon VI Koster, anonymi auctoris, capitum V—VI 2 excerptoris, apud codices Aristophanis.

Codices:	V	Venetus Marcianus 474, saec. xi (quidam xii)
	E	Estensis α.U.5.10, saec. xiv (vel xv)
	N¹	Neapolitanus II.F.22, manus prima, saec. xiv
μ	Θ	Laurentianus Conv. Soppr. 140, saec. xiv
	M	Ambrosianus L 39 sup., saec. xiv
	U	Vaticanus Urbinas 141, saec. xiv
	Ps	Parisinus Suppl. Gr. 463, a Triclinio scriptus, saec. xiv
	V⁵⁷	Vaticanus 57, saec. xiv
Tr²	Vat	Vaticanus 1294, saec. xiv, Triclini recensio altera
	Lh	Oxoniensis Bodleianus Holkhamicus 88, saec. xv
	Laur	Laurentianus 31.4, saec. xv, Vaticani 1294 apographon
	Chis	Vaticanus Chisianus R.IV.20, saec. xv
	G	Venetus Marcianus 475, saec. xv
	N²	Neapolitanus II.F.22, manus secunda, post a. 1495
	Ald	editio Aldina, a. 1498

sic inter se cognatos esse codices monuit Koster:
V ‖ EN² ‖ N¹Θ | M ‖ U ‖ PsChis | V⁵⁷ ‖ VatLhLaurGAld

b = Prolegomenon XIb 67 sqq. Koster, auctoris anonymi, saec. xiv, recensionem Triclinianam praecedentium excerpentis.

Codices: r { Reg   Parisinus 2821, saec. xiv

     R   Vaticanus 62, saec. xvi

m {
M⁹   Estensis α.U.9.22, saec. xv
Ca   Cantabrigiensis Bibl. Publ. Dd.11.70, saec. xv
Vc   Vaticanus 1385, saec. xv
P   Parisinus 2677, saec. xvi

a Reg ceteros pendere docuit Koster xxxv; cuius redactor et emendator is, qui M⁹ scripsit, Prolegomenon XIc excerpsit, et codicum **m** fons fuit.

C = codex Parisinus Coislinianus 120, saec. x ineuntis.

d = consensus codicum Prolegomeni Xd Koster, anonymi auctoris, capitis XVII excerptoris, apud codices Aristophanis.

Codices: V   Venetus Marcianus 474, saec. xi (quidam xii)
         E   Estensis α.U.5.10, saec. xiv (vel xv)
         Rs   Vaticanus Reginae Suecorum 147, saec. xiv in.
         G   Venetus Marcianus 475, saec. xv
         Ald   editio Aldina, a. 1498

sic inter se cognatos esse codices monuit Koster:
    VG || EAld || Rs

Tz = I. Tzetzae Iambi de Comoedia, XXIb Koster, saec. xii, qui ad caput V et ad **d** spectat

Ω = archetypus fontium omnium

marg.   in margine
< >   inserenda
[ ]   delenda
* * *   lacuna statuenda
m¹, m²   manus prima, manus secunda (nota tamen Tr¹, Tr²
           primam atque alteram Triclini recensionem indicare)

(1) **I**   Τῆς ποιήσεως ἡ μὲν ἀμίμητος

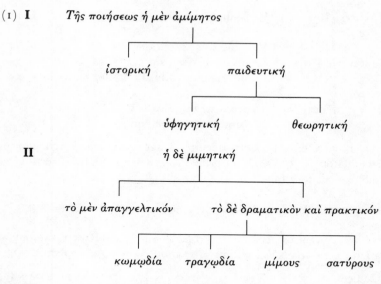

ἱστορική   παιδευτική

ὑφηγητική   θεωρητική

II   ἡ δὲ μιμητική

τὸ μὲν ἀπαγγελτικόν   τὸ δὲ δραματικὸν καὶ πρακτικόν

κωμῳδία   τραγῳδία   μίμους   σατύρους

(2) **III**   ἡ τραγῳδία ὑφαιρεῖ τὰ φοβερὰ παθήματα τῆς ψυχῆς δι' οἴκτου καὶ δέους· [καὶ ὅτι] συμμετρίαν θέλει ἔχειν τοῦ φόβου· ἔχει δὲ μητέρα τὴν λύπην.

III Cf. Aristot. *Pol.* VIII 7.1341b38 τί δὲ λέγομεν τὴν κάθαρσιν ... ἐν τοῖς περὶ ποιητικῆς ἐροῦμεν σαφέστερον, cum Iamblicho Procloque ap. Aristot. *Poet.* fragmentum V Kassel citatis. *Poet.* fr. VI Kassel fort. huc referendum, si catharseos causa (οὗ ἕνεκα) pro audientium bono (ᾧ) fabulae dandae: Philoponus in Aristot. *de Anima* p.269.28 Hayduck, διὰ τοῦτό φησιν ὅτι τὸ οὗ ἕνεκα, τουτέστι τὸ τέλος, διττόν ἐστι, τὸ μὲν οὗ ἕνεκα, τὸ δὲ ᾧ, ὅπερ καὶ ἐν τῇ Ποιητικῇ καὶ ἐν τῇ Περὶ Γενέσεως εἶπεν. |

Usque ad V fons C unicus ||
I αφ' marg. C (quid sibi velit incertum): titulus deest | ὑφηγητικήν et θεωρητικήν ad historicen refert C, corr. Bergk |
II μιμητική Kaibel: μιμητή C | ἀπαγγελτικόν Bergk: ἐπαγγελτικόν C | accusativos excerptoris esse vestigia perspexit Kaibel: μῖμοι, σάτυροι van Leeuwen |
III σ marg. C | καὶ ὅτι excerptoris vestigium

(1) **I**   Poetry is either non-mimetic, or mimetic. (Non-mimetic poetry is divided into) historical and instructive, (and this[1] is divided into) didactic and theoretical.

   II   Mimetic poetry (is divided into) narrative on the one hand, and dramatic, (directly) representing action, on the other. (The latter is divided into) comedy and tragedy, (to which we may append) mimes and satyr-plays.

(2) **III**   Tragedy removes the mind's emotions of fear by means of pity and terror. [And (he says) that][2] it aims to have a due proportion of fear. It has painful feelings as its mother.

[   ]   matter to be removed from the text
⟨   ⟩   matter to be inserted into the text
(   )   matter supplied in the translation
* * *   lacuna

I–IV Source: MS C
III Cf. Aristotle *Politics* VIII 7: 'what we mean by catharsis . . . we shall explain more clearly in the *Poetics*'; also Iamblichus and Proclus cited in *Poetics* fr. V Kassel. Fragment VI Kassel perhaps belongs here, if plays are to be performed for the sake of catharsis to benefit the audience: Philoponus on Aristotle, *On the soul* p.269.28 Hayduck 'for this reason (Aristotle) says that the purpose, that is to say the end, is twofold, divided into the for-the-sake-of-which and the for-which, as he says both in the *Poetics* and in the *On Coming to be*.'

1) C appends these divisions to 'historical': corrected by Bergk.
2) A trace of the excerptor.

(3) **IV**   κωμῳδία ἐστὶ μίμησις πράξεως γελοίας καὶ ἀμοίρου
μεγέθους, τελείας, ⟨ἡδυσμένῳ λόγῳ⟩ χωρὶς ἑκάστῳ τῶν
μορίων ἐν τοῖς εἴδεσι, δρώντων καὶ ⟨οὐ⟩ δι᾽ ἀπαγγελίας, δι᾽
ἡδονῆς καὶ γέλωτος περαίνουσα τὴν τῶν τοιούτων παθημάτων
κάθαρσιν. ἔχει δὲ μητέρα τὸν γέλωτα.

	(Tractatus)		(Prolegomenon VI)
V	γίνεται δὲ ὁ γέλως	**V**	[ὅτι] ὁ γέλως τῆς κωμῳδίας ἔκ
	— ἀπὸ τῆς λέξεως		τε λέξεων καὶ πραγμάτων ἔχει
	— ἀπὸ τῶν πραγ-		τὴν σύστασιν. ἐκ μὲν τῆς λέξεως
	μάτων		κατὰ τρόπους ἑπτά·

V Cf. Aristot. *Rhet.* I 11.1371b35 τὰ γελοῖα ἡδέα εἶναι, καὶ
ἀνθρώπους καὶ λόγους καὶ ἔργα· διώρισται δὲ περὶ γελοίων χωρὶς ἐν
τοῖς περὶ ποιητικῆς; ibid. III 18.1419b5 εἴρηται πόσα εἴδη γελοίων
ἐστὶν ἐν τοῖς περὶ ποιητικῆς (= Aristot. *Poet.* fr. II Kassel). Ioh.
Tzetzes, *Iambi technici de comoedia* 76 sqq. (Tz):

   τὸ τοῦ σκοποῦ δὲ πλάσμα καὶ λέξις ἅμα
   παρεισφοροῦσιν ἡδονὴν κωμῳδίαις
   καὶ τὸν γέλωτα τοῖς ὁμωνύμοις πλέον
   ἐσχηματισμένον τε καὶ παρῳδίαις·
80 καὶ κλήσεων πλάσεις δὲ καὶ μεταπλάσεις
   σὺν οἷς κορισμοὶ καὶ καταχρήσεις ἅμα.

IV σ marg. C | γελοίας Bergk: γελοιου C | post μεγέθους interpunxit Koster
| τελείας Baumgart: τελείου C | ἡδυσμένῳ λόγῳ add. Bergk e tragoediae
definitione Aristotelis (*Poet.* 6.1449b24sqq.) | ἑκάστῳ Bergk: ἑκάστου C, ut
Aristot. loc. cit., ubi ἑκάστῳ Reiz | post εἴδεσι interpunxerunt edd. |
δρώντων Bergk: δρῶντος C | οὐ add. Bergk ex Aristot. loc. cit. | post
ἀπαγγελίας interpunxerunt edd. | περαίνουσα Cramer: παραινοῦσα C | post
κάθαρσιν interpunxit C | post γέλωτα interpunxit Cramer |
V–VI 2 adest C || **V–VI 2 adsunt etiam fontes a, b ||**
                                     titulum ἄλλως περὶ κωμῳδίας habent
                                     VPsV⁵⁷Tr²ChisGAld, ἄ. π. τῆς κωμ. E, π.
                                     κωμ. N¹Θ, sine titulo N²UMb | ὅτι
                                     excerptoris vestigium ap. **a**: om. **Mb** |
                                     γέλως cett.: δὲ γέλως Mb | λέξεων **ab**:
                                     λέξεως Kaibel | τῆς λέξεως **a**: τῶν λέξεων **b** |

(3) **IV** Comedy is an imitation of an action that is absurd and lacking in magnitude,[1] complete, ⟨with embellished language,⟩[2] the several kinds (of embellishment being found) separately in the (several) parts (of the play); (directly represented) by person⟨s⟩ acting, and ⟨not⟩[3] by means of narration; through pleasure and laughter achieving the purgation of the like emotions. It has laughter for its mother.

	Tractatus		Prolegomenon VI
V	Laughter arises from speech, and from actions.	**V**	[He says that][4] the laughter of comedy is made up from speech, and from actions. From speech (it arises) in seven ways:

V Cf. Aristotle *Rhetoric* I 11: 'humour arises from people, words and deeds; a separate analysis of what is funny has been made in the *Poetics*'; *Rhetoric* III 18: 'how many types of humour there are has been stated in the *Poetics*'. John Tzetzes, *Verses on comedy* 76ff.:

> 'As is its aim, both form and speech as well
>   bring pleasure into comedies,
>   and laughter veiled in homonyms,
>   and parodies; words changed and changed again,
>   diminutives, and diction much abused.'

V–VI 2 Sources: **a**, Tzetzes, **b**

1) 'Magnitude' in the sense of 'grandeur'.
2) Added by Vahlen from the *Poetics*.
3) Added by Kaibel from the *Poetics*.
4) A trace of the excerptor.

(Tractatus)   (Prolegomenon VI)

V   1 κατὰ ὁμωνυμίαν   1 πρῶτον καθ' ὁμωνυμίαν, ὡς τὸ
                               'διαφορουμένοις'· [σημαίνει γὰρ
                               τό τε διαφόροις οὖσι καὶ τὸ
                               ἐπικερδέσι·] ⟨καὶ⟩ οἷον τὸ
                               'μέτρον'.

ad V 1 διαφορουμένοις cf. Eustath. p.804.47 καὶ τὸ διαφορεῖν τό τε
παρὰ τοῖς ἰατροῖς καὶ τὸ κωμικόν, sed cf. Meineke 4.627 (com. anon.
fr. 90) |

V 1 ὁμωνυμίαν Cramer: V 1 πρῶτον om. μ, ut ordinalia cetera,
ὁμω|νυμί | C | praeter ζ ΄ ad exallagen sscr. N¹: apud V
                            marg. α ΄–ζ ΄ scripsit m¹, in textu α ΄ et β ΄
                            tantum: ordinalia cetera sscr. m² (saec.
                            xv) | καθ' ὁμωνυμίαν cett.: κατ' ὁμωνυμίαν
                            V, θ' ὁ sscr. m² | δια-
                            φορουμένοις VUPsChisr: διαφορούμενος
                            EμV⁵⁷Tr²GAld, διαφορούμενον m praeter
                            Reg; casus desinentia per compendium
                            Reg; διαφόρως νοούμενον Koster; est tamen
                            exemplum incorruptum, cf. Eustath. sup.
                            cit. | σημαίνει . . . ἐπικερδέσι praebet b pro
                            οἷον τὸ μέτρον apud a | ἐπικερδέσι b praeter
                            P: ἐπικαρδέσι P | καὶ add. Bernays | μέτρον
                            exemplum incorruptum: cf. post Dob-
                            raeum Aristoph. Nub. 637 sqq.

Tractatus | Prolegomenon VI

V   **1.** From hom-
onyms

1. First, from homonyms, such
as διαφορουμένοις;[1] [this means
both 'different' and 'profitable'].[2] ⟨Or⟩ like 'metre'.[3]

V 1 Cf. Eustathius p.807.47: 'διαφορεῖν in medical writers and
comedy', but cf. Meineke 4.627 (com. anon. fr. 90).

1) Unknown in extant comedy.
2) These words replace 'like metre' in a late and untrustworthy source, **b**.
3) A pun on metrics and mensuration, captured by the modern word;
this may refer to Aristophanes, *Clouds* 637ff., where this pun is found.

(Tractatus)	(Prolegomenon VI)
V 2 ⟨κατὰ⟩ συνωνυμίαν	2 δεύτερον δὲ κατὰ συνωνυμίαν, ὡς τὸ 'ἥκω καὶ κατέρχομαι'· ταὐτὸν γάρ ἐστιν.
3 ⟨κατὰ⟩ ἀδολεσχίαν	3 τρίτον κατὰ ἀδολεσχίαν, ὡς ὅταν τις ⟨δὶς⟩ τῷ αὐτῷ ὀνόματι χρήσηται.

V 2 Cf. Aristot. *Rhet.* III 2.1404b37 τῶν δ' ὀνομάτων τῷ μὲν σοφιστῇ ὁμωνυμίαι χρήσιμοι . . ., τῷ ποιητῇ δὲ συνωνυμίαι, λέγω δὲ κύριά τε καὶ συνώνυμα οἷον τὸ πορεύεσθαι καὶ τὸ βαδίζειν· ταῦτα γὰρ ἀμφότερα καὶ κύρια καὶ συνώνυμα ἀλλήλοις. τί μὲν οὖν ἕκαστόν ἐστι . . . εἴρηται . . . ἐν τοῖς περὶ ποιητικῆς (fr. III Kassel) | Simplicius *in Categ.* 36.13 sqq. Kalbfleisch (e Porphyrio *Comm. mai. in Categ.*) ὁ Ἀριστοτέλης ἐν τῷ Περὶ Ποιητικῆς συνώνυμα εἶπεν εἶναι ὧν πλείω μὲν τὰ ὀνόματα λόγος δὲ ὁ αὐτός, οἷα δή ἐστι τὰ πολυώνυμα, τό τε λώπιον καὶ ἱμάτιον καὶ φάρος. ἀλλ' οὐδὲν ἄτοπον, φησὶν ὁ Πορφύριος, τῆς χρήσεως τὸ διττὸν ἐχούσης χρήσασθαι μὲν ἑκατέρῳ τὸν Ἀριστοτέλη . . . ἔνθα . . . περὶ τὰς πλείους φωνὰς ἡ σπουδὴ καὶ τὴν πολυειδῆ ἑκάστου ὀνομασίαν, ὥσπερ ἐν τῷ Περὶ Ποιητικῆς καὶ τῷ τρίτῳ Περὶ Ῥητορικῆς, τοῦ ἑτέρου συνωνύμου δεόμεθα, ὅπερ πολυώνυμον ὁ Σπεύσιππος ἐκάλει. |

V 2–7 κατὰ supplevi |

V 2 δεύτερον cett.: τὸ δεύτερον U | δὲ om. μVPsV⁵⁷Chis**b** | exemplum Aristoph. *Ran.* 1153 sqq. | καὶ om. V⁵⁷ | ἐστιν om. P in lacuna | definitionem synonymiae (Aristot. *Poet.* fr. III) huc fere supplendam esse moneo |

V 3 τις om. G | δὶς suppl. V⁵⁷: post ὀνόματι suppl. πολλάκις **m**, adverbium om. cett. | τῷ αὐτῷ cett.: αὐτοῦ τῷ V⁵⁷, τῷ αὐτοῦ Chis | χρήσηται cett.: -σητ- ex ? Ps, χρήσεται ΘV⁵⁷ et scripto η super ε Chis; χρήσαιτο **b** |

Tractatus	Prolegomenon VI
V **2.** From synonyms	**2.** Second, from synonyms, such as 'I'm here and am arrived': this is the same thing.[1]
3. From repetition	**3.** Third, from repetition, as when someone ⟨twice⟩[2] uses the same word.

V 2 Cf. Aristotle *Rhetoric* III 2: 'Among words homonyms are useful to sophists, . . . synonyms to poets; I mean words both standard and synonymous, like "to proceed" and "to walk"; both of these are standard and synonymous with each other. What each of these (types of words) is . . . has been stated . . . in the *Poetics*' (*Poetics* fr. III Kassel). Simplicius on Aristotle's *Categories* 36.13 Kalbfleisch (drawing on Porphyry): 'Aristotle in the *Poetics* said that synonyms are when there are several words with the same meaning, like' (Speusippus') '"polyonyms" indeed, such as "cloak", "wrap" and "mantle". But there is nothing strange, says Porphyry, in the fact that Aristotle uses both meanings (of synonymy), since the usage is double . . . (there is one usage in the logical works, but) where his concern is with most words or the multiform nomenclature of each (thing), as in the *Poetics* and the third book of the *Rhetoric*, we need the other kind of synonym, which Speusippus called the "polyonym"'.

1) The example is from Aristophanes, *Frogs* 1153ff.
2) Supplied by MS V[57]; **b** has 'repeatedly'.

(Tractatus)

V 4a ⟨κατὰ⟩ παρω-
νυμίαν, παρὰ
πρόσθεσιν καὶ
ἀφαίρεσιν,

(Prolegomenon VI)

4a τέταρτον κατὰ παρωνυμίαν,
⟨παρὰ πρόσθεσιν⟩, ὅταν τῷ
κυρίῳ ἔξωθέν τι συνάπτηται, ὡς
τὸ ⟨* * *, καὶ παρὰ ἀφαίρεσιν,
ὡς τὸ⟩ 'βῶμαξ καλοῦμαι Μίδας'
⟨ἀντὶ τοῦ 'βωμολόχος'⟩.

4b ⟨παρὰ⟩ ὑπο-
κόρισμα,

4c ⟨παρὰ⟩ ἐξαλ-
λαγήν.
[— φωνῇ
— τοῖς ὁμογενέσι]

4b [πέμπτον] κατὰ ὑποκορισ-
μόν, ὡς τὸ 'Σωκρατίδιον, Εὐριπίδιον'.

4c[ἕκτον] κατὰ ἐξαλλαγήν, ὡς
τὸ ['ὦ Βδεῦ δέσποτα' ἀντὶ τοῦ 'ὦ
Ζεῦ'.]

4b–c ἐξαλλαγήν et κορισμούς testatur Tz 80 sq. |

4c Cf. Antiatticistam in Anecdotis Bekkeri 101.32 'Αριστοτέλης
Περὶ Ποιητικῆς 'τὸ δὲ πάντων κυντότατον' (= Aristot. *Poet.* fr. IV
Kassel), exallages exemplum ut opinor |

V 4a παρὰ C: κατὰ van
Leeuwen | παρὰ πρόσθεσιν
καὶ ἀφαίρεσιν ad ὑποκό-
ρισμα transtulit Bergk, ad
ἐξαλλαγήν Koster, haud
recte: omnes enim parony-
miae sunt partes |

V 4b–c παρὰ supplevi |
φωνῇ, τοῖς ὁμογενέσι seclusi,
ad metaphoram transtuli:
ad ἐξαλλαγήν tribuit C, cf.
tamen a |

V 4a παρὰ πρόσθεσιν supplevi | ὅταν cett.:
ὡς ὅταν PsChisGb | τῷ κυρίῳ cett.: τοῦ
κυρίου Θ, τῷ κυρίως (sic) P | τι E^{ac}N²Gb:
τις cett. | συνάπτηται Dobree, Bergk,
Koster: καθάπτηται Chis, Kaibel; ἅπτηται
a praeter Chis; καθηται sscr. τα Reg;
κατάθηται cett. | * * *, καὶ παρὰ ἀφαίρεσιν,
ὡς τὸ supplevi | βώμαξ U (cf. Hsch. s.v.;
Suda I 490.8; *Et. M.* 218.16; *Et. Gud.* 292.5
de St.); μώμαξ EΘMV^{57}Tr²GN²Aldr
(defendit Koster); μῶμαξ VPsChis; μάμαξ
N¹; μίμαξ m | καλοῦμαι cett.: καλούμεν
V^{57}; καλούμενος Koster | Μίδας ab:
Μειδίας metri gratia Meineke (*FCG*
4.688), alii alia; comoediae frag. aliunde
ignotum | ἀντὶ τοῦ 'βωμολόχος' supplevi |
V 4b–c πέμπτον, ἕκτον seclusi, quia
paronymiae sunt partes |
V 4b κατὰ cett.: καθ' P | ὑποκορισμόν cett.:
ἀποκορισμόν V, sscr. ὑπο m² |
V 4c κατὰ cett.: κατ' P | ἐξαλλαγήν cett.;
ἐναλλαγήν VPsChisrM⁹CaP; ἀναλλαγήν
Vc | ὦ . . . Ζεῦ seclusi, ad parodiam
transtuli: Aristot. *Poet.* fr. IV e comoedia
ignota haustum huc refer, ubi legas 'τὸ δὲ
πάντων κυντότατον' ⟨ἀντὶ τοῦ 'κύντατον'⟩ |

	Tractatus	Prolegomenon VI
V	**4.** From par- onyms, by addition, and subtraction,	**4.** Fourth, from paronyms, ⟨by addition⟩[1] when an extra- neous element is attached to the standard term, like ⟨* * *, and by subtraction, like⟩[1] 'I'm called Midas the scrounge'[2] ⟨instead of 'scrounger'⟩.
	⟨from⟩ dimin- utives,	[Fifth,][3] from diminutives, like 'Socratiddles', 'Euripidipi- des'.[4]
	⟨from⟩ altera- tion. [by sound, by things of the same genus]	[Sixth,][3] from alterations, like ['O Clod Almighty' instead of 'O God'.][5]

V 4 Cf. for 'alteration' the Antiatticist in Bekker's *Anecdota* 101.32:
'Aristotle, the *Poetics*: "the worstest of all"' (*Poetics* fr. IV Kassel).
Alteration and diminutives are attested by Tzetzes, op. cit. 8of.

1) My supplements.
2) βῶμαξ, a comic shortening of βωμολόχος 'buffoon' (literally one who crouches by an altar in the hope of scraps) is attested in the lexicon of Hesychius and other sources: most MSS read μῶμαξ 'blamer', a form not found elsewhere. Midas is a common slave's name; the quotation is from an unidentified comedy.
3) The ordinals are misplaced, as these items are sub-types of paronymy; they were promoted to maintain the number of items when parody(?) and metaphor were lost.
4) These diminutives are common in Old Comedy, e.g. in Aristophanes' *Acharnians*.
5) The example in the MSS is displaced, I suspect, from parody, the next (lost) item. I would supply, as an example of 'alteration' fully in accord with those of Aristotle and Theophrastus (see comm.), '"the worstest of all" ⟨instead of "the worst"⟩', from the Antiatticist.

(Tractatus)   (Prolegomenon VI)

V   5 ⟨κατὰ παρ-   5 ⟨πέμπτον κατὰ παρῳδίαν, ὡς
        ῳδίαν⟩   τὸ⟩ 'ὦ Βδεῦ δέσποτα' ἀντὶ τοῦ
                              'ὦ Ζεῦ'.

     6 ⟨κατὰ μετα-   6 ⟨ἕκτον κατὰ μεταφοράν. τοῦτο
       φοράν   γίνεται ἢ φωνῇ ἢ τοῖς ὁμο-
       — φωνῇ   γενέσιν.⟩
       — τοῖς ὁμογε-
       νέσι⟩

V 5–VI 2 Cf. Aristot. *Rhet.* III 11.1412a19 ἔστι δὲ καὶ τὰ ἀστεῖα τὰ
πλεῖστα διὰ μεταφορᾶς καὶ ἐκ τοῦ προσεξαπατᾶν ... γίγνεται δὲ ὅταν
παράδοξον ᾖ, καὶ μὴ πρὸς τὴν ἔμπροσθεν δόξαν, ἀλλ' ὥσπερ ἐν τοῖς
γελοίοις τὰ παραπεποιημένα (ὅπερ δύναται καὶ τὰ παρὰ γράμμα
σκώμματα· ἐξαπατᾷ γάρ), καὶ ἐν τοῖς μέτροις· οὐ γὰρ ὥσπερ ὁ ἀκούων
ὑπέλαβεν· 'ἔστειχε δ' ἔχων ὑπὸ ποσσὶ χίμεθλα'· ὁ δ' ᾤετο 'πέδιλα'
ἐρεῖν ... | parodiam testatur Tz 79 |
V 6 Tz 81 καταχρήσεις testatur, sc. metaphoram | Cf. Cic. *Orator*
27.94 'Aristoteles autem translationi et haec ipsa' (sc. metonyma)
'subiungit et abusionem, quem κατάχρησιν vocant, ut cum
minutum dicimus animum pro parvo'; Aristot. *Rhet.* III
2.1405a35 οὐ πόρρωθεν δεῖ ἀλλ' ἐκ τῶν συγγενῶν καὶ τῶν ὁμοειδῶν
μεταφέρειν; ibid. b17 τὰς δὲ μεταφορὰς ἐντεῦθεν οἰστέον, ἀπὸ καλῶν
ἢ τῇ φωνῇ ἢ τῇ δυνάμει ἢ τῇ ὄψει ἢ ἄλλῃ τινὶ αἰσθήσει |

V 5 παρῳδίαν e Tz 79   V 5 παρῳδίαν e Tz 79 supplevi | ὦ ... Ζεῦ
supplevi | apud exallagen habent **ab**, huc transtuli |
                         exemplum e comoedia ignota, cf. *FCG*
                         4.688 Meineke | Βδεῦ cett.: ζεὺς Θ; ζεῦ
                         (sscr. m² βεῦ) U; δεῦ V⁵⁷; βδῆ Chis |
                         δέσποτα : sscr. m² δεῦ U | ὦ Ζεῦ cett.: o Ζεῦ
                         N²; ὁ Ζεῦ Ald |
V 6 μεταφοράν e Tz 81   V 6 μεταφοράν e Tz 81 supplevi | τοῦτο ...
supplevi | φωνῇ Cramer, cf.   ὁμογενέσιν huc transtuli Aristot. *Rhet.* sup.
a: φωνη C | φωνῇ, τοῖς   cit. collata: ad schema lexeos trib. **ab**, ad
ὁμογενέσι huc transtuli   exallagen C, editores alii aliquo | τοῦτο
Aristot. *Rhet.* sup. cit. col-   VMUPsV⁵⁷Chis**b**: τού sscr. τ N¹; τούτῳ
lata: ad ἐξαλλαγήν tribuit   cett. | γίνεται ἢ φωνῇ **a**, δὲ ἢ φ. γ. **b** | γίνεται
C, ad σχῆμα λέξεως **a**, quod   cett.: γίνετο N² | ἢ φPsV⁵⁷**b** praeter P: ἡ
sequuntur Meineke, Koster   cett. | φωνῇ ΘMPsV⁵⁷**r**M⁹Vc: φωνὴ cett. |
                         ἢ τοῖς cett.: ητοις V; οἱ τοῖς Chis; ἤτοις Ca |
                         ὁμογενέσιν cett.: μογενέσιν Ps | 7 τοῦτο ...
                         ὁμογενέσιν seclusi: hic habent **ab** |

Tractatus	Prolegomenon VI
V **5.** ⟨From parody⟩[1]	**5.** ⟨Fifth, from parody, such as⟩[1] 'O Clod Almighty' instead of 'O God'.[2]
6. ⟨From transference (and misapplication, from things similar) in sound or (some other perception) belonging to the same genus.⟩	**6.** ⟨Sixth, from transference (and misapplication). This happens (from things similar) either in sound or (some other mode of perception) belonging to the same genus.⟩[3]

V 5–VI 2 Cf. Aristotle *Rhetoric* III 11: 'most jokes arise through transference and the arousal of false expectations . . . (Humour) arises when it is unexpected, and contrary to one's previous expectations, but instead resembles parodic turns in jokes (the same effect is caused by puns, as they too lead one astray) and in lines of verse: the verse "stately he trod, and under his feet were his chilblains" does not run as the hearer anticipated — he thought it would say "sandals".'

V 6 Cf. Cicero *Orator* 27.94: 'Aristotle assigns (metonyms) too to transference' (i.e. metaphor) 'and misuse as well, which they call *catachresis*, as when we say "a little mind" instead of "a small mind".' Aristotle *Rhetoric* III 2: 'transference must not be from things that are remote, but from those that are of the same genus or class.' Ibid.: 'imagery is to be sought in things that are lovely in sound or force or sight or some other mode of perception'. Catachresis is attested for this part of the Treatise by Tzetzes, op. cit. 81.

1) I supply parody from Tzetzes, loc. cit.
2) This example, attached to 'alteration' in the MSS, probably belongs here (see comm.). It derives from an unidentified play of Old or Middle Comedy.
3) I have transferred these subheadings from 'alteration' in the Tractate, and from the 'manner of speaking' in the *Prolegomenon*, in the light of the parallels in the *Rhetoric*.

(Tractatus)

V   7 ⟨κατὰ⟩ σχῆμα
λέξεως.

VI   ὁ ἐκ τῶν πραγ-
μάτων γέλως·
1 ⟨ἐκ τῆς ἀπάτης

2 ἐκ τῆς ὁμοι-
ώσεως, χρήσει ⟨ἢ
πρὸς τὸ βέλτιον ἢ
πρὸς τὸ χεῖρον.⟩⟩

(Prolegomenon VI)

7 ἕβδομον κατὰ σχῆμα λέξεως.
[τοῦτο γίνεται ἢ φωνῇ ἢ τοῖς
ὁμογενέσιν.]

VI   ἐκ δὲ τῶν πραγμάτων, κατὰ
τρόπους δύο·
1 πρῶτον κατὰ ἀπάτην, ὡς
Στρεψιάδης πεισθεὶς ἀληθεῖς
εἶναι τοὺς περὶ ψύλλης λόγους.
2 δεύτερον κατὰ ὁμοίωσιν. ἡ δὲ
ὁμοίωσις εἰς δύο τέμνεται, ἢ εἰς
τὸ βέλτιον, ὡς ὁ Ξανθίας εἰς
Ἡρακλέα, ἢ εἰς τὸ χεῖρον, ὡς ὁ
Διόνυσος εἰς Ξανθίαν.

VI ὁ ἐκ τῶν πραγμάτων
γέλως secl. Cantarella, om.
Koster | post γέλως inter-
punxerunt edd. |
VI 1–2 ordinem ἀπάτης,
ὁμοιώσεως Cantarella **ab**
collatis, cf. etiam Cic. *de
Orat.* II 243: vice versa
habet C | χρήσει C: τμήσει
Bernays, cf. τέμνεται apud
ab | ἢ bis supplevi | ordinem
βέλτιον, χεῖρον ego **ab** col-
latis: vice versa habet C |

VI τρόπους δύο cett.: δύο τρόπους U |

VI 1 πρῶτον cett.: om. Vm¹,²μ | ὡς cett.:
ὡς τὸ M | ψύλλης Dindorf Aristoph. *Nub.*
145 collato: ψυχῆς **ab** | post ψυχῆς cetera
om. V⁵⁷ |

VI 2 δεύτερον cett.: om. V, sscr. m²; ἢ N¹Θ;
καὶ M | κατὰ cett.: καθ᾽ P | ὁμοίωσιν cett.:
ὁμοίων V, σι sscr. m² | βέλτιον cett.:
βέλτιστον μ | ὁ Ξανθίας cett.: Ξανθίας M |
Ἡρακλέα cett.: Ἡρακλῆν PsChisr; Ἡρακλῆ
m (in Vc -ν add. m²) | post Ἡρακλέα
cetera om. V, suppl. m² | ὁ Διόνυσος cett.:
Διόνυσος V²M | Ξανθίαν cett.: Ἡρακλῆ **m**
(in Vc -ν add. m²) | exempla Aristoph.
Ran. 494–500 ‖ **hic deficiunt ab**,
subscriptione nulla ‖

Tractatus	Prolegomenon VI
V **7.** From the manner of speaking.	**7.** Seventh, from the manner of speaking. [This happens either by sound or by things of the same genus.][1]
VI Laughter from actions:	**VI** (Laughter arises) from actions in two ways:[2]
1. ⟨From deception[3]	**1.** First[3] from deception, like Strepsiades believing that the story about the flea was true.[4]
2. From assimilation, employed ⟨towards the better or towards the worse⟩⟩[3]	**2.** Secondly, from assimilation. Assimilation is divided into two, either toward the better, like Xanthias (made to resemble) Heracles, or toward the worse, like Dionysus (made to resemble) Xanthias.[5]

1) Cf. previous note.
2) The number 'two' is paralleled in Cicero, *de Oratore* II 243, who gives first two types, and later many more. It appears that his source reflected a structural feature of the Treatise.
3) The order of the subheadings is reversed in C: at some stage the epitomised headings were rotated by 90° and recopied. The *Prolegomenon* maintains the correct order: v. comm.
4) 'Flea' is Dindorf's emendation of 'soul'; he refers the passage to Aristophanes *Clouds* 145.
5) The examples here are from Aristophanes' *Frogs*, 495ff. At this point *Prolegomenon* VI ends, and C is our sole source for VI 3–XVI.

VI   3 ἐκ τοῦ ἀδυνάτου

      4 ἐκ τοῦ δυνατοῦ καὶ ἀνακολούθου

      5 ἐκ τῶν παρὰ προσδοκίαν

      6 ἐκ τοῦ κατασκευάζειν τὰ πρόσωπα πρὸς τὸ μοχθηρόν

      7 ἐκ τοῦ χρῆσθαι φορτικῇ ὀρχήσει

      8 ὅταν τις τῶν ἐξουσίαν ἐχόντων παρεὶς τὰ μέγιστα ⟨τὰ⟩ φαυλότατα λαμβάνῃ.

      9 ὅταν ἀσυνάρτητος ὁ λόγος ᾖ καὶ μηδεμίαν ἀκολουθίαν ἔχων.

(4) **VII**   διαφέρει ἡ κωμῳδία τῆς λοιδορίας, ἐπεὶ ἡ μὲν λοιδορία ἀπαρακαλύπτως τὰ προσόντα κακὰ διέξεισιν, ἡ δὲ δεῖται τῆς καλουμένης ἐμφάσεως.

(5) **VIII**   ὁ σκώπτων ἐλέγχειν θέλει ἁμαρτήματα τῆς ψυχῆς καὶ τοῦ σώματος.

(6) **IX**   συμμετρία τοῦ φόβου θέλει εἶναι ἐν ταῖς τραγῳδίαις καὶ τοῦ γελοίου ἐν ταῖς κωμῳδίαις.

IX Cf. Aristot. *Poet.* fr. V Kassel, praesertim Proclum *in Plat. Remp.* 1 p.42 Kroll, Iamblichum *de Myst.* 1.11, ubi notandum ἄχρι τοῦ συμμέτρου ... ἔν τε κωμῳδίᾳ καὶ τραγῳδίᾳ. Cf. etiam Olympiodorum, *Comm. in Plat. Alcib. pr.* p.54.17 Westerink, eiusdem *Comm. in Plat. Gorg.* p.1.5–17, 172.6 sqq. Westerink. |

VI 3–XVI fons unicus C ||

VI 4 δυνατοῦ Cramer: δυναστου C |

VI 5 τῶν apud C invenit Koster: τοῦ edd. |

VI 6 πρόσωπα Cramer: προσαπα C |

VI 8 τὰ inserui Kaibelium secutus | φαυλότατα Bergk: φαυλοτητα C |

VII σ marg. C |

VIII σ marg. C | post σκώπτων et θέλει interpunxit C |

IX συμμετρία Bergk: σύμμετρα C | post εἶναι interpunxit C | post κωμῳδίαις interpunxerunt edd., post γελοίου C |

VI   **3.** From the impossible.

4. From the possible and inconsequential.

5. From things contrary to expectation.

6. From making the characters base.

7. From using vulgar dancing.

8. When someone who has the power (to choose) lets slip the most important and takes the most worthless.

9. When the reasoning is disjointed and lacking any sequence.

(4) **VII**   Comedy differs from abuse, since abuse rehearses without concealment the bad (actions and qualities) attaching (to people), but (comedy) requires the so-called innuendo.[1]

(5) **VIII**   The joker aims to expose faults of mind and body.

(6) **IX**   There is to be a due modicum of fear in tragedies, and of the laughable in comedies.[2]

VI 3–XVI Source: MS C.

IX Cf. Aristotle *Poetics* fr. V Kassel, especially Iamblichus *On the Mysteries* 1.11, where note 'as far as a due modicum' . . . 'in both comedy and tragedy'. Cf. also Olympiodorus *On Plato's 'First Alcibiades'* 54.17 Westerink, *On Plato's 'Gorgias'* 1.5–17, 172.6ff. Westerink.

1) Or, possibly, 'fantasy': v. comm.
2) Parallels for this entry on catharsis are discussed in the commentary under III.

(7) **X**   κωμῳδίας εἴδη· μῦθος, ἦθος, διάνοια, λέξις, μέλος, ὄψις.

   XI   μῦθος κωμικός ἐστιν ὁ περὶ γελοίας πράξεις ἔχων τὴν
σύστασιν.

  XII ἤθη κωμῳδίας τά τε βωμολόχα καὶ τὰ εἰρωνικὰ καὶ τὰ τῶν
ἀλαζόνων.

 XIII διανοίας μέρη δύο, γνώμη καὶ πίστις. ⟨πίστεις πέντε⟩· ὅρκοι,
συνθῆκαι, μαρτυρίαι, βάσανοι, νόμοι.

XIVa κωμική ἐστι λέξις κοινὴ καὶ δημώδης.

XIVb δεῖ τὸν κωμῳδοποιὸν τὴν πάτριον αὐτῶν γλῶσσαν τοῖς
προσώποις περιτιθέναι, τὴν δὲ ἐπιχώριον αὐτῷ ἐκείνῳ.

 XVa μέλος τῆς μουσικῆς ἐστιν ἴδιον· ὅθεν ἀπ᾽ ἐκείνης τὰς
αὐτοτελεῖς ἀφορμὰς δεήσει λαμβάνειν.

 XVb ἡ ὄψις μεγάλην χρείαν τοῖς δράμασι τὴν †συμφωνίαν παρέχει.

(8) **XVI** ὁ μῦθος καὶ ἡ λέξις καὶ τὸ μέλος ἐν πάσαις κωμῳδίαις
θεωροῦνται, διάνοιαι δὲ καὶ ἦθος καὶ ὄψις ἐν ⟨οὐκ⟩ ὀλίγαις.

X lemmatis signum marg. C | εἴδη scripsi Aristot. *Poet.* 6.1450a13, aliis
locis collatis: ὕλη C |
XI post ἐστιν interpunxit C | πράξεις C: πράξεως van Leeuwen | σύστασιν
Cramer: σύστασην C |
XIII πίστεις πέντε suppl. Kaibel: // ε ΄ C |
XIVa σ cum paragrapho subscripto marg. C |
XIVb σ cum paragrapho subscripto marg. C | αὐτῶν scripsi: αὐτοῦ C;
αὐτοῦ edd. | αὐτῷ ἐκείνῳ C: αὖ τῷ ξένῳ Bergk, αὐτῷ τῷ ξένῳ Bernays,
ἑκάστου τῷ ξένῳ Kaibel, alii alia |
XVa σ cum paragrapho subscripto marg. C | δεήσει Bergk: δεήσῃ C |
XVb σ cum paragrapho subscripto marg. C | τὴν συμφωνίαν C: πρὸς τὴν
ψυχαγωγίαν vel τῇ ψυχαγωγίᾳ Bernays, alii alia; τὴν σκηνογραφίαν tentavi;
vocabulum fort. ob musicae propinquitatem corruptum; si incorruptum
est, non intelligitur |
XVI σ marg. C | πάσαις edd. omnes: πάσαιστ (sic) C; num πάσαις τ⟨αῖς⟩,
cf. Aristot. *Poet.* 6.1450a8 πάσης τῆς τραγῳδίας ap. cod. B (τῆς om. cod.
A)? | διάνοιαι Cramer: διανοίαι C, διάνοια Bergk | οὐκ supplevi: cf. Aristot.
Poet. 6.1450a12 οὐκ ὀλίγοι αὐτῶν |

(7) **X**   The parts[1] of comedy: plot, character, thought, diction, song (and) spectacle.

XI   Comic plot is one structured around laughable events.

XII   The characters of comedy are the buffoonish, the ironical and the boasters.

XIII   (There are) two parts of thought, opinion and proof. (There are) five (kinds of proof): oaths, agreements, testimonies, ordeals and laws.

XIV   Comic diction is common and popular. The comic poet must endue his characters with their[2] own native idiom, and (use) the local (idiom) himself.

XV   Song belongs to the province of music; hence one will need to take its principles complete in themselves from there. Spectacle supplies as a great benefit to dramas what is in accord with them.[3]

(8) **XVI**   Plot, diction and song are observed in all comedies, instances of thought, character and spectacle in ⟨not⟩[4] a few.

---

1) The MS reads 'material', but there can be little doubt that this is corrupt for the qualitative 'parts'.
2) 'His' MS C: 'their' makes much better sense than the various emendations to 'himself' tried hitherto.
3) This is not understood, and probably corrupt. Bernays substituted 'entertainment' for *symphonia*, 'harmony, what is in accord'; 'scene-painting' is another possibility.
4) Supplied from *Poetics* 6.1450a12.

(9) **XVII** μέρη τῆς κωμῳδίας τέσσαρα· πρόλογος, χορικόν, ἐπεισόδιον, ἔξοδος.

1 πρόλογός ἐστιν μόριον κωμῳδίας τὸ μέχρι τῆς εἰσόδου τοῦ χοροῦ.

2 χορικόν ἐστι τὸ ὑπὸ τοῦ χοροῦ μέλος ᾀδόμενον, ὅταν ἔχῃ μέγεθος ἱκανόν.

3 ἐπεισόδιόν ἐστι τὸ μεταξὺ δύο χορικῶν μελῶν.

4 ἔξοδός ἐστι τὸ ἐπὶ τέλει λεγόμενον τοῦ χοροῦ.

(10)**XVIII** τῆς κωμῳδίας·

— παλαιά, ἡ πλεονάζουσα τῷ γελοίῳ

— νέα, ἡ τοῦτο μὲν προϊεμένη, πρὸς δὲ τὸ σεμνὸν ῥέπουσα

— μέση, ἡ ἀπ' ἀμφοῖν μεμιγμένη.

XVII hic adest etiam d (a quo pendent Tzetzae *Iambi de Comoedia* 7–8, 11 sqq.) ‖ μέρη τῆς κωμῳδίας· τέσσαρα C: πόσα μέρη κωμῳδίας; **d** (sine titulo) | post κωμῳδίας cetera om. VEGAld; δ' tantum habet Rs | ad πρόλογος paragraphum hab. marg. C | χορικόν Cramer: χυρικόν C | **XVII 1** σ marg. C | πρόλογός ἐστιν· μόριον κωμῳδίας C: πρῶτον· πρόλογος **d** | εἰσόδου cett.: εἰδόδου sscr. σ Rs | post χοροῦ add. μέρος **d** **XVII 2** σ marg. C | χορικόν . . . ᾀδόμενον C: δεύτερον· χορικὸν τὸ τοῦ χοροῦ διδόμενον μέλος **d** | χορικὸν cett.: χορικὸς G, χοϊκὸν Rs | μέλος cett.: μέ sscr. ο Rs (vult μέρος) | ᾀδόμενον C, quod coniecerat Dindorf: διδόμενον **d** | ὅταν . . . ἱκανόν C: om. **d** | **XVII 3** paragraphum hab. marg. C | ἐπεισόδιόν ἐστι C: τρίτον· ἐπεισόδιον **d** | χορικῶν **d**, Cramer: χορικὸν C | μελῶν cett.: με ὦν Rs (vult μερῶν) | **XVII 4** σ cum paragrapho adscripto marg. C | ἔξοδός ἐστι C: τέταρτον· ἔξοδος **d** | post χοροῦ addidit **d** εἴρηται δὲ καὶ πόσα μέρη παραβάσεως· ἡ δὲ παράβασις τοῦ χορικοῦ (ἡ δὲ παράβασις om. Ald), quae Prolegomeni Xa (Koster) laudandi causa inseruit **d** ‖ **hic deficit d** subscriptione nulla ‖ **XVII** a Tzetza auctoribus Euclidi Dionysio Crateti apud Prolegomenon suum XIaII 53 (Koster) adscripta sunt, de quibus tamen in iambis, unde pendet tratiuncula, omnino tacuerat: Euclides de tragoedia nonnulla scripsisse videtur, alia ei iniuria ascripsisse Tzetzes | **XVIII fons unicus C** ‖ post παλαιά interpunxerunt edd. | post προϊεμένη interpunxerunt edd. | μεμιγμένη Cramer: μεμηγμένη C | **hic deficit C** subscriptione nulla

(9) **XVII** The parts of comedy (are) four:[1] prologue, choral element, episode and *exodos*.[3]

    1. The prologue is (the) part of comedy (extending) as far as the entry of the chorus.

    2. The choral element is the song sung[2] by the chorus, when it is of sufficient length.[3]

    3. The episode is the (part) between two choral songs.

    4. The *exodos* is the (part) spoken at the end by the chorus.[4]

(10) **XVIII** (The kinds) of comedy (are): (the) old, which goes to excess in the absurd; (the) new, which abandons this, and inclines towards the serious; (and the) middle, which is a mixture of both.

XVII Sources: MS C, **d** (on which Tzetzes, *Verses on Comedy* 7–8, 11ff., draws)
XVIII Source: MS C.

1) 'How many are the parts of comedy? 4' **d**.
2) For 'sung' **d** has the corruption 'given'.
3) **d** lacks this clause.
4) At the end **d** adds 'it has been stated how many are the parts of the parabasis; the parabasis is part of the choral element': this refers back to *Prolegomenon* Xa, which he had already copied. Tzetzes ascribes all this material to Euclides, Dionysius and Crates in his own prose *Prolegomenon to Comedy* XIaII 53, but in his source, his own verses, ignores them entirely: Euclides wrote on tragedy, and the rest is wrongly ascribed to him by Tzetzes.

PART III

Origins and Authorship

1. Origins

We now have before us the text of the epitome as fully as it can be reconstructed from the sources discussed above: let us call this Ω. Ω is either a series of extracts from different authors, or from one alone. Secondly, it is either faithful to the original author's or authors' diction, fairly faithful, or liberally paraphrased: the same applies to the content. Thirdly, it is either an incoherent jumble of ideas, or coherently organised; if coherently organised, it is either organised by the writer of Ω or structured as in the work of one single author; coherent organisation spontaneously arising from a careless collection of pieces from different authors is unlikely.

To compare Ω with the teachings of a known writer, we can apply four negative tests:

(i) Does Ω contain forms and words too late to have been used by an alleged author Q? If so, then at the minimum it proves an element of paraphrase; at the maximum, that the author is later.

(ii) Does Ω contain thought or ideas incompatible with those of Q?

(iii) Does Ω refer to anything historically later than Q?

(iv) Is the structure of Ω too incoherent to be compatible with Q's manner?

Each of these arguments can only prove that the work is not entirely Q's; even so, Q might underlie it. The more arguments there are against Q, the less likely this becomes. But if any argument goes against Q, we can be sure that *either* another author has contributed, *or* Ω has made a change himself. Positive proof may be sought as follows:

(a) Does Ω contain forms or usages especially characteristic of Q? In particular, does it contain any such as might not be readily perceived and imitated?

(b) Does Ω contain ideas especially characteristic of Q? In particular, does it contain not only well-known ideas such as might be imitated, but also subtle developments of his ideas which are fully compatible with them?

(c) Does Ω ignore anything that postdates Q, which we would expect to be taken into account by a later author?

(d) Does Ω possess a coherent structure such as we expect of Q? In particular, does it correspond with what we would expect him to compose on a topic such as this?

Lastly, if we are endeavouring to match Ω with a lost work by Q of which traces survive elsewhere, we must ask two questions of this external evidence:

(e) Is there an excellent match between Ω and the fragments of Q, a reasonable fit, i.e. the two are compatible, or a poor fit?

(f) If the fit is good, we must ask one last question: could Ω be a forgery of the lost work?

Six possible origins of Ω must be canvassed, that it is:

1. an abstract of a work by Andronicus of Rhodes (Kayser).
2. an abstract of a work by Theophrastus (Rostagni).
3. of mixed authorship, containing some Aristotle (Bernays).
4. an abstract of a work by Aristotle.
5. of mixed authorship, including an unknown Peripatetic writer or writers.

It has never been disputed that Ω contains Peripatetic material, and there are thus no other possibilities, except that it is:

6. a forgery of any of the above.

I shall now turn to examine these possibilities: for the detail to support my conclusions I shall need to refer ahead to the commentary on occasion.

1.1 Possible Peripatetic sources: Hellenistic scholarship

The strongest advocate of the view that Ω's source Q originates in the first century B.C. or so is Kayser.[1] He argues that the inclusion of mime under the heading of dramatic poetry (*Tract.* II) fits the first century B.C. and accords with Demetrius' *de Elocutione* on the same topic. Aristotelian studies flourished, he asserts, during that period, and Andronicus' $\Pi\epsilon\rho\grave{\iota}\ \Pi\alpha\theta\tilde{\omega}\nu$ is found in the same MS as the Tractatus: therefore this is likewise by Andronicus. It is intended, thinks Kayser, to replace Aristotle's lost *Poetics* II. Atkins and Duckworth add nothing to these arguments; the latter considers the Tractate 'Aristotelian in substance'.[2]

As we shall see ad loc., nothing in the reference to mime is necessarily post-Hellenistic. Theophrastus almost certainly defined mime along with the other dramatic genres, and Demetrius and a Peripatetic opponent of Philodemus both termed mimes 'dramatic poems'. Nor am I satisfied that Aristotle himself would have excluded mime from dramatic poetry. The occurrence of (pseudo-) Andronicus' treatise in the same MS is a weak argument: we might as well attribute the Tractatus to David or Porphyry on these grounds. In fact an ascription to the Neoplatonist commentators on Aristotle's *Organon* would be more plausible, especially since they often listed poetics among the types of (false) logic, and included his *Poetics* as the last item in the canon of his logical works.[3] The reason why Andronicus is singled out is because of the tradition that he edited the works of Aristotle and arranged them in order — a tradition there is no reason to disbelieve.[4] But there is simply no evidence that Andronicus forged the works he could not find: Kayser is the earliest authority for this suggestion, which does scant justice to the successor of Tyrannio.[5] The only possible support for ascribing this material on comedy to Andronicus is a parallel attribution to an Andronicus of a classification of poetry in general in the 16th. century MS Par. 2929 (Koster XXIII, headed Ἀνδρονίκου περὶ τάξεως ποιητῶν). This is composed and written by Constantine Palaeocappa,[6] drawing on Tzetzes' Prolegomena to Lycophron (XXIIb 1ff. Koster) and to Hesiod (XXIIc 8 Koster), the Scholia to Dionysius Thrax and the *Suda*. In like fashion he is known to have ascribed his own *Violarium* to Eudocia, and invented authors for several anonymous rhetorical and grammatical tracts in Par. 2929.[7] Even if Palaeocappa meant Andronicus the Peripatetic, there is no other evidence that Andronicus ever wrote on poetry, and no similarity at all between Palaeocappa's effort and the Treatise. Koster[8] suggests that this ascription to an unspecified Andronicus was made because Palaeocappa found some work on poetry near to a tract by Andronicus in a MS like C: that is, that it results from reasoning as dubious as Kayser's. Palaeocappa's other false ascriptions depend on entries in the *Suda* and *Violarium*, and the precise explanation for this one remains unknown.

There are two strong negative arguments against a date later than the third century B.C. for the Treatise. First, it contains no trace of the influence of Theophrastus, as we shall see; and second, the sections on the causes of laughter and on comic plot give no hint of the standard devices of New Comedy as we know it — especially of recognition and intrigue as crucial to the plot — but instead there is emphasis on verbal jokes, inconsequences in plot and argument, vulgar dancing, wicked characters and so forth. All this is alien to Menander, who operates much more like the tragedians in relying on plot; but it can apply to Old Comedy without difficulty. Thus the central sections of the Treatise seem to ignore Menander, the great Peripatetic comedian. Now if the Treatise is a whole and not a compilation from various sources, this is puzzling, because its last section refers to three types of comedy, old, middle and new, yet nothing in the body of the text relates to Menander. We may conclude either that the last section is an addition to the main body of the work, or that there is another explanation. Below[9] I shall argue that in fact the 'new' comedy did not originally apply to Menander and his contemporaries, but that the division of comedy evolved before his time, and that 'new' comedy originally denoted what is familiar to us as Middle Comedy. I would ask the reader to suspend judgement on this for the time being. Thus, if the Tractate is a unity, we would expect it to cover Menander; if it is a compilation, it is especially surprising that it does not include him;[10] *only if it was composed before his plays came to be the object of study does what we find make sense.*

If so, then the latest possible date for a unified treatise of this nature must be in the time of Aristotle's immediate successors. Menander's début was in 321 B.C., the year after Aristotle's death; Philemon, whose popularity was more immediate, won his first victory at the Dionysia in 327.[11] Theophrastus seems possible: a passing reference to a 'new' comedy 'that inclined to be serious' might be the most we would expect from an author in the last part of the fourth century, or the earlier part of the third.

Hellenistic scholarship took some decades to become aware of Menander. It is clear from the researches of Strecker[12] that the labours of Lycophron, and the long-winded reply by Eratosthenes, concerned the major poets of Old Comedy like Pherecrates, Eupolis and Aristophanes. Lycophron's work was in at least nine books, Eratosthenes' in twelve or more: both elucidated glosses and peculiar forms, and there is no trace in them of theoretical material such as the Tractate contains.[13] There is an interesting shift in title. Whereas Lycophron's work was entitled simply Περὶ κωμῳδίας, implying that Aristophanes and his generation are central to comedy, 'Comedy' *par excellence*, Eratosthenes' was called Περὶ τῆς ἀρχαίας κωμῳδίας, *On Old Comedy*, showing that Menander's importance is now recognised, and the contemporary classification is definitely established. However, Chamaeleon of Heraclea Pontica, whose date is uncertain, but probably around the end of the fourth century, is credited by Athenaeus with at least six books Περὶ τῆς ἀρχαίας κωμῳδίας, also called simply Περὶ κωμῳδίας. The longer title may not be original:[14] of the two fragments Athenaeus preserves, one tells anecdotes about Hegemon of Thasos, the hexameter parodist mentioned in the *Poetics* (IX 406e, cf. *Poet.* 2.1448a12); the other (IX 374a) contains an anecdote about the comic poet Anaxandrides, again known to Aristotle. Demetrius of Phalerum wrote one book on the poet of Middle Comedy Antiphanes,[15] and another Περὶ χάριτος: cf. Demetrius, *de Elocutione* 128−99, Cicero *de Oratore* II 235−84. Another early writer on comedy who is close to the Peripatus is Lynceus of Samos the grammarian, a contemporary of Menander. The *Suda*[16] records that he was a friend of Theophrastus, brother of Duris of Samos the historian, and a comic poet in his own right, who defeated Menander. We shall meet Duris elsewhere, when he remarks that Plato was fond of the mimes of Sophron:[17] he was following Aristotle's lead in drawing attention to the mimetic character of Plato's works, which themselves denounced literary mimesis. Athenaeus quotes from the second book of Lynceus' work on Menander, Περὶ Μενάνδρου (VI 262b–c), a description of two Attic parasites. Unfortunately we do not know whether the rest of his work was equally anecdotal, but it can be presumed that it was written after Menander's death in 293/2 B.C.[18]

Neither Chamaeleon nor Lynceus ventured beyond the telling of anecdotes, judging by the scanty fragments. At least the latter did recognise Menander's importance, as one would expect of a Peripatetic scholar. But Alexandria took far longer to do so. Apart from the works of Lycophron and Eratosthenes, Euphronius, under Ptolemy II, was seemingly the first to write commentaries on individual plays of Aristophanes;[19] a contemporary, Dionysiades of Mallos, is accredited with a Χαρακτῆρες ἢ Φιλοκώμῳδοι by the *Suda*, in which he gave an account of 'the characters of the poets'. It has been well suggested that this was a precursor of Platonius' Περὶ διαφορᾶς χαρακτήρων, which reviews the differences in character of the poets of Old Comedy (II Koster).[20] Apart from Eratosthenes' title, the first solid evidence for interest in Menander at Alexandria appears in the famous question of Aristophanes of Byzantium, 'Menander and life, which of you imitated the other?'. Pfeiffer[21] argues that Aristophanes did in fact publish texts of the plays, as well as a treatise on the authors from whom Menander borrowed. He also made some remarks on Old Comedy, but these may derive from his lexicographical work or his edition of Aristophanes' plays. Finally, we are told by Athenaeus that Machon the comic poet taught him 'the parts of comedy' in his youth (τῶν κατὰ κωμῳδίαν μερῶν).[22]

Thus, by *c.* 200 B.C., Menander was a classic even among scholars, who are always tardy and grudging of fame. Whether Ω is a compilation or of homogeneous origin, it can hardly be later than this, provided that I am right about Tractatus XVIII: my interpretation is not as *ad hoc* as it may sound at present. The scholars after Theophrastus do not seem promising candidates for the authorship of the Treatise, as far as the nature of their work can be established.

1.2 Possible Peripatetic sources: Theophrastus

As is well known, it was to a great extent through the works of Theophrastus and not the esoteric works of Aristotle that Peripatetic teaching on literature was disseminated in antiquity, although the latter's dialogue *On Poets* had some impact also. If Ω wholly or partially represents a work by or later than Theophrastus, we would expect it to display some traces of his distinctive approach.

Theophrastus' literary writings are not extant. However, from various sources[23] we can form some impression of his views on several topics dealt with in Ω. He is assigned a Περὶ Γελοίου, a Περὶ Κωμῳδίας, a *Rhetoric*, a *Poetics* in one book and another *Poetics* in one book.[24]

The analysis of humour begun by Aristotle was continued by Theophrastus. Of his treatment we have one fragment only:[25]

Θεόφραστος δ' ἐν τῷ περὶ γελοίου λεχθῆναι μέν φησι τὴν παροιμίαν ὑπὸ τοῦ Στρατονίκου, ἀλλ' εἰς Σιμμύκαν τὸν ὑποκριτήν, διελόντος τὴν παροιμίαν Μέγας οὐδεὶς σαπρὸς ἰχθύς

(Ath. VIII 348a). This suggests that Theophrastus listed proverbs as one type of comic resource, just as did Demetrius.[26] They are absent from Ω. Plutarch (*Mor.* 631e) preserves a Theophrastean definition of the σκῶμμα (joke), which should also be assigned to this work.[27] Ω preserves no such definition.

The sole fragment I have located of the Περὶ Κωμῳδίας is also in Athenaeus (VI 261d):[28] Τιρυνθίους φησὶ Θεόφραστος ἐν τῷ περὶ κωμῳδίας φιλογέλως ὄντας ἀχρείους δὲ πρὸς τὰ σπουδαιότερα τῶν πραγμάτων καταφυγεῖν ἐπὶ τὸ ἐν Δελφοῖς μαντεῖον . . . etc. This anecdote surely derives from a discussion of the origins of comedy, or of the comic impulse in man. There is nothing like it in Ω.[29]

We are not told the source of all the definitions of four major genres, found in late grammarians, of which the first is assigned to Theophrastus by name: but the arguments of Rostagni and others[30] as to the common origin of all four are cogent.

(a) Tragedy. τραγωδία ἐστὶν ἡρωϊκῆς τύχης περίστασις (Diomedes *Ars Gramm.* III 8.487 Keil = XXIV 2 Koster). There is no reason to doubt Diomedes' ascription.[31]

(b) Comedy. κωμωδία ἐστὶν ἰδιωτικῶν πραγμάτων ἀκίνδυνος περιοχή (ibid.).[32] The term ἰδιωτικῶν confirms that this is a pendant to the definition of tragedy. Dosi[33] argues plausibly that this definition fits New Comedy especially well: Diomedes justifies its wording by referring to the different characters presented in tragedy and comedy (the high and mighty beside the ordinary), the topics (grief, exile and death beside love and seduction), and *anagnorisis.* Similar material is found elsewhere in relation to the probably Theophrastean concepts of ἱστορία and πλάσμα (below). Compare Aristophanes of Byzantium on Menandrian comedy as a μίμησις βίου.[34]

(c) Epic. ἔπος ἐστὶν περιοχὴ θείων καὶ ἡρωϊκῶν καὶ ἀνθρωπίνων πραγμάτων (ibid.). The terms are the same: the epic covers a wider range, divine, heroic and human affairs as well.

(d) Mime. μῖμός ἐστιν μίμησις τά τε συγκεχωρημένα καὶ ἀσυγχώρητα περιέχων (ibid.). This is ignored by the Italian scholars, perhaps because it is not understood. But the use of περιέχων is characteristic of the series.[35] Dosi[36] demonstrated that περίστασις and περιοχή are good Theophrastean terms. Be it noted that they are absent from the Tractate, whose definition of comedy is totally divergent.

I mentioned that Diomedes justified the Theophrastean definition of comedy by citing some of the differences between tragedy and comedy. He is dependent on a Greek source here, because this passage recurs not only in Euanthius XXV 2 Koster = Donatus p.21.9ff. Wessner, but also in the Scholia to Dionysius Thrax: in the two latter sources the definition of comedy is absent, but instead we find emphasis on comic plot as fictional πλάσμα, for which the evidence will be given later. The Scholia to Dionysius will serve to exemplify the other occurrences of these ideas:[37]

πολλὴ διαφορὰ τῆς τραγωδίας καὶ τῆς κωμωδίας, ὅτι ἡ μὲν τραγωδία περὶ **ἡρωικῶν** πραγμάτων καὶ προσώπων λέγει, ἡ δὲ κωμωδία ἀπήλλακται τούτων· καὶ ὅτι ἡ μὲν τραγωδία τὰ τέλη περὶ σφαγῶν καὶ φόνων ἔχει, ἡ δὲ κωμωδία περὶ **ἀναγνωρισμοῦ**· καὶ ὅτι ἡ μὲν τραγωδία ἱστορίαν καὶ ἀπαγγελίαν ἔχει πράξεων γενομένων, ἡ δὲ κωμωδία διάπλασμα[38] βιωτικῶν

πραγμάτων· καὶ ὅτι πάλιν ἡ μὲν τραγῳδία διαλύει τὸν βίον, ἡ
δὲ κωμῳδία συνίστησιν.

The use of ἡρωϊκῶν links this to the definition of comedy above: the
mention of recognition evokes Middle and New Comedy, but is
absent in the Tractate: but it is the distinction between 'history'
and 'narrative of past events' for tragic plot and 'fiction' for comic
plot that is most interesting. Theophrastus saw poetry as antithetical to truth: cf. Dion. Hal. *Lys.* 14, θαυμάζειν ἄξιον τί δή ποτε
παθὼν ὁ Θεόφραστος . . . αὐτὸν οἴεται . . . τὸ ποιητικὸν διώκειν
μᾶλλον ἢ τὸ ἀληθινόν.[39] Dosi further argued that Theophrastus laid
great emphasis on the fictional character of poetry, if it was he who
arranged Aristotle's logical works in a descending scale of logical
cogency, with Rhetoric and Poetry placed last, after the *Sophistical
Refutations*.[40] This is not proven, but he certainly contrasted them
with 'philosophical' logic: poetry and rhetoric aim at the audience,
philosophy at the facts (πράγματα). Hellenistic and later criticism
was profoundly influenced by this stress on the similarity of poetry
and rhetoric, where Aristotle would have noted their differences.
The fact that the Scholiasts juxtapose πλάσματα with περιέχει and
βιωτικῶν πραγμάτων reminds us of the four Theophrastean
definitions. Unfortunately the terms πλάσμα, ἱστορία and μῦθος (i.e.
the plot of epic) are not ascribed to Theophrastus by name. They
are first attested in Asclepiades of Myrlea of the first century
B.C.;[41] cf. also Horace, *A.P.* 338ff.

This is very different from the Tractate, which uses μῦθος to
mean 'comic plot'.[42] Plebe[43] mildly terms this and other features
unorthodox vis-à-vis Theophrastus: others may think it untheo-
phrastean. Instead of these influential Hellenistic ideas, C is closer
to Aristotle's more subtle approach. πλάσμα is definitely not
Aristotle's term: he uses it in the depreciatory sense of fiction,[44]
while he uses μῦθος for comic as well as tragic plots.[45] Moreover he
underscores the difference between history and tragedy, recognising
as purely accidental the use of historical personages by tragic
playwrights. Only the names, and not all of these, are historical;
the events are manipulated to suit the dramatist.[46] Instead this
source speaks of events that actually happened.

Theophrastus' emphasis on the dichotomy between truth and
poetry, as against Aristotle's teaching that poetry is a special form
of truth, was surely an early stage in the great Hellenistic debate as

to whether poetry was for useful learning or entertainment. Eratosthenes under Platonic influence was dogmatic in favour of the latter.[47] Traces of the dispute are widespread, e.g. in Philodemus' Περὶ Ποιημάτων V:[48] but the Tractate is silent on this, and distinguishes between didactic (unmimetic) 'poetry' and mimetic poetry at the outset, which is closer to Aristotle's subtlety than to the sweeping generalisations of later polemic.

Whether poetry was true or false, Theophrastus continued to recognise its emotional effects, i.e. catharsis. Fragments 87−9 Wimmer from his Περὶ ἐνθουσιασμοῦ show that he followed Aristotle's belief that enthusiastic music could cure bodily and psychic ills.[49] In the Περὶ μουσικῆς he wrote ἀρχὰς μουσικῆς τρεῖς εἶναι . . . , λύπην ἡδονὴν ἐνθουσιασμόν.[50] Compare Aristotle's analogy between the effects of enthusiastic music and the catharsis of pity and fear at *Pol.* VIII 7.1341b32ff. The presence of ἡδονή in Theophrastus supports the common supposition, based on Iamblichus and Proclus, that catharsis also applied to comedy in Aristotelian doctrine. Here C agrees, as it holds that comedy is cathartic: but its definition of comedy is far closer to Aristotle's *Poetics.* Now another definition of comedy mentioning catharsis is in the Scholia to Dionysius Thrax, XVIIIb4 Koster, as follows: ἔστι δὲ κωμῳδία μίμησις πράξεως καθαρτικὴ παθημάτων καὶ τοῦ βίου συστατική, τυπουμένη δι' ἡδονῆς καὶ γέλωτος.[51] At Schol. Dion. Thrax XVIIIb2 Koster (quoted above) the phrase τὸν βίον συνίστησιν is seen in connexion with πλάσμα.[52] The definition has the peculiarity that it does not state what kind of πρᾶξις comedy imitates. The oddity would be explained if this definition once stood alongside that in Diomedes: note the overlap between Diomedes' explanation of the latter definition, and the differences between tragedy and comedy listed by Schol. Dion. Thr., which include a phrase of the former definition.[53]

A fragment of Theophrastus' Περὶ λέξεως I shows that he could write on the same topics as Aristotle (here, in *Poet.* 21), with similar terminology and examples, but minor divergences in content and some elaboration.[54] Ω also covers this topic, the kinds of altered words (paronyms): in both the order, and the omission of syncope, it is closer to Aristotle than to Theophrastus.[55]

It was no doubt in this work that Theophrastus developed the concept of ἠθικὴ λέξις, diction suited to the expression of character.[56] Plebe[57] identifies a reference to this in the Tractate's description of comic diction as ordinary and popular: but this refers neither to this concept nor to particular characters. Plebe[58] does show that ἠθικὴ λέξις is to be linked to the χαρακτῆρες λόγου, which are almost certainly an invention of Theophrastus. Neither is found in Ω.

Another innovation of Theophrastus' may be the use of the term 'mimetic' for the 'dramatic' genres, harking back to Plato, since this usage is persistently associated with the χαρακτῆρες λόγου in other classifications of the *genera* of poetry. Again, this is most definitely absent from the Tractate, which employs Aristotle's terminology.[59]

Thus Ω differs from Theophrastus in numerous respects, and he seems an unlikely candidate for the authorship, total or partial, of the Treatise.

2. The question of Aristotelian authorship

Having argued on general grounds that Ω ignores New Comedy, and on particular grounds that it ignores Theophrastus, we are left with a mildly uncomfortable choice. Either Ω covers comedy in a very incomplete fashion, and merely by chance contains none of the recognisably Hellenistic material that is still current in late antiquity: or Ω is, or purports to be, wholly or largely derived from another early Peripatetic work. The next candidate to be examined must therefore be Aristotle: we have already seen a number of respects in which Ω agrees with Aristotle against Theophrastus. Consideration of whether the work is Aristotelian must proceed along several paths. We must examine Ω for evidence of Aristotelian material, and, if it is forthcoming, we must examine the structure of the whole, to see whether there is any possibility that the whole is derived from him, not merely some sections: we must also compare this with the traces of a particular lost work, *Poetics* II, known to have dealt with comedy: and we must examine the content and expression of each section.

Bernays began his discussion by reviewing the Tractate, section by section, in search of Aristotelian and unaristotelian elements, great or small. It would have perhaps been prudent, but also repetitious, to begin in the same way. I shall not do so for two reasons. First, every aspect of each section is treated in the commentary, to which the reader must refer. Also, the structural approach taken below has led me to believe that Ω deserves to be scrutinised as a whole: only then can the merits or demerits of individual sections be assessed in their proper context. This is because it is clear to me, not only, as is universally agreed, that Ω contains Aristotelian elements, but also that Ω is Aristotelian in overall structure. First, therefore, I must prove this structural proposition: only then can we properly assess the extent of the Aristotelian elements, and also the suggestion that Ω is a forgery.

The only work at all like Ω which survives complete, and to which it can be compared in structural terms, is the extant *Poetics* of Aristotle. With such a comparison we shall begin.

2.1 Structure and coherence in relation to the Poetics

In order to compare the structure of the Tractate with that of the *Poetics*, I set out in Tables below their respective structures, omitting for the present the details of the analysis of humour in V — VI. The analysis of the *Poetics* is not my own, to avoid tendentiousness, but Butcher's (pp. 1 — 3); compare the summary in R. McKeon, *Introduction to Aristotle* 668f., or F.L. Lucas, *Tragedy* 181 — 8. There is a large measure of agreement between these. The first summary of the Tractate is likewise intended not to be controversial, as it is a broad outline; to it I append the most interesting parallels in the *Poetics*. These analyses represent an unphilosophical approach; the more sophisticated headings of M.E. Hubbard, in Aristotelian philosophical terminology, give I believe a better understanding of the *Poetics*, and therefore I have added her view of the *Poetics* and an application of her analysis to the Treatise. Her translation, with the important explanatory headings, is found in Russell and Winterbottom, *Ancient Literary Criticism*, 90 — 132.

The structure of the Poetics, *after Butcher*

The structure of the *Tractatus*

I – II	The division of poetry into: (a) unmimetic, including historical and didactic (cf. *Poet.* 1, 9). (b) mimetic, subdivided by manner of imitation into narrative and dramatic (*Poet.* 3) — dramatic poetry is subdivided by the object of imitation (*Poet.* 2).
III	The aim of tragedy (tragic catharsis through pity and fear).
IV	The definition of comedy (cf. *Poet.* 6) and its aim (comic catharsis).
V – VI	The sources of laughter (cf. the sources of pity and fear, *Poet.* 13 – 4). (a) In words (b) In actions
VII	Expressed not directly, but indirectly (cf. *Poet.* 9 init.)
VIII	Arising from errors in body and mind (*Poet.* 13).
IX	The aims of tragedy and comedy compared (tragic and comic catharsis).
X	The six qualitative parts of comedy (*Poet.* 6).
XI	(a) Plot (*Poet.* 7ff., 13f.)
XII	(b) Character (*Poet.* 15)
XIII	(c) Thought (*Poet.* 19)
XIV	(d) Diction (*Poet.* 20 – 22)
XV	(e) Music (*Poet.* 6 fin.) (f) Spectacle (*Poet.* 6 fin.)
XVI	Not all six are found in all plays (*Poet.* 6).
XVII	The four quantitative parts of comedy (*Poet.* 12).
XVIII	The three stages of comedy.

The structure of the Poetics, *after Hubbard*

Chapter
(1)   I The Preliminaries to the Definition of Tragedy.
            A. The division *per genus et differentiam*
                  1. The genus we are concerned with stated
                  2. The genus divided
                        (a) According to differences of media
(2)   (b) According to differences of object
(3)   (c) According to differences of mode.
(4)   B. Each kind a completely developed and single
                  species
(5)   (Development of tragedy and comedy)
(6)   II The Nature of Tragedy
            A. According to the category of substance
            B. According to the category of quality
                  1. The deduction of its qualitative elements
                  2. These elements ranged in order of importance
(7 — 11)   3. Closer analysis of plot
(12)   C. According to the category of quantity
(13) III Excellence in Tragedy
            A. With respect to plot
                  1. Things to aim at and beware of
(14)   2. The source of the tragic effect
(15)   B. With respect to character
(16 — 18) Digression on topics of interest to the playwright
(19)   C. With respect to *mimesis* of the intellect
(20 — 22) D. With respect to verbal expression
(23) IV Epic
            A. The Similarities between Epic and Tragedy
(24)   B. The Differences between Epic and Tragedy
(24 — 25) C. The Merits of Homer
            D. How to rebut Criticisms of him
(26)   E. Epic and Tragedy, which is superior

The structure of the Treatise

Chapter		= Section in *Poetics*
	α′ The Preliminaries to the Definition of Comedy	I
(I)	A. The division *per genus et differentiam*	A.
	1. The genus we are concerned with stated	1.
(II)	2. The genus divided	2.
	(a) According to differences of mode	(c)
	(b) According to differences of object	(b)
(III)	B. The final cause of the genus	cf. B.
	(Aim of Tragedy)	
	β′ The Nature of Comedy	II
(IV)	A. According to the category of substance	A.
	B. According to the category of quality	B.
(V−VI)	1. The deduction of its qualitative elements	1.
(VII−VIII)	2. Their manner of expression	cf. *Poet.* 9
(IX)	3. The final cause attained through them	—
	(Aims of tragedy and comedy compared)	
(X)	4. Excellence in these elements	III
(XI)	(a) With respect to plot	A.
(XII)	(b) With respect to character	B.
(XIII)	(c) With respect to *mimesis* of the intellect	C.
(XIV)	(d) With respect to verbal expression	D.
(XV)	(e) With respect to song and spectacle	—
(XVI)	5. These elements in order of importance	IIB.2
(XVII)	C. According to the category of quantity	IIC.
	γ′ Iambus (lampoon)	IV
(XVIII)	A. The iambic element in Comedy	—

Finally, I summarise the main sections of each work, showing by juxtaposition how similar they are to one another:

	Poetics		*Tractatus*
1 — 3	Subdivision of poetry	I – II	Subdivision of poetry
4 — 5	Origins of poetry	III	Aims of poetry (also IX)
6	Definition of tragedy	IV	Definition of comedy
7 — 11	Plot and unity	V – IX	Humour
12	Quantitative analysis	X – XVI	Qualitative analysis
13 — 22	Qualitative analysis	XVII	Quantitative analysis
23 — 26	Epic and tragedy	XVIII	Iambic element in comedy

I must now explain these tables and explore the similarities and variations, taking each section in turn.

(a) *The subdivision of poetry*

Each work begins by defining the *genus* which concerns it. *Poet.* 1 assigns poetry proper to the class of *mimesis*, *Tract.* I delineates non-mimetic verse (loosely termed 'poetry'), thereby separating it from the mimetic, and then distinguishes narrative from dramatic, and the different dramatic genres according to the object of the representation (II): this serves to focus on comedy, causing a reversal of the manner and the object of imitation vis-à-vis the *Poetics*.

(b) *The origins and aims of poetry*

Although C is almost entirely on comedy, it is curious to say the least that discussion of the aim of tragedy, i.e. catharsis, in III precedes the definition of comedy. In the *Poetics* a discussion of the development of both tragedy and comedy precedes the definition of tragedy; origins balance ends, and there is no duplication in either work of the other. As if the *Poetics* had preceded, C omits the origins of the genres and all other detail about tragedy, to concentrate on aims. III deals briefly with tragedy alone; comedy is postponed until laughter has been explained, and is dealt with in IX, where it is compared with tragedy.

(c) *The definitions of tragedy and comedy*

The *Poetics'* definition of tragedy follows the discussion in 4 — 5 of the *efficient causes* of poetry, e.g. man's love of imitation; the definition of comedy in C follows the *final cause*, i.e. catharsis. The two definitions are extremely similar, as has long been noted. Both serve to introduce the *formal causes* of their respective genres, the qualitative and quantitative elements of drama; but in each case these are approached indirectly.

(d) *The deduction of the qualitative elements*

The analysis of humour which follows in the Tractate V — VI is not incoherent, as has been thought, but shows how humour can be obtained through the four main qualitative parts of comedy, in the order diction, plot, character and *dianoia* (v. inf. pp.69 — 76). Parallel to this in *Poet.* is a much briefer paragraph, 6.1449b31 — 1450a10, where the qualitative elements are deduced from the media, object and mode of the imitation, but I also discern correspondences on a broader scale with the discussion of plot and unity in 7 — 11 (**a** actually speaks of the *systasis* of laughter; *systasis* is also used for plot here) and the account of how to arouse the tragic emotions in 13. In particular, the section on humour continues with a distinction between comedy and abuse (VII), i.e. between the generalised and the particular (see commentary), which is parallel to the section distinguishing poetry from history in *Poet.* 9; and in the next place a discussion of comic faults constitutes a close parallel to that on tragic *hamartia* in 13 (again see commentary). The section concludes with a resumption of the final cause of both tragedy and comedy, necessarily postponed in the latter case from III; this is appropriately placed after the account of humour. Moreover, in *Poet.* 4 — 5 the comic branch of poetry develops away from personal abuse, and the absurd is defined as a kind of error or blemish that is not painful or destructive; these ideas recur together in VII — VIII, but in the context of comedy fulfilling its aims, not developing from its origins: in the teleological view this is the same process. There is no better teleologist than Aristoteles.

Although this section performs a similar function to that of parts of the *Poetics*, and its end has the same scrappy air, the structural parallel is inexact: the next section parallels *Poet.* 13 — 22, but in XVI we are back in *Poet.* 6.

(e) *The qualitative analysis*

The analysis in terms of the six qualitative elements of comedy, namely plot, character, thought, diction, song and spectacle, occupies sections X — XVI. This is paralleled by *Poet.* 13 — 22, which, however, discusses only the first four elements of tragedy; this deficiency is remedied in C by XV, where spectacle, if not song as well, is discussed with reference to 'dramas' rather than to comedy, the stated topic in X, XI, XII, XIV and XVI. The discussion concludes by stating that not all the qualitative parts are found in all comedies, but only plot, diction and song are ubiquitous. This parallels *Poet.* 6.1450a12 — 14, where we are told that not all tragedians use all the parts of tragedy, and again a23ff., where this fact is given in justification of the primacy of the plot (see below). The six parts are in the standard Aristotelian order, as adumbrated too in the analysis of humour, and there is nothing exceptionable from an Aristotelian viewpoint in the detailed accounts of them, as we shall see.

(f) *The quantitative analysis*

The division of comedy into quantitative parts (XVII) succeeds the qualitative analysis in C. A quantitative analysis is needed, cf. *Poet.* 1.1447a10, where it is promised. In the *Poetics*, however, the quantitative analysis in 12 follows the account of unity and plot, but precedes that of excellence in the four main qualities of tragedy in 13 — 22. The order in C is more logical, and yet the transition from *Poet.* 22 (on diction) to epic, which shares the same four main parts of tragedy, is easy, and the placing of *Poet.* 12 there would have been discordant. Therefore the position of this section in both works is defensible, and neither is a slavish copy of the other.

The order of sub-entries is different too, in that the choral part of comedy stands in second place, but the equivalent part of tragedy last. Most of the definitions are the same, but that of the choral part is modified (v. inf.).

(g) *Epic, iambus and the respective dramatic genres*

XVIII is at first sight unparalleled in the *Poetics*, as it analyses comedy into three apparently chronological phases. Aristotle is aware of the development of tragedy from its origins until the mid fourth century (*Poet.* 4, cf. 6.1450a25, 14.1453b27), but nowhere uses a triple division. However, the terminology used shows that the development is in terms of the decrease in iambic elements in comedy, which has parallels in *Poet.* 4, on how tragedy became serious, 5, on the evolution of comedy, and in *Rhet.* III 3 and *E.N.* IV 8 on absurdity, solemnity and buffoonery (see comm.). Now iambus is for Aristotle not a mimetic genre, as it depicts real individuals and not generalised persons or actions (e.g. *Poet.* 9.1451b11), and this accords with the exclusion of direct abuse from comedy in *Tract.* VII. We would not therefore expect or welcome a direct discussion of abusive poetry like Archilochus', to balance Homer's epic, either in terms of similarities and differences or inferiority to comedy, like *Poet.* 23—6; iambus is not poetry at all. The nearest approach to such a discussion possible for an Aristotelian treatise is what we find — an account of the disappearing iambic element in comedy: as in the *Poetics*, the dramatic genre is superior to the non-dramatic, and both works end on a note of comparison (see comm.).

Other elements of Aristotle's section on epic, namely the poetic faults detected by the critics of Homer (*Poet.* 25), reappear in Ω in the analysis of laughter. I have passed over this section, which is largely self-contained, and reserve it as a testing-ground for the conclusions reached regarding the remainder of the Treatise. Meanwhile I must dilate upon some implications of the above structural analyses. These reveal striking similarities between the two works, and supply the Tractate with a structure as clear and coherent as that of the *Poetics*: even *Poet.* 12 finds its analogue in XVII. Coincidence looks unlikely as an explanation of *either* the fact that Ω seems to have a coherent structure, *or* of that structure's resemblance to the *Poetics*. Is the former imitating the latter? Despite the similarities, I think it fair to claim that Ω is no servile copy; nor is the structure of the *Poetics* so entirely obvious itself that an ignorant forger could readily replicate it, while making the requisite alterations. Lane Cooper's rendering of the *Poetics* into comic terms in *An Aristotelian Theory of Comedy*, although intended as a scholarly exercise and not as a forgery, gives an idea of what to expect from an imitator of the *Poetics*. Cooper simply transfers the analyses of tragedy to comedy, changing all appropriate terms to fit laughter and substituting examples from Aristophanes. Several tragic notions inevitably reappear — recognition and reversal, for instance, and the *hamartia* of the comic hero.[60] Such slavishness is incautious: Ω is quite different. *Anagnorisis* and *peripeteia* are ignored: the nature of *hamartia* in comedy is broad, as Pack independently deduced it would be, including both errors and accidents.[61] There is no section explicitly comparing comedy with iambus at the end, but iambus is not mimetic in Aristotle's doctrine, as we saw, and not therefore on a par with epic. Again, the discussion of how comedy achieves its aim, through laughter, appears directly after the definition of comedy and before the enumeration of its qualitative parts, not after the listing of such parts as in the *Poetics*; yet their distribution, i.e. whether they are present in all plays, is postponed until after each has been discussed, in contrast to the parallel in *Poet*. 6. The quantitative parts of comedy are also differently placed. Again, no overwhelming primacy is assigned to plot, and great emphasis is given to verbal humour.

I shall mention further arguments against copying below, when we consider the content and diction of Ω. But, on the above evidence, the imitation is of a subtle kind, if imitation it be.

The balance and contents of Ω suggest that it is something other than a random miscellany of extracts. But they suggest more than this. The peculiar shape of the work — its opening classification of the literary *genera* to focus on comedy, its discussion of no other aspect of tragedy than its aim, catharsis, its omission of epic and of any account of the origins of comedy, can only be explained if it was originally intended to follow, or subsequently tailored to follow, a work identical in scope and content to the surviving *Poetics*, which omits every aspect of comedy except its origin, and covers every aspect of tragedy except its aim. In other words Ω was not a compilation of extracts, like the Prolegomena to Aristophanes, with no particular end in view: it is surely either an epitome, or a deliberate forgery, of the second book of the *Poetics*, specifically intended to be read in conjunction with the extant book. That such a book did once exist is the next step in the argument.

2.2 *The lost second book of the* Poetics

That a second book of the *Poetics* was not only planned by Aristotle, but also written, is clear beyond doubt. It is clear also that a large-scale treatment of comedy was envisaged, not merely a section of briefer scope like that on epic in the extant work. The evidence for these propositions is threefold: Aristotle's own statements, the fragments and the external testimonia.[62]

In the *Poetics* itself, Aristotle's remark περὶ κωμῳδίας ὕστερον ἐροῦμεν (6.1449b21) indicates clearly that he intends to give a fuller treatment of comedy later *in the same work*. His parallel promise to discuss epic certainly is kept.[63] As there is no obvious place in the extant text where it could have fallen out, it follows that Aristotle dealt with comedy in a lost part of the *Poetics* after our text breaks off. Where it does so, at the end of Chapter 26, the closing formula περὶ μὲν οὖν Χ . . . εἰρήσθω τοσαῦτα is, as Else[64] remarks, a normal formula of transition to another topic, even at the end of a book: cf. the ends of *Rhet.* I and II, and contrast the tone of finality at the conclusion of *Rhet.* III. The one MS of the *Poetics*, B, which derives from a tradition independent of the oldest MS, A, has traces of a few words after the supposedly final εἰρήσθω τοσαῦτα, which read

περὶ δὲ ׃ . ⌢ . ׃ . ωμω | [. .] ουγρ. . ω.

This is restored as compendiously written ἰάμβων(?) καὶ κωμῳδίας. If the last words really read οὐ γράψω, 'non loquitur ipse Aristoteles': but Gallavotti now wishes to read ἐφ[ε]ξ[ῆς] instead.[65] However this may be, the restoration κωμῳδίας is inevitable, and indicates some knowledge in this branch of the tradition of a discussion of comedy to follow.

In like vein, Aristotle twice states in the *Rhetoric* that he has already discussed the types of the laughable in the *Poetics* (*Rhet.* I 11.1371b33, III 18.1419b2, = *Poet.* fr. II Kassel).[66] Elsewhere he says that he has discussed synonymy there (*Rhet.* III 2.1404b37, = *Poet.* fr. III Kassel). For the tenses compare *Rhet.* III 1.1404a39, 2.b7, 28, 1405a6 referring to chapters 21−2 of the *Poetics*. The sixth-century commentator Simplicius actually quotes from the *Poetics*' discussion of synonymy (*in Categ.* 36.13 Kalbfleisch, = *Poet.* fr. III Kassel). I shall show that he is dependent on Porphyry (inf. p.172f.).

Again, in the *Politics* Aristotle promises to supply in the *Poetics* a more detailed account of catharsis, which seems to receive an echo in Iamblichus' and Proclus' discussions of the emotional effects of literature, with reference to both tragedy and comedy (*Pol.* VIII 7.1341b32ff., Iamblichus *de Myst.* 1.11, Proclus in Plat. *Remp.* I p.42ff. Kroll, = *Poet.* fr. V Kassel).[67]

Although of less value as proof of the second book's erstwhile existence, one fragment of smaller compass serves to demonstrate that material has been lost from the extant *Poetics*, into which it cannot be fitted; this material seems therefore to have been lost at the end. The learned Antiatticist, second century after Christ,[68] quotes the form κυντότατον from Aristotle's *Poetics* (*Anecdota* Bekker I 101.32 = fr. IV Kassel).[69] But *Poet.* fr. VI Kassel is rightly seen as spurious. The sixth-century philosopher Philoponus, commenting on the *de Anima*, says that Aristotle discussed the final cause in the *Poetics* and the *de Generatione* (p.269.28 Hayduck): the latter report is wrong, and the former is probably an error for the *Physics*.[70]

The value of such minor quotations is reduced by the possibility that they originated in the Περὶ Ποιητῶν, a more popular exoteric work in three books. Confusion between the *Poetics* and the *On Poets* is manifest in two places: (i) the 'Plutarchan' life of Homer 3 (I 25 Allen, = fr. 66 Rose) quotes the third book of the Περὶ Ποιητικῆς for Aristotle's version of Homer's birth, and (ii) Diogenes Laertius (II 46, fr. 75 Rose) makes a similarly erroneous reference to a third book of the *Poetics*: however, such confusion is less probable in later writers, since the dialogue seems, like the other exoteric works, to be unknown after the fourth century A.D., while the esoteric works increase in importance.[71] The *On Poets* is quoted, after a spate of references in the second century, by Diogenes Laertius and then Macrobius alone;[72] the *Poetics* are not much quoted before the fourth century, but quite often then and thereafter.[73]

In these mentions, whether by Aristotle or by others, of the *Poetics*, no evidence for a second book can be derived from such turns of phrase as ἐν τοῖς περὶ ποιητικῆς, any more than from our idiom 'in the writings on poetics': so much must be conceded to McMahon and Cantarella, who wished to deny the existence of Book II altogether.[74] But this argument cuts both ways, since such expressions as ἐν τῷ περὶ ποιητικῆς are equally devoid of significance. However, there is no lack of other evidence against their position, in addition to that already given, evidence which actually specifies that there was a second book, and not merely, as at *Poet.* 6.1449b21f., that comedy as well as epic will be discussed later.

This other evidence is as follows:

(i) The list of Aristotle's works in Diogenes Laertius V 24 includes a πραγματεία[75] τέχνης ποιητικῆς ᾱβ̄, i.e. in two books.

(ii) In Hesychius of Miletus' account of Aristotle's life and writings, p.13.75 Rose, we read of a τέχνης ποιητικῆς β̄. These entries follow the treatises on rhetoric, as they should if our *Poetics* is in question. Only one other esoteric work is known that might have become confused with our *Poetics* here, namely the Ποιητικά in one book; however, the location of this in Diogenes' list indicates that it dealt with the problems similar to those discussed in the Ἀπορήματα Ὁμηρικά, *Homeric Problems* (with which *Poet.* 25 may be compared), but with regard to other poets.[76] Hesychius was active under Justinian.

(iii) Ptolemy *al-garīb*, probably of the fourth century,[77] listed the *On Poets*, and the *Poetics* in two books, according to extracts in Arab writers (Düring p.225): we await thorough publication of a full Arabic translation of Ptolemy discovered in 1961. The version of al-Qiftī also lists a work 'On the art of poetry according to the doctrines of Pythagoras and his followers', but this is surely a conflation of two entries, 'On the art of poetry' (first listing) and 'On the doctrines of Pythagoras', which are juxtaposed in the version of ibn-abī-Uṣaibiʿa.[78]

Apart from this evidence for a two-volume *Poetics*, two further testimonia must not be overlooked, despite their late dates:

(iv) Eustratius, commenting on the *Nicomachean Ethics* (VI 7 1141a14f., fol. 95b, p.320.38 Heylbut), says that Aristotle mentions the *Margites* in the *first* book of the *Poetics* (ἐν τῷ πρώτῳ τῆς ποιητικῆς); this refers to 4.1448b30. Eustratius was writing circa A.D. 1100.[79]

(v) In A.D. 1278, William de Moerbeke concluded his translation of our *Poetics* into Latin with the *subscriptio* (according to MS O) 'primus Aristotilis de arte poetica liber explicit'.[80] Although he was using a MS close to A, the oldest direct witness for our text (dating from the mid-tenth century A.D.),[81] which has lost all traces of Book II, William shows no less awareness than did Eustratius of the tradition that such a book once existed.[82]

To summarise, the evidence for a continuation to the *Poetics* of some sort, in which comedy was discussed, is overwhelming; and the evidence that the ancient MS tradition presented this continuation as a second book is very strong.

2.3 The contents of Poetics II *compared with the Treatise*

In his discussion of the lost second book, Fuhrmann[83] asks a number of pertinent questions, which makers of reconstructions would be wise to ponder. These questions are the more important, as Fuhrmann is on the whole a follower of Bernays regarding the Tractate. The risks of reconstruction are compounded, he notes, by the state of comedy in Aristotle's day. Whereas epic and tragedy had already reached their classic form, comedy was still evolving. Therefore we must ask whether the concept of entelechy covered comedy as well as tragedy. If it did, when and by the agency of which poet did comedy attain its 'particular nature'? Was it Aristophanes, mentioned in *Poet.* 3 alongside Sophocles and Homer, the chief representatives of the other two genres? So how then did Aristotle regard the development already apparent in Aristophanes' late plays? Could the *Poetics* have ignored it altogether? How does it tally with this that the plot of comedy is said in *Poet.* 9 to obey the laws of probability?

There is a wide consensus that Aristotle had a low opinion of Aristophanes: that the concept of entelechy did apply to comedy, but that Aristophanes was an intermediate stage in its development, and of limited value. Aristotle quoted him along with later comic poets;[84] but the evidence for his attitude, for or against, is slight. Against the positive indication provided by the aforementioned passage in *Poet.* 3, the sole negative indication is the remark at *E.N.* IV 8.1128a22, where Aristotle contrasts 'old' comedies with 'new' to the detriment of the former, because of their directly abusive content. The importance of *Poet.* 3 cannot be overstressed:[85] attempts to show that Aristophanes is given there as an example of how not to write are unconvincing in the extreme.[86] But *E.N.* IV 8 is very weak evidence, as there is no proof that

Aristotle assigned Aristophanes to 'old' comedy, rather than to the 'middle' comedy to which he is said to belong in a number of sources deriving from Hellenistic scholarship. Indeed I believe that a strong case can be made that this latter arrangement arose before Menander became prominent, and that Aristophanes was thought to constitute the happy mean between 'old' and 'new'.[87] It both goes beyond and contradicts the evidence to say that Aristotle 'undoubtedly' excluded Aristophanes and the Old Comedy from his theorising,[88] or found him 'indecorous and obscene'.[89]

If Aristophanes is to be accommodated, as he surely must be, then we ought to expect an analysis of comedy in *Poetics* II very different from that of tragedy; only in New Comedy are comedy's principles in terms of plot construction closely assimilated to those of tragedy. We could say of Menander, indeed we should say of him, that plot is the life and soul of his plays: in this we can cite the remark of Menander himself ap. Plut. *Mor.* 347f. But it is harder to sustain such a proposition concerning Aristophanes. Any discussion of his humour is bound to include a section on verbal jokes,[90] and there is independent evidence for such a section in *Poetics* II, namely fragments III and IV (synonymy and the comic form κυντότατον). Therefore although we might expect similarities, we would not find as straightforward a translation of *Poetics* I into comic terms as Lane Cooper's.

From the fragments above we have already seen other aspects of the missing discussion of comedy, of the origins of laughter in character, words and deeds, and of the cathartic effect of poetry, as indicated in the *Politics*.[91] Vahlen[92] argued that the references in Iamblichus and Proclus, to which we can add those just found in Olympiodorus,[93] showed that Aristotle discussed both tragedy and comedy in this context. From this a pattern emerges, that Aristotle discussed both how comedy performs its ἔργον, namely by arousing laughter in various ways (this is paralleled by the account of how tragedy arouses pity and fear in *Poetics* 13 — 14), and how the next step in the process operated, i.e. the effect of this experience on the audience. From this alone one can discern the seriousness of the loss of the second book.

Bywater adds,[94] as a reasonable guess, that Book II treated the μῦθοι and ἤθη of comedy; Fuhrmann[95] postulates that it had not only all the same six qualitative elements, but also a quantitative analysis comparable to *Poet.* 12. He thinks a comic hero must have had an 'error', ἁμάρτημα, and also believes that the concept of *peripeteia* would have reappeared, along with the overriding importance of plot. These three ideas belong together, unless the comic ἁμάρτημα was a much less important element in the plot of comedy than in that of tragedy, as in fact I believe it was. Here Fuhrmann is introducing ideas alien to most plays of Aristophanes, and it will, I believe, become apparent that his enthusiasm has carried him too far.

Finally, before we compare all this with the Treatise, some remarks on the probable general state of *Poetics* II are in order. Judging by the extant *Poetics*, Book II cannot have been by any means easy to read; this cannot be too strongly emphasised. Why Book I is so problematic is debated. Much of its difficulty lies in the thought, but the expression too is often far from straight-forward, and some technical terms are used inconsistently. Some ascribe its brevity and allusiveness to the existence of fuller treatments in the *de Poetis*.[96] Perhaps it was left unfinished or in note form by Aristotle himself. However, modern scholars are more sanguine about its basic homogeneity and coherence than were some previous generations. The specialised terminology and contents have certainly caused corruption in the tradition. The text of the *Poetics* is in a far worse state than that of the *Rhetoric*, the only remotely comparable treatise of Aristotle's to survive. Unlike the *Rhetoric*, the *Poetics* was neglected and its most important insights misunderstood or ignored through most of antiquity; its true significance was only appreciated in the Renaissance. While we cannot be certain that the text of Book II, even if preserved intact and unabridged, would be as difficult as that of Book I, we may nonetheless feel sure that it would be corrupt and problematic in many places; far more so, if anything less than the complete text is preserved.

We may now compare the Treatise with the contents of *Poetics* II as reconstructed from the fragments, checking the items against what Ω presents. We find in both a discussion of comedy: attention to the emotional purpose of drama, both tragic and comic, viz. catharsis (coverage of both is expected from Iamblichus and Proclus); discussion of how comedy achieves this purpose, namely through humour, and the different ways in which this may be generated, with the emphases falling on words, deeds and persons, (see below), as promised in *Rhet.* III 2. One of the promised sub-types is synonymy: Porphyry confirms that it was discussed; it appears in Ω. In the same passage Aristotle promises to discuss homonymy and metaphor: the latter is in *Poet.* 21: the former, correctly paired with synonymy, is in Ω. Irony and buffoonery, mentioned just after the reference to the *Poetics'* subdivisions of the laughable in *Rhet.* III 18, supply two of the three comic characters in Ω. Regarding smaller fragments, I shall argue below that the Antiatticist's quotation of the form κυντότατον would fit well in Ω as a specimen of comic alteration to a word, *exallage* (ἐξαλλαγή). The subscription of the MS Riccardianus may indicate (if correctly restored) that iambus was dealt with in addition to comedy in *Poetics* II. No such discussion is found in Ω: but Ω does discriminate between λοιδορία (abuse) and comedy in VII, and I shall argue on XVIII that the tripartition of comedy there relates to the decline of the iambic element within it. As remarked, more than this should not be expected, as iambus is not poetry at all for Aristotle: there is no reason to think that in this respect Ω differs from what *Poetics* II is likely to have contained.

So far the section on laughter (V—VI) with its complex analysis has largely been left out of account, and can now be used as a test case. Does this too correspond with what we expect of *Poetics* II? And does it deal, as I have argued it should, with the robust humour of Aristophanes rather than the milder wit of Menander?

2.4 *The Aristotelian analysis of humour*

In *Rhet.* I 11 Aristotle divided the sources of humour (τὰ γελοῖα) into people, words and deeds (ἄνθρωποι, λόγοι, ἔργα). In Ω V—VI we find a division into λέξις and πράγματα (diction and action). As we have seen, a reference equivalent to ἄνθρωποι (people) occurs next (VII—VIII), and is no problem here. This is of course a very obvious division — but something similar is found in the *Sophistical Refutations* 4f., where objections are divided into those dependent on diction, and those outside it (οἱ μὲν παρὰ τὴν λέξιν, οἱ δ' ἔξω τῆς λέξεως). The humour from diction is closely related to this passage. A stumbling-block to Ω as a whole has been the alleged incoherence of these sections, and it will be necessary to undertake a detailed examination of them. I shall first provide a tabulation of the text as presented to us in the MSS.

A. From λέξις
   1. Homonymy
   2. Synonymy
   3. Adoleschy (repetition)
   4. Paronymy — by addition and subtraction
   5. Diminutives
   6. *Exallage* (alteration) — by the voice and similar means.*
   7. The manner of speaking.

* So C. The remark is omitted here by **a** and appended instead to the 'manner of speaking'.

B. From πράγματα
   1. Deception
   2. Assimilation (to the better, or to the worse)**
   3. The impossible
   4. The possible and inconsequential
   5. The unexpected
   6. From debasing the characters
   7. From vulgar dancing
   8. From choosing the worst when one has power to choose the best
   9. From incoherent argument.

** **a** breaks off here.

This list, especially its latter half, seems to make little sense to begin with; I shall deal first with the former.

A. *Humour from the diction*

The first three categories relate to whole words. Homonyms are the same word with different meanings; synonyms, different words with the same meaning; adoleschy means using the same word or words with the same meaning repeatedly. Paronymy and the two subsequent types relate to *parts* of words, whether they are altered by adding, subtracting, or mutating sounds and syllables. This makes fair sense, but it is problematic that paronymy, a very large category, should be on a par with the small categories of diminutives and *exallage*, the latter of which is given as a variety of altered word in *Poet.* 22. It is an almost inevitable supposition that these two categories really belong to paronymy; we might reconstruct 'fourth, by paronymy, that is by adding something to the current word, or by subtraction, or by diminutives, or by *exallage* . . .' and suppose that Ω assigned these subheadings full status because their subordinate status was not apparent in the original. Aristotelian lists are often difficult to square with the numbers attached to them, e.g. in *Poet.* 25, while one major heading, κόσμος, has been lost entirely in *Poet.* 22. This yields the structure:

1. Homonymy   (whole words; same word, different meaning)
2. Synonymy   (whole words; different word, same meaning)
3. Adoleschy   (whole words; same word, same meaning)
4. Paronymy   (parts of words; with subdivisions, addition,
                            subtraction, diminutives, alterations)

5. < ? >
6. < ? >
7. The manner of speaking.

Whether the mistaken promotion of diminutives and alterations caused the loss of the other two items to keep the number of headings at seven, or whether the reverse occurred, i.e. that they were promoted to fill a gap, is immaterial: in view of the problems in other Aristotelian catalogues this inconcinnity in transmission presents no difficulty.

Rhet. III 2 informs us that both homonyms and synonyms have been dealt with in the *Poetics*, and they dutifully reappear. This is not the only passage where they occur together — cf. *Cat.* 1, where we find homonyms, synonyms and paronyms in the same order. The *Rhetoric* provides a further pointer when it states that homonyms are useful to the sophist, but synonyms to the poet. If we turn to *Sophistical Refutations* 4f. we find the following six ἔλεγχοι παρὰ τὴν λέξιν (arguments from diction):

    1. ὁμωνυμία; 2. ἀμφιβολία; 3. παρὰ τὴν σύνθεσιν; 4. παρὰ τὴν διαίρεσιν; 5. παρὰ τὴν προσῳδίαν; 6. σχῆμα λέξεως.

It is striking that the first and last items of this list are identical to those in Ω: otherwise the latter is woven together from *Cat.* and *Rhet.* also. Some of these headings recur in the treatment of poetic problems in *Poet.* 25.1461a21 − 6, namely προσῳδία, διαίρεσις and ἀμφιβολία. We shall see how poetic problems supply good material for comedy; the *Refutations*, so similar here, do in fact use as examples sophistic criticism of poetry, including comedy(?), cyclic epic and the *Iliad* (*S.E.* 4.166a36ff.). The *Rhetoric*'s allusion to both works completes the ring. Note also that the *Refutations* define and exemplify adoleschy (3.165b15, 13.173a32ff.).

What of the lacuna of two headings which I have postulated? It must be confessed at once that only guesswork can fill it. In his *Verses On Comedy* 76ff. Tzetzes gives a list evidently derived from one very like ours: the items are ὁμώνυμα, παρῳδίαι, κλήσεων πλάσεις τε καὶ μεταπλάσεις, κορισμοί and καταχρήσεις. This is incomplete; it certainly omits synonyms, adoleschy and the parts ἀπὸ τῶν πραγμάτων. Now it may be entirely derivative, a Tzetzean farrago of misrememberings and paraphrase standing for homonyms, paronyms, paronyms and alterations, diminutives and figures of speech (if that is what σχῆμα λέξεως means). However, it is at least worth pondering the possibility that παρῳδίαι is not a blunder for παρώνυμα, but represents parody, a comic resource extremely valuable to the poets of Old and Middle Comedy. The extract's example of exallage fits parody better, with an interesting parallel in Hermogenes. κατάχρησις denotes the misapplication of a word, and this is a type of metaphor — one that readily lends itself to laughter. Metaphor has much wider connotations in the *Rhetoric* than it does for us. Aristotle himself said that most jokes arise through metaphor (*Rhet.* III 11), and earlier he mentioned that comedians use metaphors (III 3.1406b7, cf. *Poet.* 22.1458b13 et alibi). Thus metaphor is indispensable to humour, and if Tzetzes did not supply it we would have to have done so, as is done by Rutherford and Starkie without reference to him. Its position is further secured by *Rhet.* III 2.1405b28, where the use of diminutives appears alongside it, while the placing of προσῳδία in *S.E.* 4 gives some slight support to the inclusion of παρῳδία here (see comm.).

The position of metaphor as penultimate entry is vindicated by the following consideration. In C the entry in this position has subjoined to it the words 'in sound (voice) or things of the same kind': these belong to the last item in **a**, where they must be rendered 'by the manner of speaking, in the voice and similar', i.e. acting technique, gestures and so forth: even this maltreats ὁμογενέσι. The words are nonsensical when attached to *exallage*, since nobody has ever been able to specify how one can alter a word except verbally. But in the *Rhetoric*'s discussion of metaphor in III 2, Aristotle said: τὰς μεταφορὰς ἐντεῦθεν οἰστέον, ἀπὸ καλῶν ἢ τῇ φωνῇ ἢ τῇ δυνάμει ἢ τῇ ὄψει ἢ ἄλλῃ τινὶ αἰσθήσει, and cf. 1405a35 ἔτι δὲ οὐ πόρρωθεν δεῖ ἀλλὰ ἐκ τῶν συγγενῶν καὶ ὁμοειδῶν μεταφέρειν. At once all is clear. These words urged the writer to compare like with like, within some category of sense-perception (here, sound); after the loss of metaphor they have become attached to the previous surviving heading in one source, and to that following in the other.

We see in this section, then, a nexus of coherent Aristotelian ideas. Only one item remains mysterious — the last. More than one possible meaning may be culled from Aristotle, but I shall show in the commentary that this most probably refers to the performance of sentences of different syntactic types, e.g. rendering a prayer as a command, perhaps as part of a very wide category including the acting.

B. *Humour from* πράγματα

The first two headings, deception and assimilation, are the only two found in **a**. This may reflect a structural feature of the original text, in which these were given first, followed by the others after an interval. In Cicero's treatment of the *ridiculum* (*de Orat.* II 240ff.), after two kinds, 'fabula vel enarratio ficta' and 'imitatio depravata', we read: 'ergo haec duo genera sunt eius ridiculi, quod in re est . . . ' He then gives a long series of *ridiculum quod est in verbo*, but no other types *in re* until much later. It can be shown that the two treatments are not directly related, since Cicero's classification is more complicated than the Tractate's, and thus it seems best to assume that Cicero's *source* was in some way related to our treatise on comedy.

A parallel to these two heads is found in *Rhet.* III 11, but there metaphor and the deception of expectations are the main *verbal* sources of wit, as it seems. This problem will be examined ad loc. There is an interesting parallel to assimilation (ὁμοίωσις) in *Topics* III 2, where different epic characters are discussed. However, in the next series of headings we are again on familiar territory. This is not at once obvious; at first sight the list is inconsequential. The first three items — the impossible, the illogical, and the surprising, all evidently part of plot — are followed by a reference to character, then to dancing, then to character again! What can these oddities have in common? Are they not a random list, when the more critical among us expect an incisive analysis? K.K. Smith[97] attacked the list on the grounds that it

> 'neither is restricted to the single consideration of what enhances the dramatic effect of the "ludicrous" nor yet includes this subject in a larger treatment based on all six constitutive elements of comedy. The Tractate's catalogue contains the heading "Diction", but no heading for Plot, Ethos, Dianoia, Music or Spectacle. Separately the Tractate speaks of Ethos, Dianoia, Music and Spectacle, but without explaining how they may be made ludicrous.'

As Smith remarks, the kinds of the ludicrous do not correspond to the account of how tragedy achieves its effect through *hamartia*, *peripeteia* and *anagnorisis*. It has been shown above why this difference is no surprise, but instead another sign of Aristotelian authorship. As Aristotle indicates, to attain the end of tragedy, the ἔργον τῆς τραγῳδίας, pity and fear are aroused essentially through the plot, but in various passages he clearly derives laughter, the end of comedy, from multifarious other sources: contrast the crudity of Diomedes *Ars Gramm.* III 488, XXIV 3 Koster, and Schol. Dion. Thr. XVIIIb2 Koster, where tragedy is said to have its end in murders and deaths, comedy in recognition. Smith sets a worthier standard, and in fact I believe that he has correctly intuited what is required — and that Aristotle did after all supply it. The common thread running through the catch-all list of 'things' is the exemplification of how the most important qualitative parts of comedy, except diction which has already been discussed, can be exploited for humorous purposes. The recognition of this purpose obviates the inadequacy, unevenness, incomprehensibility and redundancy decried by Smith. I propose that the third, fourth and fifth types relate to plot, the sixth, seventh and eighth to character, and the ninth to thought, *dianoia*. The list is representative rather than complete, and redolent of Aristotelian acuity. We may tabulate, with explanation and parallels, as follows:

B. From πράγματα

1. Deception		[Source of wit in *Rhet*. III 11]
2. Assimilation		[Source of wit in *Rhet*. III 11]
3. The impossible		[Poetic problem in *Poet*. 25]
4. The illogical	(Plot)	[Poetic problem in *Poet*. 25]
5. The unexpected		[cf. *Poet*. 9.1452a4]
6. Debasing the characters		[Poetic problem in *Poet*. 25]
	(Character)	
7. The use of vulgar		[cf. *E.N*. IV 8 init., *Pol*. VIII 5−6]
dancing	(Character, Song and Spectacle)	
8. Choosing badly	(Character)	[cf. *E.N*. III 2]
9. Incoherent argument	(Thought)	[cf. *E.N*. III 2]

This gives us a descending amount of representation — plot, character, thought, with a smaller rôle allotted to song and spectacle in 7: this is analogous to the representation of the respective parts of tragedy in the *Poetics*. I must explain how it works.

Entries 3, 4 and 6 reappear in different guise in *Poet*. 25 among the poetic problems inherent in the art (προβλήματα τὰ πρὸς αὐτὴν τὴν τέχνην, 1460b22). It is clear that Aristotle appreciated their comic possibilities; in *Poet*. 24 he remarks that the pursuit of Hector round the walls of Troy, with the whole Greek army standing to watch, while effective in epic, would be absurd on stage; this example covers both the impossible and the illogical. Debasement of the characters follows from Aristotle's statement that comedy aims to represent men as worse, tragedy as better than in real life (*Poet*. 2.1448a16). For the comic effect of this where inappropriate, cf. 15.1454a28ff. and 25.1461b21, where the Menelaus in Euripides' *Orestes* is criticised as gratuitously nasty. In tragedy this is a fault — a character must not fall through wickedness (*Poet*. 13) — but faults in tragedy are sustenance for comedy. Similarly the unfair objections of sophists seen in the *Refutations*, and in the poetic problems of *Poet*. 25, are brought together in this list. Finally, these three entries are juxtaposed at the close of *Poet*. 25 (1461b23); their collocation gives conclusive support to this interpretation of entry 6 against another which is linguistically possible (see comm.). The intrusion of the unexpected here is not a problem, since it is appropriate before attention shifts away from the humorous potentialities of plot. Aristotle was no despiser of the surprise (cf. *Rhet.* III 11.1412a25), and at *Poet.* 9.1452a1ff. remarks on the value of logically motivated surprise in a plot — surprise brought about by the necessary or the probable. Thus the best place to discuss comic surprise is in the same context as the improbable and the unnecessary (I refer to unmotivated baseness of character, entry 6).

With entry 6, though remaining in the realm of the poetic *problemata*, we move on to character, and I believe stay there for 7 and 8. Entry 7, the use of vulgar dancing, pertains at first sight to the performance only, but consideration of *E.N.* IV 8.1127b33ff. and *Pol.* VIII 5—6 has led me to a different conclusion, that the use of vulgar dancing reflects, not only on the poet's ability to raise a laugh by staging it, but also on the character who is perpetrating such lasciviousness. Aristotle, in the passages mentioned, makes a firm distinction between those entertainments proper to respectable people, and those suitable only for the vulgar, who prefer buffoonery to wit proper. In the *Politics* he reviews the suitability of various kinds of music for the education of free men, with a marked bias against performances seen as in any way degrading. He does not discuss dancing in either context, but it is legitimate to extend his views by analogy to this field, and the epithet 'vulgar' conveys a like disapprobation: who but 'vulgar' people would use 'vulgar' dances? This is therefore a mark of *character*, just as much as the preceding and succeeding categories. For verbal parallels in Aristotle linking entries 6 and 7, see on VI 7.

The last two entries are not problematic. Choice is the essence of Aristotelian ethics, and making the wrong choice is obviously a matter of character. Logic that is disjointed and lacks sequence pertains to thought (*dianoia*), and follows naturally after erroneous choice; the link between these is explicit at *E.N.* III 2.1111b6ff., and especially 3.1112a18ff., where emphasis is laid on the fact that choice must be between possibles, just as here.

Thus I argue that the whole analysis of humour is sophisticated, far from random and skilfully woven from different strands in Aristotelian thought; that it suits its context in the Tractate as a whole, as illustrative of the four main qualitative parts of comedy; and that it corresponds closely to what we expect, on external as well as internal grounds, of the discussion of humour in *Poetics* II.

3. The problem of authenticity

It should now be clear that Ω does contain Aristotelian material, both in overall structure and the more plentiful detail of V — VI. At least some of this material is derived, I think it will be agreed, from *Poetics* II. But several questions are still unanswered. The commentary will append further details to the arguments about structure; but the essentials are already stated. Now the discrepancies between C and **a** in V — VI 2 reveal that both of them altered Ω, partly by accident, and partly by deliberate omission. Elsewhere C is effectively our only source for Ω. Clearly a great deal was omitted in C: presumably Ω was no less full elsewhere than **a** reveals it to have been in V — VI 2. Does C fairly represent the structure of Ω? Does Ω fairly represent the structure of *Poetics* II? On the analogy of the situation in V — VI 2, where we can compare C to **a**, I am prepared to answer that C probably does give a fair representation of Ω. But to bridge the gap between Ω and *Poet.* II we have to apply two methods — reconstruction from fragments of the latter, and from the parallel structure of the extant *Poetics* — which can yield no more than probable results. I am persuaded that the structure of Ω as given in C does make very good sense if it represents the major headings of *Poet.* II, and that it represents them accurately in terms of both sequence and content: I see no reason why the Tractate should not also assign them roughly the amount of prominence which each section possessed in the original lost Book II. But I must state forthrightly that this is a judgement based on probabilities. It is impossible to prove a positive. Either this explanation will best explain the phenomena, or someone will find weaknesses and propose a better one. At least I shall have shown that there are phenomena to be explained.

This caveat about probability applies equally to the question of whether this *Poetics* II, granting that this is what Ω represents, is by Aristotle, or a forgery. I have stated a case for thinking that it presupposes a preceding work practically identical to *Poetics* I: whether such a work ever existed that was not our *Poetics* I, again depends on a judgement of probability, which each reader must make for himself. I have suggested that some elements in Ω are unlikely to be forgeries, and shall suggest the same of numerous others below: again the reader must judge.

However, no such caveat governs the arguments in favour of forgery that have been advanced by certain scholars. These arguments are trying to prove a negative, and stand or fall on matters of fact. I shall now show that, wherever the facts are definitely established, the arguments which have so far been advanced are not cogent, and many are self-defeating. It will be convenient to separate form and content in examining these arguments, and I shall append to them references to arguments in favour of the authenticity of the same sections.

3.1 Aristotelian diction

Bernays was first to impugn the Tractate's language. He stated that several words are not only unaristotelian, which means, of course, unattested in the extant corpus of genuine works and fragments of Aristotle, but also of later origin. Such lexicographical arguments are very difficult. That a particular word occurs in Aristotle usually signifies very little; that it is not signifies about as much. Lack of attestation of a term before a given date is no proof that it could not have been used earlier, especially if evidence for writing of the appropriate type is scanty, as is certainly true of classical and Hellenistic literary criticism. A good illustration of the hazards is provided by *Phaedrus* 255−67, where a number of technical terms of literary criticism used by Plato are either unique, or unattested until the Roman period. Another case with far-reaching results is the usual dating of Demetrius *On Style* to the late Republic, on linguistic grounds: and this despite agreement that the work is in content early Peripatetic, very close to Aristotle and Theophrastus; it cites no writer later than the early third century B.C.[98] One method of approach is to compare the new vocabulary in C with the words attested in Aristotle in the *Poetics* only, compiled from Bonitz. These latter are as follows:[99]

ἀγγελία, ἀγερμός, ἀγώνισμα, ἀδελφή, ἀήθης, αἰτίασις, ἀκουσ-τός, ἀναγνωρισμός, ἀνάπαιστος, ἀνεκτός, ἀπαγγέλλειν, ἀπεικάζειν, ἀπεργασία, ἀποκοπή, ἀποσεμνύνειν, ἀρτικροτεῖ-σθαι, ἀτράγῳδος, αὐτοσχεδίασμα, αὐτοσχεδιαστικός, βαρ-βαρισμός, δέσις, διακωμῳδεῖν, διηγηματικός, διθυραμβικός, διθυραμβοποιητική, δραματικός, δραματοποιεῖν, ἐθελοντής, εἰ-κονογράφος, εἰκονοποιός, ἐκπληκτικός, ἐλεγοποιός, ἐμβόλιμος, ἐντολή, ἐξαλλαγή, ἐξάρχειν, ἐπεισόδιον, ἐπιστολή, ἐπιτίμημα, ἐποποιία, ἐποποιικός, ἠθογράφος, ἡμίφωνος, θέατρον, θεσπέ-σιος, ἰαμβίζειν, ἰαμβικός, ἰαμβοποιεῖν, ἰαμβοποιός, κακοδαι-μονία, καταπλέκειν, κιθάρισις, κιθαριστικός, κομμός, κωμ-ῳδεῖν, λευκογραφεῖν, μιαρός, μύθευμα, ὀρχηστικός, παρῳδία, πέμψις, περιδέραιον, περιεργάζεσθαι, πέρσις, πολλαπλοῦς, πο-λύμυθος, προαγόρευσις, προπράττειν, πτωχεία, ῥαψῳδεῖν, ῥῆσις, σατυρικός, σκάφη, σκευοποιός, σκηνογραφία, συβότης, συναγων-ίζεσθαι, σύνδηλος, τετραπλοῦς, τραγῳδοδιδάσκαλος, τραυματίας, τρίμετρον, τροφός, τρῶσις, ὕμνος, φαλλικός, χειμαίνειν, ψευδ-άγγελος, ψιλομετρία, ψυχαγωγεῖν, ψυχαγωγικός.

With these 91 words compare the ten not found in the extant writings of Aristotle including the *Poetics*, but used in C. These are in fact nearly all paralleled in Aristotle by the equivalent noun or adjective (there are no new words, poetic forms excluded, in **a**):

ἀκολουθία (VI 9); ἀνακόλουθος (VI 4); ἀπαγγελτικός (II); ἀπαρακαλύπτως (VII); ἀσυνάρτητος (VI 9); δημώδης (XIV); ὁμοίωσις (VI 2); παιδευτικός (I); παρωνυμία (V 4); ὑφηγη-τικός (I).

All except ἀσυνάρτητος and ὑφηγητικός are attested from the fifth or fourth centuries B.C. (see commentary). The *Poetics* is circa 10,000 words long, the Tractate scarcely 400, but with a far heavier concentration of nouns and adjectives in epitome: therefore 91 to ten new words is the sort of ratio to be expected.

Two terms found in Aristotle are used in an extended sense in C: ἔμφασις 'implication, innuendo' at VII, and πρόσωπον 'personage, character' at VI 6. I am not satisfied that either would be impossible for Aristotle in these senses, although on the one occasion when he does speak of innuendo, he uses a different word (ὑπόνοια): v. commentary for the possibility that the true sense is 'fantasy'.

On the positive side, C uses Aristotle's term μῦθος for 'comic plot', rather than the later πλάσμα or ὑπόθεσις. However, diction that is simply the same as Aristotle's, which means nearly all the wording of Ω, is open to the suspicion that it is merely borrowed from him. Thus XV, Γ τῆς Δ ἐστιν ἴδιον, is very characteristic, but not particularly significant; the definition of comedy in IV, almost entirely phrased as is that of tragedy in *Poet.* 6, came under heavy attack from Bernays precisely because it is so similarly worded, and yet applied to comedy: the compiler adapted the *Poetics*, argued Bernays. Instead we should look at phrases which can be held unlikely to have been forged or invented. δραματικὸν καὶ πρακτικόν in II has close parallels in *Poet.* as far as sense is concerned, but not in adjectival expression. The clearest case is III, δι' οἴκτου καὶ δέους, where we expect δι' ἐλέου καὶ φόβου for those central Aristotelian concepts 'pity and fear'. Bernays condemned the divergence as the result of the compiler's attempt to conceal his dependence on Aristotle (which he proceeds flagrantly to advertise in IV). But the variation is Aristotelian, current in both *Rhet.* and *Poet.* (οἶκτον καὶ δείνωσιν, δεινὰ ἢ οἰκτρά). One of his salient arguments against the Tractate vanishes (see comm.). But there is more: this variation has gone unnoticed for centuries; how likely is it that a forger, however competent, would have observed it?

Another objection is to ἀμίμητος ποίησις in I: is not all true poetry mimetic for Aristotle? Indeed: but once again Aristotle's terminology is less fixed than Bernays thought; he frequently refers to verse-writers and their works as poets and poetry, even when these clearly did not qualify as such by his own criterion of mimesis. The popular equation of poet with versifier was simply convenient, in the absence of a separate word for the latter (see comm. on I−II).

In favour of Ω's wording I mention among other parallels the Aristotelian ambiguity in the word ἡδονή in IV (p.157ff.), the variation between singular and plural in the list at XIII which defends the transmitted texts of *Rhet.* and *Poet.* in several places (p.220), or the parallels between XVIII, *Poet.* 4−5, and *Rhet.* III 3 (p.243).

If this defence succeeds, it follows that Ω gives an accurate sample of Aristotelian diction, such as is unlikely to have been forged. Considering the vicissitudes which the text appears to have undergone, the evidence of the diction is both surprising and intriguing: the only phrase where there is a presumption of non-Aristotelian origin is the peculiar metaphor found in III and IV (ἔχει δὲ μητέρα), which would be tolerable if οἷον has been lost in transmission (v. comm.). To refute the charge of forgery and compilation, proof is not required that Ω's diction is almost entirely

Aristotelian; the case depends above all on the content, whose expression could well have been altered during the excerption and epitomisation of the text. That the surviving wording should be subtly and thoroughly Aristotelian lends no support to Bernays. Indeed, the very looseness in terminology, to which exception has often been taken, is a typical Aristotelian feature. As Guthrie[100] remarks, Aristotle's 'commonsense sympathies led him to use words still in their ordinary meanings even after he had established them for particular purposes in specialised contexts'. For this, there are innumerable parallels in his extant work,[101] and this feature of his philosophy should be kept firmly in mind by the judicious reader of the Tractate.

3.2 Aristotelian ideas

Here we can discuss only briefly the respects in which the ideas of the Treatise have been supposed to agree or disagree with Aristotle. For full discussion, see the commentary.

I. Poetry is divided into unmimetic and mimetic. As remarked, Aristotle does use the term poetry loosely, and there is no contradiction to his ideas here. Moreover, the classification of poetry follows his lines, in contrast to other ancient classifications of the *genres*, which replicate Platonic models: mimetic poetry is *subdivided* into narrative and dramatic, instead of being *equated* with the latter only.

II. Mime is included under dramatic poetry. In *Poet.* I, mime is mentioned in the context of the nature of poetry, where it is certainly part of *poesis*: there are similar references in Aristotle's *On Poets*. As the only form of dramatic fiction, except the Socratic dialogue, that existed in his day, Aristotle could reasonably have termed it dramatic: Hellenistic writers certainly did so.

III. The purpose of tragedy is the removal of pity and fear through the agency of these same emotions. This is catharsis, although III does not use this term: instead it speaks of a balance, *symmetria*, as do certain late sources, principally Proclus and Olympiodorus. It is odd, if C is a forgery imitating Aristotle, that it should avoid his term here, and use that current in the late sources: equally odd, if it is trying to disguise dependence on Aristotle, that it should use the term catharsis in the definition of comedy in IV. Both tragedy in III and comedy in IV aim to purge the tragic and comic emotions by means of those emotions: the two are explicitly set in parallel in IX. Catharsis is too large and important a subject to be dealt with here: in the commentary on III it is argued that Ω contains the same teaching as that of Aristotle, *Pol.* VIII, where the difficulties are to be resolved by the concept of homoeopathy, and the same as that found in cognate later sources. Catharsis applied as much to epic and comedy as to tragedy, is to be linked with Aristotle's central concept of *mimesis*, and constitutes the obvious and valid retort to Plato's denigration of poetry as a lubricious stimulant of the emotions.

IV. The definition of comedy has been attacked as too slavish an imitation of Aristotle's definition of tragedy, too divergent, and too corrupt. The corruption is a surface problem, neither surprising nor worrying, for a difficult technical passage transmitted with no means of elucidation such as are supplied in *Poet.* 6, where in fact the text of the definition of tragedy has been improved from C. Two phrases have come in for particular attack. First, how can the action represented by comedy be called ἀμοίρου μεγέθους τελείου? Bernays translated 'lacking size, perfect', which would would indeed be an incompetent and impossible reversal of Aristotle's description of the action in tragedy as 'complete, possessing size' (τελείας, μέγεθος ἐχούσης). Later attempts to emend or to render ἀμοίρου as other than 'lacking' are unconvincing, and Bernays' objection has been seen as fundamental by subsequent students of the Tractate. But his reading and translation is not the only one possible. If we read 'lacking perfect size', this can be held to match Aristotle's views if we bear in mind that size is a necessary condition for the beautiful, but the laughable is part of the ugly, and also basic to comedy (*Poet.* 5.1449a34). A comic mask, for instance, is ugly and distorted. Thus it might be held that the comic action is exaggerated and distorted; such distortion is common in Aristophanes, although not in Menander. Another, better, possibility was suggested by Baumgart and Kayser, who translate 'of an action that is complete but lacking in grandeur'. The translation of μέγεθος by 'grandeur' is unusual for Aristotle, but guaranteed once in the *Poetics*, and in a significant context: early tragedy lacked μέγεθος, as it evolved from 'small' or 'trivial' plots and absurd diction and only became serious late (4.1449a19). The collocation of ideas — that comedy depends on the absurd and lacks μέγεθος — is significantly similar to this account of early tragedy, and Bernays' objection cannot bear the weight which has been placed upon it.

The second problem is ἡδονὴ καὶ γέλως, 'pleasure and laughter', of the comic emotions. Bernays objected that terms of different orders could not be juxtaposed, as γέλως is a sub-category of ἡδονή. But the juxtaposition of heading and sub-category is found in Aristotle, e.g. *E.N.* II 5.1105b25 (on pain). Again, Bernays ignores Aristotle's frequent mention of different kinds of 'pleasure', when he objects that pleasure resides in tragedy also, and cannot therefore be distinctive of and definitive of comedy. In the *Poetics* tragedy and comedy are said to produce different kinds of pleasure. The difficulty here is augmented by two Aristotelian uses of the word 'pleasure' — of a pleasurable activity, and the resultant feeling; the use of ἡδονή to denote both has caused difficulties in understanding Aristotle's accounts of ἡδονή in *E.N.* VII and X. Here ἡδονή is on a par with παιδιά, 'play', 'innocent mirth' or 'delight', while γέλως represents less innocent aspects of humour; this usage is to be distinguished from the pleasure resulting from comedy, which is produced by means of the catharsis of the comic emotions. 'Pleasure and laughter', given moderate expression by mimesis, relieve one's impulse to the immoderate display of these emotions in everyday life, and in so doing produce pleasure.

Finally, IV gives support to a broader view (held by a minority) of the celebrated phrase τῶν τοιούτων παθημάτων in the definition of tragedy, which is found to have more parallels than had been realised (p.16of.). Tragic catharsis can affect not only pity and fear, but other painful emotions also, such as anger.

V—VI have passed as Aristotelian without challenge since Cramer's remarks in 1839. In addition to the arguments above, several points deserve mention here. The division into diction and 'actions' suits comedy better than oratory, to which Cicero applies it; the underlying structure, in which the types of humour are related to the qualitative parts of comedy, has no counterpart in the analyses of Demetrius and Cicero, which are more elaborate and less incisive (comm. on V–VI). **a**'s citations of otherwise unknown comic fragments tell against a late forgery. The example of synonymy covers Aristotle's philosophical usage of the term in *Categories* 1 as of genus and species, not merely his wider usage (comm. on V 2). Note **a**'s Aristotelian use of τὸ κύριον in the explanation of paronymy (V 4). Like Ω, Aristotle recognised the comic value of diminutives (V 4) and metaphor (V 6): the account of the latter as reconstructed is close to the *Rhetoric*, as is the separation of the first two headings in VI (p.189f.). Both associate 'making alike' with superior and inferior characters (VI 2). C helps to explain a digression in *Poet.* 15 (VI 4).

VII. Comedy is distinguished from abuse by its indirect method of attack. At *E.N.* IV 8.1128a23 Aristotle makes a similar distinction, but between old and recent comedies, not between abuse and comedy itself. The two have been thought contradictory, but this disregards Aristotle's concept of entelechy: comedy, like tragedy, develops towards its essence in his system, and we shall see signs of the same development in XVIII. In any case Aristotle draws such a distinction between abuse (ψόγος) and the laughable at *Poet.* 4.1448b37.

There are parallels between comic ἔμφασις (innuendo, fantasy?) and Aristotle's remarks on dreams: see comm.

VIII. The errors of comedy are those of body and soul. This implies that they include bodily deformations, for which the characters are not culpable, as well as mistakes, for which they are. That tragic *hamartia* similarly includes accident as well as error has recently been deduced independently from the acknowledged works of Aristotle by R. Sorabji, while R.A. Pack noted that the philosopher views comic error likewise in *Poet.* 5.

IX. See on III.

X. The qualitative parts of comedy have been criticised as being slavishly taken from the *Poetics*, although such austere critics of the Tractate as Bywater admit that they are needed. The order in which the parts are given, both in Ω and *Poet.*, varies; the two works share a reversal in the sequence *ethos – dianoia* (p.213). The naming of the six parts as ὕλη 'material', for the εἴδη 'parts' of the

Poetics, has been rightly criticised: I argue that in fact ὕλη is corrupt for εἶδη.

XI. Regarding comic plot, it can be established from Ω that plot is not as paramount in comedy as in tragedy, but that it is still important. This difference from the *Poetics* inheres in the nature of the genres discussed, if one bears in mind that Ω is not dealing with New Comedy.

XII. The choice of comic characters has won praise ever since Bernays. The three cited bring together different kinds of deviance from the mean in two passages, *E.N.* II 7 and *Rhet.* III 18.

XIII. The division of *dianoia* into two parts, *gnōmē* and *pistis*, is also found in *Poet.* Lane Cooper has convinced recent editors of C that the listing of five types of *pistis* relates well to comedy, and is not irrelevant as nineteenth-century scholars thought.

XIV. This section has nothing to offer for or against, although its doctrine is certainly Peripatetic.

XV. The entries on song and spectacle in drama fill a gap in the extant *Poetics*, where these are passed over and Aristotle moves straight on to epic. The dismissal of song is rather characteristic.

XVI. The statement that plot, song and diction are present in all comedies, but the other elements are not, accords with a *locus conclamatus* in *Poet.* 6, where nearly all scholars have emended the text to imply the opposite of this (1450a7ff.), or at least refused to believe that Aristotle does mean that not all tragedians use all the parts of tragedy. That he does is confirmed by several passages elsewhere; and, in both comedy and tragedy, *Poet.* 4−5 reveals that song, diction (i.e. spoken verses) and plot are the elements basic to their development (see the commentary for the justification of these unorthodox statements). Thus the text of *Poet.* 6 can be decisively clarified, and the correct readings established.

XVII. The analysis of the quantitative parts of comedy presents difficulties similar to those over *Poet.* 12. Both analyses have been thought banal and oversimplified; but it should be remembered that analysis of this sort tends to move from the simple to the sophisticated, as scholars through the generations exercise their ingenuity on the unelaborated efforts of their predecessors. As has been remarked,[102] in the *Rhetoric* Aristotle regards the formal divisions of speeches as only a small part of the subject, of limited importance, and the same applies to drama. *Poet.* 12 is based on two fundamental Aristotelian principles, the mutually exclusive λόγος and μέλος (spoken verse and song), and the concept of beginning, middle and end; I see no reason to deny it to him (comm. ad XVII). The principles of XVII are the same, and the main quantitative parts of comedy are the same as those of tragedy, just as are the qualitative parts; the parabasis, for instance, passes unmentioned and unanalysed.[103] But for this peculiarity, which is less difficult when we recall the dropping of the parabasis even in Aristophanes' last plays, and the range of comedy about which C is generalising (cf. XVIII), I see no reason why Aristotle should not have assigned these parts to comedy. Those who do not agree should recognise that the rejection of this section no more entails the conclusion that Ω as a whole is a stupid compilation, than does the rejection of *Poet.* 12 entail a similar conclusion about that work.

There are interesting minor differences; the choral element is usefully qualified, and the definition of the exodos differs from that in *Poet.* 12, which has often been thought inane. The different definition in C has prompted me to reexamine a variant reading in the *Poetics*, which will permit the sense of ἔξοδος known elsewhere. I refer to καθ' ὅ in B, for μεθ' ὅ in the other sources, which yields 'the exodos is a complete part of a tragedy, insofar as it is' (for 'after which there is') 'not a choral song'. In a later Peripatetic classification the exodos appears twice, listed as both an independent part and a choral song (p.238).

XVIII. Many since Bernays have believed that this contains a reference to New Comedy, but it is not certain that its division of comedy into 'old', 'new' and 'middle' corresponds to that in use today. At *E.N.* IV 8 Aristotle spoke of 'old' and 'recent' comedies, and his view of the differences between them is the same as that expressed here. Moreover the two extremes — comedy that has too much of the absurd, and is too serious — are the two poles of bad metaphor at *Rhet.* III 3; the same polarity is found in the development of tragedy itself at *Poet.* 4.1449a19. Moreover a number of late sources show that the original tripartition of comedy did not include Menander: comedy before the Peloponnesian War was 'old', Aristophanes (*sic*) was 'middle', and it was in the latter's last plays that 'new' comedy appeared. The plentiful evidence for these astounding heterodoxies will be found in the commentary.

Detailed study of the text has thus led me to these conclusions:

(i) Ω is a unity, not a farrago from different sources.

(ii) Ω has a coherent structure, of Peripatetic origin.

(iii) Ω is Aristotelian in both diction and content.

(iv) Ω corresponds well to what we know of *Poetics* II, and its structure strongly suggests that it is intended to represent it.

3.3 The Treatise, Poetics II *and the question of forgery*

Any defence of Aristotle's authorship must tread a narrow path. If what we find is too slavish a copy of Aristotle, like Lane Cooper's transmogrification of the *Poetics*, then we are fully entitled to be suspicious; if it is too unlike, then it is not Aristotelian. I contend that Ω comfortably observes the mean between these two extremes, as a well-behaved Aristotelian work should. But if Ω is a forgery, intended to replace or supplement the lost *Poetics*, the forger has followed a very self-contradictory method. In III he is charged by Bernays with changing the wording to hide his dependence on Aristotle: in IV he is said to produce an 'utter travesty' of *Poet.* 6. He is loose in his terminology, and flexible in his construction of Aristotelian ideas. He shows knowledge of even more Aristotelian works than Bernays realised, notably *Cat., Top., S.E., E.N.* and *Rhet.*, as well as *Poet.* He juggles with these to produce ideas that Aristotle does not formulate explicitly in his extant work. What mere compiler, who was not a philosopher in his own right, would try to replace the lost account of catharsis, but omit the name of the very entity he is supposed to be illustrating (in III and IX)? Why say that tragedy 'takes away' ($\dot{v}\phi\alpha\iota\rho\epsilon\hat{\iota}$) the emotions of fear, when by changing two letters one could have said 'purifies' ($\kappa\alpha\theta\alpha\iota\rho\epsilon\iota$)? Yet in the next section the writer is so close to *Poet.* 6! The compiler is both bold and cowardly; he is also very clever, for example over the terminology for 'pity and fear'. I find it difficult to believe in such a forger.

In fact there is an inconsistency in Bernays' concept of the 'compiler' or 'forger'. If Ω is a forgery intended to replace the loss of the real *Poetics* II, this suggests that the forger would not have had the original before him — otherwise, why bother? Therefore Bernays may justly be asked where the forger found the Aristotelian materials — from *Poetics* II, indeed — which he agrees do constitute part of the work. Heitz,[104] a complete sceptic regarding C, made the same charge in 1865, when there was no need of theurgy to elicit an answer.

Moreover, as our knowledge of later scholarship increases, it becomes clearer than it can have been to Bernays that such a forgery during the late Roman and early Byzantine period is unlikely, and one between *c.* A.D. 600 and the copying of MS C inconceivable. Scholars like Tzetzes may confuse their materials or make false ascriptions, but they do not invent them out of thin air. Already in 1882 Bergk[105] protested that the Tractate did not derive from one of the Byzantine epigoni, but from an earlier epoch, and deserved the same respect as the writings of a modern philologist in the transcription of an ignoramus.

The Hellenistic Age and early Roman Empire are the periods in which a forgery such as Bernays postulates is a practical possibility. But, like the extant *Poetics*, the second book is not quoted directly until the end of this period. The Antiatticist seems to have known it in the late second century, unless he is quoting the *On Poets*. This is unlikely, since our quotations from the latter are mainly anecdotal, whereas this is of a particular word, a comic formation which fits well into what we know of Book II.[106] Bernays[107] considered that Proclus' discussion of the emotional effects of comedy and tragedy (= *Poet.* Fr. V Kassel) shows that he had Book II before him in the fifth century, but Bywater disagreed.[108] Simplicius in the sixth century is quoting Porphyry of the third for the discussion of synonymy;[109] his older contemporary Ammonius quotes *Poet.* 20;[110] if the latter knew Book I, there is no *a priori* reason why he should not have known Book II also. Olympiodorus, the commentator on Plato who displays knowledge of Aristotle's view of catharsis (cf. on III), may be drawing on Ammonius or other secondary sources.

However, the first definite sign of the loss of Book II is the fact that the Syriac translator of the *Poetics*, active no later than *c.* 900,[111] used an exemplar which lacked it; the lack is inferred from the Arabic translations made from the Syriac, which is largely lost. Both tenth-century Arab versions, that of Abū Bišr (extant) and that known to Avicenna[112] (now lost), comprised only the first book, although Avicenna recognises the work's incompleteness. Not much later, the oldest Greek MS, A, has no trace of Book II, although, as we have seen, Eustratius in the twelfth century, William de Moerbeke in the thirteenth and MS B in the fourteenth display awareness that it once existed.

Bywater[113] suggested that the second book vanished during the period when each book still constituted a separate papyrus roll; it is equally likely that it was not transferred from roll to codex, a process mainly occurring during the fourth century. Ammonius could still have found it on rolls in sixth-century Alexandria, where he resided. It may be germane that some philosophers at this period considered the *Poetics* the last member of the canon of Aristotle's logical treatises, after *Top.*, *S.E.*, and *Rhet.*;[114] the last item in a corpus is always vulnerable to loss, especially if regarded with the contempt towards poetry expressed by Elias[115] or the doubts earlier expressed by Philoponus.[116] It seems never to have been popular enough to merit a commentary.[117] Rostagni[118] adduced as a reason for Book II's demise the creation of the Prolegomena to Comedy, starting with Proclus' *Chrestomathy* in the fifth century. It is a pity, in this context, that we cannot date Platonius' remarks on comedy, but, to judge by his name, he ought to belong to this period. A further reason for its loss must be its content. Whereas tragedy had ceased to develop in any significant new directions by Aristotle's day, comedy was on the brink of evolving to new heights through the agency of such playwrights as Menander. Thus whereas *Poetics* I could stand as an acceptable introduction to tragedy, II, with its total silence on Menander and the rest of New Comedy, would be inadequate in any age when the latter was still popular, i.e. even in late antiquity.[119] But, with its interest in Aristophanes, the Byzantine 'Renaissance' would have had good reason to preserve *Poetics* II: therefore the fifth, sixth and seventh centuries seem the most likely time for the book to have become increasingly rare and eventually lost entirely.

From this survey it appears that the *Poetics* did exist in two books until the end of antiquity. So the forger, aiming to replace the lost second book, must have lived in the seventh, eighth or ninth centuries. *Credat qui potest.* The alternative is that the source of Ω, the *Poetics* II read by the Antiatticist and Porphyry, is a forgery which had entered the Aristotelian canon earlier. This must be assessed on the merits of the work, and how accurately it corresponds to what Aristotle himself says it contained. I have argued that in both respects forgery is unlikely. But we have the right to be suspicious: there are plenty of spurious works in the corpus.[120] Each must be judged individually. The ancestor of Ω did pass as Aristotle's work, I am certain, whether or not it was genuinely his, as I believe it was.

A last problem is the degree to which Ω is an accurate précis of *Poetics* II. We have seen that modern précis of the extant *Poetics* yield section-headings similar to those of Ω, and a similar underlying structure is apparent in both. Undoubtedly a vast amount of detail has been lost: perhaps too some digressions. But comparison between the two suggests strongly that the maker of Ω and subsequent epitomators aimed at summarising the main points of the work, rather than selected a series of minor points at random; in the latter case we would hardly expect to find a coherent structure parallel to that of the *Poetics*. But again I judge from probability.

PART IV

Poetics II:
a hypothetical reconstruction

The text and translation given above are as far as it is proper to go
in a scholarly presentation of the text as it is handed down to us.
However, in the Introduction and Commentary I have, I hope,
contrived to supply the outline drawing left by the epitomator with
some splashes of colour; better an outline, after all, than pretty
splodges with no underlying structure (*Poet.* 6.1450a29ff.). Furthermore, it is notable to what extent the sense becomes clearer if
headings and subheadings are supplied, as in Hubbard's rendering
of the *Poetics*, to which I here pay the tribute of imitation.
Therefore it may be helpful to give an expanded version of the
Treatise, on the strict understanding that this is merely a construct
whose details are endlessly debatable, which possesses no independent authority whatsoever, but is intended only to present in
a convenient form a summary of the conclusions reached in the
Commentary, as to how the interstices between the terse entries are
to be filled. It is on this proviso only, and I stress this, that the
following is offered. I have not been shy of reproducing Aristotle's
mannerisms, such as 'obviously' when it isn't, or 'as we said' when
he didn't say so explicitly. But I have been cautious in supplying
examples. The portions of the reconstruction that are in the text
and translation constituted above are in bold type: the correspondence is not verbatim. I have also included the fragments of the
Poetics at the appropriate points: these are between angle-brackets
(< >).

< ARISTOTLE, POETICS II >

Section A

THE PRELIMINARIES TO THE DEFINITION OF COMEDY

(a) *The division* Per genus et differentiam *recapitulated*

1. *The genus we are concerned with stated*

I Concerning tragedy and its parts, both qualitative and quant-itative, and the proper construction of plots, and epic poetry and its differences from tragedy, enough has been said. Now, as we said, **poetry is of two kinds, the first unimitative, which is divided into historical verse and didactic verse (this in turn consisting of verse for imparting instruction, and for theoretical speculation); the second imitative**, and it is only with the latter that we are concerned.

2. *The genus divided*

(i) according to differences of mode

II Mimetic poetry is divided according to the manner in which the imitation is achieved, and the nature of the persons imitated. **Narrative poetry differs by the manner of imitation from that which is dramatic and directly represents action.**

(ii) according to differences of object

Dramatic poetry, as was stated, represents people doing things, and these people must be either good or bad. The difference between **comedy and tragedy** is that the latter aims to represent people as better, the former as worse, than they actually are; we can compare **mimes and satyr-plays.**

(b) *The final cause of the genus*[1]

III Just as I showed above that tragedy and comedy developed
gradually to attain their natural forms, so too they exist for an end,
namely the catharsis of the emotions of the audience. If a **tragedy**
is properly constructed, it **removes the mind's emotions of fear**
and pity **by means of** the representation of **pitiful and fearful
events. Tragedy aims to achieve a balance** or equilibrium **in
the** spectator's **feelings of fear** and suchlike, by giving these
feelings a moderate and controlled expression by means of dramatic
representation. **It has painful feelings**, as one might say, **for its
mother.** I have explained above how these feelings are best
aroused by tragedy; on how catharsis works in comedy, and how
this differs from tragedy, I shall explain below when we have
looked at the nature of humour. But now I wish to discuss comedy,
supplying the definition of its essential nature from what has been
said.

Section B

THE NATURE OF COMEDY[2]

(a) *The nature of comedy defined*

IV **A Comedy is a representation of an absurd, complete
action, one that lacks magnitude, with embellished language, the several kinds of embellishment being found
separately in the several parts of the play: directly represented by persons acting, and not by means of narration:
through pleasure and laughter achieving the purgation of
the like emotions. It has laughter**, so to speak, **for its mother.**
I explained the meanings of the terms here when tragedy was
defined.

(b) *The nature of comedy according to the category of quality*

1. *The deduction of the qualitative elements of comedy*

V Since comedy achieves its aim through laughter, we must next consider how laughter arises. **Laughter is made up from** a number of different elements[3]; **it arises** principally **from speech, and from actions. From speech it arises in seven ways. First, from homonymy**, when the same word has two or more different meanings, **such as 'paying' (this means both 'defraying' and 'profitable'), or like 'metre'**, which Aristophanes puns on in the *Clouds*; **secondly, from synonyms,**[4] < when two or more words have the same meaning, such as 'cloak', 'wrap' or 'mantle';[5] > **an example is 'I'm here and am arrived', which is the same thing**, as Aristophanes jokes in the *Frogs*; **thirdly, from repetition, as when someone continually uses the same word** with the same meaning; **fourth, from paronyms, by addition, when an extraneous element is attached to the standard term, or by subtraction, like 'I'm called Midas the scrounge'** instead of 'scrounger'; to which one can append **diminutives**, forms of words which trivialise or make ridiculous, **like 'Socratiddles, Euripidipides'**, and **alteration**, when a standard word is in part left unchanged and in part altered, like < 'the worstest of all'[6] > instead of 'the worst'. Again, there is humour from **parody**, as when the letters are changed to make something absurd, **like 'O Clod Almighty' instead of 'O God'. Metaphor**, and especially **misapplication, the transference** of words from things similar **either in sound or** appearance or power or some other sensible aspect, especially if degrading or grotesque, also has humorous potential, but one must not transfer from something too dissimilar, but from **things belonging to the same class** or kind, otherwise it will be a riddle not a metaphor. **Seventh, from the manner of speaking**. This belongs to delivery. These then are the seven types of laughter dependent on diction, and diction is obviously a major element of comedy.

VI But **laughter** also **arises from the actions** on the stage, **in two ways**. As I said in the *Rhetoric*, two major causes of laughter are **from deception, like Strepsiades believing that the story**

about the flea was true in Aristophanes' *Clouds*, **or from as-similation or making alike. This is divided into two, according to whether it is employed to liken a worse person towards a better, like Xanthias disguised as Heracles** in the *Frogs*, **or a better person to a worse one, like Dionysus disguised as Xanthias.** Other instances of humour arising from the actions are faults in serious poetry, which can be put to comic account as we observed. Laughter arises **from the impossible,** or **from the possible and inconsequential** which might also be called the illogical (these are effective provided that they are used for an artistic purpose, otherwise they are flaws), or **from the un-expected,** or **from making the characters base** (in fact this is normal in comedy). From this it will be clear that the re-presentation of the action, and the moral qualities of the people engaged in it, both contribute to the aim of comedy. Moral qualities are also revealed indirectly, as **through the use of vulgar dancing** like the cordax, which also involves the elements of song and spectacle, or through bad choice, as **when someone who has the power to choose lets slip the most important and takes the most worthless.** Nor must we overlook intel-lectual qualities, since to explain actions we look to the intellects as well as moral characters of those involved, as **when the reasoning** for an action **is disjointed and lacking any sequence.** These, then, are the kinds of humour arising from the actions: they reveal the qualities of comedy that contribute to its aim, namely laughter.

2. *The rôle of personal abuse in comedy*

VII As character has a part to play in giving rise to laughter, it will be asked whether the comic poet should make fun of known people in his plays. (As we remarked in the *Rhetoric*, humour resides in people as well as in words and actions.) In fact **comedy differs** here **from abuse, since abuse rehearses without concealment the bad actions and qualities attaching to people, but comedy requires the so-called innuendo,** or fantasy through which reality is transformed and distorted. Although comedy evolved from abusive performances, in its essential nature to which it has attained it aims at a representation of how people might behave, rather than of how actual people like Alcibiades do be-have. So comic poets use invented names for the characters in their plots, such as present an appearance of reality, and do not submit individuals to abusive attack like the writers of scurrilous verses.

VIII Even so, there is a place for some mockery in comedy, since a reproach becomes acceptable if it is sweetened with wit. **The joker aims to expose faults of mind and body** in his victims, and this is amusing, provided that the fault is painless and embarrassing rather than destructive. Otherwise he lapses into buffoonery, if he is so keen to arouse laughter as to ignore everyone's feelings. There must be some restraint in these matters.

3. *The aims of tragedy and comedy compared*[7]

IX Now that we have examined the various constituents of humour, we can explain what we said above about the aim of tragedy and comedy, namely catharsis. This is the cause for the sake of which drama is performed. For just as **in tragedies there is to be a due modicum of fear** in the audience, so that the force of these emotions is reduced by their being given expression through the mimesis, to remedy evil with evil as one might say, so too **there is to be a modicum of the laughable in comedies,** with the beneficial effect of reducing the human propensity to excessive buffoonery and impropriety.

4. *Excellence in the qualitative parts of comedy*

X As we have deduced, **the parts of comedy** are six: **plot, character, thought, diction, song and spectacle**. These are the same as the parts of tragedy, and, as in tragedy, two of the parts refer to the means of the representation, one to the manner, and three to the object represented; there are no others. Regarding comedy they possess the following special features.

(a) with regard to plot

XI By **comic plot** I mean one that **is structured around laughable events**. Unless there is an artistic purpose, that is, the arousal of laughter, these events should be structured in accordance with probability, although impossibilities and illogicalities can be used comically, as we have seen.

(b) with regard to the representation of character

XII Comic characters are those who are in error in some way: typical **characters of comedy are the buffoonish, the ironical and the boasters.** As is stated in the *Ethics*, those who in character diverge from the mean deserve not praise but reproach. The buffoon errs in humour, as he will make any joke, even against himself, to please another, whereas the ironical man does so for his own amusement. Yet even the latter departs from the mean of truthfulness, just as the boaster does in the opposite direction; both are liars, but the boaster is more blameworthy, while a modicum of irony can seem witty. Not every kind of bad character is suitable, however, but only those that are not painful or destructive.

(c) with regard to the representation of thought

XIII **Thought falls into two parts**, as was stated in the *Rhetoric*, namely **the expression of opinion and the establishment of proof.** This is set out in that work. Of particular value to the comic poet are **the five kinds of proof** that do not depend on art — **oaths, agreements, testimonies, ordeals, and laws.**

(d) with regard to verbal expression

XIV We have seen already how diction is constituted, and how it can be used for verbal humour. **Comic diction is common and popular**, and uses current words rather than glosses from dialect. In tragedy all the characters speak the same dialect, but **the comic poet must endue his characters with their own native idiom, and use the local idiom himself**. Thus the Boeotian in Aristophanes' *Acharnians* uses his own dialect, and the poet uses Attic in the parabasis, but Epicharmus uses his local Doric in his plays.

(e) with regard to song and spectacle

XV The last two parts of comedy are shared with tragedy but not with epic, and as I passed over them in the discussion of tragedy I will mention them now. **Song**, however, by which I mean the combination of speech, rhythm and melody, **belongs to the**

province of music and not to poetry proper. **Consequently** the poet **will need to take its principles complete in themselves from there. Spectacle contributes as a great benefit to dramas**, both tragic and comic, scenery and costume.

5. *The qualitative elements ranged in order of importance*

XVI These, then, are the six elements which give a comedy its distinctive quality. They are not of equal importance, as **plot, diction and song are observed in all comedies, but instances of thought, character and spectacle in not a few.** If there is no plot, there is no representation of an action; but an action can be represented without a portrayal of the ethical or intellectual motives of those acting. Spectacle is entertaining but not germane to the art of poetry, as the effect of a comedy can also be obtained from reading it. But a comedy without the means of representation is inconceivable, as each comedy consists of spoken diction and choral song in its separate parts.

So much for the parts of comedy that one should use as qualitative elements.

(c) *The nature of comedy according to the category of quantity*

XVII Now for the category of quantity and **the** quantitative **divisions of comedy; they are four — prologue, choral element, episode and exodos.**

The prologue is that part of a comedy which extends as far as the entry of the chorus; the choral element is the song sung by the chorus, when it is of sufficient length; an episode is that part of a comedy **between two choral songs, and the exodos is the part** of a comedy **spoken at the end by the chorus** as it departs.

Having already dealt with the parts of comedy that one ought to use as qualitative elements, I have now finished with quantity and the quantitative divisions of comedy.

Section C

THE IAMBIC ELEMENT IN COMEDY

Comparison of the different kinds of comedy

XVIII Whereas I explained that epic shares the four main qualitative elements with tragedy, but has narrative as its medium of representation, no such comparison between iambus and comedy is possible, since iambus is not mimetic, as is obvious. However, comedy did not at once relinquish the iambic form, but developed gradually to attain its essential nature. **In the old style of comedy, there was** still **an excessive amount of the ludicrous**, even after Crates, in imitation of the Sicilians, began to substitute plots and speeches for the style of the lampoon. **Recent comedy has rejected this and inclines instead towards the serious**, but laughter and amusement are vital to comedy. Therefore **a mean between these styles, which constitutes a mixture of both,** is to be preferred, so that comedy falls into neither buffoonery nor solemnity to any excessive degree. Many claim that Aristophanes occupied such an intermediate position, both in time and in the mixture of both styles that he employed.

So much both for comedy — its nature, the number and differences of its qualitative elements and quantitative parts — and for poetry as a whole.

PART V

Conclusion: an evaluation of the Treatise

To the student of comedy rather than of Aristotle's *Poetics* or his wider philosophy, it is the limitations of the Treatise that will be most immediately apparent. We are told only how laughter is aroused; its essential nature is not discussed. We receive no new information on the origins of comedy, and only one passage indicates awareness of comedy outside Attica. Many aspects of Old Comedy remain unexamined — the rôle of political and social criticism through the 'comedy of ideas', the animal chorus, the use of fantasy and the nature of illusion in the plays, the parabasis and its parts, the centrality of the *agon*. Equally, the salient characteristics of New Comedy are not discussed, especially the prevalence of such tragic techniques as *peripeteia* and *anagnorisis*, division into five acts, stock names and types, and the loss of metrical and structural variety. What we have instead is rigorous generic criticism with a pronounced tendency to schematisation, of the type familiar from the *Poetics*. It is only if we are prepared to think about literature from Aristotle's theoretical standpoint that the Treatise begins to make sense; many today accept some of the main concepts, such as plot, but are unhappy about the schematic results of the detached dissection of literature as if it were a dead animal and not a living mode of communication and expression. I am not sure whether a perusal of the Treatise will help them to sympathise with Aristotelian method, as unfortunately the making of the epitome has led to the disappearance of all but the barest and driest bones of the analysis; it has been my aim to revivify the skeleton, a task analogous to trying to reconstruct the mastodon on the basis of its skeleton and some living relatives or descendants. Luckily part of the text has been more completely preserved in the manuscripts of Aristophanes; and we have living relatives, I allege, in the *Rhetoric* and *Poetics* of Aristotle, as well as scattered passages in his other works. Herein lies a curious paradox. Many difficulties of the *Poetics*, and many criticisms of it, have ultimately been caused by its surpassing strangeness as a creature in a class all of its own. In the whole of antiquity there is nothing else like it, and nothing else to explain it. Its text has been emended, whole chapters excised, its structure furiously debated, largely because of its extraordinary uniqueness. But it is unique no longer; and if the Treatise helps the modern student of literature to penetrate the verdure of the *Poetics* and discern the trunk and main branches within, by comparing the boughs blown clean of leaves in the epitome, then antiquity has not handed on this strange gift in vain.

Some of the Treatise's limitations on comedy are caused by its date, and others by its scope. The omission of recognition-scenes and mistaken identity is difficult to explain unless the work is mainly concerned with older comedy, as is confirmed by the Aristophanic examples preserved in *Prolegomenon* VI to Aristophanes. If Aristotle wrote it, one reason for its eventual loss is evident; Menander made it out of date almost at once. Other limitations are probably caused by the attempt to generalise over the Sicilian and Attic comedy, both 'Old' and 'Middle'; this will explain the very simple analysis of comedy's quantitative parts, and omission of the parabasis. Just as the *Politics* was preceded by the compilation of 158 *Constitutions* of cities, so the *Poetics* is linked to the *Didascaliae*, or performance-records, a huge research-project.[1] A further function of scope is that the Treatise fills gaps left by the *Poetics*, e.g. by discussing catharsis, but does not duplicate it, except in the opening recapitulation designed to reorient the reader to comic drama. Thus there are no more details on the origins of comedy, no excursus on grammar and phonetics under diction, no review of poetic faults. But this is only to be expected if the work is correctly identified. It is nonetheless the massive loss of detail that has been most damaging; the damage is more severe for our knowledge of comedy than for the understanding of Aristotelian theory. *Prolegomenon* VI gives a fleeting glimpse of lost examples and lost plays, enough to tantalise but not to enlighten.

Any estimate of the full importance of our losses is impossible, but one can guess the size of the original work. The *Poetics* is much shorter than one is prone to believe — only ten thousand words or so: in the Treatise we have well under a thousand. One receives the impression (it cannot be put more strongly) that *Poetics* II would have been shorter than *Poetics* I; if fairly represented by the headings in the Tractate, it certainly covered less ground. Five or six thousand words might be a fair estimate, which shows how drastic the epitomisation has been; even so, on this estimate, the balance need not have been seriously distorted nor the gist misrepresented. In the reconstruction I have given an example of what the full text might have looked like, with analytic headings to aid the reader.

As indicated above, it is in the understanding of Aristotelian theory, and especially that of the *Poetics*, that most is gained. I list the crucial points. In the recapitulation (I – II) of the classification of poetry we find features lacking explicit expression in *Poet.* — '*poesis*' in the popular sense of verse, subdivided into the crucial mimetic and non-mimetic categories; the position of mime is also elucidated. The next section, of great importance, is on tragic catharsis: note the flexibility of the terminology and how close it is to later references in Iamblichus, Proclus and Olympiodorus. The passage is valuable in confirming that the most usual view of catharsis is broadly correct, although I would wish to modify this view by closely integrating it into the theory of *mimesis*, which greatly increases its efficacy as a reply to Plato. It has more important and interesting ethical connotations than some believe. C also leads to new thoughts on the breadth of the tragic and comic emotions.

Comedy is then defined. The passage is difficult and has attracted an unusual amount of corruption, but the analogy with the *Poetics*' definition of tragedy is clear. Just as in the latter's analysis of the qualitative parts of tragedy in relation to unity, we find next an establishment of the main qualitative parts of comedy through the contribution they have to offer to humour. At first sight the list of 'humour from diction and humour from action' seems incoherent and over-schematic; nobody but a boor would wish to pigeon-hole all jokes, yet this is what the Treatise seems to do, in common with Demetrius' analysis of 'grace' or 'wit', and those of the *ridiculum* in Cicero and Quintilian. But in fact the list is a selection only of examples to show how each qualitative part can contribute to laughter, and fits well into its present place. Its original purpose helps to account for oddities in Demetrius and Cicero, whose approaches do not suit humour in non-dramatic genres such as oratory very well. The parallels with the *Categories*, *Rhetoric*, *Sophistical Refutations* and *Poetics* here help more to give us a fuller understanding of this passage than to throw light on those works, and here the subtlety of the Treatise can best be seen, especially in the relation of faults in serious poetry and absurd sophistical arguments to their comic equivalents. This section concludes with the drawing of a firm distinction between abuse and comedy, which counters Plato and helps one to understand how Horace is playing with Peripatetic theory in *Satires* I 4. The important account of comic errors, another source of humour, parallels the tragic error of the *Poetics*, but with interesting differences. Finally, in a section that appears digressive but in fact is properly postponed from III, as the absurd would not have been explained, the aims of tragedy and comedy are compared.

With laughter expounded, and the qualitative parts deduced from the discussion, the Treatise enumerates the six qualitative parts, beginning a discussion of how they should be used in comedy. The most significant entry in this list is the last, which throws light on an extremely controversial passage in *Poet.* 6; not all dramas possess all the qualitative parts.

Next follows the analysis of comedy in terms of quantity; consideration of this leads me to have greater faith in the parallel treatment of tragedy in *Poetics* 12, often rejected as spurious. Both analyses are rudimentary, however, and have been far surpassed by modern scholarship. Finally, comedy is divided into Old, Middle and New, according to the Aristotelian criterion of 'iambic' content. This has led to a fresh consideration of the evidence for precisely when the tripartite classification arose, and to what it applied; for some Hellenistic scholars, Aristophanes was Middle Comedy.

In the world of modern literary criticism Aristotle is clarity itself, and his maintenance of poetry's autonomy, and of the proper balance between author, text and audience, sets him far apart from Platonising sophists and their sophistries.[2] But perhaps it is best nonetheless to offer a prayer to the Muses that the spirit of Comedy be not harmed. Whenever artists surrender their creative liberties to philosophers, art itself is at risk.[3] It was understanding and autonomy together that gave to Menander's Peripatetic drama such an advantage over some Aristotelian playwrights of the Renaissance.[4]

With all the complexities, virtues and vices inherent in its philosophical approach, as the sole systematic treatment of comedy in theoretical terms surviving from the ancient world, the Treatise deserves more attention than it has received in the past sixty years. Whether or not it represents *Poetics* II, the analysis is closer to Aristotle than anything else we have. It ought to occupy a prominent place in ancient literary criticism and the history of writing about comedy and humour, as Bernays and Lane Cooper both felt; if it turns out not to offer theorists of humour and comedy a wholly new perspective, this will be owed only in part to its Aristotelian propensity for stating the obvious (not by any means always a vice). Indirectly through Cicero and Horace, and directly through Bernays and Lane Cooper, it has probably exercised a wider influence than many would surmise. But it would take too long to study its *Nachleben* here, when it remains to elucidate the details of the Treatise, and to see whether Aristotle was indeed its author, in fulfilment of his promises to discuss catharsis, comedy and humour in the *Poetics*, where Sophocles, Homer and Aristophanes are named as the greatest masters of the three genres with which he was concerned.

Notes

Part I: Introduction

1. The 'Tractatus Coislinianus'

1. *Anecdota Graeca e Codd. manuscriptis Bibliothecae Regiae Parisiensis* I 403 – 6.
2. Op. cit. 403 (my transl.).
3. Ap. *RhM* 8 (1853) 561 – 96. In this study, citations use the pagination of the revised version of 1880.
4. *CGF* 50 (my transl.).
5. As well as Kaibel loc. cit., cf. his 'Die Prolegomena . . . ' *Abh. der Königl. Gesellsch. der Wissensch. zu Göttingen*, Phil.-Hist. Klasse 2 (1897) 1 – 70, esp. 53ff., Vahlen *Poet.* ed. 3 pp.78 – 80, Bywater *Aristotle on the Art of Poetry* xx – xxiii.
6. *Handbuch der Poetik* 660 – 99. His critique of Bernays has been noticed by Kayser alone.
7. *de veterum Arte Poetica quaestiones selectae* 1 – 44.
8. Arndt, *de ridiculi doctrina rhetorica* 8 – 15; Rutherford *A Chapter in the History of Annotation* 435 – 55; Starkie *Aristophanes' 'Acharnians'* xxxviii – lxxiv.
9. Cf. commentary on V – VI.
10. *Roman Literary Theory and Criticism* 361.
11. *Literary Criticism in Antiquity* II, 138 – 43.
12. *The Nature of Roman Comedy* 308.
13. *La Teoria del Comico da Aristotele a Plutarco* 122 – 5 (with reservations).
14. *The Greek and Roman Critics* 141f., 144 – 9.
15. *Einführung in die antike Dichtungstheorie* 63 – 70.
16. *Criticism in Antiquity* 152, 204 – 6.

17. *Rend. Ac. Lincei* 30 (1975) 289—97.
18. *Aristotle's Poetics: the Argument* 186. Cf. L.F. Guillén, *Aristoteles y la Comedia media* 28f. (he provides a defective text).
19. R. Kassel, *Aristotelis de Arte Poetica*; D.W. Lucas, *Aristotle, Poetics*; C. Gallavotti, *Aristotele, Poetica.*
20. *In Praise of Comedy* 82—5: he misunderstands Lane Cooper on *Tract.* VII. Cf. Northrop Frye, *Anatomy of Criticism* 166ff.
21. *Comic Laughter*: silent.
22. *Comedy: the Irrational Vision*: again silent.

2. The Manuscripts

23. *Bibliothèque Nationale, Catalogue des Manuscrits grecs II: le Fonds Coislin* 109ff.
24. Cf. Grosch, *de Codice Coisliniano 120* 1; Glibert-Thirry (inf.) 36ff.
25. Nos. 9—11, saec. ix—x, ap. Cavalieri and Lietzmann, *Specimina Codicum Graecorum Vaticanorum.* The hands of the famous MS Parisinus 1741, saec. x, containing Aristotle's *Poet.* and *Rhet.*, are slightly more advanced: v. the plate in Roberts' *Demetrius* following p.64, and those of Harlfinger and Reinsch ap. *Philologus* 114 (1970) 28—50. So too MS Parisinus 2036 of [Longinus] *de Subl.*, cf. the plate in Roberts' ed. facing p.1. The end-papers in C have the earliest known minuscule, saec. viii—ix (Devreesse, *Introduction à l'étude des MSS grecs* 31).
26. Unfortunately the text was not deemed worthy of publication by Busse (*CAG* IV 1 p. xxxv n.2); it ends with a sentence.
27. The extracts begin at *CAG* XVIII 2 p.12.19 Busse, and end at ibid. p.150.12, both in complete sentences. Busse did not refer to this MS in establishing his text.
28. Glibert-Thirry (infra) assigned it to Theodore of Raithou. It appears to be unpublished, cf. *CAG* IV 1 loc. cit. Between 240v. and 241r. ten leaves have been cut out.
29. This has incipits and excipits in complete sentences. It is not published, but represents the thought of Aristotle accurately enough.
30. The 1977 edition by Glibert-Thirry supersedes all others. For his detailed account of MS C see pp.36—41. The numeration of the quires is a complex problem: v. his p.39 n.4. The starting-point of quire α' of the second part is especially puzzling.

31. The marginal entry at the opening, ἀφ', is obscure (cf. Koster *Mnemosyne* VIII (1955) 21): if it stands for ἀφηγήσεις or the like, it is still not a title. Koster's statement that the text is on folios 248v.—249r. is inaccurate.

32. These run from *CAG* XVIII 2 p.101.25 Busse to ibid. 172.20, ending ὁμοίως δὲ τῷ πρώτῳ σκέλει. τὸ 'μάλιστα' προτέθηκεν ὅτι πολλάκις διὰ τὴν . . . (lacuna).

33. I consulted the MS at Paris in June 1980. As will be apparent from my apparatus, and from the Plates, some minor points in it have been missed. On C's errors cf. also Glibert-Thirry 96, 115ff.

34. Prof. Sandbach suggests to me that there are traces of a system wherein σ marks the start of an entry, and — its end, at least from XIV.

35. Cf. the version of the Mutensis (saec. xiii) of Porphyry *in Cat.* 65.23 Busse; Parisinus 2064 (saec. x—xi) summarises Ammonius *in An. Pr. I* ed. Wallies viii—xii; this MS has many other summaries and epitomes, esp. of Aristotle *An. Pr.* I, e.g. fol. 156—202: cf. Tarán, *Anonymous Commentary on Aristotle's De Interpretatione* (1978): note the schematic marginalia to Olympiodorus' commentaries on Plato in MS Marcianus graecus 196Z (saec. x in.); or indeed those in our MS, folios 258r. and 260r., to David's commentary on Porphyry, and also fol. 231v. to the summary of Porphyry. A good example of large-scale schematic diaeresis is that in MS Parisinus 2064, ix—x century, accompanying Philoponus' commentary on the *Analytica Priora* (*CAG* XIII 2 p.68 Wallies); cf. also Proclus, *Comm. in Plat. Remp.* II p.83f. Kroll. A schematic work, such as Rufus' Τέχνη Ῥητορική (Spengel 1.462—70), would go easily into such a format.

36. *CAG* XXI 2 pp.279, 300 Rabe. Stephanus is later, however; he quotes the *Suda* (285.18 Rabe) and Eustratius (312.19), and mentions Sicilian piracy against the Venetians (285.12). Undated is the author of the diaereses in *Prolegomenon to Rhetoric* XI, pp.161 and 170 Rabe.

37. Cf. Zuntz, *Die Aristophanes-Scholien der Papyri* 110f.; Westerink, 'Quotations from Attic Comedy in Olympiodorus'.

38. But they did read Aristophanes: Zuntz op. cit. 120f.

39. V. comm. on *Tract.* I.

40. V. comm. on VI 1—2.

41. V. comm. on XVII. But Mrs Easterling suggests to me that this error *could*, less probably, have arisen in minuscule.

42. For these items I have relied on Koster's collations, which checking of the Venetus and of the MSS in England proves to be trustworthy; his is the definitive edition of all the *Prolegomena*, except Tzetzes' *Anecdoton Estense* which he omits.
43. Cf. Kaibel *Abh.* 9, Plebe 21.
44. Cf. Koster's apparatus criticus to *Prol.* XIII: Dindorf *Schol. Aristoph.* ad loc. records its truly execrable readings.
45. Cf. Dover, *Aristophanes' Clouds* cv n.3, against Koster.
46. p.xxxif.: Kaibel (*CGF Prol.* VI Pa, where he quotes the readings of *Prol.* VI Koster in the apparatus) ascribed this to Tzetzes, without evidence.
47. Koster xxxii.
48. *Die Aristophanes-Scholien der Papyri* 61—121.
49. Cf. Dover *Clouds* cxiv; N.G. Wilson ap. *CQ* 17 (1967) 244—56, *GRBS* 12 (1971) 557f., *CR* 27 (1977) 271.
50. Cf. Zuntz op. cit. 111f.
51. Cf. Dover op. cit. cxxf.
52. Cf. Koster and Holwerda ap. *Mnemosyne* VIII (1955) 196ff.
53. For parallels v. ad loc.
54. Cf. Wouters, *The Grammatical Papyri of Greco-Roman Egypt* 87—89, 138, 155.
55. For details of the MSS of these v. Koster xxxvif., 81ff.
56. Koster ad *Prolegomenon* XIaI 106—11.
57. Cf. Gudeman 231.
58. xxviii with n. Cf. too the sources named in the title of the *Suda*, intended to give a spurious air of authority; and, possibly, in John the Sicilian (N.G. Wilson, *Scholars of Byzantium* 145, 150).
59. This citation is the only evidence that Crates of Mallos was interested in this aspect of comedy; a pupil of his, Herodicus, did write a Κωμῳδούμενοι (Pfeiffer, *Hist. Class. Schol. from the beginnings* 242; Düring, *Herodicus* 125ff.); cf. the fragments of Crates in Mette, *Parateresis* 48, 51, 171; for another case where Tzetzes' *Prolegomena* are questionable, v. ibid. 101f. The Academic Crates of Athens left books Περὶ Κωμῳδίας on his death (Diog. Laert. IV 23), and he may be intended instead: Tzetzes gives no ethnic.
60. Cf. Koster XXIII ad loc., inf. p.45.
61. *Aristoteles Poetik* 231.
62. xxxvi.
63. ad XIc 60—5.

Part III: Origins and Authorship

1. Origins

1. p.44.
2. Duckworth, *The Nature of Roman Comedy* 308. Cf. Atkins 138.
3. Walzer, *Greek into Arabic* 129ff.; Zimmermann, *Al-Farabi's Commentary on Aristotle's De Interpretatione* lxxix, cf. Al-Farabi *in de Int.* p.28.21, 52.24, 136.14, 146.19 Zimmermann; Moraux, *Les Listes anciennes* 178ff.
4. Cf. Pfeiffer, *Hist. Class. Schol. from the beginnings* 264, with n.4.
5. On Andronicus' life v. now Moraux, *Der Aristotelismus bei den Griechen* 45ff., his editorial activities ibid. 58ff., and own writings ibid. 97ff. Two pseudepigrapha, namely a paraphrase of the *Nicomachean Ethics* and the Περὶ Παθῶν, are discussed at 136ff.: it is curious that Moraux produces evidence that parts of the latter are genuine, in view of the universal animus against it. It was of course thought to be a sixteenth-century forgery until MS C became known. Moraux records no work on poetry, but has missed the pseudepigraph of Palaeocappa discussed below. Against Andronicus' authorship of *Tract.*, v. W.L. Grant, *AJP* 69 (1948) 80ff.; Grube *The Greek and Roman Critics* 145.
6. For proof that this is a sixteenth-century pseudepigraph, v. Cohn *Philologische Abhandlungen M. Hertz . . . dargebracht* 130—3; Kayser 64; Koster ap. *Mnemosyne* VIII (1955) 23f. This is the first compilation to include a discussion of Roman comedy as well as Greek; it is in Palaeocappa's own handwriting, cf. Koster ap. *Mnemosyne* IX (1956) 319.
7. Cohn op. cit. 125f., 128f.
8. *Mnemosyne* VIII (1955) 24.
9. Ad loc. (XVIII).
10. The other writings in Koster on comedy in general all refer to Menander: Euanthius XXV Koster; Diomedes *Ars Gramm.* III 488 Keil = XXIV 2 Koster; Schol. Dion. Thr. XVIIIa1, 44, XVIIIb2, XVIIIb3 Koster, all refer to the characteristic subject-matter of New Comedy. Cf. also Platonius I 64 Koster; Anon. *Prol.* III sub. fin.; IV 17; V 3; Tzetzes *Prol.* XIaI 104; Anon. *Prol.* XIb 1, 38; XIc 43, etc. Only the

'technical' extracts on laughter, the chorus, metre, the etymology of comedy, etc., do not make some such reference.

11. *Marm. Par.* B7.

12. *de Lycophrone, Euphronio, Eratosthene comicorum interpretibus,* Diss. Greifswald 1884; but see the warning of Pfeiffer, *Hist. Class. Schol. from the beginnings* 119f., and Fraser, *Ptolemaic Alexandria* 450, 457f.

13. Eratosthenes' famous dictum on poetry as for entertainment alone was pronounced à propos of Homeric geography, not comedy or tragedy: Strabo I 15, Pfeiffer op. cit. 165f., and infra. On this dictum see further Fraser, op. cit. 759f. with nn.312 — 21. Cf. [Longin.] *de Subl.* 1.1.

14. If it was, as Wendling says (*RE* III 2103 s.v. Chamaileon), *E.N.* IV 8 shows that the term 'old' comedy was already known to Aristotle: cf. Wehrli ad Chamaeleon fr. 44. For the latter, and a useful survey of Peripatetic work on literature, v. Köpke, *de Chamaeleontis Heracleotae vita librorumque reliquiis* (1856); Wehrli, *Die Schule des Aristoteles* IX. He also wrote a book Περὶ Σατύρων, of which the sole fragment elucidates a proverb (*Suda* s.v. ἀπωλέσας τὸν οἶνον, cf. Wehrli fr. 37; Köpke p.30).

15. Diog. Laert. V 81 (Περὶ ᾽Αντιφάνους α΄).

16. S.v. Λυγκεὺς Σάμιος γραμματικός, Θεοφράστου γνώριμος.

17. Inf. p.123ff., 133ff. and Rostagni *Scritti Minori* 262ff. He wrote one book on tragedy (Köpke, op. cit. 13).

18. Körte, *RE* XIII 2472f. s.v. Lynkeus (6).

19. Cf. Pfeiffer, op. cit. 160f. The work of his successor Callistratus was similar, as it dealt with proverbs, prosopography, spelling and grammar in Aristophanes (Fraser op. cit. 467): so too Ammonius of Alexandria and Didymus (ibid. 469, 473). Note also 'Eumelus the Peripatetic', who wrote at least three books *On Old Comedy* (Schol. Aeschin. *in Timarch.* 39.4).

20. *Suda,* s.v. Διονυσιάδης . . . τραγικός; Pfeiffer loc. cit.; Körte *RE* XI 1208 — 9.

21. Op. cit. 190ff. Cf. however Gomme and Sandbach, *Menander* 127f.

22. Ath. VI 241f, cf. Gow *Machon* 6n., who thinks it means quantitative parts.

23. These are scattered and I have gathered them as best I can. A good modern collection and edition of Theophrastus' fragments, replacing Wimmer, is a major scholastic desideratum, which one trusts will soon be supplied by the project of W. Fortenbaugh and others (I am grateful to Dr R.W. Sharples

for information about this, and for showing me the project's collection of fragments in this field). Unfortunately his writings are passed over by Pfeiffer, op. cit.: their importance must not be underestimated. Cf. Regenbogen, *RE* Suppl. VII 1523−34; Wehrli, *Die Schule des Aristoteles*, Rückblick, 121ff. Grube, 'Theophrastus as Literary Critic', plays down to an excessive degree his importance and distinctness from Aristotle; cf. too Ardizzoni *ΠΟΙΗΜΑ* Ch. V.

24. Diog. Laert. V 46−8.
25. Fr. 130 Wimmer.
26. *On Style* 156, quoting Sophron.
27. V. inf. p.210f.; not in Wimmer.
28. Fr. 124 Wimmer.
29. The similarly apocryphal but unjustly scorned tale of comedy's birth in Attica, common in the *Prolegomena* and known in some form to Aristotle (*Poet.* 3.1448a36), may also be derived through Theophrastus. But in the *On Poets* Aristotle too recounted anecdotes of this sort (e.g. fr. 76 Rose), and it may go back to that work (cf. Plebe 11f., Else 118f.). A. Grilli (*RFIC* 90 (1962) 22−32) would trace it back to the Peripatetic Dicaearchus of Messene's *Βίος Ἑλλάδος*. For further Aristotelian fragments, perhaps from the *On Poets*, concerning the origins of drama v. inf. n.62.
30. First in this field was Reich, *Der Mimus* I 1.263−74. Cf. Dosi 600ff.
31. Cf. Brink *Prol.* 98n. For ἡρωϊκός v. also Dion. Thrax *Ars Gramm.* 2 on reading tragedy ἡρωϊκῶς; the Byzantine Treatise on tragedy assigned to Psellus (inf. p.238ff.), 2.12f. (οὐ τὰς τυχούσας δὲ πράξεις ἡ τραγῳδία μιμεῖται, ἀλλ᾽ ὅσα ἡρωϊκῶν καὶ πρακτικῶν ἠθῶν εἰσιν οἰκεῖα καὶ μεγαλοψύχων, καὶ μάλιστα ἐὰν τελευτῶσιν εἰς πάθη — note the Theophrastean emphasis on *ethos*, cf. inf.); and also Schol. Dion. Thr. p.451 33ff. Hilgard (inf. p.240).
32. Also in Donatus 22.14ff. Wessner = XXVI 1ff. Koster, again anonymous, but with ἰδιωτικῶν omitted. Both sources preserve other interesting detail on comedy which may be Theophrastean.
33. 609−13, cf. Russell 107, and now Fortenbaugh, 'Theophrast über komischen Charakter' 14, to whom I am indebted for a preview of his important article.
34. Pfeiffer, op. cit. 190f.; Syrianus *Comm. in Hermog.* II 23.8 Rabe. Cf. below, n.37, for Schol. Dion. Thrax on βιωτικῶν πραγμάτων: cf. also Dion. Thrax *Ars Gramm.* 2, on reading

comedy βιωτικῶς; Schol. A Hephaest. p.115.13 Consbruch
παρὰ τοῖς κωμικοῖς . . . τὸν γὰρ βίον οὗτοι μιμούμενοι . . .
(not in Koster); Cicero ap. Donatus *de Com.* V 1 (p.22.19
Wessner, = XXVI 20 Koster), 'comoediam esse . . .
imitationem vitae, speculum consuetudinis, imaginem veri-
tatis' (*de Republica* IV 11.13, p.114.5 Ziegler); Aristotle
condemned Alcidamas' similar description of the *Odyssey* as a
mirror of human life (*Rhet.* III 3.1406b12). Plebe (32ff., cf.
Dosi 605, 620) refers the idea back to Theophrastus, plausibly
enough. Cf. also [Longinus] *de Sublim.* 9.15; Richardson
'Literary Criticism in the Exegetical Scholia to the *Iliad*' n.31.

35.   Cf. Reich loc. cit. Note Posidonius' definition of poetry (Diog.
      Laert. VII 60, = fr. 44 Edelstein—Kidd): ποίησις δ' ἐστὶ
      σημαντικὸν ποίημα μίμησιν περιέχον θείων καὶ ἀνθρωπείων.

36.   601ff.

37.   p.306.21 Hilgard (assigned to Heliodorus), = XVIIIb2 Kos-
      ter. Parts of this passage recur at ibid. XVIIIb1.8—10, =
      p.173.2ff. Hilgard; XVIIIb3, = p.475.9ff. Hilgard (Helio-
      dorus); *Prol.* XIb 44—8 Koster (from XVIIIb1.8—10: both
      read πλάσματα περιέχει).

38.   Other sources read πλάσματα: cf. previous note. At *Vita Aes-
      chyli* 5 Wilamowitz (= p.331.4 Page) ἀεὶ πλάσμα is surely
      corrupt for διάπλασμα.

39.   Cited by Dosi 605, 620. A puzzling phrase in the program-
      matic passage in Theocritus' *Seventh Idyll* makes sense if the
      antithesis between poetic πλάσμα and truth was then already
      current. At 43f. Lycidas says to Simichidas ἐσσὶ | πᾶν ἐπ'
      ἀλαθείᾳ πεπλασμένον ἐκ Διὸς ἔρνος. Gow (ad loc.) found the
      expression odd, and took ἐπ' ἀλαθείᾳ closely with πεπλασμένον
      as expressing either attendant circumstances or aim. Is Theo-
      critus hereby rebutting the antithesis with a paradox about
      poetic πλάσμα — that the poet creates fictions for the sake of
      truth?

40.   p.613. The evidence is Ammonius, *in de Int.* (*CAG* IV 5)
      p.65.31ff. Busse (= Wimmer fr. 65, cf. fr. 64). See Lossau,
      Untersuchungen zur antiken Demosthenesexegese 47f.; Moraux, *Les
      Listes anciennes* 179n.; Russell[1] 94. Boethius *in de Int.* II p.12
      Meiser is not relevant: cf. II p.95—6 on *de Int.* 4.17a5, whence
      this idea ultimately derives. For the phrasing on truth, cf.
      Elias *in Categ. prooemium* (*CAG* XVIII 1) p.116.29ff. Busse (but
      Theophrastus is not named); see further the references inf.
      n.74, and Walzer *Greek into Arabic* 129ff.; we can now add
      Elias on the *Prior Analytics* p.139.5ff. Westerink (= his *Texts*

and Studies p.72).

41. Ap. Sext. Emp. *Math.* I 252 Mau; cf. Brink, *Horace on Poetry* 197f., 354, and on the importance of this triad, Rostagni on Hor. *A.P.* 338f. It recurs at Schol. Dion. Thrax p.449.5ff. Hilgard, where it is linked with the χαρακτῆρες ποιήσεως, and (with πλάσμα omitted) at Schol. Tzetzes *Exeg. in Iliadem* XXIIa2.25 Koster. Plebe (34 n.14) and McMahon (*HSCP* 40 (1929) 97ff.) stress how different this is from Aristotle, and assign it to Theophrastus. See also sup. n.39. For a different tripartition cf. Schol. Hom. *Il.* Ξ 342−51 with [Longinus] *de Sublim.* 9.13 , Quint. II 4.2 (Richardson, 'Literary Criticism in the Scholia to the *Iliad*' 271; Russell *Criticism* 109).

42. Note that it does not use ὑπόθεσις either. This was certainly current by Philodemus' time (*de Poem.* II 62 Hausrath, cf. LSJ s.v. II 3; add Hesychius s.v. and *Suda* s.v., which has the notable gloss περιοχή). Sext. Emp. *Math.* III 3 Mau does not show that Dicaearchus used it thus: in fr. 78 Wehrli (in fact a testimonium) given by Sextus, it surely means 'summary', not 'plot', pace Pfeiffer op. cit. 193: Sextus uses περιπέτεια to mean 'plot'.

43. p.125. Both he and Dosi are far too ready to assign material, especially from the Tractate, to Theophrastus, on insufficient and even contrary evidence.

44. *Phys.* VIII 1.252a5, *de Caelo* II 6.289a6, 7.289b25.

45. E.g. *Poet.* 5.1449b5; cf. Lane Cooper 49f.

46. *Poet.* 9.1451b5ff.

47. ποιητὴν γὰρ ἔφη πάντα στοχάζεσθαι ψυχαγωγίας, οὐ διδασκαλίας (Strabo I 15).

48. E.g. col. xiii 8ff. Jensen, quoting Neoptolemus of Parium (*c.* 200 B.C., cf. Pfeiffer op. cit. 166): πρὸς ἀρε[τὴν δεῖν τ]ῷ τελείῳ πο[ητῇ μετὰ τ]ῆς ψυχαγω[γί]α[ς τοῦ τοὺς] ἀκούοντ[ας] ὠ[φελεῖ]ν καὶ χρησι[μο]λ[ογεῖ]ν καὶ τὸν Ὅμη[ρον τ]έρπειν [τε καὶ ὠφελεῖν] τὸ [πλεῖ]ον. Neoptolemus' critical terms bear little resemblance to those of the Tractate or Aristotle: cf. Brink *Prol.* 93f. Those of the Homeric Scholia are likewise considerably more developed: cf. Richardson art. cit. (n.34).

49. From Athen. XIV 624a, Apollon. *Hist. Mir.* 49, Porphyry ad Ptol. *Harm.* 244 Wallis.

50. Fr. 90 Wimmer, from Plut. *Mor.* 623a. On Theophrastus' theory of music v. Rispoli, *Cronache Ercolanese* 4 (1974) 66−73, esp. n. 53.

51. καθαρτική is Koster's emendation for καθαρτικῶν, cf. Schol.[l] p.18.13 app. crit. Hilgard (καθαρτική) and Anon. *Prol.* XIb

43 Koster (καθαρτήριος): the passage is not in Hilgard, cf. Theod. Alex. *Gramm.* p.58.31 Goettling.

52. Also Euanthius loc. cit., Anon. *Prol.* XIb 43–8 Koster.

53. On the possibility that this is Theophrastean v. also Dosi 607.

54. *Griechische Papyri der Hamburger Staats- und Universitäts-Bibliothek*, ed. Snell, 36ff. For such elaboration as typical of Theophrastus, cf. Regenbogen op. cit. 1551ff.

55. V. comm. on V 4. It may have been Theophrastus who formulated the Hellenistic doctrine that to count as poetry a work must be in poetic diction, and the poetic status of verse genres that are in ordinary speech (e.g. comedy) is thus doubtful: cf. Cicero *Orator* 20.67, Hor. *Serm.* I 4.47f., and for the arguments Ardizzoni *ΠΟΙΗΜΑ* 69–78. There is no hint of this in the Treatise.

56. The Rainer papyrus containing a Peripatetic fragment on τὸ ἁρμόττον (H. Oellacher, *Soc. Roy. Égypt. de Papyrologie*, Études IV (1938) p.133ff.) is very close to *Poet.* 15.1454a24, cf. Lucas ad loc. If this too is Theophrastus, it is indistinguishable in content and expression from Aristotle.

57. 41–3, cf. Dosi 615ff.

58. Loc. cit., cf. Dosi 622f.

59. For the sources, v. comm. on I–II, where the slapdash statements of several scholars about *Tract.* I–II are also refuted.

2. The question of Aristotelian authorship

60. The same sort of recasting is done by Plebe (e.g. 58ff. on comic *anagnorisis*).

61. V. comm. on VIII.

62. Most are in Lucas' edition, xii–xiv, 49–52, 257. Other possible fragments are widely neglected. One is in Schol. Dion. Thrax p.306.9 Hilgard (not in Koster), on *tragedy*: ἄρξασθαι αὐτῆς Ἀριστοτέλης Σουσαρίωνά φησι. This must be an error for comedy, whose origins are widely associated with Susarion; unfortunately we are not told where Aristotle said this: it may have been in the *On Poets*, cf. Webster ap. Pickard-Cambridge, *Dithyramb, Tragedy and Comedy* (ed. 2, 1962) 187. This at first sight contradicts the statement that both comedy and tragedy were discovered among the Athenians, which is ascribed to Aristotle in a controversial passage of John of Sardis the Deacon (*Comm. in Hermogen.* Περὶ Μεθόδου

Δεινότητος 33, p.450.2 Rabe, ed. Rabe, *RhM* 63 (1908) 149f. = XIXa 21ff. Koster: not in Rose). But I suspect that Aristotle's attitude towards the Dorian claims was more qualified and complicated than has been thought, notably by Else; this needs consideration in another place. Aristotle probably discussed the origins of several genres in the *On Poets*, cf. frr. 676 — 7 Rose with Alfonsi, *RFIC* 20 (1942) 193 — 200. Note also Themistius *Or.* 26.316d (p.382 Dindorf), scorned by Rose (p.79) and thus generally ignored, from the *On Poets* I suspect, on the origins of tragedy: *οὐ προσέχομεν Ἀριστοτέλει ὅτι τὸ μὲν πρῶτον ὁ χορὸς εἰσιὼν ᾗδεν εἰς τοὺς θεούς, Θέσπις δὲ πρόλογόν τε καὶ ῥῆσιν ἐξεῦρεν, Αἰσχύλος δὲ τρίτον ὑποκριτὴν καὶ ὀκρίβαντας, τὰ δὲ πλείω τούτων Σοφοκλέους ἀπηλαύσαμεν καὶ Εὐριπίδου*; cf. Dicaearchus of Messene fr. 76 Wehrli; Lucas on *Poet.* 4.1449a16; Pickard-Cambridge op. cit. 78; Else, *The Origin and Early Form of Greek Tragedy* 53 with note. Themistius is also the source of a new testimonium to the *Poetics*, which deserves to be given in full: Elias, on the *Prior Analytics* p.136.25ff. Westerink (= his *Texts and Studies* 69), quotes a lost commentary of his on the latter work (cf. Westerink ad p.134.5) as follows: *αἱ γὰρ μεγάλαι φύσεις ὑπὲρ κανόνας ἐνεργοῦσαι αὐταὶ κανόνες γίνονται τοῖς μεταγενεστέροις. οὐ γὰρ ἐδεήθη, φησὶν ὁ Θεμίστιος, Πλάτων ἀποδεικνὺς τῆς συλλογιστικῆς Ἀριστοτέλους, ἵνα μὴ παρίδῃ τὰ ἴδια τῶν σχημάτων, ἀλλ' Ἀριστοτέλης τῶν Πλάτωνος διαλόγων, ἵνα ἐξ αὐτῶν ἀθροίσῃ τὰ ἴδια τῶν σχημάτων. οὕτως οὐχ Ὅμηρος τοῦ Περὶ Ποιητικῆς Ἀριστοτέλους, οὐ Δημοσθένης τῆς Ῥητορικῆς τέχνης Ἑρμογένους, τοὐναντίον δὲ Ἀριστοτέλης Ὁμήρου ἐν τῷ Περὶ Ποιητικῆς καὶ Ἑρμογένης Δημοσθένους ἐν τῇ Ῥητορικῇ τέχνῃ*. Note the interest in the *Poetics* as an analysis of Homer, as in other late sources.

63. Vahlen, *Gesammelte Schriften* I 232, compares the promise at *de Caelo* I 3.269b20, fulfilled at IV 1.

64. p.653.

65. *Aristotele, Poetica*, cf. Landi, *RFIC* 3 (1925) 551, whence Kassel's text derives.

66. These statements are repeated in the scholia to *Rhet.* at p.159 15 Spengel = *CAG* XXI 2 p.327.1 Rabe, and Schol. Neobar. fol. 82a23 (not in Rabe, cf. Vahlen *Poet.* ed. 3 p.77), but these echoes are without substance. *Poet.* antedates *Rhet.*: cf. Vahlen, op. cit. 49ff., 58f.; Rostagni *Poetica* XXVIIIf.; P. Thielscher, *Philologus* 92 (1948) 230f.

67. Again cf. the promise at *de Caelo* I 3.269b20.
68. Cf. Latte, *Kleine Schriften* 612 – 30.
69. He also quotes Aristotle's *Homeric Problems* (ibid. 84.26f.).
70. *CAG* XV: v. comm. on IX. At *Phys.* II 2.194a35 Aristotle refers to a division of the οὖ ἕνεκα in the Περὶ Φιλοσοφίας (fr. 28 Ross), and Mr Russell suggests to me that this is meant. Heitz (p.92) thinks the *Physics* is intended: Olympiodorus (*in Cat.* 23.1 Busse) did once write '*Physics*' for '*Poetics*' (cf. Moraux ap. *Mélanges Mansel* I 267f.); for erroneous references in Philoponus cf. Hayduck's *index locorum*, op. cit. 669f.
71. The *exoterica* were largely unknown to Plotinus; only Iamblichus after him was more familiar with them (*Cambridge History of Later Greek Philosophy* 98, 114); Proclus had some knowledge of them (cf. Guthrie *HGP* VI 68). On knowledge of *Poet.* in antiquity cf. Else 337 n.125.
72. Fr. 81 Rose (from Proclus) is referred to the *Poetics* (fr. V Kassel), but without complete confidence: v. n.93.
73. Cf. Lucas xxiii; Cantarella *Ac. Lincei, Rendiconti morali* 30 (1975) 290f.: v. n.62 on Themistius.
74. Cf. McMahon, *HSCP* 28 (1917) 1 – 46; Cantarella, loc. cit. 289 – 97, esp. 293. Thus Plebe (8 n.3) assumes too much from the use of the article in the citations ap. Ammonius *in An. Pr.* = *CAG* IV 6 11.23ff. Wallies, Olympiodorus *Prolegomena* = *CAG* XII 1 p.8.10 Busse, Elias *in Categ. Prooem.* = *CAG* XVIII 1 p.116.35 Busse, to which can be added Elias on the *Prior Analytics* p.136.29ff. Westerink (= his *Texts and Studies* p.69), from Themistius (cited sup. n.62): contrast Philoponus *in Categ.* = *CAG* XIII 1 p.5.12 Busse, Boethius *in de Int.* II p.6.16 Meiser. The theory of S. Haupt, ap. *Philologus* 69 (1910) 252 – 63, that Aristotle did write a *Poetics* in two books, of which the first was general and we possess but the second, is idiosyncratic not to say idiotic.
75. This term may be Aristotelian (cf. LSJ s.v. III 2): it recurs in the late scholia to *Rhet.*, *CAG* XXI 2 pp.163.20ff., 167.2ff. Rabe.
76. Cf. Lucas xiii; note also his work on Archilochus, Euripides and Choerilus, inf. p.122.
77. Cf. Düring, *Philomathes* 264ff.; Plezia *Eos* 58 (1975) 37ff., who promises a joint edition of the text with J. Bielawski.
78. Cf. Düring *Aristotle* 244, Tkatsch I 120f.; contrast Baumstark, *Aristoteles bei den Syrern* 94, 104.
79. Heitz (91) argues that this goes back to an early source, e.g. Heraclides Ponticus.

80. Ap. *Aristoteles Latinus* XXXIII, ed. Minio-Paluello.
81. Cf. Harlfinger and Reinsch, *Philologus* 114 (1970) 28—50.
82. On Avicenna's awareness that the *Poetics* is incomplete, v. inf. n.112.
83. 54f.
84. Lane Cooper 150ff. collects the instances.
85. Cf. Fuhrmann 56f., Rostagni ad *Poet.* 1448a25.
86. V. p.205f.
87. V. inf. p.244—9.
88. Tierney 243f.
89. R.G. Ussher, *Aristophanes* 41, cf. id. ap. *Greece and Rome* 24 (1977) 70f.
90. So Ussher's, *Aristophanes* 21ff.
91. Cf. Fuhrmann 61—3.
92. *Gesammelte Schriften* I 223.
93. Cf. inf. p.146ff. But Rostagni, *Scritti minori* 276—93, makes a strong case that they refer to the *On Poets*, where Plato was attacked overtly.
94. Op. cit. xxiii.
95. 60—3.
96. Cf. House, *Aristotle's Poetics* 30ff.
97. p.154.

3. The problem of authenticity

98. On our knowledge of ancient literary terminology cf. Grube, *Demetrius* 8n., 46ff., 133ff., and also D.M. Schenkeveld, *Studies in Demetrius On Style* 135—48. Both make out a strong case for dating the content, if not the diction, of Demetrius' *On Style* to 270 B.C. or thereabouts. The lexicographical arguments in favour of a later date have been much overstated.
99. Proper names, poetic forms, and the *Rhetorica ad Alexandrum* are left out of account. For a similar study of the language of the *Ath. Pol.* v. Sandys' edition, lviiff.
100. *HGP* VI 125.
101. See, for example, ibid. 105 n.1; 121 n.1; 144 n.1; 193 n.2; 309; 347 n.1; 397.
102. Russell 152.
103. Russell loc. cit., who is sceptical of the Tractate, predicts nonetheless that Aristotle would have omitted such an analysis in his work on comedy.

104. p.95f. For a useful survey of the motives for pseudepigraphy in the ancient world, and of the clues that make forgery likely, v. Syme, 'Fraud and Imposture'. The very anonymity of the Treatise is evidence against most of these. Perusal of N.G. Wilson, *Scholars of Byzantium* (1983), has confirmed my view that Byzantine scholars would have been neither able nor willing to create a forgery of this kind. The only real possibility is that mentioned inf., n.120.

105. *Philologus* 41, 581.

106. V. inf. p.181.

107. *Zwei Abhandlungen* 48.

108. *Aristotle on the Art of Poetry* xxff.

109. V. comm. on V 2, and n.93.

110. *In de Int.* p.13.1 Busse; cf. Boethius *in de Int.* II p.6.16 Meiser 'in *libris* quos Aristoteles de arte poetica scripsit'; Schol. Dion. Thrax 344.23ff. Hilgard (Heliodorus); Al-Farabi *Comm. on Ar. de Int.* p.48.7, 49.11 Zimmermann. Hermias, *in Plat. Phaedrum* p.98 Couvreur (doubtless from Syrianus) notes that Aristotle distinguished the εἴδη ποιήσεως in *Poet.*: ibid. p.241.21—3, referring to pity and fear as the tragic emotions, may also show knowledge of *Poet.*; he was active in the fifth century. See Heitz 90f. for further citations.

111. On Syriac versions v. Reynolds and Wilson, *Scribes and Scholars* 31, and Lemerle, *Le premier Humanisme byzantin* 22—30. Isḥāq ibn Ḥunain may well have been the author (see Dahiyat (inf.) n.7, and Minio-Paluello, *Aristoteles Latinus* XXXIII ed. 1 p.XII n.14, cf. ed. 2 p.XIX): Isḥāq died in A.D. 910.

112. *Avicenna's Commentary on the Poetics of Aristotle*, ed. trans. Dahiyat, p.121: 'this has been a summary of the Book of Poetry by the First Pedagogue — the portion which is available in this land, for a substantial part of it still remains'. Dahiyat produces good evidence that Avicenna used a version superior to Abū Bišr's, probably that of Yaḥyā ibn 'Adī recorded in Al-Nadīm's *Kitāb al-Fihrist* (p.602 Dodge, where it is also stated that the ninth-century philosopher Al-Kindī made a compendium of the *Poetics*). See Peters, *Aristoteles Arabus* 28—30. Abū Bišr knew no Greek (Zimmermann, op. cit. xlvii): our text of his version has lost the last leaf (it stops at 1462b5), but Avicenna's source had not (see Dahiyat op. cit. 120f. for Avicenna's paraphrase of the last paragraph).

113. Loc. cit.

114. See Walzer, *Greek into Arabic* 129ff.
115. *In Cat. prooem.* (*CAG* XVIII 1) p.116.29 Busse, esp. πάντῃ ψευδεῖς (αἱ προτάσεις) καὶ ποιοῦσι τὸν ποιητικὸν (συλλογισμὸν) καὶ μυθώδη.
116. *In Cat.* (*CAG* XIII 1) p.5.8ff. Busse, cf. Walzer op. cit. 134.
117. Assertions that Alexander of Aphrodisias composed commentaries, which were translated into Arabic, on *Rhet.* and *Poet.*, derive from a misunderstanding (cf. M. Steinschneider, *Die arabischen Uebersetzungen aus dem Griechischen*, 48ff., 93). I owe this information to the kindness of Dr Sharples, who also brought to my notice an unpublished Arabic piece entitled 'Useful Remarks on(?) Poetry by the philosopher Aristotle' in MS Carullah 1279, fols. 69v. — 70v. (Millet Library, Istanbul; cf. F. Rosenthal, *Journ. Amer. Orient. Soc.* 75 (1955) 18). A transcript and translation most kindly supplied by Dr Zimmermann shows that this is in fact a series of extracts and paraphrases of the *Topics* on choice and sameness, and not to do with poetry at all. I am grateful to Prof. Rosenthal for confirming this in correspondence. The Arabs, though interested in humour, clearly knew no Greek sources related to C (cf. Rosenthal, *Humor in early Islam* 132—8). The title, a bizarre misnomer, is perhaps due to a majuscule corruption of ΤΟΠΙΚΑ to ΠΟΙΗΤΙΚΑ.
118. *Aristotele, Poetica* ed. 2 p.xciii.
119. Although still read in sixth and early seventh century Egypt, his texts did not survive the Iconoclastic period (Gomme and Sandbach, *Menander* 2f.); Plebe 120 dates the reported book-burning of New Comedies by clerics too low, but Demetrius Chalcondyles' statement should not be rejected out of hand: we see in our own time what religious and ideological fanaticism can achieve. Cf. the banning of comedy by the Eastern Church in A.D. 691, *Acta Concil. in Trullo*, canon LXII (*Patrologia Graeca* 137, col. 728A Migne, ap. Cantarella *Aristofane* I p.115: not noted by Wilson, *Scholars of Byzantium* 12).
120. Philoponus (*in Categ.* p.7.22—31 Busse), with plausible circumstantial details apparently from Alexandrine pinacographers, and more vaguely Olympiodorus (*Prol.* p.13 11—20) and Elias (*in Categ.* p.128.5—9 Busse), report that Ptolemy Philadelphus was willing to pay so much for works of Aristotle, as of others, that forgery was encouraged: cf. Fraser, *Ptolemaic Alexandria* 325 with n.151, Moraux 'La Critique d'authenticité'. This is the least unlikely context for the

forgery of *Poetics* II, but even so it seems a most improbable achievement.

Part IV: A hypothetical reconstruction

1. Cf. *Poet.* fr. V Kassel.
2. Cf. *Poet.* fr. I.
3. Cf. *Poet.* fr. II.
4. Cf. *Poet.* fr. III. See comm. for text.
5. V. previous note.
6. *Poet.* fr. IV.
7. Cf. *Poet.* fr. V.

Part V: An evaluation of the Treatise

1. Cf. House, *Aristotle's Poetics* 33.
2. See W.B. Stanford, *Enemies of Poetry* passim.
3. 'Aristotle is a person who has suffered from the adherence of persons who must be regarded less as his disciples than as his sectaries. One must be firmly distrustful of accepting Aristotle in a canonical spirit; that is to lose the whole living force of him.' T.S. Eliot, *The Sacred Wood*, ed. 2 p.10.
4. We need not expect the analysis of comedy, as opposed to comedy itself, to be humorous. For an eloquent appeal not to confuse the two, and a defence of the value of studying the aesthetics of comedy, v. Feibleman, *In Praise of Laughter* 168 — 72.

PART VI

Commentary on the Treatise

Note, throughout Part VI, the abbreviation A. for Aristotle.

Chapters I – II: The nature and classification of poetry

In this introductory section we find a differentiation of the kinds of poetry, first explicitly by the criterion of *mimesis*, secondly, by implication, by the manner of imitation (narrative or dramatic), and third, again implicitly, by the objects imitated (men, good or bad). Cf. *Poet.* 1–3, where we find a division according to the medium employed (Ch. 1), the objects imitated (Ch. 2) and the manner of imitation (Ch. 3). Here the division by medium is assumed (there is no mention of instrumental music, for example), as if *Poetics* I had preceded, and the sequence of Chapters 2 and 3 is reversed. This reversal is logical: in *Poet.* both tragedy and epic are to be discussed, which differ less in objects imitated than in mimetic mode; in C the topic is comedy, with tragedy in a supporting rôle only, and the crucial difference between these two genres is in the actions which they imitate. Thus the divergent emphases of the two works are reflected in their introductions. But so too are their shared aims: both are *Poetics*, not *On Tragedy* or *On Comedy*, and both begin with poetry as a whole.

(a) *Mimesis and poetry in Aristotle*

In *Poet.* A. defines poetry in terms of *mimesis*. What is mimetic, is poetry; what is not mimetic is not, though it be in verse like Empedocles' writings. Bernays saw this as a fatal objection to this part of C (140f.); he has been followed by most scholars, Kayser and Lane Cooper excepted. But A.'s position is more subtle than this. What, after all, is meant by *mimesis* in his teaching? In one, Platonic, sense, even Empedocles would be a mimetic writer, since he is representing the perceived world; so too Choerilus, with his account of historical events, the Persian Wars. But A. distinguishes between poetry and history on the grounds that history represents the particular, poetry the general (*Poet.* 9); Herodotus' *History* in verse would still be history; a connected and plausible sequence of events is the key, whether these happen to have occurred or not. The essence of this process is not precisely representation, nor again fiction, but rather to be described by the Structuralist term 'reduction'. (I derive this useful term, and much of my under-standing of the Aristotelian theory of *mimesis*, from Redfield, *Nature and Culture in the Iliad*, Ch. 1; cf. also House, *A.'s Poetics* Ch. 7.) *Mimesis* reduces the complexity of the object imitated to a clear outline, in which the separate parts and their interconnections are clearly defined, and the whole is fully intelligible, and can be appreciated as a relatively simple whole. One might contrast for example Herodotus with Aeschylus' *Persae*, where the action is shaped by the dramatist to bring out more strongly the moral and theological implications of Xerxes' behaviour.

The reason why A. lays such emphasis on this reductive *mimesis* as the essence of poetry is not far to seek, namely the popular tendency to confuse poetry with composition in verse. He discussed this on several occasions, in *Poet.* 9 with amplification in 23, in 1 at length, and in the *On Poets* (frags. 72 − 3 Rose). There is a twofold attack on the breadth of applicability of this criterion:

(i) Some writers in verse do not write mimetic poetry, e.g. Empedocles (*Poet.* 1.1447b18), or, as one surmises from the discussion of Herodotus, Choerilus (9.1451b2ff.; cf. 23.1459a24, *Rhet.* III 14.1415a4, 16): note the lost Ἀπορήματα Ἀρχιλόχου, Εὐριπίδου, Χοιρίλου ἐν βίβλοις γ′ (Moraux, *Les Listes anciennes* 252, 273, 275) for A.'s interest in him. Plato had preferred Antimachus (cf. Alfonsi, *RFIC* 20 (1942) 198ff.).

(ii) Some writers in prose are none the less mimetic, e.g. the mimographers Sophron and Xenarchus, or those who wrote Socratic dialogues, or Chaeremon who mixed up all kinds of verse in his *Centaur* (*Poet.* 1.1447b10, 21). Sophron's mimes and the dialogues reappear in the *On Poets* fr. 72 Rose, where both are termed 'verbal imitations' even though not in verse:

οὐκοῦν οὐδὲ ἐμμέτρους <ὄντας> τοὺς καλουμένους Σώφρονος μίμους μὴ φῶμεν εἶναι **λόγους καὶ μιμήσεις**, ἢ τοὺς Ἀλεξαμενοῦ τοῦ Τηΐου τοὺς προτέρους γραφέντας τῶν Σωκρατικῶν διαλόγων;

(cf. Bernays 81ff.). In fr. 73 A. says that the style of Plato's dialogues was between poetry and prose: τὴν τῶν λόγων ἰδέαν αὐτοῦ μεταξὺ ποιήματος εἶναι καὶ πεζοῦ λόγου. This point obviously received the more emphasis since these were the only kinds of fiction in prose that had arisen by A.'s time.

Thus whereas popular usage distinguished poetry by the formal criterion of versification, A. offered an alternative, namely *mimesis*. The relation between these criteria can be tabulated as follows:

	'mimetic'	'non-mimetic'
prose	mime, Socratic dialogue	history etc.
verse	'poetry' proper	Choerilus, Empedocles

This represents an effective subversion of the popular division. Thus A. is justified in making bold statements such as 'Homer and Empedocles have nothing in common except that they are in verse; it is right to call the one a poet, but the other a natural philosopher rather than a poet' (*Poet.* 1.1447b17ff.). Cf. 9.1451b27 'the poet should be a maker of plots rather than verses, inasmuch as (ὅσῳ) he is a poet according to *mimesis*, and imitates actions'. However, contrary to the usual interpretation, these are not simply dogmatic statements about nomenclature, i.e. 'it is wrong to call Empedocles a poet; the category of didactic verse belongs outside what we call poetry', but constitute a sharpening of the definition of the category of poetry about which A. is concerned, namely mimetic poetry in verse, poetry *par excellence*. Plato's dialogues, as the *On Poets* expressly stated, are between poetry and prose; Empedocles occupies a similar half-way position, but on a different criterion. As Else says (p.50), Empedocles is chosen in order to make the point as drastically as possible, since he was a maker of very fine verses.

That this is so is clear from A.'s own usage of the term ποίησις. He uses the popular sense of 'poetry' and 'poet' for Solon, who is certainly unlikely to be mimetic (*Pol.* I 8.1256b33, IV 11.1296a20, *Rhet.* I 15.1375b34, *Ath. Pol.* 5.3, 6.4, 12.2, cf. Lane Cooper 12, Rostagni *RFIC* 5 (1927) 166ff.). Again, after denying Empedocles the title of poet, he cites him to illuminate details of the theory of poetry (e.g. *Poet.* 21.1457b24), and had earlier discussed his life and work in the *On Poets* (fr. 70–1 Rose), calling him Homeric and a master of poetic diction. This passage best makes sense if it is intended to soften a denial that Empedocles was a poet (cf. House, *A.'s Poetics* 30): yet it is followed by a reference to other *poems* of his (ἄλλα ποιήματα, ibid.). Another case of the popular usage is where A. warns aspiring orators not to use regular verses, lest they write *poetry* (**ποίησις** γὰρ ἔσται, *Rhet.* III 8.1408b30): cf. ποίημα similarly, of Alcidamas' excessively poetic diction, at 3.1406a31. Likewise, in discussing the openings of poems, he quotes together those of the *Iliad*, *Odyssey* and Choerilus' *Persica* (*Rhet.* III 14.1415a16). At *Poet.* 23.1459a29 he complains that most poets do not obey the vital principle of unity of action (οἱ πολλοὶ τῶν ποιητῶν): he does not say 'so-called poets'! I find that Reich, *Der Mimus* 250, takes the same position: so too Fuhrmann, *Einleitung* 59f., *Aristoteles Poetik* 39n.12; cf. Ardizzoni *ΠΟΙΗΜΑ* 58ff., 108ff.

In *Poet.* A. restricts the discussion to poetry definable by both criteria, *mimesis* and verse (τῆς ἐν ἑξαμέτροις μιμητικῆς *Poet.* 6.1449b21; τῆς διηγηματικῆς καὶ ἐν μέτρῳ μιμητικῆς 23.1459a17). In C also we find an immediate dismissal of unmimetic verse, τῆς ποιήσεως ἡ ἀμίμητος, and concentration on a genre, comedy, qualified on both counts. A. did use the term ποίησις in the popular sense of versification, and the standard objection to C on the grounds of its first two words τῆς ποιήσεως is invalid. The difference between versification and poetry proper, i.e. the definition of the latter as belonging to the genus of *mimesis*, is dealt with at the start of each work, before the genres are divided up by the mode and object of imitation.

(b) *The diaeretic method*

We have a division of poetry into unmimetic and mimetic, poetry proper. The division of an entity into itself and other subdivisions looks peculiar, but is in fact an Aristotelian procedure, as Kayser pointed out (8f.). At *E.N.* VI 8 politics (i.e. everything to do with the government of cities) is subdivided into law-giving for the framework, and politics for its detailed management (which is then subdivided into deliberative and judicial): 1141b24 τῆς περὶ πόλιν (φρονήσεως) ἡ μὲν ὡς ἀρχιτεκτονικὴ φρόνησις νομοθετική, ἡ δὲ ὡς τὰ καθ’ ἕκαστα τὸ κοινὸν ἔχει ὄνομα, πολιτική, cf. ibid. 31. Another example (noted by Sorabji, *Necessity, Cause and Blame* 297) is *E.N.* V 8.1135b12 — 8, where ἁμάρτημα is divided into ἀτύχημα 'accident' and ἁμάρτημα 'mistake': this diaeresis is in fact the key to what A. means by *hamartia* in tragedy ap. *Poet.* 13 (v. on VIII). Cf. also *Poet.* fr. VI, cited in the parallels to Tract. III. This type of division was already attacked in antiquity as illogical: Kayser cites a critique of *E.N.* VI 8 by the sixth-century commentator Elias (*CAG* XVIII *Prol. Philos.* p.31.34ff. Busse). We may agree with Elias about the logic, but must agree with Kayser that 'this subdivision in the Tractatus Coislinianus is not to be condemned, but is constructed on Peripatetic principles'.

(c) *The function of Chapters I — II*

The function of I — II as the opening of *Poetics* II is surely that of a résumé of previous divisions, leading to a focus on the topic to be discussed. The technique is paralleled at the opening of *Rhet.* III, much of it diaeretically expressed, with a surprising amount of detail. I quote:

> ἐπειδὴ τρία ἐστὶν ἃ δεῖ πραγματευθῆναι περὶ τὸν λόγον, ἓν μὲν ἐκ τίνων αἱ πίστεις ἔσονται, δεύτερον δὲ περὶ τὴν λέξιν, τρίτον δὲ πῶς χρὴ τάξαι τὰ μέρη τοῦ λόγου, περὶ μὲν τῶν πίστεων εἴρηται, καὶ ἐκ πόσων, ὅτι ἐκ τριῶν εἰσί, καὶ ταῦτα ποῖα, καὶ διὰ τί τοσαῦτα μόνα (ἢ γὰρ τῷ αὐτοί τι πεπονθέναι οἱ κρίνοντες, ἢ τῷ ποιούς τινας ὑπολαμβάνειν τοὺς λέγοντας, ἢ τῷ ἀποδεδεῖχθαι, πείθονται πάντες), εἴρηται δὲ καὶ τὰ ἐνθυμήματα, πόθεν δεῖ πορίζεσθαι (ἔστι γὰρ τὰ μὲν εἴδη τῶν ἐνθυμημάτων, τὰ δὲ τόποι)· περὶ δὲ τῆς λέξεως ἐχόμενόν ἐστιν εἰπεῖν . . .

All the material in brackets, and a good deal outside them, is strictly speaking redundant. Likewise C does not resume all that was said on tragedy and epic, but only reminds us of the location of comedy and the different kinds of poetry; it is at least as easy to justify as *Rhet.* III 1. Note that the latter recapitulation is in addition to that concluding *Rhet.* II, which is so similar to the end of *Poet.* 26. F. Solmsen suggested (*Die Entwicklung der aristotelischen Logik und Rhetorik* 31f.) that the opening of *Rhet.* III was an earlier version of the of the conclusion of *Rhet.* II, which was intended to replace it when A. had developed his logical thought. But there is a parallel at the transition from *Rhet.* I to II, although the conclusion of I is much briefer. On the unity of *Rhet.* see Grimaldi, *Studies in the Philosophy of A.'s Rhetoric* 28ff., 50ff. 'While [*Rhet.* III] might possibly stand by itself, it makes sense only in terms of what has preceded it' (ibid. 50). Surely the same must have applied to *Poetics* II; it is this peculiar relation to the preceding work in each case that, I believe, prompted the long recapitulation with which each begins.

If this is a recapitulation at the opening of *Poetics* II, it will be objected that there is no explicit reference to 'unmimetic' verse in the *Poetics*, although such a distinction is implicit in Chs. 1 and 9. However, an explicit summary of a statement implicit in a previous book is known in A. *E.N.* IX opens with the statement ἐν πάσαις δὲ ταῖς ἀνομοειδέσι φιλίαις τὸ ἀνάλογον ἰσάζει καὶ σῴζει τὴν φιλίαν, καθάπερ εἴρηται. In fact this has not been said in so many words, but can be extracted from VIII 7.1158b27, 8.1159a35ff., and 13.1162a34ff. (cf. Burnet ad 1162b32, Ross ad loc.). Cf. also *Poet.* 5.1449a32 (where the exact nature of comic *mimesis* has not been specified, but is said to have been, cf. Lucas ad loc.), or 24.1460a3 (cf. Lucas ad loc., Else 615).

Chapter I: Mimetic and non-mimetic verse

(a) *Text and expression*

C appends instructive and theoretical poetry to historical poetry, not to educational poetry. This is defended by Grube (145), who interprets it as referring to history which preaches by examples as distinct from that which aims 'merely' at establishing the facts. But Bergk's reassignation of these subdivisions to didactic poetry is surely correct. C's error is explained if the epitome was transmitted in stemmatic format, when subheadings became dislocated, as occurred in V 6 − 7 (with a leftward shift) and at VI 1 − 2 (q.v.). — ἀμίμητος does not occur in exactly this sense in A., but at *Poet.* 25.1460b32 we read that an artist's error is diminished if he did not know that a doe had no horns 'or if he painted with less realism' (ἀμιμήτως), an instance missed by Cantarella (295 n.32) in his attack on C. For the sense 'inimitable' cf. *Probl.* 29.951a6. — παιδευτική is Platonic, but not in A. according to Bonitz, whom I shall be citing for information of this kind (a concordance to A. is much to be desired); nor is ὑφηγητική, although ὑφηγεῖσθαι is common and ὑφήγησις known in other fourth-century writers, e.g. *Rhet. Al.* 1.1420b25. παίδευσις and παιδευτέον both occur (*Pol.* VIII 3.1338b5, *Rhet.* II 23.1399a13). Of 91 words in A.'s *Poetics* absent from his other works, 12 are adjectives in -ικός (sup. p.78f.). διήγησις and διηγητικός are known (this once only, *E.N.* III 10.1117b34). The concept of poetry for παιδεία goes back to the fourth century (K. Ziegler ap. *RE* Suppl. VI 2052ff., citing Aeschines III 134f.).

(b) *Interpretation*

Kaibel (*Abh.* 64, *CGF* 50) and Grube (145) suggest that non-mimetic poetry denotes prose, just as Dionysius of Halicarnassus calls the works of Herodotus and Thucydides poetry (ποιήσεις), although with an apology for so doing (*ep. ad Pomp.* III 3.777, p.240.17 Usener; for further parallels v. Norden, *Die antike Kunstprosa* I 92). Immisch demolished this by pointing out that rhetorical prose is missing (*Festschrift Gomperz* 263, cf. Kayser 22). ἀμίμητος ποίησις denotes prosy versification such as Choerilus for ἱστορική, Hesiod for ὑφηγητική, Empedocles for θεωρητική (on the sense of θεωρία in A. v. Guthrie *HGP* VI 396ff.). Kaibel and Immisch further suggested that non-mimetic is used here in a Platonic sense of narrative as opposed to dramatic poetry, where *mimesis* denotes the representation by the actors ('impersonation'), rather than A.'s *mimesis* inherent in poetry *qua* poetry. Plato, in *Rep.* III, equated mimetic with dramatic, while recognising that in epic and elsewhere a mixture of the two was common: ἆρ' οὖν οὐχὶ ἤτοι ἁπλῇ διηγήσει ἢ διὰ μιμήσεως γιγνομένῃ ἢ δι' ἀμφοτέρων περαίνουσιν; (392d5), and again

τῆς ποιήσεώς τε καὶ μυθολογίας ἡ μὲν διὰ μιμήσεως ὅλη ἐστίν
. . . τραγῳδία τε καὶ κωμῳδία, ἡ δὲ δι' ἀπαγγελίας αὐτοῦ τοῦ ποιητοῦ (εὕροις δ' ἂν αὐτὴν μάλιστά που ἐν διθυράμβοις), ἡ δ' αὖ δι' ἀμφοτέρων

(394b–c). He does not use the term ἀμίμητος, although, as we shall see, it is brought in by Proclus and is a fair inference from his words. But A. contradicts this passage when he includes dithyramb among μιμήσεις (*Poet.* 1.1447a14, cf. b26). C harmonises with this, since narrative is a *subdivision* of μιμητική (v. inf.).

Kaibel (*Abh.* 63) suggested that a mixed class, part mimetic and part narrative, has been lost here. This would follow Plato's tripartition at *Rep.* III 392d. In the problematic passage *Poet.*

3.1448a2off., A. differentiates the manner of the *mimesis*, but it is not clear whether he divides it into (i) mixed, (ii) plain narrative and (iii) dramatic, or (i) narrative, *either* mixed with speeches (as in Homer) *or* unalloyed, and (ii) dramatic. As Lucas remarks ad loc., the problem in the grouping of the clauses is insoluble on grammatical grounds; A. does not refer to the division again. Most scholars favour the bipartite division, which lays less emphasis on *mimesis* as 'impersonation', but A. does preserve relics of this Platonic and popular usage (a24, 24.1460a8), and can be careless with terminology. He probably felt the matter to be unimportant, since the mixed type would presumably include the same kinds of literature as plain narrative. If C is an accurate epitome of *Poetics* II, the bipartite division is upheld; but a mixed term could conceivably have been omitted as trivial. But such a term would have been mid-way between narrative and dramatic, not between mimetic and unmimetic; Kaibel's formulation is incompatible with the subordination of narrative to mimetic in the MS, and represents an attempt to fit its Aristotelian classification to a Platonic model, as I shall show.

(c) *Later classifications of poetry*

There are, in numerous late sources, similar but not identical classifications of poetry (to which that in Horace bears no relation, cf. Brink on *A.P.* 73−85). These are variously abbreviated, but invariably divergent from both the *Poetics* and the Tractate, by (i) equating dramatic with mimetic; (ii) introducing a mixed category; (iii) equating didactic with narrative, and assigning narrative genres like epic to the mixed category; (iv) terming narrative diegematic (or iv.a aphegematic, iv.e exegetic), not apangeltic; (v) associating the classification with three or four χαρακτῆρες λόγου. The Roman numerals after each source indicate which divergent aspects it includes:

1. Proclus' Commentary on Plato's *Republic* 392 (I 16ff. Kroll): (i), (ii), (iv). [τὸ μὲν δραματικὸν καὶ μιμητικὸν . . . τὸ δὲ ἀφηγηματικὸν καὶ ἀμίμητον . . . τὸ δὲ μικτόν — a fair representation of Plato's views.]

2. Photius' extract of Proclus' *Chrestomathy*, 318 Bekker (I 230 Westphal, p.96.17 Allen, vol. 5.155 Henry; translation in Russell, 201): (i), (iv), (v). [Here there is no mixed type, probably in error: v. inf.]

3. Proclus, *Prolegomena to Hesiod* (*Poet. min. Gr.* III 4f. Gaisford): (ii), (iv).

4. Scholia to Dionysius Thrax, p.450.3ff. Hilgard ('Heliodorus'): (ii), (iv), (v).

5. Scholia to Theocritus p.4.11 Wendel: (ii), (iv), (v).

6. < Tzetzes >, *Anecdoton Estense* III 6, p.11 Wendel: (ii), (iv), (v).

7. Probus, Comm. in Verg. *Ecl.* 329.10 — 13 Hagen, p.15 Wendel: (ii), (iv).

8. Servius, Comm. in Verg. *Ecl.* III 1.29.18f. Thilo (p.21 Wendel): (ii) [no term in (iv)].

9. Isidore *Etym.* VIII 7.11 (p.22 Wendel): (ii) [from Servius].

10. Diogenes Laertius III 50: (ii), (iv).

11. *Vita Aeschyli* 19 Wilamowitz (ad fin., p.334.9ff. Page): (i), (ii), [(iv)]: [διεξοδικά / διηγηματικά / ἀπαγγελτικά: δραματικά / μιμητικά].

12. Statements in the Scholia to Homer and the tragedians, e.g. Schol. Aristonic. Π 203, Ψ 855, Dionys. Sidon. ad Φ 218 (*P.Oxy.* 221 col. xi), Schol. exeg. Δ 303, Z 45 − 6, Schol. Eur. *Hipp.* 1240: (i).

13. Diomedes *Ars Gramm.* III 482.14ff. Keil (p.15ff. Wendel, XXIV 1 Koster): (i) (ii) (iii) (iv.e) (v) [narrative also called apangeltic].

14. Iunius Philargyrius, Comm. in Verg. *Ecl.* 1a 12ff. Hagen (p.19 Wendel): (ii) (iii) (iv.e) (v).

The diachronic relationships here are complex, but 13 and 14 are distinguished by (iii) and (iv.e), which two items are linked, as the subordination of didactic poetry to 'narrative' is eased by the ambiguity of the term 'exegetic', i.e. 'expository'. Among the rest Proclus was certainly important, but the origins of his classification lie further back, as is shown by Diogenes Laertius. Nor can the equation of dramatic and mimetic be ascribed to Platonic influence on Proclus, as it already occurs in scholia to Homer as far back as the Augustan age. Kayser (23) sought to explain the divergences by supposing that the common source for all these texts had a dual nomenclature, 'dramatic and mimetic' etc. as in Diomedes, or, we may add, the *Life of Aeschylus*. The terminology 'diegematic' / 'mimetic' is predominant, and the only cases I have found of 'diegematic' versus 'dramatic' are Dion. Hal. *Thuc.* 38.908.17, ἀποστρέψας τοῦ διηγήματος τὸν διάλογον ἐπὶ τὸ δραματικόν, [Longin.] *de Sublim.* 9.13 δραματικόν . . . διηγηματικόν, and 11 supra. 13 and 14 also share the association with χαρακτῆρες λόγου and have subheadings to narrative and dramatic, which both Proclus ap. Photius with the Scholia to Dionysius Thrax, and on the other side Diomedes supply as follows:

(a) narrative: epic, elegy, iambic, melic. The last is absent in Diomedes, and can be shown not to have been lost in the undoubted lacuna. The scholia to Dionysius subjoin these to 'narrative and mixed'; Usener, however, thought that they belong only to 'mixed', and that the 'narrative' sub-types have been lost in a hypothetical lacuna (*Kleine Schriften* II 291n.).

(b) dramatic: tragedy, comedy, satyr-play. Diomedes has mime also, as in C, where however the comic genre is first in each pair, as is fitting in a work on comedy. Mime is omitted presumed lost in the other sources; the *Anecdoton Estense* and Philodemus, *de Mus.* p.14 Kemke (*SVF* III 226.10 von Arnim), have the three types also, without mime.

A fourth difference between these sources and C is the 'mixed' category (κοινόν / μικτόν). This is absent only in Photius' epitome of Proclus. Severyns (*Recherches sur la Chrestomathie de Proclus* I.2.8of., followed by Dahlmann 65n.) believes that this absence in Photius is original, deriving straight from A.'s bipartition. To enforce this he has to deny the evident connexion between the *Chrestomathy* and the Scholia to Dionysius (also with Proclus' *Prolegomena to Hesiod*), and concludes from his assumptions that the Proclus of the *Chrestomathy* is not the Neoplatonist. This is against the evidence of the *Suda* s.v. Πρόκλος, which is also rejected by Henry, *Photius* loc. cit., cf. Russell 154, but also W.T. Treadgold, *The Nature of the* Bibliotheca *of Photius* 50n.: on Proclus Diadochus' doctrine on poetry cf. also Sheppard, *Studies in Proclus' Commentary on Plato's Republic* 162ff., Russell 199ff. It is far simpler to believe, with Kaibel (*Abh.* 64) and Rostagni (126n.1), that Photius has omitted the mixed category in epitome. He can certainly be shown to have omitted the ἀνθηρόν among the four χαρακτῆρες λόγου (Kayser 83): cf. further Mette *Parateresis* 58 n.2.

The ultimate model behind all these versions, with the exception of the refinements in Diomedes and Philargyrius, (iii) and (iv.e), is a Platonic model, with the Platonic disadvantage that it leaves no room for didactic poetry and similar genres important in the Hellenistic period and later. It is the following:

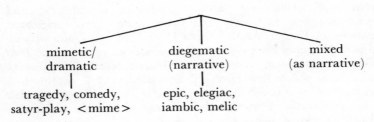

(χαρακτῆρες λόγου associated)

Diomedes, followed by Philargyrius, has a model that solves this difficulty at the price of a worse one, and also relieves the *horror vacui* of mixed types; the 'narrative' genres are assigned to 'mixed', and the missing kinds of verse are substituted under 'narrative' — moralising, historical and didactic, while in the heading itself diegematic is renamed exegetic. I quote:

'exegetici vel enarrativi species sunt tres: angeltice, historice, didascalice. angeltice est qua sententiae scribuntur, ut est Theognidis liber, item chriae; historice est qua narrationes et genealogiae componuntur, ut est Hesiodu γυναικῶν κατάλογος et similia; didascalice est qua comprehenditur philosophia, Empedoclis et Lucreti, item astrologia, ut Phaenomena Aratu'

(482.30ff. Keil). To schematise Diomedes' model:

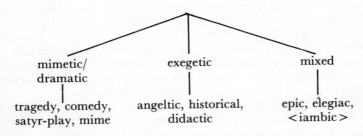

(four χαρακτῆρες ποιημάτων associated)

But this is a crude and absurd device, whether Diomedes' own or his predecessors' (among whom are Suetonius and Varro, cf. Kayser 44ff., Dahlmann *passim*). Didactic, genealogical and sententious verse is hardly narrative: these surely originated elsewhere (cf. Usener, *Kleine Schriften* II 291f.). Comparison with C, and with Diogenes Laertius loc. cit., suggests an explanation. Two of Diomedes' headings, historical and didactic, recall C's division of non-mimetic poetry into historical and paedeutic. If the heading 'non-mimetic' is transferred to narrative, as in the Platonic model, these 'non-mimetic' genres are left floating without an anchorage, and can be pirated away as in Diomedes.

The alternative to supposing that Diomedes is reconciling the Platonic model with the didactic genres outside it, taken from a source (like Ω) in which they occupied a place in a divergent model, is that C too exhibits efforts to reconcile these genres with such a Platonic model. This has been proposed by Kaibel (sup.). Dahlmann too (71f.) suggests that C's 'mimetic poetry' is the same as Plato's 'dramatic'; he does not explain how in this case 'dramatic' and 'narrative' come to be *subordinated* to 'mimetic'. He equates the 'narrative' sub-type with Plato's 'mixed' type, but himself remarks that it ought to be a third independent type, not subordinate to 'mimetic'. Nor does he explain why it is not called 'mixed'. Štabryła (*Meander* 31 (1976) 445−61) follows Dahlmann. Feibleman (*In Praise of Comedy* 82) disregards the narrative sub-type and, blind to incest, pairs its dramatic twin with its mimetic parent: similarly Plebe 123, Dosi 623.

Difficulty exists only for those who wish to connect C with Plato or Platonic models. C is resoundingly Aristotelian here, and differs from the above schemata on all five counts. Whether these, with their χαρακτῆρες λόγου, go back to Theophrastus as has been argued, or to the first century B.C., cannot be debated here (cf. Kayser 80−97; Hendrickson *AJP* 25 (1904) 124ff., 26 (1905) 249ff.; Rostagni 113f.; Dahlmann 44ff.; Grube *TAPA* 83 (1952) 79ff., *Demetrius* 50 n.66; Kennedy *The Art of Persuasion in Greece* 278ff.; Russell 138). There are grave obstacles to assuming that C presents a late reworking of this material, but the only problem if it is Aristotelian is the phrase ἀμίμητος ποίησις, where I have cut the Gordian knot with the sword of A.'s loose terminology.

Koster (on Diomedes, XXIV 1, p.118) recognises both the distinctness of C's primary division compared with the rest, and the superiority of its handling of the didactic types (*subtilior distinctio*): Russell (153) remarks that its lack of reference to style or metre is unusual, and in this it resembles the *Poetics*: moreover, its classification leaves no more room for lyric poetry than does the latter's, as he notes; both apparently subsume it under music.

Chapter II: Narrative, drama and the place of mime

(a) *Text and expression*

μιμητική, Kayser's correction for μιμητή 'imitated', an easy slip after ἀμίμητος, is supported by A.'s use of μιμητική at *Rhet.* III 1.1404a22; *Poet.* 6.1449b21; 8.1451a30. Bergk's correction ἀπαγγελτικόν for ἐπαγγελτικόν is also certain; cf. 6.1449b26, where B has ἐπαγγελίας for ἀπαγγελίας. The latter also occurs in C, ch. IV. — Kaibel thought the accusatives μίμους and σατύρους indications of a careless excerptor (*CGF* 50); Cantarella emended to μῖμος, which Koster (*Mnemosyne* VIII (1955) 20) supports by pointing to C's accentuation μίμους, but accentual errors are legion in C. Might the accusatives suggest that these types were given in a different clause or sentence, wherein they were direct objects, e.g. 'comedy and tragedy belong to this type; we may add mimes and satyr-plays'?

ἀπαγγελτικός is absent from A., but cf. ἀπαγγελία, the parallel formation διηγηματικός with the same meaning (*Poet.* 24.1459b33, 36), and ἐξαγγελτικός at *Rhet.* II 6.1384b5, 7, 11. δραματικός is Aristotelian, cf. *Poet.* 4.1448b35; so is πρακτικός, e.g. 24.1460a1, *Pol.* VIII 7.1341b34. The phrase δραματικὸν καὶ πρακτικόν has a particularly close parallel at *Poet.* 3.1448a25ff.: τῇ μὲν ὁ αὐτὸς ἂν εἴη μιμητὴς Ὁμήρῳ Σοφοκλῆς, . . . τῇ δὲ Ἀριστοφάνει, **πράττοντας** γὰρ μιμοῦνται καὶ **δρῶντας** ἄμφω. ὅθεν καὶ **δράματα** καλεῖσθαί τινες αὐτά φασιν. μῖμος is in the same sense at 1.1447 b10 and fr. 72 Rose. σάτυροι is not used to denote satyr-drama by A., although already in Aristophanes (*Thesm.* 157); we find σατυρικόν at 4.1449a20, σατυρικὴν ποίησιν ibid. 22, in connection with tragedy, with which it is in parallel here. The term was certainly current in Peripatetic scholarship (cf. Chamaeleon's Περὶ Σατύρων).

(b) *Mime*

There are two problems relating to mime: (i) could A. have considered mime a part of poetry? (ii) could he have considered mime a dramatic genre?

(i) *Was mime part of poetry?* As we saw, A. complains that popular usage did not distinguish mimetic and non-mimetic verse, or mimetic and non-mimetic prose (*Poet.* 1.1447b14), but he none the less uses the term poetry in the popular sense, when it suits him; as Lucas remarks ad 1447a28, the drift of this controversial passage suggests that he regrets the lack of a term to cover mimetic writing in both prose and verse (cf. House, *A.'s Poetics* 30ff.). Lobel's emendations here (ap. *CQ* 23 (1929) 76) are neither necessary nor desirable; it is better to read and translate as does Butcher (cf. Bernays 81ff., Rostagni and Gudeman ad loc., Montmollin 272f.: contrast Kassel, *Dichtkunst und Versifikation bei den Griechen* 24), i.e. ἡ δὲ [ἐποποιία] μόνον τοῖς λόγοις ψιλοῖς ἢ τοῖς μέτροις . . . <ἀνώνυμος> τυγχάν<ει> οὖσα μέχρι τοῦ νῦν: N.B. ἡ δὲ requires τέχνη ποιουμένη τὴν μίμησιν to be supplied, after Butcher. This is not obvious, which is why the gloss ἐποποιία entered the text and was read there by Tzetzes or his source along with the lost adjective ἀνώνυμος (Exegesis on Hesiod, *Works and Days*, Gaisford *Poet. min. Gr.* III p.11 = Colonna *BPEC* 2 (1953) 35.63, 36.70, = XXIIc 10, 16 Koster; and *de Diff. Poet.* 167 = XXIa Koster). ἀνώνυμος was in the singular, as indicated by him in the same poem, v.11 (ποιητικόν τε πᾶν ἀνώνυμον γένος). Lobel disregards this evidence, and the Arabic is also rather against him, cf. Tkatsch I p.221, II p.1 nn.85−6, p.154ff. The next sentence surely runs as Butcher renders it: the conjunction οὐδέ coordinates (cf. LSJ s.v. A2) the two items for which we have no common name, mimetic prose (e.g. mime or Socratic dialogue) and mimetic verse, in whatever metre. Poets should be known κατὰ μίμησιν (1447b15, cf. 9.1451b28) and not because they use verse: there is no name for verbal *mimesis* as a whole (*pace* Russell 13).

This passage shows that, just as A. could loosely refer to non-mimetic verse as poetry, so too he could include mimetic prose (so Fuhrmann 59f., 65). We must remember how new his distinction was; by his time, mime and Socratic dialogue were the only such mimetic forms which had evolved. Demetrius (*de Eloc.* 298) testifies to the profound impact of the Socratic dialogues by virtue of their mimetic, vivid and instructional character.

Despite their lack of versification, mimes, including those of Sophron known to A., were certainly called poems in an early Peripatetic source reported in Philodemus (cf. Kayser 24, Gudeman ad 1447b10, Brink ap. *Maia* 24 (1972) 342ff.). In the Περὶ Ποιημάτων II fr. 72 Hausrath we read:

καὶ αὐτὸς εἶν[αι ἐ]κεῖνα **ποήματα** ἔ[φη, καὶ] μὴ μόνα· καὶ γὰρ
[τὰ τοῦ] Σώφρονος καὶ τὰ [τῶν] ἄλλων μιμογρ[άφων] εἴ ποτε
ποήμα[τα λέ]γεται καὶ μὴ . . . οἱ συντιθέν[τες . . .] μίμων
ποη[. . .

Again, fr. 52:

καὶ κατὰ τοῦτο δήπο[υθεν τὰ το]ιαῦτα τέρπε[ιν τε καὶ] ποήματ'
εἶναι· κα[τὰ τὰ] κρούματα γὰρ οὐκ ἂν φθάνοιεν οὕτω ποήματα
λέγοντες. ὑπὲρ γὰρ τοῦ διὰ μηδὲν ἕτερον ἡδὺ **πόημα** τὸ [το]ῦ
Σώφρονος [εἴ]ρηκέ[ναι.

(ii) *Was mime dramatic in Aristotle's day?* Kayser (23f., 30) thought
not, and rejected the passage as unaristotelian: contrast Fuhrmann
59, 65. A. called Sophron's work, in company with the Socratic
dialogues, λόγους καὶ μιμήσεις, 'speeches and representations' (fr.
72 Rose); it is clear from Plato and the large fragment of Sophron
(Page, *Literary Papyri* 328ff.) that both normally possessed dramatic
form. Cunningham (*Herodas' Mimiambi* 10ff.) believes that mimes
were intended for acting, at first by one person, later by several, as
in the performance in Xenophon's *Symposium*. Demetrius calls
Sophron's works dramas (*de Eloc.* 156), and confirmation that this
appellation was current by the first century B.C. is provided by
Philodemus, Περὶ Ποιημάτων I 194 Sudhaus, who casually refers to
dramatic delivery in tragedy, comedy and mime. Comedy and
mime occur together in Asclepiades of Myrlea (ap. Sext. Emp.
Math. I 253, p.62.27 Mau, cf. Müller *de Ascl. Myrl.* 27, Kayser 28).
In addition to his similar list of tragedy, comedy, satyr-play and
mime, Diomedes' definition of mime is from a Greek source
connected with Theophrastus (sup. p.49). Thus there is no reason
why this section cannot be Aristotelian, and no need to invoke the
elaborate mimes of later times: Reich (*Der Mimus* I 1.252f.), von
Christ (*Literaturgeschichte*[1] 380) and Fuhrmann (loc. cit.) ascribe this
fourfold division of the dramatic arts to A. himself, and argue that
there is nothing essentially alien to him in I−II. The fourfold
division was translated into Roman terms by Varro (Kayser 51). —
Reich (loc. cit.) suggests, on the basis of the parallelism in the list
comedy, tragedy, mime, satyr-play, that A. derived comedy from
the *phallikon* plus the mime, just as he is thought to derive tragedy
from the dithyramb plus satyric drama. But the order is to be
explained by affinities of content alone, the major types first.

Chapter III: Tragic catharsis

(a) *Expression*

ὑφαιρεῖν is used at *de Caelo* II 13.294a18 to mean 'gradually remove', as here: cf. *Poet.* 21.1457b2, ὑφῃρημένον ὄνομα, elsewhere ἀφῃρημένον 'curtailed'. Ničev (35, 100f.) notes that both ὑφαίρεσις and ἀφαίρεσις are synonyms of κάθαρσις in Plato, e.g. *Sophist* 227d, *Rep.* 567c. It seems not to occur as a medical term; though not cognate with καθαίρειν, it could readily be linked with it by popular etymology: A. was himself capable of absurd etymologies, e.g. *de Caelo* I 3.270b22ff. — The passive sense of φοβερός in τὰ φοβερὰ παθήματα ('feelings of fear' not 'feelings inspiring fear') is paralleled at *Rhet.* II 5.1382b7 οἱ συνειδότες πεποιηκότι τι δεινὸν φοβεροί. With παθήματα τῆς ψυχῆς cf. παθήματα τῆς ψυχῆς *de Int.* 1.16a6; *de Anima* I 1.403a3, 11; ἔλεος καὶ ὀργὴ καὶ τὰ τοιαῦτα πάθη τῆς ψυχῆς *Rhet.* I 1.1354a17.

δι' οἴκτου καὶ δέους has been regarded (since Bernays 141ff.) as unaristotelian, for δι' ἐλέου καὶ φόβου. However, both *Rhet.* and *Poet.* prove that A.'s terminology in this matter was by no means rigid, and the phrase can be paralleled several times. Although δέος is found only once in A., fr. 182 Rose, it is of course cognate with δεινός: Plato connected the two words explicitly at *Laches* 198b. τὰ δεινά for τὰ φοβερά is frequent, e.g. *E.N.* II 3.1104b7 ὑπομένων τὰ δεινά beside b3 ὑπομένειν τὰ φοβερά; *Rhet.* II 5.1383a4; 8.1386a22 on the relation of pity to fear, τοῦτο μὲν ἐλεεινόν, ἐκεῖνο δὲ δεινόν; cf. *Poet.*14.1453b1 – 5, where τὸ φοβερὸν καὶ ἐλεεινόν is resumed by καὶ φρίττειν καὶ ἐλεεῖν, and ἢ ἐλεεινὰ ἢ δεινά at 19.1456b3. But the fluidity is not limited to τὸ φοβερόν in A.'s usage, since he twice uses οἶκτος or its adjective for pity:

(i) At *Rhet.* III 16.1417a12 the defendant is counselled to tell of things as past, unless they arouse οἶκτον ἢ δείνωσιν when represented as present, e.g. 'the story told to Alcinous, which is retold to Penelope in sixty lines'; he gives two more examples of brief summaries from poetry. δείνωσις, normally 'indignation', surely must mean 'fear' alongside 'pity' here: with *Rhet.* III 19.1419b25 (τὰ πάθη) ἐστὶν ἔλεος καὶ **δείνωσις** καὶ ὀργὴ κτέ. cf. *Poet.* 19.1456b1 πάθη . . . οἶον ἔλεον ἢ **φόβον** ἢ ὀργὴν κτέ. It is particularly significant that it is used in the context of a literary narrative, where the narrator Odysseus has no reason to excite indignation, only sympathy. The passage must be added to those on the effect of poetry, and shows that catharsis applies as much to epic as to tragedy, *pace* Hubbard ap. *ALC* 132n. For this use of δείνωσις cf. also Demetrius *de Eloc.* 130 (of σεμναὶ χάριτες):

χρῆται δὲ αὐταῖς Ὅμηρος καὶ πρὸς δείνωσιν ἐνίοτε καὶ ἔμφασιν, καὶ παίζων **φοβερώτερός** ἐστι, πρῶτός τε εὑρηκέναι δοκεῖ φοβερὰς χάριτας.

(ii) At *Poet.* 14.1453b14, on the arousal of pity and fear in tragedy, we find ποῖα **δεινὰ** ἢ ποῖα **οἰκτρά**. To my knowledge this passage has never been adduced to support C's phrasing, or itself denounced as spurious along with the latter. Far from toying with his exemplar's wording to assert his independence, the supposed forger has noticed something unperceived by modern scholars, even with the aid of modern indices, namely that A. varied his terminology for the key concepts 'pity' and 'fear': for ἔλεος and ἐλεεινά, there is οἶκτος and οἰκτρά; for φόβος and φοβερά, there is δείνωσις, δεινά and (if we trust C) δέος as well. In view of the parallels, Baumgart's idea (662ff., cf. Lucas ad *Poet.* 14.1453b14) that οἶκτος and δέος are not synonymous with ἔλεος and φόβος needs no rebuttal. The synonyms passed into critical usage, e.g. Aesch. *Ag.* Argumentum 14 ἔκπληξιν ἔχον καὶ οἶκτον ἱκανόν, of the Cassandra scene; [Longin.] *de Subl.* 8.2, οἶκτοι λῦπαι φόβοι, where note the generic alongside the specific emotions (cf. sup. p.124f.); ibid. 10.2 (δέος), 11.2.

καὶ ὅτι is certainly a sign of the process of excerption (cf. Bernays 141f.; *contra*, Grube 146, Ničev 102). It is most natural to supply 'tragedy' from the preceding sentence: ' < tragedy > wishes to have a due proportion of fear' (Lane Cooper 228), although the alternative, 'he (i.e. the author of the piece being epitomised) wishes (it, i.e. tragedy) to have a due proportion of fear' is conceivable. The personification of tragedy as an entity capable of wishing is paralleled in *Poet.*, e.g. 5.1449b9 ἡ ἐποποιία τῇ τραγῳδίᾳ . . . **ἠκολούθησεν**, ibid. 1449b12 ἡ (τραγῳδία) ὅτι μάλιστα **πειρᾶται** . . . , and particularly 2.1448a17 ἐν αὐτῇ τῇ διαφορᾷ καὶ ἡ τραγῳδία πρὸς τὴν κωμῳδίαν **διέστηκεν**· ἡ μὲν γὰρ χείρους ἡ δὲ βελτίους μιμεῖσθαι **βούλεται** τῶν νῦν.

ἔχει δὲ μητέρα τὴν λύπην was objected to by Bernays (142) as a tasteless metaphor and the opposite of Aristotelian teaching — πᾶν γὰρ ἀσαφὲς τὸ κατὰ μεταφορὰν λεγόμενον (*Top.* VI 2.139b34), cf. Guthrie *HGP* VI 382f.: yet A. does use analogies, even imperfect ones, to help out his meaning, as Guthrie points out (ibid. 302).

Gudeman (144f.) assigns it to the category of the ψυχρόν, along
with Alcidamas' saying that the *Odyssey* was a fine mirror of human
life (*Rhet.* III 3.1406b12), and schol. Aristoph. *Clouds* 638c πατὴρ
μέτρου ῥυθμός (Longinus). Baumgart (664) argued that the
metaphor is paralleled in the Aristotelian corpus at *Phys.* I
9.192a14 ἡ (ὕλη) συναιτία . . . ὥσπερ μήτηρ (recalling Plato *Tim.*
50cff.), *de Mundo* 2.391b14 ἡ γῆ . . . ζῴων ἑστία τε οὖσα καὶ μήτηρ
(this work is generally thought spurious, but see now the ed. of G.
Reale); cf. *G.A.* I 2.716a16, *de Plant.* I 2.817a28 where πατήρ is
similarly used. These are not close parallels, however; the last is
quoted from Anaxagoras. Note also Plato *Laws* III 693d εἰσὶν
πολιτειῶν οἷον μητέρες δύο τινές; Xenophon *Oecon.* 5.17 γεωργίαν
τῶν ἄλλων τεχνῶν μητέρα. In the context of poetry, note Demetrius'
ὁ γέλως ἐχθρὸς τραγῳδίας (*de Eloc.* 169). Cf. also *Poet.* 6.1450a38
οἷον ψυχὴ ὁ μῦθος τῆς τραγῳδίας, where tragedy is likened to a
living entity. The expression would be easier if the epitomator has
suppressed οἷον before μητέρα; but even if this has occurred, it still
seems vague and unsatisfactory. On the meaning v. inf. p.16of.

(b) *Objections to Aristotelian authorship*

The main objections to the content of this section are two:

(i) the brevity with which tragedy is treated led Atkins (139) to
argue that C displays an unaristotelian disrespect for tragedy as the
supreme art. But C nowhere states any preference; tragedy in fact
receives more attention than any genre except comedy herself. The
treatise is on comedy, and it is as absurd to criticise the choice of
topic as to complain at the composition of several books on *Homeric
Problems* when A. could have been discussing Sophocles. Indeed the
objection rebounds against itself: the limitation of the account of
tragedy to the *aim* thereof, while comedy receives full coverage, is
explained if most aspects of tragedy, except for catharsis, have
already been treated in a preceding discussion — which is what the
extant *Poetics* contains, along with a promise to speak later of
comedy.

(ii) Bernays (141ff.) recognised that this passage is concerned
with the emotions caused by tragedy, and accepted the sentence on
συμμετρία, although not, as we shall see, in the correct interpretation. However, he rejected the opening sentence as an
unhelpful paraphrase, and attacked the conclusion as the erroneous
deduction of a commentator who came, by a logical method, to the
precise antithesis of A.'s theory. The second problem thus amounts

to nothing less than whether C represents A.'s views on catharsis, and those views are of course hidden in the thunder and smoke of furious debate.

(c) *Aristotle's theory of tragic catharsis*

Bernays himself was not the first to conscript the now celebrated passage from *Pol.* VIII, which has a cross-reference to *Poet.*, for service in the mêlée (*Grundzüge der verlorenen Abhandlung des Aristoteles über Wirkung der Tragödie* (1857), republished in *Zwei Abhandlungen*), but since his essay it has been widely accepted that the idea of catharsis derives from medicine ('purgation') rather than from religion ('purification'). Accepted too is his translation of the crucial clause in the definition of tragedy, δι' ἐλέου καὶ φόβου περαίνουσα τὴν τῶν τοιούτων παθημάτων κάθαρσιν (*Poet.* 6.1449b27), as 'through pity and fear achieving (carrying forward) the *katharsis* of these emotions', i.e. emotions of pity and fear (but see p.160f.). Nor is it to be doubted that the emotions affected are those of the audience, rather than of the actors or characters; so much is clear from the *Politics*. Only by ignoring the *Politics* altogether, as does Else (441f.), can one apply the purification to the actions in the play. The parallels presented below underline the importance of the *Politics* and exclude this interpretation; Else (447) admits that his interpretation does not fit comedy at all. Cf. Vickers, *Towards Greek Tragedy* Appendix I, for an eloquent refutation of his views, and Bernays 4f. against Goethe's, which anticipated them.

In Bernays' view, A. intends to convey that a physiological change takes place in the 'patients' who obtain tragic catharsis. Probably the best modern statement of this view will be found in Lucas' *Poetics* Appendix II (also Fuhrmann 95ff.). As Lucas explains (p.279), 'what is purified (or diminished) is the emotional capacity of the spectator over a considerable period of time after the performance, what purifies is the emotional experience given by the performance itself'. The treatment of *enthousiasmos*, which might be termed 'possession' or 'frenzy', was homoeopathic: enthusiastic music had a cathartic effect, and tragedy is thought to have a similar effect on persons of an emotional disposition, and in a similar manner. Indeed, in a neglected passage in *Rhet.* III A. refers to an orator inspiring his hearers to such a frenzy by using elevated diction, which is also suited to poetry because poetry is something that is inspired — ἔνθεον ἡ ποίησις, 7.1408b14ff.: the notably Platonic expression is sly parody, as the next sentence ironically indicates; there is similar subtle mockery of Plato at *Probl.*

30.954a35ff., where, among ἔνθεοι, Maracus was *even* a better poet
when he was out of his mind (for such parody in A. v. Quandt,
TAPA 111 (1981) 181 — 7).

This theory of catharsis will then be an *ad hoc* bastion erected
against Plato's attack on poetry as a pernicious stimulant of the
emotions — A. countering that in fact it helps to keep them in
check. Such a redoubt, unconnected to the rest of A.'s defences of
poetry, suffers from the weakness that it shelters only those prone to
excessive emotions, in terms of humours those with an excess of
black bile, while the rest of us continue to be exposed to the
onslaught of emotional stimulation. The best audience for a
tragedy will thus consist of neurotics (in Waldock's arresting
formulation ap. *Sophocles the Dramatist* Ch. 4), or rather of
melancholics. This, then, will be the reason why the theory has
hardly any afterlife in antiquity, that it was *ad hoc* and inept.

Whether it was in fact unconnected with A.'s wider theory of
mimesis will be discussed later; here the emphasis in Bernays'
approach must be questioned. Physiology and psychology were for
A. interdependent: catharsis was both physical and psychological,
'since the process actually worked on the humours through the
emotions' (Lucas 286). There is not a word about humours or
black bile in *Pol.* VIII 7; conversely, the Peripatetic discussion of
melancholia in *Probl.* 4.880a22, 30.953a10 — 955a (cf. Lucas 284)
contains no reference to catharsis or poetry as an effective
treatment for the condition. Thus it begs the question to state that
the late sources, which present the theory in the form that the
moderate exercise of the emotions makes them more controllable in
everyday life, misrepresent it. The two approaches are perfectly
compatible in Aristotelian theory, since the emotions are physiological events in the mind; but in *Rhet.* and *Poet.* little weight is
placed on this (cf. Fortenbaugh 139). As Else (440f.) remarks,
Bernays' emphasis is

> 'inherently and indefeasibly *therapeutic*. It presupposes that we
> come to the tragic drama as patients to be cured, relieved,
> restored to psychic health. But there is not a word to support
> this in the *Poetics*, not a hint that the end of drama is to cure
> or alleviate psychological states. On the contrary it is evident
> in every line of the work that A. is presupposing *normal*
> auditors, normal states of mind and feeling, normal emotional
> and aesthetic experience.'

But we must not be misled: all of us are emotional to some degree and thus benefit from tragedy (cf. πᾶσι γίγνεσθαί τινα κάθαρσιν, *Pol.* VIII 7.1342a14); however, we do not go to the theatre specifically to do so. As House (112f.) remarks, in the most sensible treatment of the question known to me, A. never suggests any such thing, but mentions the pleasure derived from tragedy a dozen times over. Although we obtain benefit from tragedy, we go for the fun of it.

The purpose of the catharsis of pity and fear, as House argues forcefully, is not to drain our emotional capacities so that we are no longer able to feel these emotions; instead it is to predispose us to feel emotion in the right way, at the right time, towards the right object, with the right motive, and to the proper degree. It is important for a good man to feel pity and fear in the appropriate circumstances (*E.N.* II 6). Catharsis 'brings our emotions nearer to those of a good and wise man', i.e. to equilibrium or emotional balance, the Golden Mean. The restoration of balance naturally causes pleasure. I should add that House related catharsis to the Aristotelian mean independently of the *symmetria* of the Tractate, about which he is scornful (p.41); cf. Plebe 18f., who points out that A.'s discussion of excess and deficiency in laughter follows that of ἐγκράτεια and ἀκρασία, i.e. self-restraint, and that he terms those those who achieve the mean in it εὐτράπελοι . . . οἷον εὔτροποι, i.e. well-balanced: *E.N.* IV 8. Lessing had already argued along House's lines (cf. Bernays 1ff.).

To refute the purely medical interpretation one can point to indications that the theory of pleasurable catharsis is after all related to the main body of A.'s theory of literature, namely *mimesis*, just as, for him, the emotions involve cognition (Fortenbaugh 142ff.). At *Poet.* 14.1453b12 the phrasing not quite certainly insists that tragedy must aim at tragic pleasure from pity and fear *by means of mimesis* (τὴν ἀπὸ ἐλέου καὶ φόβου διὰ μιμήσεως δεῖ ἡδονὴν παρασκενάζειν τὸν ποιητήν), cf. Else 410ff., House 116. If διὰ μιμήσεως bears this weight, A. is drawing a distinction between pity and fear in 'real life', which are not pleasurable, and the imitation of these in drama, which leads to the tragic pleasure. This is surely clear from earlier in *Poet.* 14, where he repudiates 'the horrible' as a source of fear on the stage: this produces the wrong kind of pleasure, because it is not mimetic, but is itself revolting. Cf. also 4.1448b10ff., *Rhet.* I 11.1371b5ff., where A. states that we derive pleasure from imitations even of objects repellent in actuality, and this pleasure is one of learning, that 'this is that'. Although A. provides no hint that we are to extrapolate from this to a wider theory of literature, much of his emphasis on the importance of plot and logical sequence will follow from such a theory, e.g. the revulsion, τὸ μιαρόν, (the opposite, certainly, of *katharsis*) produced by the unaccountable misfortune of a decent man or good fortune of one who is vile and worthless (Ch. 13). In such cases our moral sense is dissatisfied: these reversals therefore fail to elicit the appropriate emotions, and so there is no catharsis. Such plots upset Plato; here is the answer to his complaint — they are alien to tragedy, since they elicit the wrong response. To arouse the proper response, the tragic events must be well motivated, so that we can understand the reasons behind them; and quintessential to *mimesis* is its presentation of broad outlines, at the proper scale, with a logical beginning, middle and end, so that the whole forms a rational nexus intelligible to the observer. Thus it can be argued that catharsis is an integral part of Aristotelian theory, and that the presentation of rationally motivated tragic events *in mimesis* is needed to bring it about; such events in actual experience and not mimetically presented will have no cathartic effect, quite the contrary. Note that the concepts of mimesis and catharsis are juxtaposed in *P. Herc.* 1581 fr. I; v. inf. In reaching this conclusion I am persuaded by a growing body of recent criticism, led by L. Golden (*TAPA* 93 (1962) 51 − 60, *CP* 64 (1969) 145 − 53, cf. Redfield, *Nature and Culture in the Iliad* Chs. 1 − 2). These scholars harmonise the structural and therapeutic aspects of catharsis, as Else (443) indicated was necessary.

How, then, does the cathartic process operate? By representing pitiful and fearful events artistically, it arouses pity and fear in the members of the audience, each according to his own emotional capacity, and by a homoeopathic process so stimulates these emotions as to relieve them by giving them moderate and harmless exercise; and with relief comes pleasure. If the tragic events are badly motivated, and the characters tormented incomprehensibly, we are simply shocked; our feelings are not worked through and made comprehensible. But when catharsis is achieved, the process is clearly homoeopathic: pity and fear, aroused by the drama, act on the latent emotions of pity and fear in the spectator, and I do not understand why Lucas (278) objects to the idea that A. could have said anything 'so clumsy as that pity and fear purify pity and fear', since this is the vital principle involved, that of homoeopathy. Any difficulty is eased in Greek by the ambiguity of πάθη, which can mean actual feelings, or proneness to have an actual feeling (Hardie, *A.'s Ethical Theory* 96).

(d) *Comic catharsis*

Although we have less evidence as to what emotions were purged by comedy, there is certainly enough to show that comedy had a cathartic effect on emotions of some kind according to A.'s theory. As in the case of tragedy, there are narrower and broader interpretations. Fuhrmann (63, 67 without argument) believes that A. could not have specified *any* particular emotions worthy of mention, to balance pity and fear, but would only have discussed the laughable. He therefore rejects this part of the Tractate. We shall see that he almost hit upon the truth, as laughter is one of the *emotions* to be purged. In the narrow interpretation, the emotions to be purged would be scorn and over-confidence: 'as the unstable man might be helped by tragedy to maintain his composure in time of trouble, so comedy might help him maintain his dignity and refrain from contempt in prosperity' (Lucas 288). But Lucas is prepared to entertain a broader interpretation, which conflicts with his view of tragic catharsis. He considers whether the Old Comedy, involving the imaginary suspension of many of those restraints and restrictions which make civilised life possible, might not lead to a catharsis of the impulses to defy convention and contemn authority: 'A. might have reserved his full treatment of *katharsis* for the section on comedy, because it provided the more important illustration'. He refers in support to Iamblichus (*Poet.* fr. V Kassel), where the obscenities in the Mysteries are excused as the means used to free the hearers from the harm they might incur in real experiences. Lucas sees two difficulties in this: first, that the emotions purged by comedy are common to all men, whereas those purged by tragedy, in his view, are not; this is a reason for rejecting as too narrow his view on tragedy. Second,

> 'comedy and obscene ritual work, on this theory, by providing emotions roused by imitations as a substitute for emotions roused by actual experience. But while the substitute emotions afforded by comedy are ones that mankind in general considers desirable, those afforded by tragedy are the opposite, and one would have supposed that most people experienced in the course of their lives as much pity and fear as they wanted'

(ibid. 288—9). This misses the point: tragic misfortunes *on the stage* reveal to the audience how much worse off they might be, as the poet Timocles (of late Middle Comedy) put it in a noteworthy fragment ap. Ath. VI 223b (fr. 6). This is particularly clear from *Rep*. X 606a, c, where Plato attacks the theatre for arousing emotions which in real life would shame us, *both in tragedy and comedy*, namely weeping and laughter; both types of emotion are wrong, although both are desired by human nature. Homoeopathy is the obvious answer to this; the simulated and real emotions are not the same, since the causes of the former lose their reality when the mimesis ends, but those of the latter remain with us in our lives. Thus are the emotions purified, made bearable and reduced to moderation, by their arousal through mimesis, and thus is their arousal justified.

(e) *The Tractatus on catharsis*

What does C offer on catharsis? The first sentence of III states that tragedy takes away the emotions of fear by means of pity and fear. Bernays criticises this as an unhelpful paraphrase, but its sole defect is the expression φοβερὰ παθήματα for the expected 'emotions of *pity and* fear'. The compendious expression is due to the epitomator or A. himself (cf. *Poet.* 14.1453b9 τὸ φοβερόν for τὸ φοβερὸν καὶ ἐλεεινόν above, b1; cf. also Else 514 n.22 on b17).

This sentence makes four contributions to our knowledge. First, the use of ὑφαιρεῖ reminds us of the fluidity of A.'s terminology, as in οἴκτου καὶ δέους; secondly, παθήματα τῆς ψυχῆς confirms once for all that it is not the tragic events that somehow receive catharsis, but our emotional reactions; further, as is usually believed, the emotions are *diminished* by the cathartic process, not somehow transformed — the change is quantitative; lastly, it puts into clear relief the stark and inescapable fact of homoeopathy, that pity and fear do cast out the devils of pity and fear in their own name.

Bernays' objection to this sentence was at least partly grounded in a surprising and self-contradictory resistance to the straight-forward doctrine in the *Politics*, and led him to argue that πάθημα and πάθος do not mean the same: the former is the disposition of the soul to emotion, the latter is the emotion itself. In fact both can mean either (cf. Hardie loc. cit., Bonitz, *Ar. Stud.* V). Thus τὰ φοβερὰ παθήματα will be the same as δέος, and in the definition of tragedy ἔλεος καὶ φόβος will be the same as τῶν τοιούτων παθημάτων. C removes the last mystery about homoeopathy, and concurs with our conclusions from the interrogation of the other witnesses to A.'s theory.

The second sentence is more problematic: 'tragedy wishes to have a due proportion (συμμετρία) of fear'. The interpretation depends on whether the author is making a fresh point, or restating his previous one. We must also note that in IX the need for due proportion is applied to comedy as well as to tragedy, and the similar terms in Iamblichus and Proclus (*Poet.* fr. V Kassel) and in Olympiodorus, below. In both III and IX 'to have' is slightly odd, and 'to generate' would be a better rendering of the idea.

Bernays (142) assumed that the fear must be in due proportion so as not to oust pity, for if the tragic events are too terrible, pity is driven out. This is Aristotelian doctrine at *Rhet.* II 8.1386a22, τὸ δεινὸν . . . ἐκκρουστικὸν τοῦ ἐλέου . . . <οὐ γὰρ> ἔτι ἐλεοῦσιν ἐγγὺς αὑτοῖς τοῦ δεινοῦ ὄντος. If a balance between the two tragic emotions is to be struck, then something analogous must be found for comedy, since IX specifies that there is to be a συμμετρία or balance of the ludicrous in comedy. Bernays (151) identifies the balancing factor as τέρψις, innocent delight, circumscribing laughter within the limits of the light-hearted type of jesting worthy of free and educated citizens. The sentiment that laughter of this kind is more appropriate to comedy is shared by A. with C, as we shall see (VII); a parallelism between ἔλεος and φόβος in the definition of tragedy, and ἡδονή and γέλως in that of comedy, certainly seems desirable.

This is a reasonable interpretation, well within the scope of Aristotelian thought; but another is at least as firmly based. This is well put by Lane Cooper (228), who suggested that 'the latent fear of the spectators is to be aroused by tragedy, and so reduced to moderation'. This possesses four advantages:

(i) We have already seen a use of τὰ φοβερὰ παθήματα in a compendious sense, including pity, about which there can be no doubt. Here too we need to supply pity; it is more straightforward to do so in *conjunction* with fear rather than in opposition thereto.

(ii) Although Bernays' restriction on fear may seem acceptable here, it is unwelcome as the burden of IX. IX ends the section (V—VIII) on how comedy achieves its end; it is followed by the list of qualitative parts, and by dint of both position and wording we deduce that it sums up the preceding discussion of laughter, the means to comedy's end, and recalls, by its comparison of tragedy and comedy, this chapter and the next. In this place we do not expect a relatively trivial limitation on the internal balance of the emotions excited by the drama, but instead a statement of the end towards which these emotions are aroused. Cf. Bergk, *Philologus* 41 (1882) 581f., against Bernays.

(iii) As Ničev remarks (v. inf., his p.102), Plato saw catharsis of the psyche in terms of the replacement of ἀμετρία by συμμετρία (*Sophist* 227cff., esp. 228c). The terminology is closely similar to that in the later sources, infra.

(iv) External evidence in support of this interpretation is supplied by later sources, who discuss Aristotelian views on tragic and comic catharsis.

(f) *External sources for Aristotelian catharsis*

First, Iamblichus *On the Mysteries* 1.11 (*Poet.* fr. V Kassel) uses very similar phraseology:

αἱ δυνάμεις τῶν ἀνθρωπίνων παθημάτων τῶν ἐν ἡμῖν πάντῃ μὲν εἰργόμεναι καθίστανται σφοδρότεραι, εἰς ἐνέργειαν δὲ βραχεῖς (βραχεῖαν Bernays) καὶ ἄχρι τοῦ συμμέτρου προαγόμεναι χαίρουσι **μετρίως** καὶ ἀποπληροῦνται, καὶ ἐντεῦθεν ἀποκαθαιρόμεναι πειθοῖ καὶ οὐ πρὸς βίαν ἀποπαύονται. διὰ δὴ τοῦτο ἔν τε **κωμῳδίᾳ καὶ τραγῳδίᾳ** ἀλλότρια πάθη θεωροῦντες ἵσταμεν τὰ οἰκεῖα πάθη καὶ **μετριώτερα** ἀπεργαζόμεθα καὶ ἀποκαθαίρομεν.

Verbal parallels with *Rep.* X 606a – b show that a rebuttal of Plato is intended; note especially ἀλλότρια πάθη θεωροῦν and ἀπὸ τῶν ἀλλοτρίων εἰς τὰ οἰκεῖα in Plato. Note also the Aristotelian play on potentiality and actuality (δύναμις and ἐνέργεια).

So too Proclus, in Plat. *Rep.* I 49 Kroll (*Poet.*fr. V Kassel): τοῦτο δ' ἦν τὸ τὴν **τραγῳδίαν καὶ κωμῳδίαν** ἐκβάλλεσθαι ἀτόπως, εἴπερ διὰ τούτων δυνατὸν **ἐμμέτρως** ἀποπιμπλάναι τὰ πάθη . . . , cf. ibid. 50.22, where he charges that, on the contrary, comedy and tragedy possess τὸ ἄμετρον . . . ἐν ταῖς τῶν παθῶν τούτων προκλήσεσι. Translations of the relevant passages will be found in Lane Cooper, 82 – 5. Whether they derive ultimately from *Poet.*, or, as Rostagni cogently argues (*Scritti Minori* 278ff., 291), from the *On Poets*, does not affect their evidential value in this context. See however Sheppard, *Studies on Proclus' Commentary on the Republic* 110ff. for a salutary warning against Bernays' and Rostagni's tendency to accept some of Proclus' terms, especially ἀφοσίωσις, as Aristotelian; these may well be typical Neoplatonist religious colouring.

Ničev (in *L'Énigme de la catharsis tragique dans Aristote*, 1970; 'Olympiodore et la catharsis tragique', *Studi Ardizzoni* 639 – 56) has rendered a valuable service in drawing attention to passages on catharsis in the sixth-century commentator Olympiodorus. Since these are little known, I give their essentials here.

(i) Olympiodorus knows of five types of catharsis, one of which is 'Peripatetic or Stoic' (*in Plat. Alcib. pr.* 54.17 Westerink, = *SVF* III 133.8 von Arnim), briefly described as 'the Aristotelian, which cures evil with evil and leads to a balance by means of the strife of opposites' (ὁ Ἀριστοτελικός, ὁ κακῷ τὸ κακὸν ἰώμενος καὶ τῇ διαμάχῃ τῶν ἐναντίων εἰς **συμμετρίαν** ἄγων, ibid. 146.3). The strife of opposites is a new and unparalleled element, probably imported from Stoic theory: cf. ibid. 54.19 ὁ Στωϊκὸς (sc. catharsis) διὰ τῶν ἐναντίων τὰ ἐναντία ἰᾶτο . . . ἵνα ἐκ τῆς εἰς τὸ ἐναντίον περιφορᾶς τὸ σύμμετρον ἀναφάνῃ (for confusions in Olympiodorus see my 'A Fragment of A.'s *Poetics* from Porphyry', n.12). But the phrase κακῷ τὸ κακὸν ἰώμενος, 'curing evil with evil', accords with the other evidence, as does the use of συμμετρία as the outcome of the process.

(ii) At the start of his commentary on the *Gorgias*, Olympiodorus defends Plato from the charge of double standards, in that he wished to expel dramatists from his Republic, but brings on dramatised characters in his dialogue. This Peripatetic attack already appears in Athenaeus XI 505c, who quotes A.'s *On Poets* for the additional detail that Plato was not the first to invent the dialogue form (fr. 72 Rose). Duris is quoted at 504b for Plato's high regard for Sophron's mimes: this is part of the same indictment (cf. Riginos *Platonica* 174ff.; Duris was a disciple of Theophrastus, cf. Ath. IV 128a: v. Rostagni *RFIC* IV (1926) 446, V (1927) 171ff.). Thus it appears that this passage in Olympiodorus has a pedigree going back to A. or his school. The defence of Plato is that the characters do not escape unexamined as in comedy and tragedy, but are subjected to scrutiny and chastised where necessary, as in the cases of Gorgias and Callicles (*in Plat. Gorg.* 1.5—17 Westerink). Cf. also Anon. *Prol. de Platone* 14 Westerink (translated by Russell, 178ff.).

(iii) Olympiodorus notes that Plato wished, in the *Republic*, to expel tragedy and comedy: comedy because it told 'old wives' tales', tragedy because it provokes the emotions in us and increases our sense of grief (ibid. 172.6ff. Westerink). The defenders of tragedy, he continues, argue that it presents heroic deeds, and does not let the emotions remain within us in an inflamed state, but calls them forth and expels them:

οἱ δὲ θέλοντες εἰσφέρεσθαι τὴν τραγῳδίαν ἀπολογοῦνται ὅτι δεῖ εἰσφέρεσθαι, πρῶτον μὲν ἐπειδὴ ἡρωϊκὰ πράγματα μιμεῖται, ἔπειτα ἐπειδὴ οὐκ ἐᾷ ἐν ἡμῖν μένειν τὰ πάθη φλεγμαίνοντα, ἀλλὰ προκαλεῖται αὐτὰ καὶ ἐκβάλλει,

ibid. 11ff. The defenders of tragedy are unnamed, but it is safe to assume that A. is their leader; both pleas are Aristotelian, in that tragedy μιμεῖται σπουδαίους, but the phrasing recalls Theophrastus' definition of tragedy as ἡρωϊκῆς τύχης περίστασις. Although Olympiodorus was familiar with the works of Proclus, his phraseology is independent; Ničev remarks (*Studi Ardizzoni* 644) that he had knowledge of Academic, Peripatetic and other sources, some now lost. Here the closest similarity is to Proclus' προκλήσεσι beside his προκαλεῖται; he also introduces the medical metaphors ἰᾶσθαι and φλεγμαίνειν (already metaphorical in Plato, v. LSJ s.v.). There is thus no doubt that he is another independent witness from late antiquity in favour of a homoeopathic process leading to balance (συμμετρία) as its *outcome*.

Another witness from the age of Justinian was first adduced by Reich (*Der Mimus* 204ff.), to wit the mellifluous rhetor Choricius. Orating in defence of the dramatic arts (Λόγος ὑπὲρ τῶν ἐν Διονύσου τὸν βίον εἰκονιζόντων, XXXII, pp.344–80 Foerster), Choricius deploys not only the argument that the moderate exercise of the emotions through drama renders them more tractable in the lives of the spectators, but also an extended medical analogy (pp.367ff.). Except for catharsis itself, many familiar terms are present, ἴασις, ὀργὴ καὶ λύπη, κουφός, and the Aristotelian statement that a certain amount of relaxation (σύμμετρος ἀνάπαυσις) helps us to continue our work with greater diligence (σπουδαιότερον ἔχεσθαι τῶν πραγμάτων); for this idea cf. *E.N.* X 6.1176b34ff., *Pol.* VIII 3.1337b36ff. (for this argument applied to literature, v. also Lucian *Vera Historia* I 1). However, the name of A. or of any other philosopher nowhere appears, Plato excepted, whose love of Sophron's mimes is mentioned (p.348: this is part of the usual Peripatetic indictment); indeed, in all the multifarious quotations and references which bedeck Choricius' verbosity, philosophy is conspicuous by her absence, doubtless because of the hostile ideological climate of his era. Whence he derived his material is thus obscure, but despite its imprecisions, his is recognisably a vulgarising version of the same theory. Cf. also Augustine, *Confessions* III 2, with Rostagni *Scritti Minori* 292f. The idea of catharsis is also current in the Homeric scholia, e.g. the AT scholia to *Il.* A 1: the poet opens with the word 'wrath' ἵν' ἐκ τοῦ πάθους ἀποκαθαριεύσῃ τὸ τοιοῦτο μόριον τῆς ψυχῆς (quoted by N.J. Richardson, *CQ* 30 (1980) 274); on catharsis of anger v. inf. p.161.

A papyrus from Herculaneum (*P. Herc.* 1581), published excellently by M.L. Nardelli and unknown to me until these pages on catharsis were finished, throws much new light on the whole topic (*Cronache Ercolanese* 8 (1978) 96 − 103). The author is probably Philodemus, the book Περὶ Ποιημάτων IV: the source is a writer very close to A., but I think that the adduction of catharsis to support the idea that poetry is useful suggests that it is not A. himself, unless the *On Poets* had a discussion in such popularising terms. Fr. I gives the propositions that a poet imitates a complete action (μιμητής ἐσ[τι πρά]ξεως τελέας), and that poetry is useful in attaining virtue, by purifying 'the part', i.e., presumably, the emotional part of the soul, as in the Homeric scholium just cited (ἡ ποι[ητι]κὴ χρήσιμον πρὸς [ἀρε]τήν, καθαίρουσα, [ὡ]ς ἔφαμεν, τὸ μόριον). The text indicates that both propositions have already been explained. The rest of fr. I is damaged, but relates catharsis to ethical goals, and fr. II talks of the emotions prevalent even among the most self-disciplined, fear among the brave, envy among the proud etc., although catharsis is not mentioned here: the emphasis is certainly ethical; the implication is that all need catharsis to some extent. The remaining fragments are less complete. Fr. III and III bis deal with ἁμαρτία in contrast to κατόρθωμα, the whole placed in relation somehow to the ἀρετή of the good poet. Nardelli restores ἐπιδει[κνύει ἐν τῷ] λόγῳ [τὴν] κά[θαρσιν τῶν] ἁμαρτιῶν[- - - -. Catharsis of hamartia is not meant in Else's sense, but cf. [Longin.] *de Subl.* 33.1, a notable parallel since success in composition is the topic. Nardelli has missed this, but the parallel raises the further unexpected problem of how this topic relates to the fact that, as she rightly points out, in tragedy hamartia is necessary for a successful play and thus the achievement of catharsis: cf. my remark about τὸ μιαρόν above. Fr. IV refers to [ἐ]λέου κάθα[ρσις τρα]γική and ἐλεινά: ἀλλότρια (cf. sup. on Iamblichus 1.11) occurs in IV and V, which is still concerned with φοβερά and tragedy.

These later sources clarify the ethical emphasis in catharsis, the nature of the medical analogy, the effect on the mind of the audience, and the end result of the operation, i.e. the achievement of proportion or balance in the emotions. This is not a finished product, but a process in time, the moderate exercise of the emotions (a conclusion already extracted from περαίνουσα by Else 230). In A.'s epigoni, the notion of proportion or balance always appears in *this* context, not in that of the relation between different emotions aroused to accomplish the catharsis, a much more trivial point.

(g) *The genesis of the tragic emotions*

The third sentence in this section is that tragedy has pain (λύπη) for its mother. Antithetical to this is the statement in IV that comedy's mother is laughter (v. p.16of.). Kaibel (*Abh.* 55) thought these once formed a zeugma, 'tragedy has pain for its mother, but comedy has laughter', now unyoked by the epitomator. Cf. pain and pleasure as *archai* of music in Peripatetic theory sup., p.50.

Bernays (142ff.) saw this as a cautionary example of how a 'commentator', by an apparently logical method, can draw a conclusion exactly opposite to Aristotelian doctrine. In his view, the 'compiler' was influenced by *Rhet.*, where he found fear and pity defined as types of 'pain' (λύπαι; *Rhet.* II 5.1382a21, 8.1385b13), and consequently believed with logic on his side that the chief concept common to both, pain, ought to be designated the basis of tragedy, which depended on these two emotions. But, continues Bernays, this 'compiler' did not reflect that in *Poet.* A. speaks of a pleasure (ἡδονή) of tragedy, i.e. the opposite of pain, and refers to a 'harmless joy' in discussing catharsis at *Pol.* VIII 7.1342a16. Thus ἡδονή and not λύπη is the theory's requirement here. In castigating this as a 'gross misunderstanding' Bernays is obliged to posit a glaring discrepancy between *Rhet.* and *Poet.*. In *Rhet.*, whose definitions are essential to *Poet.*, pity and fear are feelings of pain, yet tragedy should, according to *Poet.*, create pleasure by stimulating these same painful feelings. For this contradiction, says Bernays, there is no remedy by means of formal logic. We will not follow him into his speculations as to how the contradiction might have been overcome by A. in the account of catharsis, where the definitions of pity and fear as λῦπαι would be abandoned, after *Philebus* 47e−50a; it suffices to remark that if the definitions given in *Rhet.* were valid for *Poetics* I, as they are (13.1453a5), it is special pleading to suggest that they were not equally valid in *Poetics* II.

It is not difficult to see how Bernays has gone astray, and why. The how is his identification of the cause of catharsis with its effect, the οἰκεία ἡδονή of tragedy. In this *Poet.* marks an advance on the *Philebus*. The mother of tragic catharsis is pain; but its offspring is pleasure (cf. Rostagni, *Poetica* lvii n.2). The reason why he erred is surely his reluctance to embrace the homoeopathic nature of catharsis, in which pity and fear drive out pity and fear. Such a formulation is unavoidable in all our sources. It is no more problematic than curing a fever by piling on blankets, and modified too in A.'s formulation at *Poet.* 14.1453b12 by the insistence on *mimesis*.

(h) *Conclusion*

III constitutes an account of catharsis which concurs with our knowledge of A.'s theory from other sources, and offers new information in harmony with the old. It is very different from Plato's emphasis on the wanton arousal of the spectator's passions and their external expression, such as is also seen in *Prol.* IV 20ff. Koster, τῆς μὲν τραγῳδίας σκοπὸς τὸ εἰς θρῆνον κινῆσαι τοὺς ἀκροατάς, τῆς δὲ κωμῳδίας τὸ εἰς γέλωτα. The reader will have noticed that the notorious term itself nowhere appears, although we have not long to wait. This reflects no discredit on C: on the contrary. If the author of this piece, Bernays' 'good Unknown', was really using *Rhet.* and *Poet.* to compile a replacement for A.'s lost treatment of catharsis, it is astounding that he does not adduce the definiendum, but instead uses terms also found in our Neoplatonist sources. If he is trying so hard to be authentic, we would expect him to dilate on the Aristotelian term. On the other hand, A. himself is celebrated (to put the matter politely) for his casual use of his own jargon. Instead of adhering to one term consistently, he is prone to express the same idea in different terms: *rem tene, verba sequentur*. Bold indeed would be the forger of such a paragraph.

Chapter IV: The definition of comedy

(a) *Text*

The text presents grave difficulties: however, as Baumgart (665f.) remarked, the closely parallel definition of tragedy in *Poet.* 6 is almost as corrupt, and there Kassel actually cites C in his app. crit. to confirm the reading παθημάτων of the Riccardianus and the Syriac, against μαθημάτων in the other *fontes*. We may presume that the definitions of the terms given in *Poet.* 6 would not have been repeated in *Poetics* II; in their absence, so technical and difficult a paragraph would be unprotected from the grossest of corruptions by the tenth century A.D., especially when it was being copied in the context not of other writings on literature, but of commentaries on Aristotelian philosophy. Thus it is no surprise to encounter problems.

γελοίου C: γελοίας Bergk. Presumably the corruption arose through a compendium or in anticipation of μεγέθους. As Kayser (31) noted, τελείου could stand as a two-termination adjective

agreeing with πράξεως, cf. *E.N.* VII 13.1153b16: contrast *Poet.*
6.1449b24 πράξεως σπουδαίας καὶ τελείας, cf. 7.1450b24. But I shall
suggest that it is corrupt for τελείας, a corruption that would be
almost inevitable after μεγέθους. — Before χωρίς Vahlen inserted
ἡδυσμένῳ λόγῳ as in *Poet.* 6, where Kassel prints ἡδυσμένῳ λόγῳ
χωρὶς ἑκάστῳ τῶν εἰδῶν ἐν τοῖς μορίοις. Lucas, supplying τῶν
ἡδυσμάτων after τῶν εἰδῶν, states the standard interpretation thus:
'this is a complicated way of saying that rhythm alone is used to
make more alluring the language of the dialogue, rhythm with
melody is used in the sung parts' (ad loc.). A. glosses the sentence
just below (1449b28):

λέγω ἡδυσμένον μὲν λόγον τὸν ἔχοντα ῥυθμὸν καὶ ἁρμονίαν [καὶ
μέλος], τὸ δὲ χωρὶς τοῖς εἴδεσι τὸ διὰ μέτρων ἔνια μόνον
περαίνεσθαι καὶ πάλιν ἔτερα διὰ μέλους.

Else (57) has shown that μέτρα means stichic verse-metres, and
without Vahlen's supplement the phrase lacks its essential definiens
(cf. Kayser 34). It is scarcely conceivable that this was left to be
supplied from *Poet.* 6. — Corruption of χωρὶς ἑκάστῳ to χωρὶς
ἑκάστου is very easy, owing to the frequency of χωρίς as a
preposition with the genitive in later Greek, and Reiz' emendation
of this corruption in *Poet.* 6 has been accepted by editors. Its
recurrence here is mere coincidence.

τῶν μορίων ἐν τοῖς εἴδεσι beside the τῶν εἰδῶν ἐν τοῖς μορίοις of
Poet. 6 has been criticised, e.g. Kayser 35; but the situation is not
simple. In *Poet.* the μόρια are the *quantitative* parts of tragedy ('each
of the kinds (of embellished speech) in the (different) parts (of the
play)'). After explaining χωρὶς τοῖς εἴδεσι, A. proceeds to the
qualitative parts of tragedy, beginning **μόριον** τραγῳδίας ὁ τῆς
ὄψεως κόσμος. Yet the qualitative μόρια are later, persistently,
termed εἴδη, and also μέρη at 1450a8 (cf.1449b16). A further set of
εἴδη describes four kinds of whole plays in terms of certain
qualitative criteria (18.1455b32ff.) which are compared with four
μέρη, probably including character. Meanwhile, the quantitative
parts of tragedy, mentioned in the definition and therefore, one
presumes, important, do not reappear except in Ch. 12, where they
are termed μέρη in contradistinction to the qualitative εἴδη. It may
be helpful to tabulate these usages, along with those of C: the result
shows that the usage in both fluctuates similarly, and it would be
hazardous to conclude that it is wrong, as did earlier editors.
(Baumgart's (669) defence of the phrase, involving the suppression

of ἐν, is misguided, cf. Kayser 35.):

	εἶδος	μέρος	μόριον
qualitative parts	Poet. 6, al. Tract. X cj. (ὕλη MS)	Poet. 6, al. —	Poet. 6 —
quantitative parts	— Tract. IV MS	Poet. 12 Tract. XVII	Poet. 6 Tract. XVII

The cause of C's reading δρῶντος καὶ δι᾽ ἀπαγγελίας is evident. Such corruption would inevitably ensue from the easy misdivision of the sentence as follows: χωρὶς ἑκάστου τῶν μορίων ἐν τοῖς εἴδεσι δρώντων, καὶ οὐ δι᾽ ἀπαγγελίας δι᾽ ἡδονῆς καὶ γέλωτος κτλ. Here δρώντων would be altered to agree with ἑκάστου, and οὐ omitted because it was thought to impair the sense. In a similar way Renaissance editors of *Poet.*, until Giacomini in 1573, misdivided the definition of tragedy to read . . . δρώντων, καὶ οὐ δι᾽ ἀπαγγελίας <ἀλλὰ> δι᾽ ἐλέου καὶ φόβου . . ., in order to explain a polar expression which they did not understand. For the loss of οὐ cf. XVI infra, and *Poet.* 6.1450a30 (lost by A, Lat); 17.1455b17, 18.1456a28 (lost in all sources except the Arabic); *Rhet.* II 8.1386a23, III 9.1410a30, 18.1419a34 (all lost in MS A). This omission deserves none of the expostulations hurled at it by some sceptics.

(b) *Interpretation*

This section is attacked by Bernays (145f.) as 'eine jämmerliche ungeschickte Travestie der aristotelischen Definition der Tragödie, obendrein durch Lücken verstümmelt und durch Fehler verwirrt'. He considers the definition such a travesty that its compiler could not have had A.'s own definition before him. He has been followed by many, although as usual the individual charges in the indictment have been rebutted by scholars acquiescent in the whole, and only Plebe (122) protests that 'il *Tract. Coisl.* tuttavia si aggira nell'ambito di un aristotelismo non del tutto deformato come vorebbe il Bernays'.

Apart from the main problems (below), exception has even been taken to πράξεως γελοίας; K.K. Smith (147) wrote that 'as a matter of technical fact, the Poetics always uses φαῦλος as the dramatic opposite of σπουδαῖος. And we can actually find in the Poetics A.'s own wording for this part of the definition of comedy (49a32): ἡ κωμῳδία ἐστὶν ὥσπερ εἴπομεν μίμησις φαυλοτέρων.'

However, this sentence opposes the *characters* of those imitated, and not their actions; Smith's quotation continues by discussing what the φαυλότεροι *do*, and at once refers to the absurd: . . . φαυλοτέρων μέν, οὐ μέντοι κατὰ πᾶσαν κακίαν, ἀλλὰ τοῦ αἰσχροῦ ἐστι τὸ γελοῖον μόριον. Again, compare 4.1448b34ff.: ὥσπερ καὶ τὰ σπουδαῖα μάλιστα ποιητὴς Ὅμηρος ἦν, . . . οὕτως καὶ τὸ τῆς κωμῳδίας σχῆμα πρῶτος ὑπέδειξεν, οὐ ψόγον ἀλλὰ τὸ γελοῖον δραματοποιήσας. Here the representation of the serious and the absurd is counterpoised. Better still is *E.N.* X 6.1177a3 'we say that serious matters are better than absurd ones' (τὰ σπουδαῖα τῶν γελοίων). Cf. too *Rhet.* III 18.1419b3f. (quoting Gorgias), Aristophanes *Frogs* 391f., Theophrastus fr. 124 Wimmer. — The point of mentioning the ridiculous here is, as Bernays (19f.) said, to make a *material* distinction between the *formally* identical comedy and tragedy, whose action is to be taken seriously, as it is performed by serious ('good') characters, just as the reference to representation 'through persons acting and not through narrative' distinguishes in *form* the *materially* identical tragedy and epic. For all his condemnation of the definition, Bernays was prepared to use it to explain A.'s definition of tragedy; and right to do so, I believe.

The main problems in IV are: (i) the meaning of ἀμοίρου μεγέθους τελείου; (ii) the meanings of ἡδονή and γέλως, and how these are connected with comic catharsis; (iii) the sense of ἔχει δὲ μητέρα τὸν γέλωτα.

(i) **ἀμοίρου μεγέθους τελείου**. Even if not corrupt, this presents difficulties. Interpreters disagree over whether ἄμοιρος bears its usual sense of 'lacking'; whether μέγεθος means 'size' or 'grandeur, sublimity'; and whether τελείου, 'complete' or 'perfect', depends on μεγέθους or refers back to πράξεως. The translations are ordered according to these three problems:

(a) ' . . . of a laughable action, of undivided' (ἀμοίρου) 'and completed length' (Grube 146, Plebe 122).
(b) ' . . . of an action that is ludicrous and imperfect,' (ἀμοίρου) 'of sufficient length' (Lane Cooper 228, Feibleman *In Praise of*

Comedy 83).

(c) '. . . of an action that is ridiculous, incomplete(?)' (ἀμοίρου), 'and of an uncertain' (*sic*) 'magnitude' (Starkie, *Aristophanes' Acharnians* p.xl).

(d) '. . . of an action that is ludicrous and unfortunate' (ἀμοίρου) 'and of adequate magnitude' (Atkins 140).

(e) ' . . . of an absurd action, lacking sublimity' (μέγεθος) 'but complete' (Baumgart 667f., Kayser 33f.: this is easier if τελείου is emended to τελείας).

(f) ' . . of an absurd action, complete, that lacks size' (Bernays 147, after Vahlen *Poetica* (1874) 77: this too is better with τελείας).

(g) ' . . . of an absurd action, that lacks perfect size' (cf. Russell 205).

The normal meaning of ἄμοιρος is 'with no share in, lacking', as A. twice uses it (*de Caelo* III 7.306a3, *E.N.* I 13.1102b12). The word may verge on the related ἄμμορος 'unfortunate' at Plato, *Laws* IX 878b, but the senses 'undivided', 'imperfect' and 'incomplete' are nowhere attested; of the first four versions, Atkins' is the least intolerable. The earliest editors supposed that the word is corrupt, but there is no reason to believe this. If we accept the normal meaning of ἄμοιρος, it clearly must accompany μεγέθους at least. If μεγέθους and τελείου do not belong together, two interpretations are possible — that of Bernays, which yields a manifest absurdity, as a complete but instantaneous action offers no scope for dramatic presentation, and Baumgart's. Both really require the simple emendation τελείας.

Baumgart takes μέγεθος, 'magnitude', in the broader sense of 'grandeur, sublimity', rather than the more usual sense of 'length' or 'size' found at XVII 3. It is usually held that μέγεθος does not mean 'grandeur' until Demetrius (*de Eloc.* 5, al.), but in fact it is certain that A. does so use it once in *Poet.*, and in a significant context; the author of this Treatise may have been equally inconsistent. At 4.1449a19 on the evolution of tragedy we read: ἔτι δὲ τὸ μέγεθος· ἐκ μικρῶν μύθων καὶ λέξεως γελοίας διὰ τὸ ἐκ σατυρικοῦ μεταβαλεῖν ὀψὲ ἀπεσεμνύνθη. Lucas comments: 'like "greatness" in English μέγεθος can refer both to physical length and to grandeur of content; the same ambiguity extends to μικρῶν μύθων, "short", or "trivial".' In fact the emphasis is much more on grandeur of content (cf. Else 223 n.3), since A. adds, as if it is an item different from ἔτι δὲ τὸ μέγεθος, that tragedy also increased the number of episodes — ἔτι δὲ ἐπεισοδίων πλήθη (a28). It follows that comedy, like the less serious early stages of tragedy, was held not to possess grandeur in plot and diction. If Bernays' rendering were the only one possible, its absurdity would indeed be troubling, and it would look like a thoughtless reversal of the definition of tragedy, σπουδαίας καὶ τελείας μέγεθος ἐχούσης. But there σπουδαῖος looks back to what has preceded, and μέγεθος may also, even though A. explains it in Ch. 7 as the size a play requires for the natural development of its action (he also refers to the length of a play in performance as another kind of μέγεθος). If Baumgart is right, C employs the terminology as if *Poet.* 7 had not been written, but experience teaches that A. is quite capable of such writing. I am convinced that this is the correct interpretation.

If however τελείου belonged with μεγέθους, as the copyist of C indicated with his punctuation, we would have to translate 'lacking perfect size', understanding μέγεθος in the more usual sense of *Poet.* 7; it will not do to translate τελεῖος as 'sufficient' or 'adequate'. A comic action must certainly possess size: cf. *Poet.* 9.1451b13 on the composition of comic plots 'according to what is probable'. A comedy itself has size too: at *Rhet.* III 14.1415a9ff. A. notes that tragedy, comedy and epic have prooemia to show the purpose of the work that follows, since if it is clear and the matter is a small one no proem is needed. It does not ensue that the size of the comic *action* must be perfect, however, as beauty resides in size *and* arrangement (τὸ γὰρ καλὸν ἐν μεγέθει καὶ τάξει ἐστίν, *Poet.* 7.1450b37), but the absurd is part of the ugly (τοῦ αἰσχροῦ ἐστι τὸ γελοῖον μόριον, 5.1449a34), just as the comic mask is ugly and distorted. A comic action needs size, but it will be all the funnier if it is exaggerated or otherwise distorted, as are so many of the plots of Aristophanes. This interpretation does offer the tiny advantage that it avoids emending τελείου, and explains the change in order between *Poet.* (**τελείας**, μέγεθος ἐχούσης) and C (ἀμοίρου μεγέθους **τελείου**), which Baumgart and Bernays do not. As Else (256) says, 'τελεῖος has the twin implications of completeness and seriousness'. This rendering permits it to retain something of the latter nuance in *Poet.* 6, while denying it to comedy here. But Baumgart's and Bernays' are linguistically possible, and only Bernays' contradicts Aristotelian doctrine.

(ii) **δι' ἡδονῆς καὶ γέλωτος** has been assailed on four fronts:

1. Bernays (145, followed by Grube 147) objected to γέλως being called a πάθημα and not a πάθος, but Bonitz (sup. p.144) demonstrated that A. used the terms interchangeably. Fuhrmann

(65) thinks he could not have called γέλως and ἡδονή πάθη either, but cf. inf.

2. Bernays (146) objects that ἡδονή and γέλως, pleasure and laughter, are not on the same level, since γέλως is a sub-category of ἡδονή (cf. [Longinus] *de Sublim.* 38.6, ὁ γέλως πάθος ἐν ἡδονῇ). This is indeed Aristotelian doctrine; at *Rhet.* I 11.1371b35 A. contends that παιδιά, ἄνεσις and ὁ γέλως are τῶν ἡδέων. But he is perfectly capable, as we saw (p.124f.), of putting two terms, one subordinate to the other, on the same level, analysing an entity into itself and other subdivisions. The subordination of the individual emotions (πάθη) to pleasure and pain, which are consequent upon them, is upheld at *E.N.* II 5.1105b21: λέγω πάθη μὲν ἐπιθυμίαν ὀργὴν φόβον θάρσος φθόνον χαρὰν . . . ἔλεον, ὅλως οἷς ἔπεται ἡδονὴ ἢ λύπη (cited by Kayser 36, to support Bernays); but A. continues δυνάμεις δὲ καθ' ἃς παθητικοὶ τούτων λεγόμεθα, οἷον καθ' ἃς δυνατοὶ ὀργισθῆναι ἢ λυπηθῆναι ἢ ἐλεῆσαι. Here, just as in C, individual emotions, in this case anger and pity, are in parallel with pain, which seemed in the previous clause to belong to a higher plane. Had he used pleasant feelings as his example, we would have found (e.g.) θαρσῆσαι ἢ ἡσθῆναι ἢ χαρῆναι, and this parallel proves beyond doubt that he was capable of placing pleasure and pain in the ranks of the less generalised emotions on occasion.

3. An ambiguity in A.'s use of ἡδονή (not in his understanding of it) provides the reply to another criticism of C, again Bernays' (146), namely that ἡδονή belongs also to tragedy and is not therefore an attribute distinctive of comedy in Aristotelian theory. The answer is simple (Baumgart 671, Kayser 36): the Stagirite distinguishes many kinds of pleasure (*E.N.* X 3, cf. *Pol.* VIII 3.1338a7), one of which is peculiar to tragedy, while the others are not. This is often explicit in *Poet.*, e.g. 14.1453b10 οὐ πᾶσαν δεῖ ζητεῖν ἡδονὴν ἀπὸ τῆς τραγῳδίας ἀλλὰ τὴν οἰκείαν, 23.1459a21, 26.1462b13; best of all is 13.1453a35 (on plots ending well for the good and badly for the bad): ἔστιν οὐχ αὕτη <ἡ> ἀπὸ τραγῳδίας ἡδονὴ ἀλλὰ μᾶλλον **τῆς κωμῳδίας οἰκεία**. Cf. Bonitz s.v. ἡδονή 3. The same answer applies to Tierney's (253) view that ἡδονή is the end and not the means of both tragedy and comedy in *Poet.*: in that work we are never told what the means of comedy are.

4. The recognition by A. of different tragic and comic pleasures also resolves the doubts of Atkins (140) and K.K. Smith (147). Atkins accepted that laughter could undergo catharsis in comedy, but objected that pleasure, as the end of art, could hardly do the same, and Smith rejected as nonsense the (correct) inference from C that 'the poet must arouse that pleasure which is derived by

mimesis from pleasure and laughter' (this represents a transposition
of *Poet.* 14.1453b11f. into comic terms). Provided that 'pleasure' is
here being used ambiguously, there is no difficulty; I have suggested above that just such an ambiguity resides in A.'s use of the
term.

Although highly critical of the Tractate as a whole, Smith (155)
came round to defending its use of the pair γέλως and ἡδονή:

'when I try to fix upon two Greek words to reproduce the
kind of satisfaction which I wish to express, I am led inevitably back to ἡδονή and γέλως, the former to express innocent
mirth and delight, the latter to express malicious fun or ridicule. For ἡδονή is used of specific pleasure as well as of general, and γέλως is the Greek word for the source of laughter as
well as for the laughter itself . . . *Properly interpreted*, therefore,
the definition of the catharsis of comedy as preserved in the
Tractate appears to me to be genuinely Aristotelian.'

Although the epitome's state preempts certainty, Smith is surely
correct. He criticises Lane Cooper's rendering (71 − 5) of ἡδονή as
the pleasant accessories (ἡδύσματα), such as beautiful music, diction
and so forth; indeed, Cooper must be wrong, since these are not
peculiar to comedy but found in tragedy also, whose definition
ought therefore to have included ἡδονή; moreover, comedy is not
associated with beauty in *Poet.*, but with ugliness (5.1449a34, cf.
E.N. IV 8.1128a22ff.). Smith's view finds support in *Rhet.* I, where
A. links laughter with innocent amusement (παιδιά) and relaxation
as among pleasant things: ἐπεὶ ἡ παιδιὰ τῶν ἡδέων καὶ πᾶσα ἄνεσις,
καὶ ὁ γέλως τῶν ἡδέων, ἀνάγκη καὶ τὰ γελοῖα ἡδέα εἶναι
(11.1371b33ff.). This passage is that in which he refers to the
analysis of humour in the *Poetics*. For the same conjunction of
laughter with innocent play cf. *Rhet.* II 3.1380b3 ἐν παιδιᾷ, ἐν
γέλωτι . . . and *E.N.* X 6.1177a3, βελτίω λέγομεν τὰ σπουδαῖα τῶν
γελοίων καὶ μετὰ παιδιᾶς. In the definition of comedy παιδιά could
hardly appear, since it denotes purely an activity and not an
emotion distinct from that activity, unlike laughter; so we find
ἡδονή instead. This confusing use of ἡδονή is to be censured,
although perhaps if we had the full text the usage would have been
explained. An analogous confusion is perpetrated by A. even as he
distinguishes two different senses of ἡδονή — thus can his views on
pleasure in *E.N.* best be understood: cf. G.E.L. Owen, *Proc. Arist.
Soc.* 72 (1971−2) 135−52):

'ἡδονή . . . has at least two distinct though related uses. We can say "Gaming is one of my pleasures" or, alternatively, "Gaming gives me pleasure" . . . In the first use the pleasure is identified with the enjoyed activity, in the second the two are distinct and their relationship is problematic'

(138). Cf. Hardie, *A.'s Ethical Theory*[2] 411f. Whether or not the two accounts of ἡδονή in *E.N.* VII 4 and X 1ff. are compatible, incompatible or answering quite different questions, is fiercely debated (against Owen see Gosling, *Proc. Arist. Soc.* 74 (1973−4) 15ff., and differently Kenny, *The Aristotelian Ethics* 233ff., Guthrie *HGP* VI 383); but it is clear that the first account deals with pleasurable activities in the context of restraint and excess, the second with the resulting feeling and its nature. A. is well able to distinguish these, but does not have separate terms for them. A similar ambiguity between ἡδονή for pleasurable activity and the resultant feeling will explain how it can here both submit to catharsis and result in ἡδονή.

It is instructive to compare the distinction drawn by K. McLeish (*The Theatre of Aristophanes* 15ff.) between 'farce' and 'comedy' proper, within the overall category of comedy. Because 'comedy' (unlike 'farce')

'springs from character rather than action, its effect is seldom hilarious, but more often a kind of serious pleasure, an inward smile at the frailties and foibles of humanity . . . Whereas farce eschews serious themes, comedy very often embraces them'

(16). These are blended in Aristophanes. Such is surely the distinction made here; the first corresponds to γέλως, the second to ἡδονή. It reappears in XVIII, where there is an antithesis between the ludicrous and the serious within the development of comedy, as the former declines and the latter increases, although the Treatise seems not to have made this distinction about action and character. Theophrastus in his *Characters* show inklings of it; for his higher valuation of ethos against plot, which is surely connected with the rise of New Comedy, cf. Plebe 39−48.

That ἡδονή refers to innocent merriment is supported by Demetrius' analysis of χάρις 'grace' in *On Style*. He distinguishes between types of 'grace' that are loftier and more dignified, namely those of poets, and others that are more everyday and comic,

resembling jokes — which are not far from buffoonery (128). At
163−72 he discusses the difference between χάρις and τὸ γελοῖον,
which differ in their objects, mode of expression, style and aim —
the εὐχάριστος aims to give pleasure, the buffoon to be laughed at
(168). They differ too in where they occur — laughter and
pleasantry occur in satyr-plays and comedies; tragedy often admits
pleasantry, but laughter is its enemy (ἔνθα μὲν γὰρ γέλωτος τέχναι
καὶ χαρίτων, ἐν σατύρῳ καὶ ἐν κωμῳδίαις· τραγῳδία δὲ χάριτας μὲν
παραλαμβάνει ἐν πολλοῖς, ὁ δὲ γέλως ἐχθρὸς τραγῳδίας, 169). Finally,
at 180 he pairs χάρις with ἡδονή, when discussing metrical effects.
All this suggests first, that his χάρις is equivalent in sense to ἡδονή
in C; and second, that the term ἡδονή is chronologically prior to
χάρις, since it is so much more imprecise and confusing, as we have
seen. χάρις may be Demetrius' own invention to replace ἡδονή; on
his inventiveness vis-à-vis A. v. Grube, Demetrius 32−8. Note the
ascription of a Περὶ Χάριτος to Demetrius of Phalerum ap. Diog.
Laert. V 81. The germ of this usage is present in the type of the
χαρίεις and his mild wit at E.N. IV 8.1128a31: cf. Plebe 70.

The phrase ἡδονὴ καὶ γέλως recurs in the Peripatetic definition
of comedy ap. Schol. Dion. Thrax XVIIIb4 Koster and elsewhere
(quoted sup. p.51). I suggested that this may derive from Theophrastus. The Scholia also comment on reading comedy βιωτικῶς
(XVIIIb1.3 Koster): τουτέστιν ἱλαρῶς . . . ἀντὶ τοῦ ἐν ἡδονῇ καὶ
γέλωτι. (The only other collocation of these words known to me is
Soph. Ajax 382.)

(iii) ἔχει δὲ μητέρα τὸν γέλωτα. For the grave doubts over this
metaphor v. sup. p.137f. Why is λύπη, the common denominator of
pity and fear, balanced not by its opposite ἡδονή but by γέλως? The
answer was adumbrated above; γέλως connotes 'the source of
laughter', 'humour' as much as laughter itself (LSJ s.v. γέλως II),
but ἡδονή would have been still more confusing here, as it could
have been understood as (a) pleasant amusement or jocularity
(παιδιά or Demetrius' χάρις), (b) the pleasure that is the outcome
of comedy, i.e. of comic catharsis, or (c) pleasure in general. The
real difficulty lies in the use of λύπη in 'pain, the mother of
tragedy', when it seems clear, in C as in Poet., that it is pity and
fear that are the 'mother' of tragedy and of the pleasure
appropriate to tragedy. We have seen how, in E.N. II 5, A. equates
specific painful feelings like fear with the genus to which they
belong (sup. p.124f.), and it may be that he is only using λύπη as a
compendious expression for such feelings. However, this use of λύπη
lends support to a minority view in the dispute over τὴν τῶν

τοιούτων παθημάτων κάθαρσιν (*Poet.* 6.1449b27, from the definition of tragedy). This is normally taken to refer back to pity and fear as the emotions purified, but the use of λύπη generically ('painful feelings') in III suggests that 'the purification of such emotions' refers not only to pity and fear, but to painful emotions in general, including for example anger. Lucas (ad loc.) cites parallels which now look rather more significant, e.g. *Poet.* 19.1456b1, on the rôle of the intellectual element in tragedy to arouse emotion οἷον ἔλεον ἢ φόβον ἢ ὀργὴν ἢ ὅσα τοιαῦτα; add *Rhet.* I 1.1354a17 ἔλεος καὶ ὀργὴ καὶ τὰ τοιαῦτα πάθη τῆς ψυχῆς, and cf. II 1.1378a22, III 19.1419b26, *Pol.* VIII 7.1342a12. Such painful emotions evidently have a part to play in tragedy; to pity, fear and anger we might add from the lists in *E.N.* II 5.1105b21 and *Rhet.* III 19 envy, strife and hatred as painful emotions deserving purgation (cf. House 101f., Taplin *Greek Tragedy in Action* 169ff.). This has the important advantage that it provides a more complete rebuttal of Plato; at *Rep.* X 606, after rejecting the stimulation of pity by tragedy and of laughter by comedy, he says that the same applies to sexual appetite, anger and all other emotions of desire, pain and pleasure (περὶ ἀφροδισίων δὴ καὶ περὶ θυμοῦ καὶ περὶ πάντων τῶν ἐπιθυμητικῶν τε καὶ λυπηρῶν καὶ ἡδέων ἐν τῇ ψυχῇ).

One suspects that A. concentrates so much on pity and fear because they relate neatly to his account of the tragic hero and *hamartia* in *Poet.* 13−4. If a broader definition of the tragic emotions is conceded, the discrepancy between their apparent precision and the greater vagueness of their comic equivalents is obviated. A. is then saying no more and no less than that tragedy depends on painful emotions, comedy on pleasant ones, for their respective effects.

Chapters V−VI: The analysis of humour

The vital issues in V−VI have already been adumbrated, namely (a) the sources of the text (sup. p. 8−12), whether the subheadings have a logical Aristotelian arrangement, and whether they correspond to the testimonia and fragments of *Poetics* II (p.66ff.). There is also (b) the relation of other analyses of humour to the Tractate's.

(a) *The arrangement of the list*

Prolegomenon VI, our most detailed source for V−VI, exhibits a clear pattern of entries. The item is numbered, named, subdivided if necessary, equipped with an example, but not usually defined. If these are the standard elements, not too much is missing in **a**, only the examples of 'addition', exallage, metaphor and manner of speech, if the reconstructed text is correct. This type of list is not unusual in A. In *Poet.*, the catalogues of linguistic elements in 20 and of types of words in 21 are equipped with definitions as well as examples; neither has ordinal numerals. So too the enthymemes in *Rhet.* II 23. But other lists lack definitions, e.g. the apparent enthymemes in II 24, or the four types of ἐρώτησις (with ordinals) in III 18, where only three receive examples. I suggested above (p.71f.) that the lists which relate most closely to ours are those of sophistical arguments at *S.E.* 4–5 and of poetic faults in *Poet.* 25. The list in *S.E.* divides into six arguments from diction and seven not dependent on it. A. gives, without ordinals, examples of arguments from homonymy and ambiguity, and only afterwards defines these two, since they are cognate. Next he gives instances of synthesis, diaeresis and prosody; the manner of speaking has a more extensive exemplification and is assumed to be less self-evident in meaning. The second half of the list begins with the statement that there are seven types, and these are named with ordinal numerals, and furnished with definitions and examples.

I have set out this list at length because it offers the key to a contradiction in our evidence. A. in *Rhet.* III 2.1404.b37 leads us to expect an account of homonymy and synonymy in the *Poetics*, and Porphyry (v. inf. on V 2) says that he defined synonyms in the *Poetics*, and gives the definition; but none is preserved in **a**. Therefore this is either unaristotelian, or heavily condensed itself (we shall see other evidence that this is so). From *S.E.* 4 we can suggest that the headings were originally listed and exemplified first, and only later did A. pause to define and distinguish between the different permutations of words and meanings: homonyms, or the same word with the different meanings, synonyms, different words of the same meaning, and *adoleschia*, the repetition of the same word with the same meaning, can all be slotted into a convenient paragraph, perhaps alongside paronyms or different forms of a particular word too. Such a paragraph might be omitted when the extract was made, because it was thought too obvious or irrelevant to comedy.

The presence of quotations from unidentified comedies in **a** is a strong argument against the idea that this is a Byzantine re-expansion of a summary, done by a scholar who supplied examples from Aristophanes, then popular. Examples can be identified from the *Acharnians* (possibly), *Clouds* (one, possibly two more) and *Frogs* (three). Even assuming that the doubtful cases are certain, there remain three otherwise unknown fragments, which is hardly expected in a late fabrication of the kind postulated.

There are divergences between **a** and C, meagre though the latter is in comparison: **a** does not name aphaeresis, but can be shown to have lost it, presumably through a failure to perceive that paronymy is a large class including more than prosthesis; a similar failure had already contributed to the mistaken promotion of diminutives and exallage in the common tradition. A remark originally attached to metaphor has ended up joined to the item preceding in C, and to that following in **a** (v. inf. on V 6). The first two items in the second part of C's list are in reverse order, and so are the subheadings; C has suffered a mechanical dislocation here (inf. on VI 2).

There is a further point to be made about Tzetzes' verses *On Comedy* 78f. His phrasing

> . . . τὸν γέλωτα τοῖς ὁμωνύμοις
> ἐσχηματισμένον τε καὶ παρῳδίαις

contains a hint of extra knowledge. The term ἐσχηματισμένον ἐν λόγῳ or simply σχῆμα is familiar from ancient sources, meaning 'to pretend one thing and mean another' (e.g. Demetrius 287−98). This use of σχῆμα goes back to Zoîlus the contemporary of Isocrates (ap. Phoebammon Περὶ Σχημ. 3.44 Spengel, cf. Rutherford 195). But it not clear whether, like πλάσμα, this is a later adaptation or distortion, or whether it represents something in the original. Conceivably there was some reference to it at the opening of Chapter V, or in VII, where ἔμφασις is probably employed to express the same idea. The two are equivalent in Peripatetic literary criticism, e.g. Demetrius *de Eloc.* 287ff. (v. inf. on VII).

In *Rhet.* I 11 A. says that the *Poetics* divides the laughable into persons, words and deeds (ἄνθρωποι, λόγοι, ἔργα; 1371b35). Here, however, we find a division into diction and actions, λέξις and πράγματα, which reappears (perhaps mediated through Theophrastus' Περὶ Γελοίου, cf. Kayser 36f.) in Demetrius *On Style* 132, 136 (ἦσαν . . . αἱ μὲν ἐν τῇ λέξει, αἱ δὲ ἐν τοῖς πράγμασιν), and Cicero *De Orat.* II 243. Arndt (4), accompanied by K.K. Smith (153), suggests that λόγοι and ἔργα are not the same as λέξις and πράγματα, but as usual A.'s terminology is less fixed than scholars imagine: earlier in *Rhet.* I 11 he has πράγματα instead of ἔργα (τὰ διὰ χρόνου ἡδέα ἐστίν, καὶ ἄνθρωποι καὶ πράγματα, 1371a29).

The great majority of scholars has accepted the analysis of humour as Aristotelian. Thus Cramer (403): 'scriptor pleniorem eum' (sc. Aristotelis tractatum de Poetica) 'quam qui ad nos pervenit, praesertim ἐν τοῖς περὶ γελοίου, habuisse videtur'; Bernays (168) 'das *videtur* ist viel zu schüchtern und hat auch wohl die Besorger der spätern Abdrücke eingeschüchtert, welche diesen Fingerzeig ganz unterdrückt haben' (it is ironic that I am now saying the same of other parts of Bernays' own work); cf. Arndt 9, Rutherford 435ff. (although he rejects **a**), Starkie *Aristophanes' Acharnians* xxxviiiff., Lane Cooper 8, 13f., 138, Atkins 141f., M.A. Grant *Ancient Rhetorical Theories of the Laughable* 32, J.F. D'Alton *Roman Literary Theory and Criticism* 361, G.E. Duckworth *The Nature of Roman Comedy* 308, Grube 141, 147, Dosi 637n.43, Fuhrmann 67ff.

(b) *Other analyses of humour and their relation to the Tractate*

There survive five other analyses of the sources of humour, by Demetrius (*On Style* 136ff.), the *Auctor ad Herennium* I 6.10, Cicero (*de Orat.* II 239ff.), Quintilian VI 3.35ff., and Hermogenes Περὶ Μεθόδου δεινότητος 34, 2.453f. Spengel, p.451.11 Rabe.

(i) Demetrius' list concerns a milder form, χάρις not γέλως; on its origin cf. sup. p.159f. It is divided into three — 'charm' from diction (λέξις, 137−45), from style (ἑρμηνεία, 146−55), and from subject-matter (πράγματα, 156−62). The unnumbered list is more sophisticated than ours, with more subheadings. At the outset (136) he gives no sign of tripartition, but refers simply to λέξις and πράγματα.

A. From diction	B. From style	C. From content
1. Brevity	1. Imagery	1. Proverbs
2. Arrangement	2. Recantation	2. Fables
3. Figures	3. Parody	3. Release from fear
4. Metaphor	4. Allegory	4. Comparisons
5. Exotic compounds	5. The unexpected	5. Hyperbole
6. Unique expressions	6. The inconsequent	
7. Invented words	7. Riddles	
8. Application of words	8. Antithesis	
	9. Persiflage	

(ii) Cicero's list is less complicated and falls into but two sections, *in verbo* and *in re*, although, as was remarked, two kinds of the latter, namely invented anecdotes and mimicry or caricature, are placed before the remainder and separated from them. Passing over these, the subheadings, which are not numbered by Cicero, are approximately as follows:

A. From diction	B. From content
1. The ambiguous (*amphibolia*)	1. Narratives (fables, anecdotes)
2. The unexpected	2. Comparisons
3. Word-play (παρονομασία)	3. Mimicry or caricature
4. Quotation of verses, proverbs	4. Exaggeration or understatement
5. Taking words literally	5. The telling detail
6. Allegory	6. Irony
7. Metaphor	7. Innuendo
8. Irony	8. Assumed incomprehension
9. Antithetical expressions	9. Hinted ridicule
	10. The illogical
	11. Personal retorts

(iii) Quintilian does not recognise, save *en passant* at VI 3.7, 25, the dichotomy between speech and action as sources of laughter; instead, different types are intermingled in a long and rambling list, with far more sub-types than its extant predecessors. To quote Quintilian against himself, 'si species omnes persequi velimus, nec modum reperiemus et frustra laborabimus'. It would be wasted labour to discuss him here, as Arndt (41 – 62) has shown that he was dependent on Cicero for theory, and Roman collectors of the *dicta* of famous men for examples, with no direct recourse to Greek writers (so too J. Cousin, *Études sur Quintilien* I, 324 – 46; Plebe 78 – 80).

(iv) Hermogenes' analysis of 'speaking comically' is in fact the same as that of the *Auctor ad Herennium*. Hermogenes lists three heads, parody, the unexpected and 'making the images contrary to the nature of things': περὶ τοῦ κωμικῶς λέγειν· κατὰ παρῳδίαν . . . παρὰ προσδοκίαν . . . ἐναντίας ποιεῖσθαι τὰς εἰκόνας τῇ φύσει τῶν πραγμάτων. There is no division into words and actions. There are examples from oratory, as we might expect in a rhetorical handbook, except that Aristoph. *Wasps* 45 is cited for parody. This suggests that Hermogenes is drawing on a broader account of humour, like Demetrius', where these items occur in the same sequence, though separated by others; there the first two are assigned to style, the third to content. Plebe 26 proposed that each represents a major category, verbal, factual and mixed: but the parallel in the *Auctor ad Herennium* proves that they are excerpted from a Hellenistic source that lacked such categories.

(v) The *Auctor ad Herennium* has a much longer list than Hermogenes, but like his it is not subdivided. It is given in the context of introducing a speech to a restive audience. There are seventeen types, unnumbered, unillustrated and unexplained, as follows:

(1) ab apologo, (2) fabula verisimili, (3) imitatione depravata, (4) inversione, (5) ambiguo, (6) suspicione, (7) inrisione, (8) stultitia, (9) exsuperatione, (10) collectione, (11) litterarum mutatione, (12) praeter exspectationem, (13) similitudine, (14) novitate, (15) historia, (16) versu, (17) ab alicuius interpellatione aut adrisione.

11 — 13 reappear in the same order in Hermogenes, who stands towards the *Auctor* as **a** does to C, since he provides examples but fewer headings. It is difficult to perceive any relation between these and Cicero's arrangement, although many of the same types appear. One curious similarity is that the opening types recall Cicero's two isolated types of humour *in re* at *de Orat.* II 243, *fabella vel enarratio ficta* and *imitatio depravata.* But the originator of this list has dropped the distinction between *res* and *verba*, if ever he knew it.

The attempt of Mayer (*Theophrasti ΠΕΡΙ ΛΕΞΕΩΣ* 208) to show that the first three of these analyses and the Tractate's all go back to Theophrastus reveals the unlikelihood of his hypothesis. In fact the Treatise must be sharply distinguished from the rest, since their purposes differ. Demetrius is dealing with smiles not bellylaughs, and in a far wider range of literature; the others are orators, and oratory has its own standards and proprieties when compared with comedy, which ought to have many more resources of the absurd. Yet their classifications are more detailed, and in lists of this kind this is an indicator of a later date, though a hazardous one (cf. inf. p.239 — 41).

If, as argued above, our analysis is closely tied to the main qualitative parts of comedy, and exemplifies the comic potentialities of each without exhausting them, three consequences follow: (i) it was written for its present place, not imported by some compiler from another source; (ii) it is neither so clumsy nor so

Procrustean as has been thought, so that we should be less worried
by minor gaps and refrain from stretching categories beyond their
proper bounds to fill them; (iii) it is superior to those of the other
writers, who simply catalogue types of humour in an inherited or
arbitrary order with no underlying structure. As Arndt (13)
suggests, the types that are shared probably derive from the
analysis of comedy, and he makes the very strong point that the
whole category of πράγματα is most ill-suited to genres other than
the dramatic; oratory depends on speech, perhaps too on gesture,
but action, from dancing to the throwing of tomatoes, is generally
speaking unwelcome. Thus the Treatise has a good claim to
priority here.

Chapter V: Verbal Humour

The heading

(a) *Expression*

In introducing verbal humour **a** and C diverge: **a** has 'laughter has
its structure' (or 'system': ἔχει τὴν σύστασιν) rather than C's
'laughter arises' (γίνεται). Cf. *Poet.* 6.1450a32 **ἔχουσα** . . .
σύστασιν πραγμάτων, 13.1453a31 διπλῆν τὴν σύστασιν **ἔχουσα**, and
Tractatus XI: comic *plot* is 'that which is structured around absurd
actions' (ἔχων τὴν σύστασιν). For the construction of σύστασις with
ἐκ cf. *Poet.* 7.1450b35 πρᾶγμα ὃ συνέστηκεν ἐκ τινῶν. The
construction in C is common in A., e.g. *Rhet.* III 3.1405b34 τὰ
ψυχρὰ ἐν τέτταρσι γίνεται κατὰ τὴν λέξιν; 1406b5 τὸ ψυχρὸν ἐν ταῖς
μεταφοραῖς γίνεται; 11.1412a26 γίνεται (τὰ ἀστεῖα) ὅταν . . . ; *S.E.*
4.165b23ff. τρόποι δ᾽ εἰσὶ τοῦ ἐλέγχειν δύο· οἱ μὲν γάρ εἰσι παρὰ τὴν
λέξιν, οἱ δ᾽ ἔξω τῆς λέξεως, illustrates **a**'s use of τρόποι. — In the
heading **a** has ἐκ, C ἀπό, although in that of VI both use ἐκ. Both
have κατά throughout V, except παρά in the sub-types of paronymy
(C); in VI **a** uses κατά, C ἐκ. The fluctuations are paralleled in A.
For ἐκ and ἀπό cf. the list in *Rhet.* II 22 – 3 (ἐκ predominates). In II
24 παρά prevails; so also in *S.E.* 4. Closest is *Poet.* 25 with κατά, e.g.
κατὰ μεταφοράν, κατὰ προσῳδίαν, κατὰ τὸ ἔθος τῆς λέξεως
(1461a16ff.). Cf. also the mix of κατά with ἐκ at 22.1458a25.
Demetrius' list of χάριτες is still more varied.

(b) *The 'systasis' of laughter and the plot of tragedy*

a's expression ὁ γέλως ἔχει τὴν σύστασιν is unexpected and, if original, suggests an interesting interpretation of this section which squares with theoretical considerations. In *Poet.* the effect of tragedy, the arousal of pity and fear, is brought about principally through the plot, or 'structure of the events' (σύστασις τῶν πραγμάτων). This is most explicit in 13 and 14, which discuss the various kinds of *systasis* and how they generate the tragic emotions. Now the function of comedy is to engender pleasure and laughter, according to C; in V—VI we are told how these arise — not through intrigues of plot, ignorance of identity, or recognition-scenes, which are ignored, but through all kinds of verbal jokes, and aspects of plot, character and thought, a multifarious array of sources of the kind Aristophanes employs. The parallelism of comedy and tragedy is not yet; however, this is not for lack of trying on the author's part. He supplies comedy with a definition parallel to that of tragedy, and his concern to duplicate pity and fear has led to the problematic pair 'pleasure and laughter', of which only the latter receives clarification. Now the section on how comedy performs its function, V—VIII, is analogous to *Poet.* 7—11, where *systasis* is the means through which tragedy achieves its end. I therefore suggest that the phrase 'laughter has its *systasis*', otherwise so odd, is another example of terminology intended to stress the parallels between tragedy and comedy.

Systasis is a key technical term in the broader context of Aristotelian philosophy, as well as in *Poet.*: cf. Brancato, *La σύστασις nella Poetica di Aristotele* 5ff. In Brancato's formulation, *systasis* is a sensible reality, composite and complete, consisting of parts harmoniously and indissolubly connected, conducive to a good end. From the essence of the σύστασις perfect in size and order (μεγέθει καὶ τάξει) derives the function and pleasure (ἔργον, ἡδονή) appropriate to every σύστασις. The plot of tragedy is tantamount to its purpose (τὸ οὖ ἕνεκα), since nature and function are one (τὸ τί ἐστι καὶ τὸ οὖ ἕνεκα ἕν ἐστι, *Phys.* II 7.198a25). Brancato (10) suggests that this was so of comedy also. That it was becoming so is shown by *Poet.* 9.1451b12, where comic poets are said to construct their plots according to probability; but it was left to Menander to make comedy function primarily through its plot, in this respect, as well as in characterisation and appropriateness in diction, taking the path marked out by A. Moreover, within the production of the effect of tragedy is subsumed a considerable amount of what is surely ἦθος, and comes into the province of his

Ethics: much of the effect of tragedy attained through plot in *Poet.*
13 depends on the characters of those involved, whether good or
wicked. A.'s admission that spectacle too can produce pity and fear
(14.1453b1) widens further the range of means to tragedy's end,
although he notes that the poet needs an outlay to use spectacle,
and it is not germane to the poet's craft. At least three of its six
parts are potentially implicated in the purpose of tragedy, and
διάνοια too must be adduced from 6.1449b37: character is more
important in this than is generally recognised — cf. 6.1450a21, (οἱ
μιμούμενοι) τὰ ἤθη συμπεριλαμβάνουσιν διὰ τὰς πράξεις. Note how
he continues ὥστε τὰ πράγματα . . . τέλος τῆς τραγῳδίας, where
πράγματα evokes the heading of *Tract.* VI, and likewise subsumes
ethos and *dianoia*. Cf. also 14.1453b13.

There is thus a larger area of similarity between the way in
which tragedy and comedy arouse their desired emotions than
might appear: both draw on more than one of the qualitative parts.
Hence the use of *systasis* here, if it is correct (the parallel makes me
suspect that it is), is more than a mere terminological sleight of
hand. The sources may be reconciled by supposing that the original
ran roughly thus: ὁ δὲ γέλως τῆς κωμῳδίας ἔκ τε λέξεων καὶ
πραγμάτων ἔχει τὴν σύστασιν. ἐκ μὲν τῆς λέξεως < γίνεται >
κατὰ τρόπους ἑπτά.

Chapter V 1: Homonymy

(a) *The examples*

In **b** the gloss on διαφορουμένοις has ousted the further example
οἷον τὸ μέτρον, but **b** is derivative in other respects (sup. p.9f.) and
the chance that this is original is slender. When single words are
involved, in the case of diminutives, **a** gives two examples: thus οἷον
τὸ μέτρον should stand.

The source of the pun διαφορουμένοις is unknown; the parallel in
Eustathius 804.47 protects it from emendation and confirms one's
expectation that it is drawn from comedy. The gloss, absent from
the Byzantine lexica, is probably wrong, since διάφορος is found
with both meanings but the verb formed from it is not. The sense of
διαφορεῖσθαι at Aristoph. *Birds* 338, 355 'to be torn in pieces' might
however be relevant, as it is easier to think of appropriate puns:
this may be the reference intended by Eustathius, cf. Van der Valk
ad loc. Cf. also A. *Div. Somn.* 2.464b13, inf. p.203, and *Poet.*
8.1451a34 (em. Butcher). — Dobree pointed to a likely source of
the pun on μέτρον, namely *Clouds* 638ff., where Socrates talks of

poetic metres, and Strepsiades misunderstands him to mean 'measures' of corn: the joke continues for over ten lines, followed by another, less seemly, pun on δάκτυλος. The passage is prominent and in a play known to this writer (cf. VI 1).

(b) *Aristotle on homonyms and their uses*

A.'s interest in homonyms is evident. At *Categories* 1 he defines homonyms, synonyms and paronyms in that order as follows:

ὁμώνυμα λέγεται ὧν ὄνομα μόνον κοινόν, ὁ δὲ κατὰ τοὔνομα λόγος τῆς οὐσίας ἕτερος, οἷον ζῷον ὅ τε ἄνθρωπος καὶ τὸ γεγραμμένον . . . συνώνυμα δὲ λέγεται ὧν τό τε ὄνομα κοινὸν καὶ ὁ κατὰ τοὔνομα λόγος τῆς οὐσίας ὁ αὐτός, οἷον ζῷον ὅ τε ἄνθρωπος καὶ ὁ βοῦς . . . παρώνυμα δὲ λέγεται ὅσα ἀπό τινος διαφέροντα τῇ πτώσει τὴν κατὰ τοὔνομα προσηγορίαν ἔχει, οἷον ἀπὸ τῆς γραμματικῆς ὁ γραμματικὸς καὶ ἀπὸ τῆς ἀνδρείας ὁ ἀνδρεῖος.

These definitions are framed for the purposes of logic, and we shall see that A. uses the terms in broader senses also; for useful and rigorous surveys v. J. Barnes ap. *CQ* 21 (1971) 75 – 9, and L. Tarán ap. *Hermes* 106 (1978) 73 – 99.

Homonyms have dubious uses too: sophists use them to prove white black. Homonyms, paired with ambiguity (*amphibolia*), head the list of sophistries dependent on diction at *S.E.* 4.165b30ff. After exemplifying amphiboly, i.e. ambiguity produced by the collocation of more than one word, he defines homonymy as when τοὔνομα κυρίως σημαίνῃ πλείω, οἷον ἀετὸς καὶ κύων (cf. *Rhet.* II 24.1401a13ff.). Thus homonyms, standard words of dual or multiple meaning even on their own, are first among the types listed in both *S.E.* 4 and the Treatise. The links with sophistry and humour are both made explicit by A. himself. At *Rhet.* III 2, after listing types of words studied in *Poet.* 21 – 2, he continues that homonyms are useful to the sophist, synonyms to the poet; all the items (referring back over the whole paragraph) have been defined in the *Poetics*. Confirmation that homonyms have humorous uses comes in *Rhet.* III 11 on wit (1412b10ff.). Simplicius preserves his definition of synonyms, but that of homonyms is lost; if parallel to that of synonyms it must have run ὁμώνυμά ἐστιν ὧν ἓν μὲν τὸ ὄνομα λόγος δὲ ἕτερος: cf. *Cat.* 1a1, inf. on V 2.

This entry is expected, and in the right position, for an Aristotelian analysis of humour. Later writers neglect it. Demetrius lacks it entirely, perhaps because it is less a source of χάρις than of γέλως. Cicero (*de Orat.* II 253) refers to *ambigua* more broadly, although the term *amphibolia* also occurs in his writings; they are first among the verbal kinds. Quintilian echoes Cicero at VI 3.47ff.; at VII 9 he discusses *amphibolia*, in which he subsumes ὁμωνυμία, as a source of legal confusions; cf. VIII 5.21, Hor. *A.P.* 449 with Brink ad loc., Theon 2.81 Spengel, Tryphon 3.203 ibid. The scholiasts to Aristophanes were ready to speak of ambiguity, but neglected the term ὁμωνυμία (Rutherford 296 – 309, 438f.); they are more indebted to collections of tropes and figures than to any analyses of humour. — Examples of this type of humour can be multiplied indefinitely, but more readily from Aristophanes than Menander (Starkie *Acharnians* xli – xliv, Lane Cooper 229f.).

Chapter V 2: Synonymy

(a) *Genus and species in the example and in Aristotle*

a's example is from the *Frogs*, where Euripides criticises the prologue of Aeschylus' *Choephori*: on the line ἥκω γὰρ ἐς γῆν τήνδε καὶ κατέρχομαι he exclaims that Aeschylus has said the same thing twice, since ἥκω and κατέρχομαι mean the same, ἥκω δὲ ταὐτόν ἐστι τῷ κατέρχομαι (1157). Thus the apparent gloss ταὐτὸν γάρ ἐστιν in **a** is really part of the quotation and confirms its provenance (for this use of ταὐτόν ἐστι cf. *Rhet.* I 2.1357b9). Euripides is being sophistical; both verbs convey that Orestes has arrived, but κατέρχομαι adds that he is back from exile. Bernays (171) criticised the example for ignoring the difference, but in fact it exemplifies exactly the semantic overlap stipulated for synonyms by A. in *Cat.* 1, quoted above, where synonyms are species of the same genus, e.g. man and ox are both animals (cf. *Metaph.* I 6.987b10, *E.N.* V 2.1130a33 συνώνυμος, ὅτι ὁ ὁρισμὸς ἐν ταὐτῷ γένει). Here ἥκω is the genus, and κατέρχομαι a species. Now at *Rhet.* III 2.1405a1, in discussing their utility to poets, A. gives as an example of synonyms τὸ πορεύεσθαι καὶ τὸ βαδίζειν. Again we find paired verbs of motion, where the first is general and the second specific: 'τὸ πορεύεσθαι is the genus, and τὸ βαδίζειν is one of its species, just as τὸ πέτεσθαι is another, τὸ νεῖν another' (Rutherford 439f.). The examples are strikingly similar; A. often used verbs of motion as illustrations (*Rhet.* III 5.1407b23, 39; *Poet.* 20.1457a17ff., etc.). Both cover synonymy in the narrow sense of genus and species, as well as the popular sense of different names for the same thing (cf.

LSJ s.v. συνώνυμος). Rutherford did not see this, and rejected **a**'s example because he thought A. did not use 'synonymy' in the popular sense. But Aristophanes' joke depends on the narrower sense as well; in the Athens of 404, being back and being back from exile are quite different, yet συνώνυμα. Moreover A. *did* use synonymy in the wider sense too, just as he used 'poet' and 'poetry'; so we learn from *Poet.* fr. III Kassel, a definition of synonymy in popular terms preserved by Simplicius (v. testimonia ad V 2). This can be decisively confirmed by neglected statements of Porphyry, as I have shown in *CQ* 32 (1982) 323ff.

(b) *Porphyry's fragment of the* Poetics

The passage of Simplicius just cited also contains a little-noticed testimonium to this lost part of the *Poetics*. The passage is at once followed by a quotation of Porphyry's lost *Greater Commentary on the Categories* (Simplic. *in Categ.* 36.15 – 31 Kalbfleisch). For A.'s use of synonymy in linguistic questions, in a different sense from that in his logic, Porphyry refers to the *Poetics* and the third book of the *Rhetoric* (he means 2.1404b37ff.). From his words we can draw three inferences: first, he knew a discussion of synonymy in the lost part of the *Poetics*; second, A. used the term there in the popular sense; third, the latter did not use the term *polyonyma*, but used *synonyma* in this popular sense of 'things with many names'. This last seemingly contradicts the definition from the *Poetics* that preceded, 'synonyms . . . like things with many names (*polyonyma*), e.g. . . . '. In fact the definition is quoted by Simplicius from Porphyry, and the reference to polyonyms is a gloss by Porphyry and not part of A.'s wording. For, in the passage that follows, Porphyry has a polemical point to make against his predecessor Boethus, who claimed that A. ignores the polyonymous sense of synonymy, Speusippus' *polyonyma* (fr. 68 Tarán): Porphyry retorts that this sense *is* found, but elsewhere, where it is relevant, namely in the linguistic contexts of *Rhet.* and *Poet.*, not the logical context of the *Categories* on which Boethus is commenting. Thus a polemical aside inserted by Porphyry into A.'s definition will explain the inconsistency perfectly, as well as the presence of the ironical particle δή in that aside. As soon as the definition from *Poet.* concludes, we find ourselves within a quotation from Porphyry, and the definition must belong, for the reason just given, within that quotation. For Simplicius' indirect manner of quotation, cf. *in Categ.* 38.15ff. Kalbfleisch, where he requotes 36.25ff. without naming his source. If I am right, it follows that *Poet.* fr. III Kassel is to be ascribed to

Porphyry not Simplicius, and the former's testimony must be added in any case. The presence of an actual quotation by Porphyry from the text of *Poet.* will refute the suggestion (by Tarán, art. cit. n.40) that he cites it merely because of the cross-reference in *Rhet.* III 2.

I have found no other definite citations of *Poet.* in Porphyry. At *Vita Pyth.* 41 his mention of A.'s account of metaphor could refer to *Poet.* 21.1457b6ff. In the Gedaleian commentary wherein he cited *Poet.* on synonymy he also listed patronymics, comparatives, superlatives and diminutives as sub-types of paronymy (Simplic. op. cit. 38.1f.): this is paralleled in the Treatise as I reconstructed it independently (inf. p.175ff.). There too he discussed the relation of homonymy to metaphor, a probably Aristotelian topic (Simplic. op. cit. 32.22ff., cf. Porph. *in Cat.* 67.4 Busse, beside Ar. *Rhet.* III 2.1405a3 referring to *Poet.*). He knew other lost works by A. on literature: Erbse (ap. *Zetemata* 24 (1960) 61ff.) confirms that his frequent quotations of the *Homeric Problems* in his *Quaestiones Homericae* are direct.

Porphyry's polemic confirms Barnes' and Tarán's arguments (artt. cit.) in favour of divergent uses of *synonymia* in A. The example in **a** conforms with even the stricter usage of *Cat.* 1, and causes no difficulty. We should reconstruct A.'s definition of synonymy in *Poet.* as given in the testimonia to V 2, minus the words οἷα . . . πολυώνυμα. There is a striking parallel for the remainder at *Top.* I 7.103a10, ὧν ὀνόματα πλείω τὸ δὲ πρᾶγμα ἕν, οἷον λώπιον καὶ ἱμάτιον. The examples are characteristic: λώπιον καὶ ἱμάτιον recur at *Top.* VI 6.149a4, *S.E.* 6.168a30, *Phys.* I 2.185b20, III 3.202b13, *Metaph.* III 4.1006b26; φάρος does not appear.

There is no reason to suppose that the treatment of synonymy has been lost from *Poet.* 21, in view of its association with humour in *Rhet.* (*pace* Hubbard *ALC* 119, Fuhrmann *Aristoteles Poetik* 9). Rutherford (loc. cit.) extended synonymy to pejorative and ameliorative epithets, and others followed. But at *Rhet.* III 2.1405a10ff., the source of this notion, A. clearly subsumes such epithets in *metaphora* (cf. a14, 24).

Chapter V 3: Repetition *(adoleschia)*

a has lost a word for 'more than once'; Byzantine scribes supply two possibilities. V[57], a contaminated MS of scholarly pretensions, reads τις <δὶς>, while M[9] and its progeny add πολλάκις, a reasonable try but palaeographically inferior. — For ὀνόματι χρῆσθαι cf. *de An.* II 5.418a3 χρῆσθαι . . . ὡς κυρίοις ὀνόμασι.

A. uses ἀδολεσχία, a term with no precise English equivalent, in two contexts — logic, and character. In neither is it a desirable trait. In *S.E.* those seeking to win arguments try to induce it in their opponents: it is defined as repetition of the same thing (τὸ πλεονάκις ταὐτὸ λέγειν, 3.165b16). For example: ἆρά ἐστιν ἡ ἐπιθυμία ἡδέος; τοῦτο δ' ἐστὶν ὄρεξις ἡδέος· ἔστιν ἄρα ἡ ἐπιθυμία ὄρεξις **ἡδέος ἡδέος** (13.173a39). τὸ ἀδολεσχεῖν results from repeating a term in a definition (*Top.* V 2.130a34), or asking the same question repeatedly (VIII 2.154a27). In *E.N.* III 10 he defines garrulous people (τοὺς φιλομύθους καὶ διηγητικοὺς καὶ περὶ τῶν τυχόντων κατατρίβοντας τὰς ἡμέρας ἀδολέσχας . . . λέγομεν, 1117b33); cf. *H.A.* I 11.492b2 μωρολογίας καὶ ἀδολεσχίας. In *Rhet.* II 13 the old are thus characterised (1390a9). Adoleschy results from stating the obvious (22.1395b26, III 3.1406a32f.), and can be obscure (12.1414a24). Thus A. uses adoleschy in two ways — of the repetition of a particular word, or of a wider fault, whether of style, like Alcidamas' verbiage, or of character (cf. Theophrastus' ἀδολέσχης, *Char.* 3, a long-winded and repetitious purveyor of unwanted, trivial and obvious information). The narrow sense predominates in the example, as it did in those of homonymy and synonymy; but doubtless it can cover *loquendi cacoethes* in general, as well as comic 'catch-words', just as synonymy too has a broader definition. Rutherford wished to include parodies and travesties in adoleschy (441f.); he is again followed by Starkie and Lane Cooper. But his citation of *Rhet.* III 3.1406a32ff. in support will not do: there poetic speech in oratory is censured for inappropriateness as well as verbosity, and parody demands the former above all.

Demetrius (212) defends Ctesias against the charge of being ἀδολεσχότερος because he repeats the same word for the sake of vividness. Here, as in A., adoleschy is a defect of serious style, and as such ought to have a comic application: yet the analysis of χάρις ignores it. Cicero and Quintilian are equally silent: it is very much an Aristotelian term. The sources of Plutarch's essay on adoleschy (Περὶ ἀδολεσχίας, *Mor.* 502b–515a) are obscure; he quotes two witticisms of A. against garrulous people at 503b. Although A. nowhere associates it directly with comedy, as a sophistical fault he can hardly have failed to note its humorous potential.

Chapter V 4: Paronymy

a omits C's subdivisions 'addition and subtraction', but its explanation clearly refers to the former, and example to the latter. These omissions represent the last stage in the tradition's tendency to reduce the scope of paronymy, which began by discarding diminutives and exallage, as in both **a** and C.

(a) *Paronymy in Aristotle and others*

A.'s definition of paronyms in *Cat.* 1 was quoted above: cf. *Top.* II 2.109b5, *Phys.* VIII 3.245b11, *E.E.* III 1.1228a36 (ὁ θρασὺς παρὰ τὸ θράσος λέγεται παρωνύμως). The substantive παρωνυμία happens not to occur in his works, but cf. ὁμωνυμία, συνωνυμία, παρώνυμος, παρωνυμιάζειν. In the preceding types A. used both a broader and a narrower sense, that in the *Organon*: there may be a like discrepancy here. Arndt (9ff.) suggested that A. used παρωνυμία to denote not only grammatical alterations but deliberate and unusual verbal modifications, the later *paronomasia* or *adnominatio*, cf. *Auct. Herenn.* IV 21.29, (*adnominatio*) 'multis et variis rationibus conficitur . . . addendis litteris . . . demendis . . . transferendis'; also Cic. *de Orat.* II 256 'alterum genus est, quod habet parvam verbi immutationem, quod in littera positum Graeci vocant παρονομασίαν, ut "Nobiliorem, mobiliorem" Cato'; Rutilius Lupus I 3 (*Rhet. min. lat.* p.4 Halm); Quint. VI 53, IX 3.66ff., discussing tropes. But the terminology fluctuates: παρωνυμία replaces παρονομασία at Aquila Romanus p.30.32 Halm (where it is not to be emended away), Plut. *Mor.* 853b, while Trypho 3.196 Spengel uses the *latter* to denote inflectional changes.

Deeming that παρωνυμία should have the latter sense, Bergk and Koster would transfer its subdivisions elsewhere. But the presence of these in A.'s *Poetics* defends them. At 21.1457b1 we read of extended, curtailed and altered words; these are then defined with examples. Poetic diction is raised above the everyday by lengthening words and so forth (22.1458a21ff.); lengthenings, shortenings and alterations of words make a major contribution (a34ff.). All these types can be used deliberately for comic purposes (b13ff.). In *Rhet.* III 11 A. mentions παραπεποιημένα (altered words?) as humorous, but exemplifies only jokes based on altering letters (1412a28ff.). Are these equivalent to paronyms? Demetrius, on how to invent new words, indicates that they are (*de Eloc.* 97f.):

ποιητέον . . . παρὰ τὰ κείμενα **παρονομάζοντα** αὐτόν, οἶον ὡς
. . . 'Αριστοτέλης τὸν αὐτίτην οἶον τὸν μόνον αὐτὸν
ὄντα. Ξενοφῶν δὲ 'ἠλέλιξέ' φησιν . . . **παραποιήσας**
ὀνόματι.

Thus we must choose between jokes based on inflectional changes, as defined in *Cat.* 1 (these would seem have to little humorous potential, except for some grammatical jokes in the *Clouds*), or changes in general, later *paronomasia* and *paronymia*. The latter must be right, because of the example **a** gives. Starkie (*Acharnians* liii) usefully lists several types, but it is not certain that he should have included compounds: cf. *Poet.* 21 1457a31ff. Demetrius, however, made them akin to coinages (*de Eloc.* 98).

(b) *The subdivisions of paronymy*

The treatise offers a curious pattern at this point, which recurs twice. Paronymy, fourth in this list, is third in the otherwise identical list in *Cat.* 1, where adoleschy is absent. The insertion of a third item into such Aristotelian lists recurs thus:

Cat. 1a1ff. Cf. V 1−4	*Poet.* 22.1458b2 cf. V 4	*Poet.* 25.1461b23 cf. VI 3−6
Homonyms	Lengthened words	The impossible
Synonyms	Shortened words	The illogical
< Adoleschy >	< Diminutives >	< The unexpected >
Paronyms	Alterations	Debasing the characters

The striking parallel reinforces my confidence in assigning diminutives and exallage to paronymy.

1. Addition and subtraction

(i) *Expression and text*: The subdivisions παρὰ πρόσθεσιν καὶ ἀφαίρεσιν correspond to the first two items in A.'s list of altered words in *Poet.* 21−2. Although this pair is Aristotelian and frequent, e.g. *Phys.* III 6.206a15, it is not used by him in a grammatical context: LSJ s.v. give Trypho precedence. A.'s terms are far from constant, and may be listed as follows:

(a) addition: ἐπεκτεταμένον (ὄνομα) *Poet.* 21.1457b2, 35, 1458a3; ἐπέκτασις 22.1458a23, b2.

(b) subtraction: ὑφῃρημένον (ὄνομα) 21.1457b2; ἀφῃρημένον 1458a1, 3; ἀποκοπή 22.1458b2. The terms for 'alteration' are consistently ἐξηλλαγμένον and ἐξαλλαγή. ἀφῃρημένον is related to ἀφαίρεσις as 'subtracted' to 'subtraction', and presents no difficulty. πρόσθεσις is unparalleled in the series.

Bernays (173f.) attacked the definition and example in **a** as the work of a compiler expanding the headings of C. He alleged that τὸ κύριον, the standard Aristotelian designation of the current word, was misunderstood as referring to a proper name, and that the compiler therefore chose an example which comprised the name Midas. There is a contradiction in his argument: the hypothesis presupposes either two stages of expansion, the addition of the definition and then that of the 'inappropriate' example, or that **a** did contain matter lost to C anyway. Moreover the 'compiler' still knew an example absent from extant comedies and other sources. In fact τὸ κύριον is not misinterpreted. For A., an altered word did depart from τὸ κύριον (*Poet.* 22.1458a23, b1ff.); in any case the oddity in the example is βώμαξ, not the unaltered Μίδας. That the example contains a proper name is a coincidence paralleled at 21.1458a4 (lengthening in Πηλείδου/ Πηληϊάδεω) or Theophrastus' Περὶ Λέξεως I (sup. p.51, Ἀχιλλεῖος/ Ἀχιλλήϊος).

τι συνάπτηται is Dobree's conjecture in a copy of Kuster's *Aristophanes* (Cambridge Univ. Library Adv. a.79.20 ad loc.). Unlike other efforts, it accounts for the sigma in the majority reading τις ἅπτηται, and incidentally introduces a favourite word of A.'s in a common construction, e.g. συνάπτειν τῷ μέτρῳ τὸ ποιεῖν *Poet.* 1.1447b13, cf. Bonitz s.v. I now find that Koster has had Dobree's idea independently (his Addenda): also Bergk. Kaibel proposed <τῶν> ἔξωθέν, Koster τι <παρόμοιον>. I see no reason to alter the text further. Lane Cooper (234) suggests that one might see the two headings addition and subtraction as indicative of the process involved in addition, i.e. the removal of the standard ending, and then the addition of the novel suffix: the parallels in A. disprove this.

(ii) *The example*: Meineke (iv 688) refers the example to New Comedy, Edmonds (i 962) to Old. We must choose between μώμαξ, βώμαξ, μῶμαξ, μάμαξ, and μίμαξ. The last is a worthless conjecture by **m**, while μάμαξ is meaningless. The comic suffix in -αξ -ακος has a long vowel, so μῶμαξ is wrong (cf. Herodian I 524.16 Lentz τὸ ᾱ θέλει ἔχειν ἐκτεταμένον, e.g. θώραξ . . . βώμαξ). βώμαξ is also found in the Antiatticist 85.17 Bekker, in Hesychius, Agathias 2.30 and elsewhere, while μώμαξ is without parallel, and surely results from a minuscule corruption of β to μ: if β- is an emendation or error in U, it is a happy one (but contrast Koster xi and ad loc.). Nouns in -αξ bearing a derogatory force are common in comedy, as Starkie (*Acharnians* liii) proves: cf. Björk, *Das Alpha Impurum* 48f., 260 — 8. The inapplicability of this example to 'lengthening' has not been remarked: whether from βωμός 'altar' or μῶμος 'blame', no extra syllable is involved. Sense and syllables suggest that it is *shortened* from βωμολόχος, the gloss usually applied to βώμαξ; the example of 'lengthening' must be lost, unless it is the κυντότατον of the Antiatticist.

Μίδας has been subjected to various changes, mostly asinine, to restore a purely iambic rhythm instead of iamb plus cretic. But the metre is acceptable if comic lyric is the source, and the name eminently so: Strabo (VI 304) lists it as a typical name for Phrygian slaves, as is confirmed by Aristoph. *Wasps* 433, Euphron fr. 2. Thus the speaker is probably a slave, Midas. The only emendation worth whispering is Koster's in his Addenda, from a variant in V[57], which does produce iambic rhythm, and leaves Midas unmetamorphosed, but certainly no king.

The context of Aristophanic examples, and the metre, are inadequate evidence for attribution. Even in non-choral parts of Middle Comedy, there was considerable metrical variety (Hunter *ZPE* 36 (1979) 23 — 38).

2. Diminutives

C's ὑποκόρισμα denotes the endearing or belittling name itself (cf. Aeschines 1.126, Charisius p.37 Keil, Eustath. 1540.54), **a**'s ὑποκορισμός the use of such names, cf. Ar. *Rhet.* III 2 infra. The sense of this is better, and Tzetzes has κορισμοί.

At *Rhet.* III 2.1405b28ff., where he has been speaking of ameliorative and pejorative epithets, A. defines diminutives as diminishing both good and bad, and quotes from Aristophanes' *Babylonians*:

ἔστιν ὁ ὑποκορισμὸς ὃ ἔλαττον ποιεῖ καὶ τὸ κακὸν καὶ τὸ ἀγαθόν, ὥσπερ καὶ ὁ Ἀριστοφάνης σκώπτει ἐν τοῖς Βαβυλωνίοις, ἀντὶ μὲν χρυσίου χρυσιδάριον, ἀντὶ δ' ἱματίου ἱματιδάριον, ἀντὶ δὲ λοιδορίας λοιδορημάτιον, καὶ νοσημάτιον.

A. thinks of comedy in choosing examples; he discerned the comic potential in the distortion caused by diminutives. He thinks of the commonest suffixes, -άριον and -άτιον; a's examples use the third type of like frequency, -ίδιον, and may be Aristophanic too (cf. Starkie's list, *Acharnians* liv). Bernays (178) objects that Σωκρατ-ίδιον, Εὐριπίδιον are inept examples, as they are proper not common nouns, chosen owing to a misunderstanding of τὸ κύριον. Note his compulsion to associate diminutives with paronymy; but he is wrong to argue that diminutives of proper names are so rife in Greek as to be inconspicuous. Σωκρατίδιον is a comic formation absent from everyday speech such as the Socratic dialogue: cf. *An. Ox.* IV 273.8 Cramer (γίνεται τὰ ὑποκοριστικὰ . . . διὰ <τὸ> γελοῖον, ὡς τὸ παρὰ Ἐπιχάρμῳ Πριαμιλλύδριον), schol. Dion. Thr. 356.1 Hilgard, Herodian II 858.32ff. Lentz, schol. Aristoph. *Clouds* 80, 92, 223.

Porphyry, in a work that shows cognizance of *Poet.* II, confirms the assignation of the diminutive to paronymy (sup. p.173). But why is it not simply subsumed by 'addition'? Its particular emotive effect and suitability for comedy were noted by A. (cf. Dover on *Clouds* 92, Amundsen *SO* xl (1965) 1ff.). But there may have been another reason. Herodian (loc. cit.) lists several varieties of diminutives *shorter* than the current word, e.g. πίθηκος πίθων, δραπέτης δράπων, Διονῦς παρὰ τοῖς κωμικοῖς . . . παρηγμένον ἀπὸ τοῦ Διονύσου. Thus diminutives may subsume both 'addition' and 'subtraction', being distinguished rather by emotive effect. If so, they are in the right place in the list of sub-types.

Starkie (loc. cit.) thinks A. included ameliorative and pejorative epithets under this head at *Rhet.* I 9.1367a33ff., where diminutives are conspicuous solely by their absence. At III 2 they occur together, but only because of their like effect in persuading the dicasts, not because they are equivalent.

3. Exallage

V, Triclinius and **b** read ἐναλλαγήν; V alone has authority. Enallage is familiar later as a standard rhetorical figure, denoting supposed innovations to nouns or verbs, e.g. Ap. Dysc. *Synt.* 157.12;

cf. Rutherford 310f. It was also called ἀλλαγή and ἐξαλλαγή
(Alexander 3.33 Spengel). The latter *difficilior lectio* has rightly
been preferred by all editors.

While enallage does not appear, exallage is typical of A.
ἐξαλλάττειν is the *mot juste* for the elevation of diction above the
everyday level (*Rhet.* III 2.1404b8, al., *Poet.* 22.1458a21); so too in
Demetrius, who as usual reflects early Peripatetic teaching (*de Eloc.*
77). If, as Arndt thought (11ff.), this is the usage here, paronymy
ought to depend on exallage, which is textually impossible. But
ἐξαλλαγή also occurs in the more specific sense of a particular type
of alteration to a word, following addition and subtraction (e.g.
Poet. 22.1458b2). A. defines it as when part of a word is left
unchanged, but part is altered; as an example he cites a word with
an additional medial syllable (ἐξηλλαγμένον ἐστὶν ὅταν τοῦ
ὀνομαζομένου τὸ μὲν καταλείπῃ τὸ δὲ ποιῇ, οἶον τὸ 'δεξιτερὸν κατὰ
μαζὸν' ἀντὶ τοῦ 'δεξιόν', 1458a5ff.). Similarly Theophrastus, in
series with addition, subtraction and syncope, has ἐξηλλαγμένον or
μικρὸν ἠλλοιωμένον, and an example with an extra medial syllable,
λιβανωτός/ λιβανός (Περὶ Λέξεως I, sup.).
    The Treatise maintains A.'s terminology, whereas later series of
altered words do not: ἀλλοίωσις is especially common. Cf. Philo of
Judaea's four kinds of change, πρόσθεσις, ἀφαίρεσις, μετάθεσις and
ἀλλοίωσις, in Περὶ 'Αφθαρσίας Κόσμου 113 (he draws on the
Peripatetics, quoting Theophrastus in 117, cf. Kayser 38); Phoebammon 3.45ff. Spengel, on the four principles underlying all
figures, ἔνδεια, πλεονασμός, μετάθεσις and ἐναλλαγή; Dion. Hal.
Comp. Verb. 39, μετασκευῆς . . . ἀφαιρέσεως λέγω καὶ προσθήκης καὶ
ἀλλοιώσεως; [Plut.] *Vit. Hom.* 41 (ἀλλοίωσις); Theophrastus just
cited, where perhaps apocope rather than syncope should be
restored, cf. Simplic. *in Cat.* 10.28 K. (ἀποκοπή and ἀφαίρεσις).

a's example, Βδεῦ for Ζεῦ, is letter-substitution rather than the
insertion of a syllable; cf. the παρὰ γράμμα σκῶμμα at *Rhet.* III
11.1412a28ff., discussed along with παραπεποιημένα, which may
mean paronyms. Plutarch cites a pun from Aristophanes on
Λαμίας/ Ταμίας as a paronym (*Mor.* 853b), and **a**'s example may
belong here, since the symmetry of changes to the beginnings and
ends of words by addition and subtraction, and the middles in
exallage, handsome as it is, omits substitutions of this type, and A.
does not specifically exclude them from exallage (cf. Rutherford
444f., Lane Cooper 236f.). But I prefer to retain the symmetry, and
hesitantly assign the example to the lost heading 'parody' restored

from Tzetzes, since A. and Theophrastus in their examples apply paronymy to changes affecting whole syllables.

A perfect example of exallage in the Aristotelian sense is the comic superlative κυντότατον quoted from the *Poetics* by Bekker's Antiatticist 101.32, = *Poet.* fr. IV Kassel. This expansion, by the interpolation of a syllable, of the epic form κύντατον is exactly paralleled by A.'s δεξιτερόν, also with a 'comparative' ending, beside δεξιόν (Theophrastus has a noun instead). Lane Cooper assigned it to paronymy, wherein exallage must be its rightful home. The source of the quotation is unknown, but the anapaestic metre suggests Old or Middle rather than New Comedy, and there are close parallels in Aristophanes, e.g. αὐτότατος (*Plut.* 83): Eubulus even had κυντατώτατον (Antiatticist loc. cit. = fr. 85). Cf. Porphyry's subordination of superlatives to paronymy (v. p.173). Heitz (93f.) thinks A. used the form himself, and therefore it must be from the *On Poets*, but this is incredible: clearly, like **a**, he gave no source.

Bernays (177f.) proposes that exallage is also related to word-choice, i.e. the substitution of words of the same genus: he builds on the subheading τοῖς ὁμογενέσι in C. For efforts to fit the subheadings to exallage see also Arndt loc. cit., Rutherford 444, Fuhrmann 68. None has shown how a verbal modification can be made other than φωνῇ, which is itself pleonastic. Moreover, to translate ὁμογενέσι as if it read τοιούτοις is very strained (so W.L. Grant). The subheadings do not belong here at all. Yet Bernays' error contains an insight whence the truth proceeds, as I shall show.

Chapter V 5: Parody

I argued that diminutives and exallage belong in Aristotelian theory to paronymy, and have displaced two other main headings, reported by Tzetzes, parody and metaphor (sup. p.69ff.). Even if Tzetzes is quoting incorrectly, we would be tempted to postulate these types: metaphor at least is inevitable. I have shown how earlier writers on the Treatise tried to introduce them where they do not belong. But neither has vanished entirely, if indeed the example Βδεῦ for Ζεῦ is of parody not exallage. It operates by the change of a single letter, and is not necessarily what we think of as parody, i.e. the depraved imitation of a recognisable piece of serious writing. Instead it corresponds to parody in the narrower usage of Hermogenes, Περὶ Μεθόδου Δεινότητος 34, whose brief discussion of comic speech is Hellenistic in origin (sup. p.165f.). Hermogenes' example is the skit on Alcibiades' lisp from Aristoph. *Wasps* 44f. (cf. schol. on *Wasps* 1167): ὁλᾶς; Θέωλος τὴν κεφαλὴν κόλακος ἔχει. But contrast the pun quoted as paronymy by Plutarch (sup.). On ancient use of the term cf. Rau, *Paratragodia* 7ff., and especially Householder ap. *CPh* 9 (1944) 1ff. If used in the broad sense, parody is a bigger category than the others; if of individual words, then extensive parody or burlesque is nowhere dealt with, a serious omission, as Dr Carey points out to me. The problem would be solved if A. used parody, like the first four items, in both a broad and a narrow sense, but this remains a conjecture. — Cf. also the parallel position of prosody, or quibbles over an accent or breathing, as penultimate entry before σχῆμα λέξεως in *S.E.* 4, the list of sophistical arguments from diction.

In *Poet.* παρῳδία means a burlesque in hexameters, which stands in the same relation to epic as does comedy to tragedy; both represent men as worse than they are (2.1448a12). The closest parallel is *Rhet.* III 11.1412a25ff. (quoted in the *comparanda* to this section), where the order of topics is as follows: 'saying novel, strange things' is a source of urbanity, 'and is effected when the sequel is unexpected, as in the humorous writers who employ παραπεποιημένα; jokes based on altering the letters have the same effect: and also in verse' ('comic verse', says the scholiast) 'such as the disappointment of our expectations in the line "Stately he trod, and under his feet were his chilblains", when we anticipate "sandals".'

This passage demands careful attention. A. is discussing a particular comic effect, the disappointment of expectations. This is brought about in several ways — παραπεποιημένα, which amount to paronyms; play on letters, which is not entirely the same as παραπεποιημένα, as καί at a29 reveals; and by some unnamed phenomenon ἐν μέτροις, where A. quotes a hexameter poem of the ilk of Homer's *Margites*. Editors agree that ὅπερ . . . ἐξαπατᾷ γάρ is parenthetic, as these jokes are elucidated later; but it is not clear whether καὶ ἐν τοῖς μέτροις is a new heading, or belongs with παραπεποιημένα. Against the latter combination I urge that it would be odd indeed in A.'s time to say 'in the comic writers' (ἐν τοῖς γελοίοις) 'and in verse', since nearly all comic writing was in verse anyway. It might be the use of *another's* verse, cf. Demetrius 150. Above all one must disagree with Cope ad loc., who thinks that the replacement of 'sandals' by 'chilblains' is a play on *letters* (cf. *de Gen. et corr.* I 1.315b14f.). We do at least find the same

collocation of ideas — alterations to words, whether by exallage or
by letter-play, and verse-parody, in the context of raising laughter,
and this supports the supplement of parody in the Treatise.

ὦ Βδεῦ δέσποτα is paralleled in Aristoph. *Lys.* 940, where Bentley
proposed Βδεῦ from **a** against Ζεῦ in the codices. This rightly won
little favour, and *P. Hibeh* 6.25 (*Com. Adesp. Nov.* 258.25 Austin) has
ὦ Ζεῦ δέσποτα also; the phrase is clearly a cliché (cf. also Aristoph.
Birds 835 ὦ νεοττὲ δέσποτα; *Ach.* 247; *Wasps* 389). Thus **a** has
another unknown comic fragment. The joke should derive from
Old or Middle Comedy, as it presupposes the pronunciation of ζ as
[zd], which tended to be replaced by [z] in Attic from the mid
fourth century, cf. Threatte *Gramm. Attic Inscr.* I 547, Allen *Vox
Graeca*[2] 54ff. A. was interested in the pronunciation of zeta (*Metaph.*
I 9.993a5). The mild obscenity is not beyond his sense of humour,
cf. *Rhet.* III 3.1406b15.

Chapter V 6: Transference *(metaphora)*

There are three reasons why this heading is required here, though
lost in both C and **a**. (i) Only if such a heading has been lost can
the subheadings attached to the preceding item in C, and to that
following in **a**, be explained; otherwise they are exceedingly
problematic. (ii) A. lays great emphasis on transference as a source
of verbal humour. Modern scholars without exception have felt
that *metaphora* ought to be in this list; judging by its associations,
this is the most appropriate place for it. (iii) Tzetzes refers to
catachresis at this point in his list of the sources of the absurd, *Iambi
de Comoedia* XXIb Koster 81. Even if he is misquoting (cf. sup.
p.11), the first two reasons suffice.

(a) *Transference in Aristotle*

Metaphora had for A. a wider meaning than does 'metaphor' today:
the *transfer* of names that belong to one thing to something else. In
Poet. 21 four types are distinguished, only the last of which is
metaphor in our usage: the name of the genus may be applied to a
subordinate species, that of a species to the genus, within a genus
the name of one species may be transferred to another, or the
relation may be one of analogy, i.e. as p is to q, so x is to y
(1457b6ff.). Although in *Rhet.* A. gives more attention to analogical
metaphor, it was Theophrastus who limited the name to this type:

in the papyrus of his Περὶ Λέξεως (40ff.) the first two classes are termed μετουσία, the third is lacking, and only the fourth retains the name μεταφορά.

A. has much to say about transference. It is paramount in both poetic and prose diction (*Rhet.* III 2.1405a4, *Poet.* 23.1459a6) but especially suited to iambic poetry (1459a10). Its proper effect is to elevate the diction above the commonplace, like other types of modified diction, e.g. paronyms (*Rhet.* III 2.1405a8ff., 6.1407b31ff., *Poet.* 22.1458a21ff.). To master it demands talented observation of similarities (*Rhet.* III 11.1412a10ff., *Poet.* 22.1459a7, cf. *Top.* VI 2.139b32ff.); to err in it courts disaster — obscurity (*Poet.* 22.1458a25, *Rhet.* III 3.1406b8), bombast, or absurdity (ibid. τὸ γελοῖον — χρῶνται γὰρ καὶ οἱ κωμῳδοποιοὶ μεταφοραῖς). That comic poets use metaphor receives corroboration elsewhere, e.g. *G.A.* V 4.784b19 εὖ δὴ οἱ ποιηταὶ ἐν ταῖς κωμῳδίαις μεταφέρουσι σκώπτοντες, τὰς πολιὰς καλοῦντες γήρως εὐρῶτα καὶ πάχνην (= Meineke *FCG* 4.604, Adespoton): *Poet.* 22.1458b13 counsels moderation in the use of elevated diction, since all its kinds, including metaphor, can be employed for absurd effects on purpose (ἐπὶ τὰ γελοῖα). Good metaphor is thus a mean between commonplace and the unintelligible on one axis, and between bombast and absurdity on the other.

The main account of metaphor in the context of humour is *Rhet.* III 10 — 11. A. starts from the syllogism that learning is pleasant, words have meanings, so those that make us learn are pleasant. We know current words but not glosses (hence glosses duly fail to appear as a source of laughter): metaphor teaches us most; similes have the same effect, and, if done well, are amusing (1410b10 — 18). Most jokes arise from *metaphora* and disappointed expectations (1412a18). After illustrating other jokes — including those from paronymy and, I have suggested, from parody — he remarks that jokes based on homonyms or on transference must be fittingly done to succeed (1412b11f.). Instances of jokes based on similes follow. Next, proverbs too are classified under *metaphora* (1413a15); their comical potential is not mentioned, but cf. Demetrius 156. Finally he adds a further category to *metaphora*, namely hyperbole, comparison that exaggerates the shared element. His examples, the comparison of a man with black eyes to a basket of mulberries, and that of bandy legs to parsley, both involve comic 'faults of the body' (*Tract.* VIII). See McCall, *Ancient Rhetorical Theories of Simile and Comparison*, Ch. II.

A. sees *metaphora* as a most important source of wit in oratory and laughter in comedy. This establishes the right of metaphor to a place in our list, if it is indeed Aristotelian. Metaphor, paronymy (?) and parody (?) are closely associated in *Rhet.* III 11: metaphor and paronymy by addition are juxtaposed at *Poet.* 22.1458a22. Here the sequence is reversed, but the placing of metaphor before paronymy in the Treatise would have disrupted the logical progression in the first four items (homonymy etc.). It is the significant detail of the subheadings φωνῇ and τοῖς ὁμογενέσι which proves that metaphor was indeed present at this point. We saw that these headings are difficult under exallage, and they will be seen to be equally intractable under σχῆμα λέξεως. Only as relics of a discussion of metaphor can they be explained.

(b) *The comments on metaphor in the Treatise*

In summarising the *Rhetoric* I passed over some crucial sentences in the advice there proferred on how best to use metaphor. One must not transfer from things remote, but from those of the same genus or species, so that the relationship is clear when the metaphor has been enunciated (ἐκ τῶν **συγγενῶν** καὶ τῶν **ὁμοειδῶν** μεταφέρειν, III 2.1405a34ff., cf. 3.1406b8). Further, one must transfer from things that are beautiful, whether in sound or meaning or the image they present to the sight or any other of the senses (ἀπὸ καλῶν **ἢ τῇ φωνῇ** ἢ τῇ δυνάμει ἢ τῇ ὄψει ἢ ἄλλῃ τινὶ αἰσθήσει, 1405b17ff.). Since he continues by discussing pejorative and ameliorative epithets and diminutives, clearly comic metaphor would be drawn ἀπὸ φαύλου ἢ αἰσχροῦ not ἀπὸ καλῶν, i.e. by transference from inferior members of the same class: this is also clear from 1405a15ff., ἐάν τε κοσμεῖν βούλῃ, ἀπὸ τοῦ βελτίονος **τῶν ἐν ταὐτῷ γένει** φέρειν τὴν μεταφοράν, ἐάν τε ψέγειν, ἀπὸ τῶν χειρόνων. Lastly, he stipulates that analogical metaphor should be reversible between things of the same kind (ἐπὶ θάτερα **τῶν ὁμογενῶν**, 4.1407a14ff.). The crucial words are emphasised: they are the words of the subdivisions which cause such perplexity. That they derive from a discussion of metaphor is surely beyond doubt; from what part of the discussion do they come?

In **a** at least, the entries are mutually exclusive: ' < metaphor > occurs by voice (sound) or by (things belonging to) the same kind'. Likewise C's format usually represents uncoordinated items or statements; but it is difficult to understand these thus. τοῖς ὁμογενέσι cannot mean 'and the like', nor ἄλλαις αἰσθήσεσι (1405b19): it must mean 'belonging to the same class or kind'. The proximity of the legitimate idea of membership of the same class surely rules out such a loose and unattested usage. If so, both sources seem to have paired uncoordinated statements, that (a) the similarities on which transference depends lie in the perceptions, of sound (φωνή), sense, sight etc.; (b) transference should be between things of the same class (τὰ ὁμογενῆ). In Ω these separate statements have been run together: the case of ὁμογενέσι has presumably been made to conform with that of φωνῇ. For a possible reconstruction, v. sup. p.94. — No example survives: on metaphor in Aristoph. see Taillardat, *Les Images d'Aristophane*.

(c) *Catachresis*

Tzetzes lists κατάχρησις 'misuse' at this juncture in his verse catalogue. This could be a misunderstanding of σχῆμα λέξεως as a frequent 'figure of speech', but does correspond well to the occurrence of metaphor in Ω. Cicero tells us that A. 'includes in *metaphora* both metonyms and misuse, which they call *catachresis*, as when we say "little-spirited" for "mean-spirited"' (*Orator* 27.94, cf. *de Orat.* III 169). The example is the same as that of metaphor at *Poet.* 22.1458b25ff. (Lucas ad b31 thinks that ὀλίγος exemplifies 'glosses', but it is a current word unless applied to single indivisible entities by transference, cf. μύριον for πολύ at 21.1457b11ff.) It is doubtful whether A. used the term κατάχρησις itself. Cicero is listing a series of later subtleties with their own nomenclature (ὑπαλλαγή, μετωνυμία, ἀλληγορία), all subsumed in Aristotelian *metaphora*. It is the later grammarians who are said to use the term (*pace* LSJ s.v. κατάχρησις and *ALC* ad loc., relying on a f.l.). But at *de Caelo* I.270b24 A. does use the appropriate verb when criticising Anaxagoras for misusing αἰθήρ (κατακέχρηται τῷ ὀνόματι τούτῳ οὐ καλῶς). — On catachresis later v. Trypho 3.192 Spengel, ii 3 West, Quint. VIII 6.34−7, Charisius IV 273 Keil, [Plut.] *Vit. Hom.* 18, Silk *Interaction in Poetic Imagery* 210f. If Tzetzes did not find κατάχρησις or καταχρῆσθαι in his source, it would have been familiar as a close cogener of metaphor (cf. Rutherford 209ff.).

(d) *Later writers on metaphor*

For Demetrius (142), metaphor is a χάρις dependent on λέξις, and precedes compounds, unique expressions and coined words (cf. *Poet.* 21.1457b3 μεταφορά, κόσμος, πεποιημένον; Arndt 18 wrongly assigns all these to exallage). Cf. also παραβολή (146), ἀλληγορία (151), proverbs (156); εἰκασίαι (160) and hyperbole (161) depend on πράγματα. Cicero makes a similar distinction (*de Orat.* II 242, 261f.), which may owe something to the existence of *Tract.* VI 2 (q.v.). Cf. also Quint. VI 3.57, 67ff., X 1.12. See further McCall op. cit.

Chapter V 7: The form of the diction

Although there is no doubt that this is an Aristotelian rubric, its meaning is difficult (cf. Else 490).

(i) Discussing apparent enthymemes, A. gives first place to syllogisms that appear to be such because of the manner of their expression, but are not syllogisms at all: these depend on the 'form of the diction' (*Rhet.* II 24.1401a1 − 7). He refers especially to antitheses, which are cited alongside metaphor (cf. III 10.1410b28ff.). Homonyms are listed next; cf. *S.E.* 4, where the last type of verbal sophistry is 'from the form of the diction', while the first is homonymy, as in Ω.

(ii) At *Rhet.* III 8.1408b21, 'the form of the diction must be neither versified nor lacking in rhythm'. This refers to the articulation of units of prose by clausulae.

(iii) *Poet.* 19 links 'the form of the diction' to its performance. Different types of sentences, interrogative, minatory, declarative etc. demand different modes of performance. We need to recognise them to perform them aright, but this pertains to acting, not to poetic criticism; Lucas ad loc. notes that this was especially true in an age without punctuation or stage-directions (1456b9ff.). This is a ripost to carping criticisms of Homer by Protagoras.

(iv) *Poet.* 19 directs us to *S.E.* 4, where the sixth and last fraudulent verbal argument is 'from the form of the diction' (166b10ff.), and consists in obfuscation by the confusion of grammatical categories, of gender, number, transitivity etc., e.g. 'to be healthy' and 'to cut', both of active form in Greek, belong in different categories, one intransitive, the other transitive. At 6.168a24ff. A., using as usual divergent terms, divides verbal sophistries into two groups: homonymy, amphiboly (here λόγος) and this item (here ὁμοιοσχημοσύνη) rest on the need to make a distinction where it is not made by language, the remainder on the blurring of an existent distinction. In 22 he gives further cases of such arguments, named ὁμοίως λεγόμενον· τὸ δὲ λέγεται μὲν οὐχ ὁμοίως, φαίνεται δὲ διὰ τὴν λέξιν (178a23); again he compares homonyms.

The later 'figures of speech', such as antithesis, developed from his remarks in *Rhet.* Cicero (*de Orat.* II 263) lists antithetical expressions (*verba relata contrarie*) as ninth and last of the types of verbal wit, after allegory, metaphor and irony. Demetrius lists third under verbal humour 'graces from the employment of figures' (149 αἱ ἀπὸ τῶν σχημάτων χάριτες), instancing anadiplosis and anaphora. Thus this meaning, though not straightforwardly Aristotelian, has later parallels (the usage of σχῆμα in *Rhet. Al.* is still non-technical, despite Grube *Demetrius* 143, 162).

We have too much choice here, and no guidance from a definition or example, except for the false aid of **a**'s subheadings, which C has under exallage. Meineke and Koster kept them here, thinking of voice and gestures in acting (this sense of σχήματα is known, e.g. *Poet.* 26.1462a3). But in this case φωνή ought to be coordinated with σχήματα, which it is not, and the hypothesis does not explain C's text. But although the subheadings are alien here, parallels in *Poet.* do suggest that the acting is somehow relevant.

Rutherford (445ff.) and his followers, and Fuhrmann 68ff., confine this type to grammar and syntax, as in *S.E.*, and believe that this provides plenty of mirth, in Old Comedy at least (e.g. *Clouds* 669ff.). Yet, as Arndt (12) says, later writers ignore grammatical jokes, whose scope is ludicrously restricted, but cite σχῆμα λέξεως as antithesis and the like. The dilemma is to be resolved thus. In several cases — homonyms, synonyms, adoleschy, paronyms and (?) parody — we have seen the Treatise employ terms in a broader and more popular fashion than did the *Organon*. *S.E.* has a narrow, logical definition relating σχῆμα λέξεως to grammar and syntax, but *Rhet.* and *Poet.* have a broader usage applying to prose style, e.g. in antithesis; is it not likely that the Treatise followed suit? Unfortunately we may never know for certain, but the analogy of the other headings is strong.

Chapter VI 1 – 2: Deception and assimilation

(a) *Text*

The problems are two: (i) why does **a** break off after only two headings? (ii) Which gives the correct order of these headings, **a** or C? These problems are in fact connected.

(i) The abrupt close of **a** was initially attributed to a lazy excerptor, in which case δύο must be either an addition or an alteration of ἐννέα. This seems arbitrary, and Arndt (13) improved on Bernays by remarking a bizarre parallel in Cicero *de Orat.* II. At

240 Cicero distinguishes two kinds of wit, one founded on facts, the other on words ('duo enim sunt genera facetiarum, quorum alterum re tractatur, alterum dicto'). Then he cites *two* types of the former without stating that they are the only two, or indicating that they are given by way of example: 're, si quando quid, tanquam aliqua fabella narratur . . . , sive habeas vere, quod narrare possis, quod tamen est mendaciunculis aspergendum, sive fingas' (240f.). After the true or false anecdote, caricature: 'in re est item ridiculum, quod ex quadam depravata imitatione sumi solet'. At 243 he sums up with the surprising statement that these are the two kinds of jest dependent on facts ('ergo haec duo genera sunt eius ridiculi, quod in re positum est'), and at 244 moves on to the *ridicula in dicto*. Finally, at 264ff., he returns to types of laughter dependent on facts, which are now said to be numerous, beginning with anecdotes, comparisons, caricatures and understatement. I shall show how the two segregated items relate to VI 1—2; there seems no doubt that Cicero's source for some reason introduced them before the rest, and separated them off in some way; but, since they all fell under πράγματα, they are put together in C.

(ii) The order of items differs in our sources. It is easier to believe that C's brief stemmatic headings have been misplaced, than continuous prose in **a**. Cicero sides with **a**, and, as we shall see, Demetrius does likewise; C's order is backed by A., *Rhet.* III 11.1412a18, but this is reversed in his ensuing discussion.

At first glance the reversal of the sub-types of *homoeosis* — 'towards the better' and 'towards the worse' in **a**, reversed in C — seems an irrelevant problem. Bonitz' index shows that A. had no preferred order, e.g. *G.A.* II 1.731b28; but *Poet.* 16.1454b26 and *Top.* III 2, significant parallels both (infra), favour the former sequence. In fact both reversals can be explained at one blow if the epitome originally had these items and sub-entries at a different orientation from the other types, and they were rotated 90° in copying and made uniform with the rest, as shown below. When the headings are written out horizontally, we obtain the text as in C, and the two reversals are explained by a single movement. In C the entries in question are by the margin; if they had for reasons undivined been omitted and placed in the margin, tidying-up with the results we see would be likely. Perhaps this is connected with C's repetition of ἀπὸ τῶν πραγμάτων and ὁ ἐκ τῶν πραγμάτων γέλως. If in the archetype the first two were given under the former heading and the rest under the latter, a scribe might well conclude that they belonged together and add them in the margin. — From this observation I draw two conclusions: that these headings were indeed distinct in the archetypal epitome, just as in **a** and Cicero; and that the stemmatic format was not the creation of the scribe of C, which agrees with other indications about the history of the text.

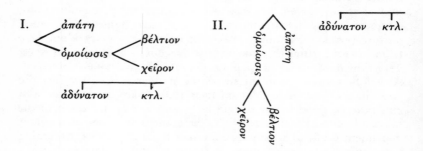

(b) *The meaning of 'pragmata'*

πράγματα has been variously translated as 'things', 'content', 'matter'. The subheadings reveal some features of plot, some of character and one of *dianoia*. When is a joke verbal, and when is it not? Lane Cooper (239): 'if the humour disappears when the joke is translated . . . , we have to do with "laughter from the diction"; if not, then "laughter from the things"': Fuhrmann (69) likewise denied that these kinds possess a greater cohesion. I argued above that they possess the shared characteristic that they exemplify the major qualitative parts of comedy, apart from diction. But the basic point is surely correct: this is a broad category embracing all humour that is not purely verbal, with a division like that in *S.E.* 4.

Now the notion of likeness is fundamental to A.'s teaching on the link between speech and πράγματα. At *de Int.* 1.16a6ff. we are told that words correspond to mental events, and that these are *likenesses* of 'things' (παθήματα τῆς ψυχῆς, καὶ ὧν ταῦτα ὁμοιώματα, πράγματα ἤδη ταῦτά, cf. Rutherford 448). In *S.E.* 1.165a7 we read more simply that we use names as tokens for 'things'. The point is clearest in *Rhet.* III 2, where A. refutes Bryson's sophism that indecent language does not exist, since the same 'thing' is signified whichever term is used; this is untrue, because one term is more closely assimilated ('made more alike') by putting the 'thing' before our eyes (ἔστιν ἄλλο ἄλλου . . . ὡμοιωμένον μᾶλλον . . . τῷ ποιεῖν τὸ πρᾶγμα πρὸ ὀμμάτων, 1405b9ff.). This process of 'making alike', for which the Greek will be ὁμοίωσις, operates upon terms whose impact may be augmented or lessened by the use of transference, epithets or diminutives, as A. hastens to tell us: one can slant a case by denigration or amelioration (ἀπὸ τοῦ βελτίονος, b21ff.). This recalls the Treatise's 'making alike, towards the worse or towards the better'.

At III 11 A. justifies his statement that wit arises from metaphor that operates by analogy and by vividness (τῷ πρὸ ὀμμάτων ποιεῖν, 1411b22). Vividness demands the term that is 'made more alike' to the 'thing', as we have seen; A. continues that transference depends on the recognition of unobvious *likenesses*; he quotes Archytas' equation of lawyers and altars, both the refuge of the wronged (1412a10ff.). Cf. the ubiquitous modern jokes beginning 'What's the difference between p and q?', where p and q turn out to have an unexpected similarity despite their difference.

Here, then, we have parallels to *homoeosis*, and to complete the pattern we need only read on in the *Rhetoric*. Most witticisms arise through metaphor and from the *deception* of expectations, when the mind says, 'so it is, and I missed it' (a17ff.).

Now these parallels are divergent in one important respect; the Treatise is speaking of πράγματα and not λέξις, and this applies to its examples as well. Strepsiades is led to believe the story about the flea; this is deception *on the stage*, not in the minds of the audience, and differs from *our* surprise when our expectations are falsified in *Rhet.* III 11. Again, the 'making alike' is not the discovery of an unexpected relation, as between an anchor and a clothes-hook, in that the objects attached to each hang upwards and downwards respectively: it is a 'making alike' *on stage*, when the slave Xanthias is physically disguised as Heracles, and Dionysus as Xanthias. Thus these two headings represent the translation onto the stage of two fundamental principles of humour which A. expounds in the *Rhetoric* in a verbal context only, as the needs of oratory dictate. False tales and depraved imitations, Cicero's first two kinds of laughter *in re*, are surely the same; a similar pattern reappears in Demetrius, where the five types of χάρις ἐν πράγμασι are proverbs (*de Eloc.* 156), *tales*, whether true or invented (μύθους . . . προσπλάσσομεν προσφόρους καὶ οἰκείους τοῖς πράγμασι, 157), comical errors, mistaking the harmless for the fearsome (159; again a kind of deception?), *comparisons* (εἰκασίαι, 160) and hyperboles (e.g. 'randier than a cucumber' (161 — 2): such ἀδύνατα combine the Tractate's third heading with the the the second, *homoeosis*).

Thus these two items are Aristotelian, but applied to the *stage-actions* of comedy, as they could not be in *Rhet*. This conclusion explains why both Demetrius and Cicero have headings under πράγματα, an unsatisfactory term especially for rhetoric: both mitigate it by noting the excellence of jokes that mix 'diction' and 'action' (*de Eloc.* 133, *de Orat.* II 248). It also shows A.'s attitude to the dichotomy of 'form' and 'content', which played no small part in Hellenistic literary theory: from Philodemus (Περὶ Ποιημάτων V col. ix 25ff. Jensen, cf. IV col. iii Gomperz) we learn that some saw λέξις as the sole source of poetry's attraction, others thought her purely didactic and dependent on content for her worth, Neoptolemus argued for compromise, while Philodemus held that the dichotomy is false (cf. L.P. Wilkinson, *Greece and Rome* 2 (1932 – 3) 144 – 51). Via Horace, the dichotomy has had a wide influence. It is transcended in the *Poetics*, and its formulation here serves only as a heuristic device with which to analyse humour, with none of the dogmatic intentions found elsewhere.

Chapter VI 1: Deception

a's example is from Aristophanes' *Clouds*. The MSS read ψυχῆς, but Strepsiades is not deceived about the soul in our *Clouds*; hence Dindorf's excellent conjecture ψύλλης (the error is easy in minuscule). At *Clouds* 145ff. Strepsiades hears how Socrates measured the distance that a flea could jump by dipping its feet in wax, removing the bootees that formed, and with these measuring the distance from his head to Chaerephon's eyebrow whence it had leapt. Strepsiades exclaims at the ingenuity. Starkie (*Acharnians* lxiii) comments: 'the illustration is not very apt, but it may descend from A., who was not always happy in such matters'.

However, it is just conceivable that Dindorf's conjecture is superfluous, and the reference is to the lost first version of the *Clouds* performed in 424/3 (cf. Dover, *Aristophanes' Clouds* lxxx – xcviii, *Aristophanic Comedy* 105n.). The *Didascaliae* attested the first *Clouds*, and even if A. was not himself responsible for them, we might expect both versions of the play to attract his attention by virtue of their target.

I made clear above the difference between deception here and in *Rhet*. III 11, where the process is in the minds of the audience, not objectified on stage. Rutherford (449) denies that A. could have used the notion as found here, and thinks the compiler has reinterpreted it. However, he trusts C, and this too includes these headings under πράγματα. Contrast Starkie *Acharnians* lxiii, who is followed by Lane Cooper 243f. We need look no further than the *Thesmophoriazusae* to see deceit on a large scale — Euripides' offers of the dancing-girl to the Scythian, and the chorus' frustrations of the latter's efforts to catch her (cf. Fuhrmann 69). — Cooper (loc. cit.) speculates on an overlap with 'the unexpected'. He also refers to an important passage in *Poet.* 24, 1460a19−25, where Homer is praised for his ability to make his characters lie convincingly, by means of the fallacy that if *q* follows *p*, and *q* exists, *p* must exist too. The emphasis on the response of our ψυχή recalls *Rhet.* III 11.1412a20; this type of παραλογισμός is also the fourth kind of sophistical argument from πράγματα in *S.E.* 5. In *Poet.* 24 it appears in a discussion of the illogical and impossible, alongside which we see it here, where the sophistical proof bamboozles characters on stage. — Plebe (22, 29f.) emphasises the importance of ἀπάτη in A.'s theory of humour.

Chapter VI 2: Assimilation or 'making alike'

Bernays emended χρήσει to τμήσει, comparing τέμνεται in **a**. For τέμνειν of logical division cf. *de An.* III 8.431b24, al. But χρήσει and τέμνεται are not mutually exclusive: Ω might have read e.g. ἡ δὲ ὁμοίωσις εἰς δύο τέμνεται, χρήσει ἢ πρὸς τὸ βέλτιον, cf. *Poet.* 16.1454b26 τούτοις χρῆσθαι ἢ βέλτιον ἢ χεῖρον (χρῆσις is frequent in A.). Mr Russell suggests to me that χρήσει might be for χρήσῃ injunctively used as in later rhetorical treatises, but I am not convinced. — ὁμοίωσις, the active verbal noun from ὁμοιοῦν, has as basic meaning 'a making alike', first in Plato, e.g. *Rep.* V 454c, and *de Plantis* II 6.826b34, τοῦ αὐτοῦ εἴδους καὶ τῆς αὐτῆς ὁμοιώσεως. Cf. ὁμοίωμα similarly at *E.N.* VIII 10.1160b22, *Pol.* VIII 5.1340a18, *Rhet.* I 2.1356a31; ὁμοιότης at *Top.* VI 2.140a12, *S.E.* 15.174a38f. Its earliest use as a rhetorical term is in the title of a work ascribed by the *Suda* s.v. to Theramenes of Ceos, but his dating is doubtful (McCall, op. cit. 5ff.). The author of *Rhet. Al.* uses παρομοίωσις (11.1430b20ff.), and McCall's arbitrary emendations on *a priori* grounds to ὁμοίωσις are wisely ignored in Fuhrmann's text. Anaximenes is illustrating types of *gnômai*, among which *paromoeosis* designates remarks where resemblance is discerned in things apparently dissimilar (cf. sup. p.191). A. uses this term at *Rhet.* III 9.1410a24 to cover homoeocatarcton and homoeoteleuton in balanced clauses (cf. Demetrius 25f., Dion. Hal. *Lysias* 14). Note

the sophistication of the terminology then current. Later writers use
homoeosis for 'comparison' in general, cf. Dion. Thrax 19.12;
Philodemus *Rhet.* IV p.177 col. xviii 2ff. Sudhaus; Iulius Rufinianus
22 p.44 Halm; Charisius IV 277 Keil; Rutherford 274). It means
'simile' at [Plut.] *Vit. Hom.* 84, 'imitation' in Plutarch *Mor.* 53c;
ἀφομοίωσις means 'comparison' at 988d.

In our Treatise no technical sense is required: 'resemblance'
suffices. I argued that these types are analogous to those in *Rhet.* III
11 (sup. p.191): a particularly interesting parallel is *Top.* III
2.117b10, where comical comparisons exemplify methods of choice
between items related in order of merit to a third term:

βέλτιον . . . τὸ τῷ βελτίονι αὐτοῦ **ὁμοιότερον**, καθάπερ τὸν
Αἴαντα τοῦ Ὀδυσσέως φασὶ βελτίω τινὲς εἶναι, διότι ὁμοιότερος
τῷ Ἀχιλλεῖ . . . σκοπεῖν δὲ καὶ εἰ **ἐπὶ τὸ γελοιότερον** εἴη
ὅμοιον, καθάπερ ὁ πίθηκος τῷ ἀνθρώπῳ, τοῦ ἵππου μὴ ὄντος
ὁμοίου· οὐ γὰρ κάλλιον ὁ πίθηκος, ὁμοιότερον δὲ τῷ ἀνθρώπῳ.
πάλιν ἐπὶ δυοῖν εἰ τὸ μὲν **τῷ βελτίονι** τὸ δὲ **τῷ χείρονι ὁμοιότερον**, εἴη ἂν βέλτιον τὸ τῷ βελτίονι ὁμοιότερον.

It is important that when A. thinks of items similar but superior or
inferior to each other, his examples are individuals in epic or
tragedy, and comic pairs like men and apes, horses and asses. This
recalls our example from the *Frogs*, with the series Dionysus,
Heracles and Xanthias (man, lion and donkey?), and reinforces
one's confidence that both heading and examples are Aristotelian.
Note the citation of the unheroic Dionysus and Heracles in this
play by Schol. Dion. Thrax XVIIIb3 Koster: εἴ μοι λέγεις, ὅτι καὶ
ἡ κωμῳδία ἡρωϊκὰ ἔχει πρόσωπα . . . , in a possibly Theophrastean context, cf. sup. p.48ff.

The Aristophanic example illustrates the comparison between
comic characters effected by their physical disguise which, as Lane
Cooper shows (239−43), is ubiquitous in comedy; it must not be
thought, however, that disguise is all this heading includes (cf.
Fuhrmann 69). It is extended by Starkie (*Acharnians* lxiiff.) to cover
metaphors, epithets and imagery in general. While we have seen
strong grounds for ascribing metaphor to 'diction', as A. does
consistently, Demetrius lists proverbs (156), comparisons (160) and
hyperbole (161f.) under πράγματα, and we saw parallels in Cicero
de Orat. II 240ff., 266. One suspects therefore that comparisons
more generally were included here (cf. Arndt 13f.). At *Rhet.* III

11.1412b32ff. A. discussed 'images' (εἰκόνες), proverbs and hyperbole, with illustrations from comedy, alongside metaphor. Their separation from metaphor here may help to explain why later writers were reluctant to accept A.'s usual subordination of imagery to metaphor (McCall op. cit. 51). Surely all the Treatise did was to reiterate the general principle of *Rhet.* III 11 and show how it can be applied to stage-actions (πράγματα), before turning to the three remaining major parts of comedy which contribute to those actions; a livelier approach than the later rigid classifications, whose creators, one suspects, elaborated the first two items, but neglected the rest because of their close relation to A.'s literary theory.

Chapter VI 3: The impossible

A. lists τὸ ἀδύνατον in *Poet.* 25 as a problem inherent in the poetic art itself (1460a20). In serious poetry impossibility may be used successfully if it achieves some intended effect such as ἔκπληξις, as in the pursuit of Hector; if carelessly employed, absurdity results: cf. 24.1460a12ff., where the pursuit of Hector is said to be laughable if put on stage, although effective in epic. A. appreciated the comic potentialities of impossibility, and it is in harmony with his theory that it should appear here, especially as in *Poet.* ἀδύνατα are not given under problems inherent in λέξις (1460b11ff.). Cf. also *Rhet.* II 19.

This category reappears in Demetrius' account of frigidity (124), where hyperbole is defined as of three kinds — comparison ('they run like the wind'), making one thing superior to another ('whiter than snow') or stating the impossible ('her head reached the sky'). Comic poets in particular use this figure (126). Cf. 161 on hyperbole, which follows comparison directly; how the two are connected is easily seen (so Cic. *de Orat.* II 267, cf. Quint. VI 3.64 − 7). — Starkie's examples (*Acharnians* lxiv) trespass on adoleschy and the inconsequential. Lane Cooper (244ff.) does much better to stress the violation of the laws of nature, as in the building of Cloudcuckooland or Trygaeus' ascent to heaven. Unfortunately we lose **a** at this point, and the guidance of its examples; but the impossible is a vital resource in Aristophanes, and hardly present in New Comedy.

Chapter VI 4: The possible and inconsequential

A.'s extant works do not contain ἀνακόλουθος, first attested according to LSJ in Epicurus *Ep.* 2 p.41 U., while the noun is at Demetrius 153. Nor does ἀκολουθία at VI 9 occur before Chrysippus *SVF* II 68.31, although A. often uses both ἀκολουθεῖν and ἀκόλουθος of logical sequence. It would hardly have been beyond his wit to have used either form.

The possible and inconsequential is the same as the illogical, or indeed the possible and implausible. This is clear from *Poet.* 24 — 5. At 1460a14ff., referring to serious poetry, A. states that the plausible impossibility is preferable to the implausible possibility; cf. 1461b14ff. That this category too belongs under πράγματα is proved by a digression from ethos at *Poet.* 15.1454a37 — b8; A. enunciates the right circumstances for using the *deus ex machina* (presumably an ἀδύνατον) and warns against illogicality in the events (ἄλογον μηδὲν εἶναι ἐν τοῖς πράγμασιν, b6). It is remarkable that he next recommends that the playwright should make the characters like us but better, the converse of 'making the characters base' in the series in *Poet.* 25 and here. The parallels help to explain the digression, otherwise difficult (e.g. for Else, 464 — 82). His initial reference to defects in characterisation leads naturally to plot, since a character's acts ought to be motivated, if not by considerations of ethos, then by exigencies of plot; this entails a discussion of impossibility and illogicality, as these are strongly associated together in A.'s mind; he then returns to baseness of character whence he set out.

To what extent does this entry contradict the assumption, supported by the reference to comic poets constructing their plots διὰ τῶν εἰκότων at *Poet.* 9.1451b13, that comic poets as much as their tragic counterparts should aim at logical consistency? As Lane Cooper remarks (244f.), minor inconsistencies in comic plots can be humorous, but major ones, if unintended, will harm the play. By analogy with his attitude to epic, we may be sure of A.'s view: the admissibility of inconsistency depends on its effect, i.e. whether it causes laughter; whether an illogicality is major or minor will concern him far less than this.

Demetrius 152f. pairs the unexpected with the inconsequential (ἀνακολουθία); Cicero too links 'sentences that do not hang together' (*discrepantia*) with the unexpected (*praeter exspectationem, de Orat.* II 281 — 5) among the types of laughter *in re*. Perhaps this connexion was made by A. (cf. *Rhet.* III 11.1412a24). Starkie (*Acharnians* lxvff.) and Lane Cooper (247f.) identify the inconsequential with the irrelevant, but the parallels cited above suggest that the latter belongs more with adoleschy, and with the last heading in this series, disjointed arguments.

Chapter VI 5: From the unexpected

A. was no despiser of the unexpected, cf. *Rhet.* III 11, *Poet.* 9.1452a1ff. (on the value of the well-motivated but surprising turn of events in tragedy as generative of pity and fear). The absence of surprise from the poetic problems in *Poet.* 25, or indeed from *Poet.* 15, is readily explained; surprise is not a problem but, rather, an asset unless badly motivated, in which case it falls into the class of the illogical, like Aegeus' timely arrival in Euripides' *Medea* (25.1461b20); cf. Lane Cooper 249, Plebe 28. προσδοκία is an Aristotelian term (*E.N.* III 6.1115a9, al.): Kayser (41f.) traces it elsewhere. Cf. Demetrius 152f., Cic. *de Orat.* II 281ff., Quint. VI 3.84, and Hermogenes sup. p.165. Rutherford (450) shows that the unexpected was not much recognised as a type of humour by Aristophanic commentators, but rather more than was the impossible: they prefer παρὰ τὴν ὑπόνοιαν. — For parallels to the insertion of the unexpected as third item into the series known from *Poet.* 15 and 25, cf. sup. p.176.

Chapter VI 6: Debasing the characters

Prima facie two interpretations are possible, of which only one has been canvassed: (i) 'from making the masks grotesque', (ii) 'from debasing the characters'. This turns on two words, πρόσωπον and μοχθηρός.

πρόσωπον is used of the physical mask at *Poet.* 5.1449a34, cf. *Probl.* 31.7.958a17. Whether it is also used by A. to mean 'characters' in a drama is questionable. At *Poet.* 5.1449b4 it must mean 'masks' primarily, although in the absence of more than one actor, the masks *are* the characters. προσωπεῖον, evolved to distinguish a 'mask' from a 'character', is first in Theophrastus. πρόσωπον as 'dramatic part, character' occurs in Demetrius, *de Eloc.* 130, 134, 195, and is well established in Alexandrian scholarship by 200 B.C. In C this sense occurs in XIV. μοχθηρός is scarcely used of physical appearance, e.g. perhaps Andocides I 100; for the ugliness of comic masks see *Poet.* 5.1449a34.

Parallels in A. support 'debasement'. Comedy is one of the genres which aim to represent men as worse than they really are; this is enunciated in *Poet.* from the start (e.g. 2.1448a16). We are twice told that the tragic hero must suffer calamity not as a result of μοχθηρία but through some error (13.1453a9, 15), and the passage of the μοχθηρός from bad to good fortune is the most untragic outcome of all (1452b35). If the character is wicked in a not unpleasant manner, it is also potentially funny — and laughter is the enemy of tragedy. In 15 A. states that the ἤθη must be χρηστά, and we saw above on VI 4 how this leads into criticism of baseness that is not necessary to the play. Likewise at *Poet.* 25.1461 b19ff. illogicality and nastiness (μοχθηρία) are paired as poetic faults when there is no artistic justification for them: nastiness is resumed under the term βλαβερά (b23). As usual, the dangers that threaten serious poetry are the stuff of comedy, and this entry makes best sense if it completes the series given in *Poet.* 15 and 25, turning from plot to character, after the insertion of the un-expected, which applies to plot. Moreover the phraseology can be exactly paralleled in *Rhet.*: at III 19, A. mentions various *topoi* by which one can present the litigants as good and bad characters (πόθεν σπουδαίους δεῖ **κατασκευάζειν** καὶ φαύλους, 1419b19f.).

Given these parallels it is safe to accept that the meaning is the same here, and thus the entry is related to ethos, like the two which follow, rather than to ὄψις; yet we can be sure that gratuitously base comic characters were given grotesque masks to complement their behaviour, and a tinge of the other meaning may still be present.

In comedy we do not expect the characters to be criminally wicked, but, as Lane Cooper says (250−2), lowered to make them absurd without being objectionable. Most of Aristophanes' char-acters of any standing, whether living, abstract or divine, are thus caricatured — Euripides in the *Thesmophoriazusae*, Demus in the *Acharnians*, Dionysus in the *Frogs* — although the portrait of Cleon goes further towards satire. Even Menander's characters have human failings fully in view, although few of them could be termed μοχθηροί. Although debasement is ubiquitous in Aristophanes, it was little noted by scholiasts (Rutherford 452). Fortenbaugh ('Theophrast über komischen Charakter' 15) argues that this entry's subordinate position indicates a move away from Aristotle's statement that comedy depends on inferior characters, towards Theophrastus' view that it depicts private individuals, and depends less on choice than on continuous character-traits such as are seen in the *Characters*: but VI 8 shows the importance of choice, and Bernays' equation of this passage with *Poet.* 2 is still valid. Caricature is not listed as a χάρις by Demetrius, who points out (163) that the charming is concerned rather with gardens of the nymphs and Cupids, things not meant for laughter, whereas Irus and Thersites are: cf. 167 also, Cicero *de Orat.* II 266.

Chapter VI 7: Vulgar dancing

After headings related to *Rhet.* III 11 and to *Poet.* 15 and 25, we have three different types. Bernays (179) suggested that the entire topic of deportment is meant, but we need to make a further connexion: the heading relates not only to song and spectacle, but also to character, as in the entries preceding and following.

A. does not discuss dancing itself, apart from indicating that dancers imitate ἤθη (*Poet.* 1.1447a27f.); but a man's amusements and pastimes are an important guide to, and influence on, his character (*E.N.* IV 8), and music is strongly formative (*Pol.* VIII 5.1340b8ff.):

(οἱ ῥυθμοί) ἦθος ἔχουσι . . . κινητικόν, καὶ τούτων οἱ μὲν **φορτικωτέρας** ἔχουσι τὰς κινήσεις οἱ δὲ ἐλευθεριωτέρας. ἐκ μὲν οὖν τούτων φανερὸν ὅτι δύναται ποιόν τι τὸ τῆς ψυχῆς **ἦθος** ἡ μουσικὴ παρασκευάζειν.

Vulgar music produces vulgar characters, and vice versa. In *Poet.* 26 tragedy's opponent charges that impersonation in tragedy is vulgar, as witness the wagglings of mediocre flautists at performances. The charge of vulgarity applies to the acting, runs the reply, not to the poetic composition; nor is all movement to be condemned, if all dancing is not to be. This is A.'s position.

As usual, tragic faults are comic virtues. The acceptance of vulgar dancing to characterise vulgar persons is probably a ripost to Plato, *Laws* VII 801b−802d, where both poetry and dancing are to be subject to censorship (cf. Else 22f.), and 815c, where he is concerned about dances portraying drunken nymphs and satyrs (Else 83). At *Rhet.* III 8.1408b36 A. notes that trochaic metre is 'suited to the comic dance' (κορδακικώτερος, cf. *Poet.* 4.1449a22, 24.1460a1). Theophrastus' Desperately Reckless Man (*Char.* 6) dances the cordax sober and without a mask. The Byzantine Treatise on tragedy ascribed to Psellus, which has Peripatetic sources, notes that in tragedy only the chorus, not the actors, danced (11.74: cf. p.238 inf.). — Apart from *Pol.* VIII 5.1340a8ff., this entry is also connected with the preceding by verbal parallels at *Rhet.* III 1.1403b34ff., where μοχθηρία and τὸ φορτικόν are associated.

Chapter VI 8: Poor choice

C reads φαυλοτητα, emended by Bergk. Kaibel further proposed <τὰ> φαυλότατα by haplography, which provides an object, instead of an adverb with the object to be supplied. For the corruption cf. *Rhet.* III 11.1413a29 (Ross). — The shift from a series of ἐκ entries to ὅταν is paralleled in the long series of *topoi* in *Rhet.* II 23.

Does τῶν ἐξουσίαν ἐχόντων mean 'those in power' or 'those in whose power it is' to choose? The latter is the original meaning of ἐξουσία (cf. *E.N.* VIII 14.1163b22, al.), but the former is already in A. (e.g. *E.N.* I 5.1095b21). The phrase has no exact parallel in the corpus, but is current in the fourth century, e.g. Xen. *Mem.* II 6.24 ἐξουσίαν ἔχωσι κλέπτειν, Dem. 18.428.17; A.'s frequent usage of ἐξουσία to mean 'possibility' with other verbs supports the second interpretation, e.g. τοῖς μὲν ἐξουσία τυγχάνειν (*Pol.* VII 13.1331b40). So Bernays (181), Starkie (*Acharnians* lxxi) and Lane Cooper (255ff.): contrast Russell's rendering, 'when someone who has power passes over great prizes and receives a small reward' (205). A. is not referring to anti-authoritarian elements in comedy.

Mistaken choice is well illustrated by Starkie, e.g. Dionysus' intention to bring back Euripides from the dead, when he could have Sophocles instead (*Frogs* 76f.). This reveals character; like vulgar dancing, it concurs with the general debasement of ethos predicated to comedy by A. On how προαίρεσις reveals ethos, cf. *E.N.* III 2, especially 1112a1ff. (τῷ προαιρεῖσθαι τἀγαθὰ ἢ τὰ κακὰ ποιοί τινές ἐσμεν . . . καὶ προαιρούμεθα μὲν λαβεῖν ἢ φυγεῖν τι: this also illustrates the use of λαμβάνειν); choice is between possibles (προαίρεσις οὐκ ἔστιν τῶν ἀδυνάτων, 1111b20, cf. III 3.1113a11): compare the stress on possibility here. Conversely, character reveals choice (ἔστιν ἦθος τὸ τοιοῦτον ὃ δηλοῖ τὴν προαίρεσιν, *Poet.* 6.1450b8, cf. *Rhet.* II 21.1395b13). For the connexion of φαῦλος and μοχθηρός cf. e.g. *E.N.* X 5.1175b28.

Chapter VI 9: Disjointed logic

ἀσυνάρτητος is first in Dion. Hal. *Thuc.* 6, but A. does use συναρτᾶν and συνάρτησις, and the similar negative compounds ἀσύναπτος, ἀσύνδετος. For συναρτᾶν in a logical context v. *Part. An.* I 1.640a6 (the use in Stoic logic is not relevant). On ἀκολουθία v. on VI 4; for the phrasing cf. *Rhet.* I 13.1373b8 κἂν μηδεμία κοινωνία πρὸς ἀλλήλους ᾖ, and Epicurus *Nat.* 14.9 ὁ μηθὲν ἀκόλουθον συναρτῶν.

Lane Cooper (257, cf. 49ff., 62n.) points out that A. uses λόγος to refer to units as disparate as a single sentence and a complete epic. Here it must refer to a speech in a play at the maximum: violation of the laws of causality in the plot as a whole is surely covered by the 'possible and inconsequential'. Starkie (*Acharnians* lxxiv) considers parody under this head, which possesses no justification at all, except the perceived lack of this type in the classification; he has led Lane Cooper astray (259). Bernays (182f., with Rutherford 453, Fuhrmann 70, Russell 205) takes the most straightforward view, that incoherent speeches are meant, where the diction diverges from the norm neither in word-form nor word-choice, but the logic is absurd.

This entry exemplifies how *dianoia* can be exploited for comic purposes. Note how *dianoia* is defined in relation to λόγος at *Poet.* 19.1456a36, ἔστι κατὰ τὴν διάνοιαν ταῦτα, ὅσα ὑπὸ τοῦ λόγου δεῖ παρασκευασθῆναι. In this chapter A. reminds us that emotional effects may at times need rhetoric (λόγος) to bring them about (1456b2−8): cf. 15.1454a18. If an example is needed, cf. *Phys.* II 6.197b27, Demetrius 153, quoting a speech in Sophron.

Chapter VII: Comedy and abuse

(a) *Expression*

λοιδορία is found in A. (*Rhet.* III 2.1405b32, cf. *Phgn.* 4.808b37, *E.N.* IV 8.1128a30). He twice uses ψόγος of abuse as a literary form (*Poet.* 4.1448b27, 37, cf. *Rhet.* I 9.1367a34, 1368a34); but the divergence is trivial, cf. *E.N.* loc. cit. ἀπαρακαλύπτως is already in Plato, e.g. *Rep.* VII 538c συνόντα αὐτοῖς ἀπαρακαλύπτως, but happens not to occur in A. For the phrase cf. Antiphanes fr. 167, παρακάλυμμα τῶν κακῶν, of wealth. With τὰ προσόντα κακά cf. Plato *Menex.* 234c, Dem. 18.276, both of personal attributes, *Rhet. Al.*

2.1422a5: Bonitz cites no example in A. διεξιέναι is frequent, e.g. *Poet.* 4.1449a31; for an interesting parallel in *Rhet. Al.* 35, v. inf. With δεῖται governed by an abstraction cf. *Poet.* 5.1449b12, a sentence of similar structure; for the verb cf. 14.1453b8.

ἔμφασις, however, has aroused comment. Certainly it does not mean 'emphasis' in the modern sense, despite Feibleman *In Praise of Comedy* 83. A. uses it to mean only 'reflection', as of mirrors (*Meteor.* I 8.345b15ff.), and 'appearance, impression' in dreams (*Div. Somn.* 464b11f., cf. Chrysippus *SVF* II 24.20 von Arnim). There is a natural development from 'appearance, suggestion' to the sense 'innuendo' here. Bernays (149) thinks it a term used by late oratorical handbooks, although otherwise the wording is not unaristotelian (cf. Grube 147). Tiberius in the Augustan era defined ἔμφασις as ὅταν μὴ αὐτό τις λέγῃ τὸ πρᾶγμα, ἀλλὰ δι' ἑτέρων ἐμφαίνῃ (Spengel 3.65): Trypho (ibid. 199) says ἔμφασίς ἐστι λέξις δι' ὑπονοίας αὐξάνουσα τὸ δηλούμενον; cf. [Plut.] *Vit. Hom.* 26, *Auct. Herenn.* IV 54.67, Quint. VIII 3.83ff., IX 2.3, 64f. (where cf. Demetrius 291). Thus orators speak with emphasis when their words convey more than one meaning. These senses of ἔμφασις are frequent in Demetrius, despite Grube *Demetrius* 137f., e.g. 171 ἔστι τοῦ ἤθους τις ἔμφασις ἐκ τῶν γελοίων 'there is some indication of a man's character in his jokes', 287 μετὰ ἐμφάσεως ἀγεννοῦς 'with an insinuation'; 288 makes the important point, very close to the tenor here, that λοιδορία can be softened by ἔμφασις, which can hardly mean 'clear expression' as Grube would have it. Demetrius cites Plato's tacit reproach to those absent at Socrates' death, which is conveyed simply by Phaedo's saying 'they were in Aegina'; this is more effective than any direct λοιδορία. In 289 the writer tells how Demetrius of Phalerum dealt likewise with the arrogance of Craterus: cf. also 291. The date of the *On Style*, later than A. if by only a half century, precludes a decision as to whether the latter could have used the term in this way: as will appear, on the one occasion when he refers to innuendo, he speaks of ὑπόνοια, and so does Theophrastus (v. p.210). Yet A. himself was the first to use ἐμφαίνεσθαι in the sense 'to be implied', according to LSJ s.v. II 3 (e.g. at *Rhet.* II 21.1394b20f.), and the idea in this section was already current in his day: at *Rhet. Al.* 35.1441b15ff. Anaximenes urges that you retail in sequence the life of the man to be abused, rather than mock him; not only are σκώμματα best avoided in favour of exposition, but unpleasant topics should be referred to obliquely — δεῖ μὴ σκώπτειν ὃν ἂν κακολογῶμεν, ἀλλὰ **διεξιέναι** τὸν βίον αὐτοῦ . . . Cf. also Philochorus, fr. 170 Jacoby (ap. Ath. II

37e): men in their cups not only hint at their own natures, but reveal openly those of others as they talk freely (ἐμφανίζουσιν . . . ἀνακαλύπτουσιν).

One straw in the wind points to A. here. I remarked above on the use of ἔμφασις for 'appearance' in his *Div. Somn.* 2: another term there recurs in his remarks on comedy, viz. διεστραμμένον (of the distorted comic mask at *Poet.* 5.1449a36), when he notes the need for a good dream-interpreter to recognise distorted forms of familiar items:

δεινὸς δὴ τὰς ἐμφάσεις κρίνειν εἴη ἂν ὁ δυνάμενος ταχὺ δι-
αισθάνεσθαι καὶ συνορᾶν τὰ διαπεφορημένα καὶ διεστραμμένα
τῶν εἰδώλων, ὅτι ἐστὶν ἀνθρώπου ἢ ἵππου ἢ ὁτουδήποτε

(464b12ff.). διεστραμμένον recurs at *de Insomn.* 3.461a16; 'horrible visions', ὄψεις τερατώδεις, at a22, cf. *Poet.* 14.1453b7ff. on the horrible through ὄψις (cf. *Vit. Aesch.* 7 Wilamowitz). Parallels between *Poet.* and A.'s remarks on dreams and their interpretation extend also to the importance of discerning likenesses (cf. *Poet.* 22.1459a7) or the reference to manic and melancholic types (cf. 17.1455a33): this topic merits further investigation. If *emphasis* originally meant 'appearances' in dreams, its application to comedy is best understood as 'fantasy' and fills a gap in the Treatise that has long been felt. The comic presentation of reality is in this case distorted, to use A.'s analogy, like a reflection in water disturbed by the breeze, and not given directly. See further Schofield, 'A. on the Imagination'.

Whether ἔμφασις has these connotations or not, its main sense is certainly 'innuendo', and τῆς καλουμένης implies that it is a known term. For the later sense related to ἐνάργεια, e.g. in the Homeric scholia, v. Richardson *CQ* 30 (1980) 277 n.43: add schol. *B* 670, *Σ* 207.

(b) *Parallels in Aristotle*

Bernays (loc. cit.) drew attention to *E.N.* IV 8.1128a20, where A. illustrates the difference between educated and base humour by contrasting the recent comedy with the old, which used direct abuse and not innuendo:

ἡ τοῦ ἐλευθερίου παιδιὰ διαφέρει τῆς τοῦ ἀνδραποδώδους καὶ αὖ
τοῦ πεπαιδευμένου καὶ ἀπαιδεύτου. ἴδοι δ' ἄν τις καὶ ἐκ τῶν
κωμῳδιῶν τῶν παλαιῶν καὶ τῶν καινῶν· τοῖς μὲν γὰρ ἦν

γελοῖον ἡ **αἰσχρολογία**, τοῖς δὲ μᾶλλον ἡ **ὑπόνοια· διαφέρει δ'**
οὐ μικρὸν ταῦτα πρὸς εὐσχημοσύνην.

On this one occasion when he refers to 'innuendo' he employs a
different term for it, not ἔμφασις (if the latter does not mean
'fantasy'); but surely we know by now that his terminology
fluctuates, and that our evidence for the use of literary terms at this
period is so patchy as to render perilous such statements as 'A.
could not have used this term' (Grube 147).

A more important difference between this sentence and *E.N.* IV
8 is that there A. is making distinctions *within* comedy (cf.
Tractatus XVIII), whereas here the essential nature of comedy
itself is in question. This appears to bring to light a contradiction
(cf. Starkie *Acharnians* xxxix); does comedy admit direct abuse
(λοιδορία, αἰσχρολογία) or does it not? Such a contradiction was
thought by Plebe (10ff.) to be basic to A.'s view, but it is a false
dichotomy, to resolve which we need only adduce the account of
comedy's development in *Poet.* 5, especially 1449b7 (Κράτης πρῶτος
ἦρξεν ἀφέμενος τῆς ἰαμβικῆς ἰδέας ποιεῖν λόγους καὶ μύθους). Like
tragedy (1449a14ff.), comedy for A. developed *towards its essence* (for
parallels in eristic, cf. *S.E.* 34.187b17ff.); essentially comedy differs
from the lampoon in that it is a mimetic form according to A.'s
sense of *mimesis*, describing οἷα ἂν γένοιτο rather than γενόμενα,
fiction rather than fact. The contrast is clearly drawn in *Poet.* 9
between comedy's use of randomly chosen names and iambus'
attacks on known individuals. That the contradiction is unreal is
remarked by Baumgart (68off.), who suggested that ἔμφασις
denoted part of the mimetic process, by which direct insults are
modified into indirect comment of more general significance and
acceptable form: cf. Lane Cooper 259f.

For A.'s opposition to λοιδορία or αἰσχρολογία see not only *E.N.*
IV 8, but also *Pol.* VII 7.1336b3 – 23, where he urges the lawgiver
to ban αἰσχρολογία from the state, especially in the case of the
young, who should not witness comedy or iambus until they are of
a proper age. This is an advance on Plato's attitude in the *Republic*
in that comedy *is* admitted into the state, but close to *Laws* XI
935 – 6, where comic or iambic poets are forbidden to ridicule any
particular citizen, and humorous verse is permitted only under
censorship; cf. *Phileb.* 49e, Fortenbaugh *A. on Emotion* 20f..

(c) *Aristotle's redefinition of comedy against Plato*

Chapter VII makes an important point in the reply to Plato's indictment of comedy; A.'s vision of comedy's teleological development towards its essence, combined with the observed evolution of comedy in his own time, enable him to dissociate it from the personal abuse in which it originated, and by which its repute was for Plato tarnished. (The evolution of comedy from an excess of some kind is recognised by *Tract.* XVIII, as well as *E.N.* IV 8.) Such dissociation is intimately connected with the classification of comedy as a mimetic art, for mimetic art in A.'s theory is quite different in essence from the direct representation of historically existent persons or events, although the two may coincide under certain conditions. Thus the definition of comedy as essentially exclusive of abuse is integral to Aristotelian theory, and could have been predicted for it. In fact I find that was predicted by Else (188; cf. Fortenbaugh's important remarks, loc. cit.):

'Personal abuse was as repugnant to A. as it had been to Plato. The new thing we see in him is not a change of attitude towards ἰαμβισμός, but *a new conviction that "comedy" should be defined to exclude it* . . . [He] . . . was able to see the triumph of the "true" (i.e. non-iambic) idea of comedy as a historical process spreading over centuries, from Homer to his own day. Thus the ψόγοι are not merely the worst variety but the earliest stage.'

As is the horrible to the tragic (*Poet.* 14.1453b9), so is the abusive to the comic; true comedy, for A., must be distanced from the object of its derision by the generalising process crucial to all mimetic poetry. Cf. Bernays 148ff., Lane Cooper 259f., Grube 142.

If the above interpretation is correct, what are the implications for A.'s view of what we traditionally call the 'Old' Comedy of *Eupolis atque Cratinus Aristophanesque poetae*? Did he share Plutarch's disdain for Aristophanes as vulgar and crude?

Else (311) perceives Aristophanes as very much an 'iambist', especially in early plays such as the *Knights*. It follows that these plays are neither comedies nor mimetic, i.e. not poetry at all in the strict sense. However, we have rather little with which to compare them, and must be careful not to be influenced by modern standards of what constitutes slanderous abuse. As Lane Cooper (260) remarks, the indirect method of abuse is not foreign to Old Comedy: even in the *Knights* Aristophanes names his target, Cleon, once only, and that at 976; Athenian over-ambitiousness and love of speculation are censured only indirectly in the *Birds*; and Tzetzes

(*Prol.* XIa1.69ff. Koster) cites *Wasps* 16 as an example of indirect humour. This is corroborated by the hypothesis to Cratinus' *Dionysalexandros*, which tells us that Pericles is there mocked δι' ἐμφάσεως (*P.Oxy.* 663 fin.). Although Lane Cooper's arguments that A. admired and valued Aristophanes are weak for lack of evidence, Else's contrary belief (105) leads him to suggest that A.'s reference to Homer, Sophocles and Aristophanes together, surely as the three ἄκροι of their respective genres (*Poet.* 3.1448a27f.), either is interpolated, or gives the comedian as a representative of the 'iambic' kind of comedy, of which A. disapproved; this is most unpersuasive (cf. Fuhrmann 54f.). Apart from this passage, there is simply no firm evidence; to say that Aristophanes 'cannot have held any key position in [A.'s] theory of "comedy", since he is not identified with any significant major step in either its introduction or its ultimate triumph' (Else 311) is absurd, as Euripides is unmentioned in the account of tragedy's evolution, but plays a major rôle in the *Poetics*. The teaching of this chapter does not contradict the evidence of V—VI that Aristophanes was very important in A.'s theory of comedy.

Although he echoes the standard view that A. was uninterested in Old Comedy or repudiated it as vulgar, Whitman (*ACH* 2ff.) found the distinction between ψόγος and τὸ γελοῖον vital to an understanding of Aristophanes, who, he argues, relies but little on the former (op. cit. 36, 268). I suggest below that Aristophanes actually constituted a mean for A., between excessive buffoonery and plays that had become rather tame or serious (v. on XVIII).

(d) *Alcibiades and Tzetzes*

Else (313f.) cogently argues that the reason why Alcibiades is given in *Poet.* 9 as the example of a historical individual is because he was a favourite butt of Old Comedy, which A. is censuring as in this instance too 'iambic'. The name of Alcibiades is associated with a bizarre tradition that he had a law passed curtailing direct abuse, and this began the 'Middle' Comedy: he was so offended at Eupolis' *Baptae* that he either drowned the poet in the sea or gave him a good ducking, reciting his verses derisively as he did so, and had a law passed that comedy should henceforth attack individuals only through innuendo (schol. Aristid. III 444 Dindorf = XXb Koster, Platonius I 16ff. Koster, Tzetzes *Prol.* XIaI 70, 87ff. Koster: cf. Cicero *ad Att.* VI 1.18, whence we learn that Eratosthenes proved this story of Eupolis' death chronologically impossible). It is a curious coincidence remarked by Kaibel (*Abh.* 56) that in Tzetzes this tale is linked with λοιδορία ἀπαρακάλυπτος, the mark of the first stage of comedy, as against veiled abuse. (His other formulations are σκῶμμα ἀπαρακάλυπτον, and τὸ ἀπαρακαλύπτως κωμῳδεῖν). After the law was passed, comedy was veiled and not direct in its abuse of citizens (κωμῳδεῖν ἐσχηματισμένως καὶ μὴ προδήλως), and this was practised by Eupolis, Cratinus, Pherecrates, Plato comicus and Aristophanes — by the poets of what we call 'Old' Comedy, in fact. The verbal parallel between Tzetzes and C is interesting, but the relationship is surely indirect. Economy of hypotheses might suggest that Tzetzes acquired this phrase from the same source as the classification of humour in his *Iambi* (Περὶ Κωμ. 76ff.), especially as it comes from the same part of the Tractatus, but this cannot be proved: the only similar passage in the *Iambi* is more remote (sup. p.163). There is a further parallel in his *Schol. in Exeg. Iliad.* p.29.3 Hermann (= XXIIa2.7ff. Koster), where writers of lampoons are known by abusing ἀνεπικαλύπτως: unnoticed links between other parts of this passage and Schol. Dion. Thrax 449.5ff. Hilgard may suggest its source. This is compatible with his statement in his scholia on his *de Diff. Poet.* 113 (Koster XXIa) that comic laughter is mixed with abuse only if he means 'veiled abuse'.

(e) *Later writers*

Aristotelian ideas of comedy and innuendo have considerable influence later. Demetrius' use of the term *emphasis* is illustrated above; at 292 he notes that innuendo is a valuable resource in criticising potentates for their faults (ἁμαρτήματα). Powerful populaces too need this mode of address, such as the Athenians with their flatterers Cleon and Cleophon (294). Flattery is shameful, open censure hazardous; the covert hint is the middle course, and the best. The sequence of thought is the same here (v. inf. on VIII). We shall see that he is aware of the standard Peripatetic distinction between σκῶμμα and λοιδορία also. Cicero (*de Orat.* II 236) defines the main, if not the sole, kind of humour as remarks which point out something unseemly in a manner that is not itself unseemly ('haec ridentur vel sola, vel maxime, quae notant et designant turpitudinem aliquam non turpiter'). But this is a slight touch, and innuendo is listed at 278ff. only as one means of raising a laugh in court. Cicero's needs were at variance with those of a treatise on comedy.

Horace is much concerned with comedy and abuse in *Serm.* I 4, where he playfully traces Lucilius' satiric lineage to Old Comedy,

and in his own satires' defence ironically asks whether comedy itself
is poetry at all — it is not enough to write in verse (40f.). Comedy
is little removed from everyday speech; and thus he slips into
discussing a situation typical of New Comedy, comically leaving
the poetic status even of comedy itself in limbo. For this he shares a
source, possibly Theophrastus, with Cicero *Orator* 20.67 (cf.
Ardizzoni *ΠΟΙΗΜΑ* 69 – 78). His jesting with Peripatetic literary
criticism can best be appreciated against this background. In the
development of his satire away from Lucilius, as in that of
Callimachus' *Iambi* away from Hipponax, A.'s theory of how
comedy evolved is seen in action (cf. Plebe 61ff. on Callimachus,
also 81 – 112 for attitudes to comedy and invective during the
Roman Empire).

Chapter VIII: Error in comedy

(a) *The nature of comic error in Aristotle*

This chapter, with the last, represents the division of the sources of
laughter into people, as well as words and actions, enunciated at
Rhet. I 11.1371b35f. Furthermore, at *Poet.* 5.1449a34 A. defined the
absurd as some 'fault' ('error') or blemish which is not painful or
destructive (τὸ γελοῖόν ἐστιν **ἁμάρτημά** τι καὶ αἶσχος ἀνώδυνον καὶ
οὐ φθαρτικόν); that comedians are concerned with such errors is
confirmed by *Rhet.* II 6.1384b9 – 11: οἷς ἡ διατριβὴ ἐπὶ ταῖς τῶν
πέλας **ἁμαρτίαις**, οἷον χλευασταῖς καὶ κωμῳδοποιοῖς: note the
equivalence of ἁμαρτία here and ἁμάρτημα in *Poet.* 5. On *hamartia* in
general v. S. Saîd, *La Faute tragique* 9 – 36; J.M. Bremer, *Hamartia*;
T.C.W. Stinton *CQ* 25 (1975) 221 – 54; J. Moles *CQ* 29 (1979)
77 – 94; R. Sorabji, *Necessity, Cause and Blame* 295 – 8.

Here we find expressly stated for the first time that the errors of
comedy are those of body and soul, a new detail owed to C. The
bodily blemish was already implied, however, in the distorted
comic mask which A. cites as an example of τὸ γελοῖον at *Poet.*
5.1449a36, and in the joke about white hair, a physical defect but a
mild one, endorsed by him at *G.A.* V 4.784b19. Cf. also *Rhet.* III
11.1413a13, 15.1416a14.

As Else (189) perceived, comic error is the counterpart of tragic
error in A.'s thinking. It appears in the equivalent position in the
Treatise, namely the section on how comedy achieves its ἔργον,
laughter, but late in the discussion, just as tragic error does not

appear until *Poet.* 13. But the two ἁμαρτίαι are distinct in nature. Tragic error brings suffering (πρᾶξις φθαρτικὴ ἢ ὀδυνηρά, 11.1452b11), but comic error is free of any suggestion of pain or destruction. The two are as different in use and scale as the coherent plot of tragedy and continuous laughter of comedy to which each contributes. Comic error is inevitably less important to the plot as a whole, simply because its consequences are less far-reaching, until New Comedy at least, where error is basic to the plot: cf. Salingar 84f.

Pack (*CP* 33, 1938) suggested that tragic and comic error are in another respect less close than might be expected; his conclusions are based on the acknowledged work of A. and he eschews the Tractate. In *Rhet.* I 13 and *E.N.* V 8 three classes of harmful acts are defined according to their shared characteristics as follows:

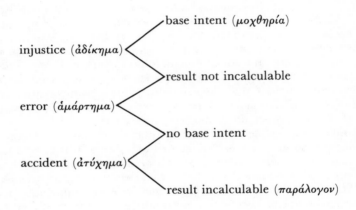

base intent (μοχθηρία)

injustice (ἀδίκημα)

result not incalculable

error (ἁμάρτημα)

no base intent

accident (ἀτύχημα)

result incalculable (παράλογον)

ἁμαρτήματα are here cast as a mean, and this view of 'error' has seemed to many to accord with *Poet.* 13 on the nature of the proper tragic plot well enough, although, as Stinton has shown, wider senses cannot be ruled out. But an ugly face or mask such as amuses in *Poet.* 5 is, as a physical blemish, an ἀτύχημα for which its possessor is not responsible, while faults of mind can in theory at least comprise faulty general principles as much as faults in reasoning about particulars, and faulty principles amount to baseness, μοχθηρία, some kinds of which are most germane to comedy. Thus comic 'error' might seem wider than the tragic type in that it admits mockery of physical blemishes, strictly misfortunes, and mental errors, including misdemeanours, which are excluded from the *hamartia* of tragedy. But recently Sorabji (loc. cit.), basing himself on *E.N.* V 8.1135b12, where ἁμάρτημα is used generically of the whole class of accidents and mistakes, and on the usage of *Poet.* 13, has made a strong case that tragic *hamartia* no less than its comic equivalent includes accidents as well as mistakes: on the method of diaeresis in *E.N.* V 8 cf. p.124f. Thus C's usage is exactly right. This use of 'faults' excludes the hypothesis that A. made mental errors or failures of knowledge (ἄγνοια) the basis for his interpretation of comedy (Tierney 243ff., H.W. Prescott ap. *CP* 24 (1929) 32−41): with Aristophanes in mind, he had to adopt a wider view.

(b) *Mockery in Aristotle and Theophrastus*

A. uses σκώπτειν and σκῶμμα of comic poets on several occasions (*Rhet.* III 2.1405b30 of Aristophanes; *de Sensu* 5.443b30 of Strattis; *E.N.* VII 10.1152a22 of Anaxandrides). At *E.N.* IV 8 he discusses mockery in greater detail. He censures the buffoon, who disregards people's feelings in his attempts to raise laughter, rather than speak with propriety and not grieve the object of his mockery (1128a7). The humorist ought to be prepared to put up with the same treatment himself; and there should be legal limits, as the σκῶμμα is a kind of λοιδόρημα (abuse, slander), but the civilised man can set himself proper limits anyway. As well as the insistence on the painlessness of comic laughter, notice its uneasy relation to λοιδορία; so too are these juxtaposed in adjacent Chapters of C.

An important fragment of Theophrastus (ap. Plutarch *Mor.* 631e: not in Wimmer) supplies both a definition of the σκῶμμα and the missing connexion between comic error and innuendo: 'a joke, as Theophrastus says, is concealed criticism of an error; hence from his own mind the hearer supplies to the innuendo what is missing, as one who knows and believes it'. The second sentence is probably Theophrastus rather than Plutarch: current translations are inaccurate: the Greek runs [ὀνειδι]σμὸς γάρ ἐστιν [τῆς] ἁμαρτίας παρε[σχηματισμένος τὸ] σκῶμμα κατὰ τὸν Θεόφραστον· ὅθεν ἐξ αὐτοῦ τῇ ὑπονοίᾳ προστίθησιν ὁ ἀκούσας τὸ ἐλλεῖπον ὡς εἰδὼς καὶ πιστεύων. The story that follows about Theocritus of Chios, executed by Antigonus I (633c), may also derive from Theophrastus' Περὶ Γελοίου. Just before, Plutarch noted that we are more liable to be offended by the jokes of clever men than of fools, because 'in the case of the clever man we know that cunning is compounded with his offensiveness — indeed his joke seems to be deliberate abuse purposely delivered' (631d trans. Clement —

[δοκεῖ γὰρ] τὸ σκῶμμα λοιδόρημα δε[δογμένον] εἶναι). Plutarch also gives advice of a Peripatetic tint on restraint in humour and avoidance of obscenity in polite conversation (imitated by Macrobius *Sat.* VII 2f.: cf. also Philodemus *Rhet.* IV p.173.25 Sudhaus). See Arndt 23−4, K. Mittelhaus *de Plut. praec. ger. reip.* 48ff.

Demetrius echoes some of these distinctions: at 128 (cf. 168) he distinguishes two kinds of χάρις, the loftier and more dignified, and the more commonplace and comical, resembling banter: αἱ μέν εἰσι μείζονες καὶ σεμνότεραι, αἱ τῶν ποιητῶν, αἱ δὲ εὐτελεῖς μᾶλλον καὶ **κωμικώτεραι, σκώμμασιν** ἐοικυῖαι. At 172 he suggests that the σκῶμμα is a sort of comparison, and gives the examples 'Egyptian clematis' for a tall and swarthy person, or 'a sheep at sea' for a fool on the water (note the criticism of personal appearance and conduct here). But if jokes go further than this, they are to be avoided as we would avoid abuse (εἰ δὲ μή, φευξόμεθα τὰ σκώμματα ὥσπερ λοιδορίας). He implies that, as A. thought, the σκῶμμα shades into the insult. Lastly, as mentioned on VII, innuendo is deemed useful in admonishing the ἁμαρτήματα of others (292ff.), while avoiding insult; this recalls both Theophrastus' definition and the juxtaposition of ideas in C: if the epitomator has not omitted an explicit statement of the link between VII and VIII, these Peripatetics do no more than spell out a definite implication of these sections. Platonius (II 14ff. Koster) remarks that Aristophanes was particularly successful at admonishing the ἁμαρτάνοντες while preserving a mean. Cicero (*de Orat.* II 236) defines the matter of humour as blemishes, whether of behaviour or physique; but good taste and moderation must be observed, to avoid buffoonery. Cf. Quint. VI 3.28f., 37 (from Cicero).

Chapter IX: The aims of tragedy and comedy

On the place of this chapter on catharsis in the structure of the whole, v. sup. p.58; for its doctrine see on III, especially p.144f. On the exact range of feelings that constitute the tragic emotions, and the use of τοῦ γελοίου alone without τοῦ ἡδέος, cf. sup. p.16of. Baumgart 685f. retained σύμμετρα and made A. the subject of θέλει, but cf. sup. p.137. on θέλει ἔχειν in III. This would also require συμμετρίαν.

Either here or in III would be the only logical place to fit *Poet.* fr. VI Kassel, were it genuine. Fr. VI is however to be rejected, because it makes a purely philosophical point about the nature of

212 Part VI: Commentary

the final cause — that it is in fact twofold, as it operates both for
the end and for the benefit of any affected by the attainment of the
end (on the doctrine, cf. A. Gräser, *MH* 29 (1972) 44−61). A.'s
general avoidance of explicit use of the categories and causes in
Poet., and the fact that Philoponus' reference in the same context to
the *De Gen.* is certainly erroneous, suggest that the Neoplatonist
may merely be misquoting the *Physics*, cf. p.116 n.70. However,
there is no reason why A. should not have believed this about
poetry also, provided that he did relate the final cause of drama to
catharsis; after all, one of the most widely held modern objections
to his theory is that it seems to posit that art exists for a higher end,
rather than for its own sake. By considering this doctrine, we can
discern his answer. The final cause of tragedy is twofold; first, the
plot, and secondly, the enjoyment of the audience, who derive
catharsis from the plot, and from catharsis benefit by obtaining
pleasurable relief (*Pol.* VIII 7.1342a14). Plot is identified as the
end of tragedy at *Poet.* 6.1450a23 (ὁ μῦθος τέλος τῆς τραγῳδίας; cf.
the important remarks of Hubbard ad loc.), and the same is said of
comedy at *Rhet.* III 14.1415a11ff., where A. says that prologues in
drama and prooemia in epic are needed to indicate what the piece
is about so that the audience is not left in suspense. He sums up:
'the most necessary and indeed unique function of the proem is to
make clear what is *the end for the sake of which* the piece is composed'
(τὸ ἔργον τοῦ προοιμίου . . . δηλῶσαι τί ἐστιν τὸ τέλος οὗ ἕνεκα ὁ
λόγος, a21f.). Clearly the final cause does apply to literature.

Thus, I argue, A. held that a piece of literary art exists for two
purposes: first, as an end in itself, considered in relation to other
complex and composite creations whose end is the form each finally
attains; and second, in relation to the audience. The score of a
symphony mouldering in a cupboard has attained one of its ends,
namely the complex form intended by its composer; but it does not
fulfil the other, namely its effect on the audience, until it is
performed. Cf. A.'s remark that tragedy has its potentiality
(δύναμις) even without performance (*Poet.* 6.1450b18). The one is
the cause 'for the sake of which', οὗ ἕνεκα; the other is that 'for
which', ᾧ.

Chapters X−XVI: The qualitative parts of comedy

On the position and function of this section in the whole cf. sup.
p.60. The entries it contains display the mixture of descriptive and
prescriptive comments familiar from *Poet.* I. Whether they were

accorded similar weightings and amounts of discussion cannot be known on general grounds. As Fuhrmann (66) notes, C is our only source for qualitative parts of comedy. Bernays (154, cf. McMahon 34) thought that the whole section was inserted by the excerptor following vague hints in A., e.g. *Poet.* 24.1459b10, where epic has the same four main parts as tragedy: but in any case comedy must have had the same six parts, as these depend on the manner, medium and object of *mimesis* (6.1450a10f.).

The qualitative parts do not always recur in the order given here. In *Poet.* they are treated in the sequence plot (13—14), character (15), thought (19) and diction (22), but when introduced at 6.1449b31ff. the series is reversed in order of ascending importance to give spectacle, song, diction, character, thought and plot; other orderings occur elsewhere, as tabulated below:

Poet. 13—22		P	C	T	D		
Tract. V—VI	D	P	C	T			
Tract. X		P	C	T	D	So	Sp
Tract. XVI		P	[T	C]	D	So	[Sp]
Poet. 6.1449b31		P	T	C	D	So	Sp
Poet. 6.1450a9		P	C	D	T	Sp	So
Poet. 6.1450a13	Sp	C	P		D	So	T

Key: P(lot), C(haracter), T(hought),
D(iction), So(ng), Sp(ectacle).

The entries occur in sequence from left to right, except for those at *Tract.* XVI (given in two groups of three, of which the latter is in square brackets) and *Poet.* 1449b31 (reversed). The spacings are intended to emphasise the underlying regularities. Notice the reversal in character and thought shared by the two works.

Chapter X: The six qualitative parts of comedy

Text: The scribe did not realise until too late that he was copying a heading, and ran on from IX, switching to capitals only for the word ὕλη: he also supplied a lemma-sign in the margin to indicate an important heading. This implies that he was copying a text with a format similar to ours, and not one presented in any less cramped fashion (he was therefore copying an epitome, and was not himself the epitomator); and that his exemplar made no use of capital as opposed to small letters, which suggests that it was in majuscule. Cf. sup. p.7.

ὕλη has been objected to, rightly (Bernays 153, Grube 147). This term could be used of literary *materies*, e.g. Demetrius 163 (διαφέρουσι τὸ γελοῖον καὶ εὔχαρι πρῶτα μὲν τῇ ὕλῃ· χαρίτων μὲν γάρ ὕλη νυμφαῖοι κῆποι, ἔρωτες . . .), cf. Philodemus *Poem.* II fr. 68 Hausrath; *Prolegomenon* V 2ff. Koster divides comedy into 'old' and 'new' according to date, dialect, subject-matter (ὕλη), metre and presentation. But this sense of ὕλη is not appropriate. What would be appropriate for the six parts enumerated is A.'s term εἴδη, which is used of these same parts in *Poet.* (v. sup. p.152f.). Out of its literary context, to a scribe copying philosophical abstracts, the term might well be puzzling. The text was surely corrupted by confusion of Δ with Λ (*ΕΙΔΗ* to *ΕΙΛΗ*) and then corrected to apparent sense (*ΕΙΛΗ* would be homophonous with *ΥΛΗ*): cf. *Poet.* 4.1449a8, where B has ἡδέσι for εἴδεσι, and 19.1456a33, where, for εἰδῶν in B and the Arabic, A reads ἡδ', the Latin *iam*. For graphic confusion of Λ and Δ followed by the restoration of intelligible words cf. Plut. *Mor.* 361f ὄναρ εἶδε corrupted to ἀνεῖλε; 388c ὁμιλίᾳ corrupted to ὃ μὴ διὰ; Galen, ap. *SVF* II 323 εἴπερ εἶδεν MSS, εἰ περὶ ὕλην cj. von Arnim.

Chapter XI: The plot of comedy

On the use of μῦθος and no other term for 'plot', see p.50. κωμικός appears in A. at *Pol.* III 3.1276b5. For περί with the accusative cf. *E.N.* III 1.1109b30 ἡ ἀρετὴ περὶ πάθη τε καὶ πράξεις; for the plural cf. *Poet.* 6.1450a16 ἡ τραγῳδία μίμησίς ἐστιν . . . πράξεων, and a21 τὰ ἤθη συμπεριλαμβάνουσιν διὰ τὰς πράξεις. The plurals are generalising, and need not imply that a particular comic plot is concerned with more than one πρᾶξις. On the rephrasing of A.'s πραγμάτων σύστασις (*Poet.* 14.1454a14) cf. 6.1450a32 μῦθον καὶ σύστασιν πραγμάτων (where καί indicates a synonym), and sup. p.168f.

A. uses μῦθος of comic plots, just as of those of tragedy. The vital step that differentiated comedy from iambus in its evolution was the adoption of generalised plots: *Poet.* 5.1449b5 τὸ **μύθους ποιεῖν** . . . ἐκ Σικελίας ἦλθε . . . Κράτης πρῶτος ἦρξεν ἀφέμενος τῆς ἰαμβικῆς ἰδέας καθόλου ποιεῖν λόγους καὶ **μύθους**. Like those of tragedy, comic plots are constructed according to probability: *Poet.*

9.1451b12 συστήσαντες τὸν μῦθον διὰ τῶν εἰκότων. Fuhrmann (60) suggests that this refers to comedy after Aristophanes, but we shall see that this is not a necessary assumption. What is more important is what we are not told; namely, whether plot is as important to comedy as it is to tragedy. Atkins, for example (140), complains that there is less emphasis on plot than in *Poet.*, and uses this as an argument against authenticity. In support he might have advanced the replacement of the discussion of plot and unity at *Poet.* 7 – 11 with the analysis of humour at V – VI: also the suggestion that impossibilities and incoherence can be used for comic effect (VI 3 – 4). Again, he could have urged that the opening sentence of *Poet.* has as third topic 'how plots must be constructed if the poetic composition is to turn out well'. Notice that A. says ποίησις not 'tragedy', and this accords with his remark in *Poet.* 9 (above) about the construction of comic plots. Consequently Lane Cooper (49f.) presumes that for A. plot would have been 'the life and soul' of comedy.

In fact there are traces of the importance of plot in the Tractatus also. In IV comedy is stated to be a representation of an action (πρᾶξις); also, in VI, as argued above, the first five types of laughter from 'actions' (πράγματα) correspond to plot, the *systasis* of 'actions', compared with three to character and one to thought (διάνοια) — and we have A.'s statement that the qualities of actions are determined by character and thought (*Poet.* 6.1449b38). So in the parts of the laughable these are all subsumed under πράγματα, which receives a prominence rivalled only by that of diction. The use of the impossible or illogical for humorous purposes does not restrict the importance of plots constructed on a probable basis. In *Poet.* 25 A. allows the impossible or illogical provided that it achieves some higher purpose (1460b22ff., cf. on VI 3). Impossibilities are no obstacle to coherence — many of Aristophanes' best plots are logically constructed around a gross impossibility. The indispensability of plot is clear also from XVI, where with diction and song it is one of the three qualitative parts of comedy that are omnipresent. Finally, one must reemphasise the importance of plot as a sign of comedy proper in *Poet.* 4 and 9, as opposed to iambus (cf. on VII – VIII, and Else 200 – 3); plot is fundamental to the whole theory of mimesis, as it supplies an outline by reduction which we can easily take in.

Nonetheless the correspondence is not as exact as it might be. The analysis of laughter gives more space to diction than to plot, and these chapters do correspond to *Poet.* 7 – 11 on plot and unity in the plan of the work. While the generalising power of plot is crucial to comedy, laughter is raised through many other means; it would be misconceived to give plot the same importance in Sophocles and Aristophanes, despite Whitman *ACH* 277f.: his suggestion that the mythopoeic factor in Aristophanes is the controlling one, that 'the comic fantasy . . . is at once the source and the final end of Aristophanean art' (ibid. 259f.), does undervalue other comic resources. Just as in σύστασις (v. p.168) there are limited agreements between tragedy in *Poet.* and comedy in the Treatise, so there are limited correspondences over plot; cf. Dale *Papers* 139–55 on how *dianoia* in *Poet.* and *Rhet.* do not quite correspond. Plot is not as fully paramount as in *Poet.*, because the Treatise is not dealing with Menander.

Chapter XII: The characters of comedy

Bernays (159ff.) perceived a subtle relation between this section and *E.N.* II 7, IV 7f. and *Rhet.* III 18. Comical characters like buffoons and boasters are flawed (cf. *Tract.* VIII on ἁμαρτήματα); they err by excess away from the mean, but not to a criminal degree (οὐ κατὰ πᾶσαν κακίαν, *Poet.* 5.1449a33). The three characters given here are found in the above-mentioned passages; at *E.N.* II 7 boasting and irony are defined as excess and deficiency of pretension, while excess and deficiency in humour leads to buffoonery and boorishness respectively:

ἡ προσποίησις ἡ μὲν ἐπὶ τὸ μεῖζον ἀλαζονεία καὶ ὁ ἔχων αὐτὴν
ἀλαζών, ἡ δ' ἐπὶ τὸ ἔλαττον εἰρωνεία καὶ εἴρων <ὁ ἔχων>.
περὶ δὲ τὸ ἡδὺ τὸ ἐν παιδιᾷ . . . ἡ ὑπερβολὴ βωμολοχία καὶ ὁ
ἔχων αὐτὴν βωμολόχος, ὁ δ' ἐλλείπων ἄγροικός τις,

1108a21ff. A. lists other median and extreme characters, such as the flatterer, his opposite the bad-tempered man, the shameless man, etc. The passage shows that C is supplying examples only and not a comprehensive list; Bernays is wrong to think that other types could not easily be named by one who exhaustively understood the three labels (loc. cit.); indeed such characters as the Flatterer or Bad-tempered Man gave titles to plays by Menander, and feature in Theophrastus' *Characters*, which represent a dilation on a passage such as this (Ussher, *Greece and Rome* 24 (1977) 71–9, suggests that the *Characters* are based on prototypes in Old Comedy).

At *E.N.* IV 7 boastfulness and irony are contrasted as extremes related to truthfulness; for an understanding of A.'s view of these the whole chapter is instructive. Both types are blameworthy, but the boaster more so; moderate use of irony seems witty (χαρίεις). In the next chapter A. turns to buffoonery and its contrary, boorishness: the same juxtaposition, but with different detail, occurs at *E.E.* III 7.1233b39ff., as is noted by Fortenbaugh, 'Theophrast über komischen Charakter' 6f. The boor is entirely insensible; hence boors are the butts of comic poets (cf. *E.E.* III 2.1230b19). Here it is the buffoon who can in certain circumstances appear to be witty (1128a14f.), but his slavish humour differs from that proper to a free and educated man.

This is taken up at *Rhet.* III 18, on the use of laughter in court: 'the number of types of humour has been stated in the *Poetics*, of which some are suited to a free man and others are not . . . Irony is more respectable than buffoonery, as the former makes the joke for his own benefit, but the buffoon to please another' (1419b6ff.). Note the direct connexion between irony and buffoonery, found elsewhere only in C. The boaster is absent, since he aims to impress not to amuse; yet he does occur in C, and if some compiler of plodding pedantry is responsible he has been acute as usual. Bernays remarks (163, cf. Arndt 7f.) that nobody would wish to impute to him such a brilliant power of combination; he has not only found the passage in *Rhet.* where two of the characters are given, but also had the wit to add a third from the *Ethics* — a type not drawn at random from the almost innumerable deviations from the mean there listed, but linked to the ironist along a different axis. A diagram may help to show the subtlety of his choice:

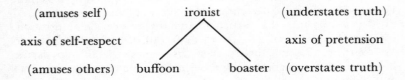

(amuses self)	ironist	(understates truth)
axis of self-respect		axis of pretension
(amuses others) buffoon	boaster	(overstates truth)

The ironist and boaster occur together in Aristophanes, *Clouds* 449. As Cornford said (*The Origin of Attic Comedy* 137f.), these fit Old Comedy especially well. 'The special kind of irony practised by the Impostor's opponent is feigned stupidity . . . The *Eiron* who victimizes the Impostors masks his cleverness under a show of clownish dullness' . . . , e.g. Demos' surprising sagacity at *Knights* 1121ff. Lane Cooper has numerous examples of these character-types (262 – 5, cf. 117 – 23), and recently McLeish has analysed the main characters in Aristophanes according to a similar pattern, with interesting results (*The Theatre of Aristophanes* 53ff., 74ff., and n.46). This approach was pioneered by Süss, *RhM* 63 (1908) 12 – 38, reprinted in *Aristophanes und die alte Komödie* ed. Newiger, esp. p.23. — As in *Poet.*, there is no emphasis on one particular character as comic hero, that valuable formulation of modern scholarship; nor does anything contradict the implicit presence of such a concept. On ἦθος v. Schütrumpf, 'Die Bedeutung des Wortes ēthos in der Poetik des Aristoteles'.

Dosi (620) assigns this section to Theophrastus, but we have seen that ethos played a larger part in his theory (sup. pp.49ff.): this tendency may have been affected by the rise of New Comedy, and later theorists like Neoptolemus probably continued it (Brink *Prol.* 111, 144). The *Characters* are on a much larger scale; the βωμολόχος is not directly represented. Cf. sup. on VIII for irony at Demetrius 291, cf. Cicero *de Orat.* II 270; the latter's sequence under- or over-statements, irony and farcical jests among humour *in rebus* surely relates to εἰρωνεία, ἀλαζονεία and βωμολοχία (sup. p.165).

Chapter XIII: 'Dianoia' in Comedy

(a) *'Dianoia' in Aristotle*

As in tragedy, *dianoia* is the point at which rhetoric impinges on comedy; it is the means of intellectual expression and cognition. How a man reasons about an event will be determined by his ethos, but he will set out his perception of it and reasoning in a speech. A. divided *dianoia* into the particular and the general demonstration, e.g. *Poet.* 6.1450a6, cf. b11. At 19.1456a34ff. he relegates *dianoia* to his *Rhetoric*, but nonetheless then gives more detail: 'to *dianoia* belongs everything effected by speech. Its sections (μέρη) are proof and refutation, the arousal of the emotions . . . and making matters important or unimportant'. *Dianoia* has the function of producing pity and fear, just as actions do. From this we can conclude that *dianoia* ought to be a source of humour also — a conclusion confirmed at VI 9 on inconsequent reasoning.

In line with his brevity in *Poet.* 19, we would expect A. to refer only to those aspects of *dianoia* which have comic potential, and otherwise to redirect us to the *Rhetoric*. There is no reason to think that C does anything else. A γνώμη is a generalising maxim, normally concerned with desirable or undesirable courses of action

(*Rhet.* II 21.1394a21ff.). There is certainly such an entity as a comic generalisation. Next C gives five subcategories of πίστις ('proof'), namely oaths, agreements, testimonials, ordeals and laws. Cramer discerned that these are the five kinds of 'simple proofs' of *Rhet.* I 2.1355b35, where A. divides πίστις into two categories, those which can be used as they are, and those which have to be invented, such as logical proofs about the facts of a particular case (τῶν πίστεων αἱ μὲν ἄτεχνοί εἰσιν, αἱ δ' ἔντεχνοι. ἄτεχνα δὲ λέγω ὅσα μὴ δι' ἡμῶν πεπόρισται ἀλλὰ προϋπῆρχεν, οἷον μάρτυρες βάσανοι συγγραφαί). The ἄτεχνοι πίστεις are listed at I 15.1375a24f. as νόμοι, μάρτυρες, συνθῆκαι, βάσανοι and ὅρκος (*sic*).

(b) *The five sub-types*

The presence of these types gives rise to two problems — why they appear at all, and why the πίστεις ἔντεχνοι do not appear alongside them.

The first problem has been resolved by Lane Cooper (265–81, cf. Koster ad loc.). Bernays considered these entries a shocking example of what the compiler could contrive (155f.); Kaibel suppressed them entirely. Cooper comments (266) 'the general animus against the epitomator has been such that no one, hitherto, has tested this part of his scheme by applying it to Aristophanes.' This he does. Oaths are plentiful, e.g. *Frogs* 305ff.; agreements not rare, e.g. *Thesm.* 1160ff.; also the appearance of witnesses, e.g. *Wasps* 936ff.; tests and ordeals are conspicuous, e.g. Aeacus' flogging of Dionysus and Xanthias at *Frogs* 642ff.; the citation of laws, either bogus or humorously misapplied, is less frequent, but cf. Northrop Frye, *Anatomy of Criticism* 166, 169.

C's position was shared by A. In *Rhet.* I 15 he shows himself aware of appeals to these πίστεις in drama. He quotes Antigone's famous appeal to everlasting divine laws, when discussing νόμοι (1375a33ff.). Witnesses are of two kinds, ancient and modern. The ancient include poets such as Homer, or oracles, or proverbs. Comedy offered more scope for such appeals than did tragedy, especially to βάσανος. But it remains problematic that no mention of the ἔντεχνοι πίστεις is made in C. Of course they may have been omitted during the epitomisation that produced the peculiar // εʹ restored as πίστεις πέντε, cf. εἰσὶν δὲ πέντε τὸν ἀριθμόν (1375a24). Cf. Lane Cooper 281:

'there can be an admixture of a serious kind of *dianoia* — that is, of "artistic" proofs — in a comic play, and the more so as the play verges toward a more serious type of comedy; but this is only saying in another way that the Tractate is right in singling out the 'inartistic' proofs as characteristic of speeches in comic drama'.

πίστις is relevant to *anagnorisis* (*Poet.* 16.1454b28f.), but, as we have it, C is silent on this major feature of New Comedy. A. uses the term compendiously for the ἔντεχνοι πίστεις at *Rhet.* I 1.1355a5. On his usage v. Grimaldi, *Studies in the Philosophy of A.'s Rhetoric* 58ff.

Lane Cooper was also impressed on textual grounds by this section (p.265f.), especially by its variations in order, which we can tabulate as follows:

Tractate	*Rhet.* I 2.1355b37	*Rhet.* I 15.1375a24	[*Rhet. Al.* 16−8]
ὅρκοι		νόμοι	
συνθῆκαι		μάρτυρες (-ίαι)	
μαρτυρίαι	μάρτυρες	συνθῆκαι	μαρτυρία
βάσανοι	βάσανοι	βάσανοι	βάσανος
νόμοι	συγγραφαί	ὅρκος	ὅρκος
	[καὶ ὅσα τοιαῦτα]		

μαρτυρίαι as well as μάρτυρες appear in *Rhet.* I 15.1376a17, 22; C is closer to A. than he realised. μαρτυρία occurs here because it does not imply the appearance of witnesses in the flesh — an unlikely contingency when e.g. a god is called upon. Likewise συνθῆκαι are preferable to συγγραφαί in a comic context, as the former have no necessary implication of agreements based on a *written* document. — *Pace* Lane Cooper loc. cit., the plural ὅρκοι should not be used to emend the singular ὅρκος at 1375a24: the singular is certainly *difficilior lectio*. Compare the converse, a plural διάνοιαι in a list of singular items at *Tract.* XVI; also *Poet.* 6.1450a13 ὄψεις ἔχει . . . καὶ μῦθον κτλ.; λέξεις καὶ διανοίας at a30; and τὰς ὄψεις at 26.1462a16 (v. p.228). The fluctuation from plural to singular or vice versa at the beginning or end of lists of this kind, mediated presumably by the notion of particular instances, seems integral to A.'s style; the occurrences support each other.

Chapter XIV: The diction of comedy

(a) *Appropriateness in Comic Diction*

The entry on comic diction has an Aristotelian demand as its fundamental precept, as Bernays remarked (165), namely that poetic diction be not too dissimilar from everyday speech. By diction (λέξις) is meant that of *spoken* verse, not the words of songs, which are part of μέλος (Else 236f., 567f.).

(i) *Parallels in Aristotle*: At *Rhet.* III 3.1405b35ff. he censures the use of glosses and compounds in oratory, and refers to *Poet.* 22.1459a8ff., where we find a similar demand for appropriateness according to genre. The idea recurs in *Rhet.* III 7. A. warns against using a high style for a trivial subject, and vice versa — otherwise, comedy results (κωμῳδία φαίνεται), e.g. πότνια συκῆ 'lady fig', 1408a12ff. The diction should be appropriate to every type of person, according to age, sex, nationality, disposition and level of education (a25ff., cf. 2.1404b16f., Hor. *A.P.* 114−8). Note in his mention of a Spartan or Thessalian a hint of local dialect, as in the second part of C's entry.

Given A.'s emphasis on propriety of diction, we certainly expect comedy to use diction that is commonplace and popular; for comedy is an imitation of inferior characters (*Poet.* 5.1449a32), and we have just been told that the characters of comedy are buffoons, impostors and people who feign stupidity (XII). It follows that they will speak in no elevated manner. However, there is a place for elevated diction in comedy; A. made clear in *Rhet.* (just cited) that elevated diction applied to low personages or trivial subjects was a fertile field for wit; contrast the Peripatetic view in Cicero and Horace (sup. p.207f.), evidently based on New Comedy, which excludes from comic diction the λέξις ξενική implied in *Tract.* V.

Bernays (165f.) suggested that A. was here opposing the fantastic and uneven style of Aristophanes to such rounded and unified diction as Menander's, which Plutarch defends in his *Comparison of Aristophanes and Menander* (*Mor.* 853a), and in *Table Talk* (*Mor.* 711f−712d). While Plutarch's point that Menander suits his diction to every nature, disposition, and period of life does accord with Aristotelian desiderata, and his distinction between two types of theatre audience (cf. *Pol.* VIII 7.1342a18ff.) and rejection of excessive buffoonery are Aristotelian attitudes also, there is simply no evidence that A. shared his disapproval of Aristophanes' verbal jokes, or of ἀνομοιότης in his diction. The Tractate's emphasis on verbal humour gives no support to such a view either.

(ii) *Expression*: The phrase κοινὴ καὶ δημώδης is interesting. δημώδης goes back to Plato (LSJ s.v.), but the conjunction 'common and popular' occurs twice elsewhere, in contexts that may be significant, especially as there are two remoter parallels in Peripatetic writers. The first is [Longinus] *de Sublim.* 40.2:

> 'many poets and other writers who are not naturally sublime,
> . . . and who in general use common and everyday words
> (κοινοῖς καὶ δημώδεσι τοῖς ὀνόμασι) . . . nevertheless acquire
> magnificence and splendour . . . solely by the way in which
> they arrange and fit together their words. Philistus, *Aristo-*
> *phanes* sometimes, Euripides generally, are among the many
> examples'

(trans. Russell; my italics). Secondly, Iamblichus in his *Life of Pythagoras* 23.104 Nauck (88 Hemst., = 60 Deubner), explaining that Pythagorean treatises are written in riddling language for the benefit of initiates only, remarks that they do not employ common and everyday diction (τῇ κοινῇ καὶ δημώδει . . . λέξει). To the ignorant they seem absurd and like old wives' tales, full of nonsense and adoleschy (γελοῖα καὶ γραώδη, λήρου μεστὰ καὶ ἀδολεσχίας). Although the *On Sublimity* displays hardly any direct familiarity with A.'s writings, Iamblichus probably was acquainted with lost writings of his on literature (cf. *Poet.* fr. V Kassel). Cf. also Theophrastus fr. 65 (incompletely quoted by Wimmer), ap. Ammonius *in de Int.* 66.2 Busse: 'it is the function of poetry and rhetoric to choose the more elevated words, not those that are common and hackneyed' (τὰ σεμνότερα τῶν ὀνομάτων, ἀλλὰ μὴ τὰ **κοινὰ** καὶ **δεδημευμένα**); and Demetrius 164, on the difference between charming and laughable diction: whereas charm is brought about by ornament and beautiful words, humour employs ordinary and commonplace words (τὸ γελοῖον καὶ ὀνομάτων ἐστὶν εὐτελῶν καὶ **κοινοτέρων**).

(iii) *The scope of the entry*: The parallels show that we have a genuine Peripatetic doctrine. What would we expect A. to have said in a section on comic diction such as this? In his account of excellence in tragic diction A. reminds us of the possible range of types of word, such as compounds and metaphors, and where they are best used. In C we would not expect the discussion of types of word to reappear, as these are already treated in the context of the opportunities they present for verbal play (*Tract.* V, cf. *Poet.* 22.1458 b13 − 1459a4). But we would expect to find an assessment of the level of diction appropriate to comedy, and that is what C offers.

(b) *The use of dialect in comedy*

There is no parallel in *Poet.* 22 to the remarks about dialect which follow. Although the general sense is clear, the text needs repair before we can proceed.

(i) *Text*: C reads δεῖ τὸν κωμῳδοποιὸν τὴν πάτριον αὐτοῦ γλῶσσαν τοῖς προσώποις περιτιθέναι, τὴν δὲ ἐπιχώριον αὐτῷ ἐκείνῳ. Following Bernays' lead, Lane Cooper renders 'the comic poet must endow his personages with his own native idiom, but must endow an alien with the alien idiom'. This is obtained by replacing αὐτῷ ἐκείνῳ with αὖ τῷ ξένῳ, αὖ ἑκάστῳ τῶν ξένων (van Leeuwen), vel sim. (v. app. crit.). These proposals depart greatly from the exemplar. Koster, rightly satisfied with none, attempts a new approach by putting the local speech into the first clause: . . . τοῖς <ἐγχωρίοις> προσώποις περιτιθέναι, τὴν δὲ ἐπιχώριον †αὐτῷ ἐκείνῳ†. The obeli show that all is not well, and <ἐγχωρίοις> is drastic. The difficulty with all the solutions except Koster's is that they imply that the ξένος is not a πρόσωπον (Bernays suggested τοῖς <ἄλλοις> προσώποις); yet Koster's solution is no simpler. The clue lies in αὐτῷ ἐκείνῳ, which is perfectly acceptable Greek, as Vahlen proved (*Opusc. Acad.* II 558ff., with further unsatisfactory conjectures affecting other parts of the entry): the comic poet is not technically the subject of the sentence, being governed by δεῖ, and ἐκείνῳ will most naturally specify that the αὐτῷ, with which it is in concord, refers back to early in the sentence, but not to the subject; therefore it designates the comic poet. But we have another αὐτός in this sentence, and if the reference of αὐτῷ ἐκείνῳ is correctly identified, this αὐτός must denote someone else. Its only possible referend is τὰ πρόσωπα. This preserves the balance between the two parts of the sentence intimated by δέ, but gives a quite different sense — 'it is required that the comic poet endue the characters with his ancestral speech, and/but himself with the local (speech)'. All is not quite correct, but it is not difficult to see what has happened: αὐτοῦ is corrupt for αὐτῶν, never a difficult change, and very easy here, as it follows a noun to which it does not refer, and *precedes* that to which it does. Thus sense is restored with one minimal change, and I translate: 'the comic poet must endow his characters with their ancestral speech, but (use) the local (speech) himself.' For resumptive αὐτὸς ἐκεῖνος cf. my article in *CQ* 34 (1984) 'αὐτὸς ἐκεῖνος: a neglected idiom', with numerous parallels, and esp. Plato *Phaedo* 97d, *Prot.* 171c, A. *Meteor.* II 4.361b6, *Poet.* 16.1454b34, *Pol.* VIII 5.1340a27. We shall consider the sense in a moment.

(ii) *Expression*: πάτριος with the genitive is rare: cf. *de Caelo* II 1.284a2, τοὺς πατρίους ἡμῶν . . . λόγους; Proclus, *Prolegomena to Hesiod* 1.4 Pertusi, τὴν πάτριον τῶν Ἑλλήνων φήμην (cf. Plut. *Mor.* 527d). The usage is related to the sandwiching between adjective and noun: elsewhere it takes the dative. On the use of πρόσωπον to mean 'character' in drama v. on VI 6. — In *Poet.* A. defines γλῶττα as a term used in the dialect of others (21.1457b2ff.). Roberts (272) implies that the sense 'language, tongue, dialect' here is not Aristotelian, but it occurs at *Rhet.* I 2.1357b9f.: 'τέκμαρ and πέρας mean the same in the ancient tongue' (κατὰ τὴν ἀρχαίαν γλῶτταν). For περιτιθέναι with this construction cf. *Rhet.* I 9.1368 a29 μέγεθος περιθεῖναι (ταῖς πράξεσι); *Vit. Aesch.* 5 Wilamowitz (p.331.15ff. Page) ὄγκον τῇ φράσει περιθεῖναι, βάρος περιτιθέναι τοῖς προσώποις (one of the sources for this *Life* is Peripatetic, cf. the reference to Dicaearchus at 15, and the cognate terminology, e.g. μέγεθος at 16); Neoptol. fr. 9 ap. Philodem. Περὶ Ποιημ. V col. xiii Jensen. ἐπιχώριος and κωμῳδοποιός both occur in A. twice.

(iii) *Interpretation*: Grube suggests (148) that C refers to the fact that 'in comedy the language is uniform, and does not change, as in tragedy, to Doric in choral lyrics'. This is unlikely; there is no reference to μέλος, but λέξις solely is in question. As often, Bernays is on the right track: he thinks that C says that comic poets must in Dorian lands write in Doric like Epicharmus, in Athens Attic like Aristophanes; whereas in tragedy nobody can let Oedipus speak in Boeotian, in comedy the use of dialects and even barbarian languages is frequent. With the text proposed, this is in the first clause — that local comic characters will each speak their local dialect, and strangers theirs; to each his own. The second clause now says that the poet himself speaks the local dialect. This can only refer to the parabasis or similar passages where the chorus acts as the playwright's own mouthpiece. For the poet's rôle in the parabasis cf. Aristoph. *Peace* 733ff. with schol., Pollux IV 111, Platonius I 36 Koster; Dover, *Aristophanic Comedy* 49ff. If so, New Comedy is certainly ruled out here, as it has no parabasis.

The same interest in the use of dialect in different kinds of comedy is found in a misunderstood passage of Demetrius on 'weight' in syllables and the breadth of Dorian speech. 'This is the reason why comedies were not written in Doric, but in the pungent Attic. The Attic dialect has about it something terse and popular (δημοτικόν), and so lends itself naturally to the pleasantries of the stage' (177; Roberts' translation). Led astray by the hunt for 'late' ideas, Roberts comments: 'the general standpoint here is surely late. The past tense is itself significant.' He apparently believes Demetrius to mean that all comedies were always in the Attic dialect. Grube is silent: but the passage makes sense if an ellipse of Aristotelian doctrine is supposed: 'this is the reason why, < when comedy was introduced into Attica from a Dorian area,> it was not in Doric.' The assumed and easy familiarity with Peripatetic doctrine (cf. *Poet.* 5.1449b6) is typical of Demetrius. Like C, he was interested in the fact, unusual for a genre of Greek literature, that the dialect of comedy was not fixed.

Chapter XV: Song and spectacle in drama

Although they are marked by separate marginal symbols in C, I have limited the entries on song and spectacle to a single chapter, since I believe this represents the amount of space they received in the original full text. In particular, the dismissal of song implies that nothing else was said about it.

(a) *Song*

The entry on song, i.e. both words and melody, was heavily abbreviated by the copyist, once he realised what it was saying; elsewhere he is sparing with compendia. Bergk corrected δεήσῃ at *Philologus* 41 (1882) 581. Both expression and sentiment are typical of A. (cf. Bernays 156). αὐτοτελεῖς ἀφορμάς is not paralleled exactly, but αὐτοτελής is found with ὁρισμός at *Top.* I 5.102b13, with θεωρίαι at *Pol.* VII 3.1325b20. For ἀφορμαί as the starting-point of an enquiry cf. *de Caelo* II 12.292a16. Cf. also ὁρμῆς αὐτοτελοῦς *SVF* III 32.12 von Arnim. With μέλος τῆς μουσικῆς ἐστιν ἴδιον cf. *Top.*

V 6.136a36 ἀπόφασις φάσεως οὔκ ἐστιν ἴδιον; Poet. 13.1452b33; 19.1456a34 τὰ περὶ τὴν διάνοιαν ἐν τοῖς περὶ ῥητορικῆς κείσθω· τοῦτο γὰρ ἴδιον μᾶλλον ἐκείνης τῆς μεθόδου; 20.1456b34, 37 etc. The thought that song is part of music recurs at Pol. VIII 6.1341a15 (χαίρειν τοῖς καλοῖς μέλεσι . . . μὴ μόνον τῷ κοινῷ τῆς μουσικῆς).

In accord with C, A. says little about song in Poet.; he was not ignorant of the subject, as witness references to flute-playing in comedy at Pol. VIII 6.1341a35f. and the cordax at Rhet. III 8.1408b36. In Poet. 6 song is a part of tragedy, but he forbears to define it on the grounds of obviousness (1449b35). Later he dismisses it in five words, as the greatest of the pleasure-giving elements, in a passage which minimises the qualitative parts other than plot (1450b16). Among passing references (Poet. 12 cf. Tract. XVII, Poet. 17.1455a25 − 32), one of tragedy's advantages over epic is its possession of music (26.1462a16). The dismissal of μέλος does not in itself show that he despised this aspect of comedy, any more than his dismissal of dianoia in tragedy reveals similar contempt. Even so it is regrettable that we receive no further details about it from C. A.'s lack of interest in this aspect of drama was remedied by his pupil Aristoxenus, as is seen in Psellus' treatise on tragedy (inf. p.238).

(b) Spectacle: text and interpretation

The entry on spectacle (ὄψις) is equally uninformative, for a different reason. It is perfectly comprehensible — 'spectacle supplies a great benefit to drama, namely . . . ' — until we reach συμφωνίαν 'harmony, agreement'. Bernays (157f.) suggested that the term is corrupt, and compared Poet. 6.1450b16 where spectacle is said to be attractive or entertaining. He therefore wished to substitute 'entertainment' (ψυχαγωγίαν) as the great need which spectacle supplies. The change is not easy, and against it cf. 1450a33, where the most important attractants in a tragedy are asserted to be parts of the plot. However, we have seen that A.'s emphasis could vary in arguments about relative importance, and I doubt not that he could have called ψυχαγωγία a μεγάλη χρεία: Eratosthenes even held that entertainment was poetry's sole end (Strabo I 15). But I wonder whether σκηνογραφίαν is not the original text, corrupted by the proximity of 'music'. A. mentions scene-painting at Poet. 4.1449a18: Lucas ad loc. suggests that costumes not scenery were the major constituent of ὄψις, but see his remarks on 1449b33.

Baumgart (691f.) defended the paradosis, adducing *Pol.* VII 15.1334b10 for metaphorical use of συμφωνία. Asking whether education should proceed by the acquisition of reasoning or the formation of habits, A. says that these must work together in perfect harmony (συμφωνεῖν συμφωνίαν τὴν ἀρίστην): cf. *Top.* IV 3.123a33ff. M. Fantuzzi (*LCM* 7 (1982) 24f.) defends συμφωνία as a late and banal synonym for σύστασις, comparing Hsch. s.v. συστάσεις, glossed σύνοδοι, συμφωνίαι, and Pollux VI 158 σύστασις, συμμετρία, συμφωνία. But what is then the sense of 'spectacle contributes plot'? Fantuzzi cites *Poet.* 14.1453b1−6, where the two are juxtaposed — but opposed; and 6.1450a13, where (after Vahlen) he retains ὄψις and thinks it embraces the other εἴδη. This is most improbable, cf. inf. p.230. Holwerda (Koster's Addenda, p.220) conjectured < παρὰ > τὴν συμφωνίαν, meaning 'along with' συμφωνία. In this case we are no wiser than with the transmitted text, which Lane Cooper translated as 'spectacle is of great advantage to dramas in supplying what is in concord with them'. He comments only (284): 'this remark would apply to the *Frogs* and the *Birds*'. Better, surely, to admit incomprehension. For χρείαν παρέχει cf. *H.A.* I 6.490b30; of music, Philodemus *de mus.* p.67 Kemke (= *SVF* III 225.14 von Arnim).

Despite the interpretative problems, it may usefully be asked why the entry speaks of 'dramas' and not 'comedies'. According to *Poet.* 3.1448a28, both Sophocles and Aristophanes wrote 'dramas', but the word is used to denote tragedy alone at five other places in the *Poetics* (Kassel's index). There is no necessity to interpret the term more widely than 'comedy' here; it is, even so, desirable to do so. *Poet.* has no autonomous discussion of song and spectacle after plot, character, thought and diction; we arrive at once at epic, which possesses the same four elements, lacking song and spectacle (24.1459b10). The omission is hardly noticeable, precisely because these elements *are* absent from the epos: but it is surprising that song is not discussed somewhere in *Poet.* (Solmsen, ap. *CQ* 29 (1935) 192, records astonishment). We have already seen C complement the *Poetics* and remedy the latter's omissions, e.g. tragic catharsis; coverage of the qualitative parts of drama as a whole would be improved if the account of song and spectacle here is à propos of tragedy as well as comedy, and nothing contradicts this except the general heading (X) under which all these parts are discussed.

(c) *Aristotle's attitude to spectacle*

A.'s attitude to spectacle has received a bad press of late (e.g. from Taplin, *The Stagecraft of Aeschylus* 25, 477ff; for another view, cf. Cantarella *Scritti minori sul teatro greco* 121−9). Taplin blames the *Poetics* for neglect of the visual side of tragedy:

> 'there are really three separate though connected insinuations in *Poet.*: that the play is best appreciated when read, that the visual aspects of a play in performance are mere externals put there to satisfy the spectators, and that the visual aspects of the tragedy are in the sphere not of the dramatist but of theatre mechanicals.'

If this is indeed so, C is slightly out of tune, as it does claim that 'spectacle' is important in some way. However, I am not convinced by Taplin's attack. In the passages quoted to illustrate the view that tragedy should be able to have its full effect without being seen on stage, Taplin slights that telling particle καί — '*even* without performance', which changes the emphasis (*Poet.* 6.1450b18, where cf. Hubbard in *ALC* 100 n., who suggests that this passage is irrelevant; 14.1453b4; 26.1462a11 only avers that one can gain a general impression of a tragedy by reading it). At 17.1455a22ff. A. insists that the playwright must envisage the performance, not only to avoid inconsistencies but to discover τὸ πρέπον. A passage in *E.N.* shows that he approved of enjoyment of 'spectacle'; he is discussing restraint regarding sensual pleasure: οἱ χαίροντες τοῖς διὰ τῆς ὄψεως . . . οὔτε σώφρονες οὔτε ἀκόλαστοι λέγονται· καίτοι δόξειεν ἂν εἶναι, III 10.1118a1ff. This also applies to things heard, such as songs and acting (μέλεσιν ἢ ὑποκρίσει, ibid. a8). He censures vulgar demands for sensationalism (rightly, cf. Taplin 477 n.1), but it is no inevitable consequence that he deem spectacle in general mere inessential show.

Taplin skims over one vital passage — *Poet.* 26.1462a15ff., which reads in the MSS ἔτι οὐ μικρὸν μέρος τὴν μουσικὴν καὶ τὰς ὄψεις, δι' ἧς αἱ ἡδοναὶ συνίστανται ἐναργέστατα. A. has just remarked that tragedy has all the same qualitative parts as epic, and surely will then refer to the *two* elements which epic lacks, song and spectacle. Spengel deleted καὶ τὰς ὄψεις because of δι' ἧς (cf. Else 643), but the plural ὄψεις can be justified (Else, cf. sup. p.220), and Vahlen proposed αἷς or δι' ἅς, comparing 6.1450b16, where ὄψις is mentioned along with music as an attractive aspect of tragedy. Moreover ἐναργής in the next sentence is strongly connected with ὄψις (cf. *Prob.* 7.886b35, *Rhet.* III 11.1411b24ff., with MS A's text). Therefore this neglected passage assigns a more important rôle to 'spectacle' in the production of pleasure.

The most serious charge is that A. introduces ὄψις in the wide sense of observation of those involved in the action, so that as tragedy is a representation of people in action, it is *of necessity* a part of tragedy (*Poet.* 6.1449b31ff.). Yet he later slips into saying that ὄψις related more to the σκευοποιός and χορηγός than to the poet (1450b16−20, 14.1453b1−8). So the narrower sense (to do with costumes, masks etc.) is allowed to damage the reader's appreciation of the importance of visual presentation in general. This charge sticks. The narrower sense is certainly present in *Tract.* XVI, where ὄψις is not present in all comedies. That it should reappear is not surprising. In *Poet.*, after 6.1449b32, the narrow use predominates: as often, the terminology shifts in meaning without warning. I do not however believe that A. altered it with malicious intent. His terminology often develops as he writes, towards the attainment of its final form; and we must bear in mind where and when he was writing. Much of *Poet.* replies to Plato's attack on poetry in the *Republic*, and one of Plato's strongest objections was to the sensual ensnarement of stage enactments. A. meets this by reinterpreting the concept of mimesis, while rejecting the prevalent pandering to the lower appetites of the audience; this evidently included gaudy costumes and elaborate χορηγία (cf. *E.N.* IV 2.1123a23, on which see Sifakis ap. *AJP* 92 (1971) 410−32). Another response is to emphasise what can be gained from reading dramatic texts. But A. was not so blind as to underplay ὄψις altogether; his undoubted caution is a function of his closeness to Plato. It is on the *Republic* that blame must ultimately rest for the bias against art in performance. It is unjust to criticise A., defender of poetry's value and autonomy against his master's strictures, for originating the very attitudes which he sought to rebut.

Chapter XVI: The distribution of the six parts

This fascinating entry, whose basic meaning is beyond doubt 'plot, diction and song are found in all comedies, but thought, character and spectacle are not', throws light on a dark corner of the *Poetics*. Bernays (167) was first to compare the *locus conclamatus* at 6.1450 a7ff., but only to say that one ought not to emend the thought into *Poet.* 6. Lane Cooper too is hesitant (284f.). But it is by no means certain that we need to emend *Poet.* to make the two conform:

rather, we must refrain from emendation.
The passage runs in Kassel's text as follows:

ἀνάγκη οὖν πάσης (τῆς add. B) τραγῳδίας μέρη εἶναι ἕξ . . .
τούτοις μὲν οὖν †οὐκ ὀλίγοι αὐτῶν† ὡς εἰπεῖν κέχρηνται τοῖς
εἴδεσιν· καὶ γὰρ †ὄψις ἔχει πᾶν† καὶ ἦθος κτλ.

Lucas puts the problem thus (ad loc.): 'after saying that every
tragedy *must* have all six parts, why add that "not a few" poets use
them all?' This is not necessarily what the Greek says: πάσης τῆς
τραγῳδίας must, and πάσης τραγῳδίας may, mean 'tragedy as a
whole', i.e. considered as a genre, individual members of which do
not invariably offer the full range of options available, as we shall
see (cf. Else 245). There is simply no need for obeli round οὐκ
ὀλίγοι αὐτῶν, where ὡς εἰπεῖν as often qualifies a statement that is
numerically too bold (v. Bonitz s.v. εἰπεῖν). Vahlen (*Beiträge* 23f.,
256) rightly followed some apographs in reading the easy correction ὄψεις, and there is no difficulty in the plural beside the
other singulars in the list, as I shall show; but he interpreted it to
mean that the element of spectacle, in the broad sense as at
1449b32, subsumed everything else within it. C rules this out, as
ὄψις is said here *not* to be ubiquitous. Instead the third sentence is
normally taken to mean 'the whole (sc. δρᾶμα, i.e. drama as a
whole) has spectacle etc.'. The ellipse of the noun with πᾶν is
surprising not to say incredible, especially since δρᾶμα has not
occurred since Ch.3. In fact I am sure that ἔχει πᾶν is corrupt, and
suggest that we read ἔχοιεν ἄν referring back to the poets, i.e. 'they
could have instances of spectacle and character' etc. This obviates
the abrupt change of subject: the corruption is easy after that of
ὄψεις to ὄψις.

The passage as just interpreted is supported elsewhere in *Poet.*.
Unless we read it thus, it directly contradicts what immediately
follows, when A. speaks of tragedies lacking one of the constituent
elements, in this case ethos (which C says can be lacking in
comedy): ἄνευ μὲν πράξεως οὐκ ἂν γένοιτο τραγῳδία, ἄνευ δὲ ἠθῶν
γένοιτ' ἄν· αἱ γὰρ τῶν νέων τῶν πλείστων ἀήθεις τραγῳδίαι εἰσίν
(1450a23ff.). The standard view is that ἀήθης means *deficient in*
character, not devoid of it altogether, but A. next says by way of
illustration that Zeuxis' paintings have *no* ethos (οὐδὲν ἔχει ἦθος,
28f.). Worse still for this view, he continues:

ἐάν τις ἐφεξῆς θῇ ῥήσεις ἠθικὰς καὶ λέξεις καὶ διανοίας εὖ
πεποιημένας, οὐ ποιήσει ὃ ἦν τῆς τραγῳδίας ἔργον, ἀλλὰ πολὺ

μᾶλλον ἡ καταδεεστέροις τούτοις κεχρημένη τραγῳδία, ἔχουσα
δὲ μῦθον

(29ff.). Vahlen (*RhM* 28 (1873) 185) emended to λέξει καὶ διανοίᾳ,
but, as Else remarks,

> 'the context calls for a mention of *all* the other parts that
> count for anything (*all of them together will not do what a plot can
> do, even without them*), and the confrontation is much more
> effective if the other parts appear as separate elements (ἐφεξῆς
> θῇ, "sets down one after the other", just as they come)'

(p.258n.131: my italics). Cf. C. Lord, *J. Aesthetics and Art Criticism*
28 (1969–70) 55–62: E. Belfiore, 'A.'s use of *praxis* in the *Poetics*'
sub fin. Against Vahlen's emendation (*Beiträge* 22, 255f.) ὡς εἴδεσι
for τοῖς εἴδεσι at 1450a13 see Gudeman ad loc., Allan *CQ* 21 (1971)
81, House, *A.'s Poetics* 73f.

Thus C does agree with *Poet.*, if only we leave the latter's text
largely unaltered. Before proceeding to the implications, a word on
three textual matters in C. At *Poet.* 6.1450a8, as we saw, there is a
choice between reading πάσης τραγῳδίας with A, or πάσης τῆς
τραγῳδίας with B. Here we face a similar dilemma. All editors read
πάσαις κωμῳδίαις, but the last letter of πάσαις is in fact the ligature
stigma, and this suggests that the article may have been lost —
hence πάσαις τ<αῖς>. But the sense is unaffected whichever
reading is adopted. — I have kept the plural διάνοιαι in the list of
parts, the rest of which are in the singular: Bergk (*Philologus* 41
(1882) 581) and Kaibel made the regularising emendation διάνοια.
This is unnecessary: cf. p.220 on *Rhet.* I 15.1375a24, and above on
Poet. 6.1450a13, a30. Koster defends C's plural as relating to the
parts of διάνοια in XIII (ad loc.). — I read ἐν <οὐκ> ὀλίγοις, cf.
οὐκ ὀλίγοι at 1450a12. 'A few' is surprising here (cf. Grube 148); it
could be defended from 1450a25, where A. casually remarks that
most recent tragedies are 'without character', again a strong
statement. But loss of οὐκ is extremely easy to parallel: cf. sup.
p.153. — θεωρεῖσθαι is frequent in A., e.g. *Poet.* 17.1455b2;
20.1456b34, 37; 22.1458b16; 25.1460b7.

The realisation that not all tragedies or comedies possess all the
qualitative elements is important, because it helps us to understand passages in *Poet.* concerning tragedies particularly rich in a
given element, such as character-plays (18.1456a1). It also explains

6.1450a9 καθ' ὅ ποιά τις ἐστὶν ἡ τραγῳδία 'according to which (qualitative part) the tragedy belongs to a particular type', such as a character-play: and 12.1452b14, where it would be silly to say 'the qualitative parts of tragedy which one must use' if the six parts were all automatically present in every tragedy. For A., these qualitative parts are on a scale ranging from zero upwards.

But C tells us more yet with its statement that plot, diction and song are omnipresent, but thought, character and spectacle are not. The omnipresence of μέλος might be thought to imply an earlier rather than a later date, before the lyrics of comedy came to be so irrelevant to the action that literary texts omit them, with only *XOPOY* to mark their place (cf. Koster, *Autour d'un manuscrit* 117−35). Even so the existence of this indication, coupled with such remarks as *Dyscolus* 230ff. that a group of drunkards is coming, proves that choral songs continued to be performed in New Comedy. In fact this omnipresence is reassuring, as in late writers we do find the assertion that New Comedy did not need a chorus (ἐν τῇ νέᾳ χοροῦ οὐκ ἔδει, *Prolegomenon* V 10f. Koster, cf. Platonius I 24ff., 31ff., 42, 56 of *Middle* Comedy: cf. K.J. Maidment *CQ* 29 (1935) 1−24, Brink on Horace *A.P.* 189f., Sifakis *AJP* 92 (1971) 410−32, Hunter *ZPE* 36 (1979) 23−38).

The omnipresence of plot, song and diction accords with the discussion in *Poet.* 5 about the origins of comedy (1449b1ff.). After a reference to the chorus, which seems to be present from the first, A. says that it is unknown who invented masks, prologues, a multiplicity of actors and suchlike; 'Crates was first to relinquish the iambic form and construct generalised speeches and plots' (λόγους καὶ μύθους). In other words, μέλος and personal abuse were the most basic elements, but when the iambus was given up generalised λόγοι and plots appeared — λόγος of course meaning spoken verses as opposed to sung lyrics; ὄψις is implied by the introduction of masks, but something more grandiose than the use of masks must be meant in C, as there were no comedies that did not use them. The primacy of plot, diction and song in A.'s teaching is confirmed by his account of the development of tragedy in 4.1449a15ff., where a similar pattern appears; in the beginning was the chorus, Aeschylus increased the actors from one to two and made λόγος take the primary rôle — i.e. made spoken verses predominate over lyric; furthermore in μέγεθος (cf. sup. p.155f.) tragedy became dignified late, developing from trivial *plots* and absurd *diction*. Thus μῦθος, λέξις and μέλος are the rudiments of both tragedy and comedy, and it is proper that they receive priority here. Cf. too p.114f. n.62.

Chapter XVII: The quantitative parts of comedy

On the sources for XVII see p.12 − 16. **d**'s corruption διδόμενον in XVII 2 has perfect parallels at *Poet.* 18.1456a28 διδόμενα Ξ, ᾳδόμενα Σ; 26.1462a7 διάδοντα A, διάδοντα recc., ᾳδοντα Spengel; Plato *Rep.* II 364c; Anacreon *PMG* 402c; Schol. Theoc. p. 3.10 Wendel. — This section supplies a quantitative analysis of comedy closely corresponding to that of tragedy in *Poet.* 12, which has itself often been rejected as spurious. Bernays (167f.) and Zieliński (*Die Gliederung der altattischen Komödie* 3f.) believed that the excerptor found this passage interpolated into *Poet.* and adopted it thence. More recently *Poet.* 12 has been less harshly viewed, and the whole matter is complicated. I shall begin with the individual sections of C, comparing *Poet.* 12, and proceed to wider considerations.

(a) *The heading*

The Treatise has no explicit statement that this set of parts (μέρη) is quantitative, in contrast to *Poet.* 12, which begins μέρη δὲ τραγῳδίας οἷς μὲν ὡς εἴδεσι δεῖ χρῆσθαι πρότερον εἴπομεν, κατὰ δὲ τὸ πόσον καὶ εἰς ἃ διαιρεῖται κεχωρισμένα τάδε ἐστίν, πρόλογος ἐπεισόδιον ἔξοδος χορικόν. It is possible that such a reference existed in Ω. Note the variation in the order of the four parts; in the epitome χορικόν holds second place. Both positions are logically defensible, and neither text need be altered to obtain conformity. Another difference is that *Poet.* 12 ends with a recapitulation of the opening, to which exception has been taken, although it does mark the chapter off as a definite unit, whereas the epitome lacks any such repetition. — Else (362 n.13) claims that the asyndetic form of listing is itself unaristotelian. This is untrue: cf. *Rhet.* I 15.1375a24, which also provides a parallel for C's statement that there are so many parts, before the list is set down in asyndeton.

(b) *The prologue*

In the definition of the prologue, C is closer than is **d** to *Poet.* 12, which reads ἔστιν δὲ πρόλογος μὲν μέρος ὅλον τραγῳδίας τὸ πρὸ χοροῦ παρόδου. **d**'s use of an ordinal, postponement of μέρος, and failure to state that we are dealing with a part *of comedy*, reveal a distance from the others, in accord with its conversion of the heading into a question: **d** is, I believe, a schoolmaster's potted version intended for rote learning. C's statement that the prologue is a μόριον does not occur of the other parts, whereas *Poet.* repeats the formula μέρος ὅλον of episode and *exodos* too: on its significance see Lucas ad 1452b19, 20. It is fair to assume that the epitomator preserved one such use, but left it to be supplied in the other cases.

Taplin (*The Stagecraft of Aeschylus* 471) charges that the use of 'prologue' in the Treatise and in *Poet.* 12 is too wide, and that the term ought to be limited to a formal opening speech if the passages are genuine, and not extended to include the whole opening scene. But this is a popular term (cf. Aristoph. *Frogs* 1119), and flexible use of popular terms is characteristically Stagiritic (the extension in usage is marked by μέρος ὅλον, cf. Lucas ad 52b19); if A. did write *Poet.* 12, it is important to remember that he had literally hundreds of plays to generalise about, and was not writing an exhaustive account. Certainly the definition does scant justice to the complexity of fifth-century practice, and may conceivably depart from fifth-century usage, but should we fairly demand anything better from an account on this scale?

A. refers to comic prologues at *Rhet.* III 14.1415a8ff., *Poet.* 5.1449b4. Note that the prologue is called 'the section up to the *entry* of the chorus' (εἴσοδος). The terminology is consistent with the use of ἐπεισόδιον, an act introduced by a new entry, which anticipates the recent and valuable emphasis on entries and exits as crucial to the articulation of Greek tragedy. The entry of the chorus is given its technical name πάροδος at *E.N.* IV 2.1123a23, *Poet.* 12.1452b17, 20, 22, where, apart from 1452b20, a choreographic distinction is in question.

(c) *The choral element*

The χορικόν comes next. In *Poet.* 12 it is discussed both after the opening list of parts and at the end; in neither place are we told what it is, but only its constituent elements — parodos, stasimon etc. C and **d** give the obvious definition that it is μέλος sung by the chorus; **d**'s corruption διδόμενον and omission of ὑπό reveal further its distance from the original (cf. *Suda* s.v. ᾿Αρίων = Aristot. fr. 676 Rose: πρῶτος . . . ὀνομάσαι τὸ ᾀδόμενον ὑπὸ τοῦ χοροῦ). C also proves its superiority by adding 'when (the song) has sufficient size', an important qualification, which helps to accommodate the comic *Agon*, since one of the more legitimate complaints against *Poet.* 12 is that it defines the episode as the part between complete choral songs, but neglects to tell us what a complete choral song actually is (Taplin 472f.).

Even this *caveat* will not satisfy critics, however. Indeed there is a great deal left unremarked about Attic Comedy of the fifth century. The parodos is not separately distinguished, and, above all, the parabasis is ignored altogether (**d**'s reference to it at the end is an addition possessing no authority, v. sup. p.13). However, it is not clear that fourth-century comedy would demand such a detailed analysis. According to Platonius I 31 Koster, Middle Comedy spurned the parabasis.

'If he (A.) tried to generalise from the practice of authors all the way from Epicharmus to Anaxandrides, he might have called a portion of a comedy intervening between two portions more distinctly musical an episode . . . The *Poetics* casts a rapid glance at the tragic chorus, but . . . does not delay over a function that in A.'s time was falling, or had fallen, into disuse. In his time there may have been little need for a long treatment of the choral element in comedy'

(Lane Cooper 55, 59; cf. sup. p.86). In terms of Old Comedy the analysis is very inadequate; three causes could have contributed to such inadequacy — the need for a broad chronological sweep, A.'s lack of interest in the formal elements of drama as of rhetoric, wherein he contrasts himself with the writers of previous handbooks (*Rhet.* I 1.1354b16ff.), and his tendency to prescribe for a writer working at a time when the chorus had assumed a subsidiary rôle as a mere interlude. He does refer to comic and tragic choruses at *Pol.* III 3.1276b5, cf. *Poet.* 1.1447b25ff.

Probably the greatest obstacle to acceptance of *Poet.* 12 has been the logical status of the choral part. The problem is identical here. Else (362) complains:

'instead of (A.'s) organic division between . . . speech and song, defined by the absence and presence of melody, we find here a purely mechanical division based on no principle and carried through in the crudest possible manner. Of the four "parts", the first three . . . are obviously thought of as *scenes*, "separated" from each other by the choral elements . . . The distinction between them is simply their position in the play: prologue at the beginning, *exodos* at the end, "episodes" in between. Thus the list presents the absurdity of a genus (χορικόν) set down side by side with three instances — they are not species — of another genus which is not even named.'

They *are* species of course; an instance is the prologue to the *Medea*. A later Peripatetic source in 'Psellus' (v. inf.) supplies the genus, but Else's point is valid; a stage in the argument is missing, one not difficult to supply. I simply refuse to be shocked. The analysis combines a division into beginning, middle and end (cf. *Poet.* 7.1450b26ff.) with the song/speech distinction, both of which are fundamental to Aristotelian theory, and employs terms already current in the theatre to express these ideas. Is this really so crass? — With μέγεθος ἱκανόν cf. 1451a14 ἱκανὸς ὅρος τοῦ μεγέθους.

(d) *The episode*

The definition of the episode is the same as in *Poet.*, except for the omission of μέρος ὅλον κωμῳδίας and substitution of δύο χορικῶν for ὅλων χορικῶν. For Lane Cooper's defence of the term v. sup.; cf. K. Nickau, *MH* 23 (1966) 155—71. Taplin (472) objects:

'This term and related words do not have the meaning "act" elsewhere in the *Poetics*, elsewhere in A., or in earlier comedy. Primarily it has, as one might expect from the first prefix, the same kind of associations as the English "episodic", viz. parenthesis, digression, subplot, interlude.'

But the ἐπ- in 'episode' has the primary implication not of irrelevance but of cumulation, as in ἐπεισάγω or ἐπεισέρχομαι, in that episodes open with the entry of a new character in addition to those who have already appeared: cf. *Rhet.* III 17.1418a33 δεῖ τὸν λόγον **ἐπεισοδιοῦν** ἐπαίνοις, οἷον Ἰσοκράτης ποιεῖ· ἀεὶ γάρ τινα **εἰσάγει**; Soph. *O.C.* 730 τῆς ἐμῆς ἐπεισόδου; Pollux IV 108. Moreover both senses of ἐπεισόδιον are present in *Poet.* At 4.1449a28 an increase in 'episodes' is one of the innovations that led to fully developed tragedy. A.'s penchant for unity is hardly likely to commend to him plentiful digressions and irrelevancies as a mark of tragedy's full development (cf. 18.1456a31). But it is an easy step from the primary sense to that of a self-contained or irrelevant intrusion, such as the jack-in-the-box appearances of impostors and busybodies in the latter part of an Aristophanic comedy, which are, incidentally, not always marked by a choral song. This is ἐπεισοδιώδης, 'full of episodes', but to good comic effect; a tragedy with similar scenes, like Aegeus' in the *Medea* perhaps, would swiftly attract the same epithet, but mockery and opprobrium too. Cf. Taplin 472 n.1, and Lucas ad 1455b21.

(e) *The exodos*

The last item is the ἔξοδος. There are important differences
between its definition and that in *Poet.* 12, which reads in MS A
ἔξοδος δὲ μέρος ὅλον τραγῳδίας μεθ' ὃ οὐκ ἔστι χοροῦ μέλος, but in
MS B ἔξοδος δὲ μέλος . . . καθ' ὃ οὐκ ἔστι χοροῦ μέρος. B has
confused μέλος and μέρος; its variant καθ' ὃ seems never to have
been considered. If A's text is right, the discrepancy is that the
Tractate states that the *exodos* is 'the utterance of the chorus at the
end', *Poet.* that it is 'the whole part of a tragedy after which there is
no choral song'. The definition in *Poet.* is repeated by Tzetzes, Περὶ
τραγικῆς ποιήσεως 24f.:

> ἡ δ' ἔξοδός τις τυγχάνει χοροῦ λόγος,
> μεθ' ὃν χοροῖς οὐκ ἔστι τι λέγειν μέλος (μέρος v.l.).

His testimonium to A's μεθ' ὃ does not of course prove it correct.
That his source is *Poet.* is proved elsewhere in the same poem:

> ἄλλοι δὲ τὸ στάσιμον χοροῦ φασι μέρος
> ἄνευ ἀναπαίστου καὶ τροχαίου τῶν μέτρων

(51—2); cf. 12.1452b23. Note μέρος corrupt for the μέλος of all
other sources for *Poet.* (Tzetzes' readings are rather neglected in the
editions; yet Kassel ad loc. is wrong to compare b23 with v.38,
where Tzetzes is quoting 'Euclides'). At 68f. ἄλλος τις is cited for
the definition of κομμός at b24. See also p.134 for his knowledge of
1.1447a28ff., where he had a text somewhat better than ours;
εὐσύνοπτος at *de diff. poet.* 3 possibly derives from 7.1451a4.
This definition is at odds with the proper ancient usage.

'In the fifth century the word was evidently used of the music
which accompanied the final exit of the chorus: see *Wasps* 582
(and scholia), Cratinus fr. 276 K. Even the late theorists
follow this obvious sense, and do not share the useless definition of *Poetics* (see e.g. Pollux 4. 108 . . .)'

(Taplin 472f.). Among these 'late theorists' is the Treatise, whose
definition contains one striking peculiarity: the *exodos* is said to be
the closing *utterance* (λεγόμενον) of the chorus. This is the same
peculiarity as the statement at *Poet.* 12.1452b22 that the *parodos* of
tragedy is the first λέξις of the chorus. As Dale said (*Papers* 35), the
term seems to be used because the *parodos* may contain stichic
marching metres like anapaests instead of lyric μέλος. The same is
true of the *exodos* of comedy in a considerable proportion of

Aristophanes' plays. Thus it is clear that the two passages are bred in the same stable, but one is not the sire of the other, due to the different definitions of the ἔξοδος.

A later source may help to illuminate the problem. A Byzantine scholarly analysis of tragedy, almost certainly by Michael Psellus (A.D. 1018 – 1078/9), has recently been published by R. Browning (ap. *Studies Presented to George Thomson*, 67 – 81, cf. Glucker ap. *Byzantion* 38 (1968) 267 – 72, Kassel *RhM* 116 (1973) 104 n.25). This lists the parts of tragedy as prologue, episode, exodos, choricon, and ἀπὸ σκηνῆς (1). These are not defined, but subdivisions of the choral element are supplied, namely parodos, stasimon, emmeleia, kommos, and exodos. This is more complex than *Poet.* and goes back to good sources, but what is important is that the *exodos* is listed twice, once as one of the five major parts, applied to the 'last act' to balance the prologue, and once as a choral element, i.e. τὸ ἐπὶ τέλει λεγόμενον τοῦ χοροῦ.

Now Psellus is not drawing directly on *Poet.* — witness such interesting statements as 8 (tragedy) τὰ πάθη μᾶλλον μιμεῖται ἢ τὰς πράξεις, although the analysis is in Peripatetic terms; but his duplication of *exodos* does suggest a solution to the difficult definition in *Poet.* — that the text is wrong. We need not search far for an improvement; the *difficilior lectio* of the Riccardianus καθ' ὅ yields the translation 'the exodos is a complete part of a tragedy, *insofar as* it is not a choral song'. For καθ' ὅ meaning 'insofar as' cf. *Metaph.* IV 18.1022a14ff. With this reading, the unparalleled extended sense of *exodos* is implied, but joined by the narrow sense attested elsewhere, and the qualification added that it may not be an independent part of tragedy at all, but instead subordinate to the choral part. The *exodos* is not then explicitly defined, which parallels the lack of definition of the choral element in *Poet.* If this is correct, the reading which yields the extended sense alone is an easy vulgarisation of B's more difficult text. But it may be felt that this reading is unacceptable, since it destroys the symmetry of the definitions; moreover, the *exodos* of tragedy never amounts to a full lyric, only to marching metres. If the discrepancy with the Treatise stands, we may ascribe it to the divergence between comedy and tragedy in this regard.

The fact remains that *exodos* was an unhelpful term at the best of times. As Lucas notes ad loc., in tragedy the last choral song 'can be a long way from the end of the play. Thus the *exodos* of the *HF* extends from 1038 to 1438.' Old Comedy is still more multifarious. As Dover remarks (*Aristophanic Comedy* 53), the end is sometimes merely a formula. In Menander there has been a drastic change;

the chorus do not appear at the end, but we find vestiges such as the prayer with which the *Samia* closes,

εὐμενὴς ἔποιτο Νίκη τοῖς ἐμοῖς ἀεὶ **χοροῖς**.

Thus for A. we might expect to find the term *exodos*, as far as comedy was concerned, coming to mean 'the last act', to provide a formal balance to the prologue. Whether this change also occurred in tragedy is obscure, but it seems likely if, as Taplin has argued (*LCM* 1 (1976) 47 − 50), fourth-century tragedy developed a five-act structure. If so (and Menander often does reflect tragic practice) we can see that the definition in *Poet.*, whichever text is read, is neither facile nor inapplicable, provided that the quantitative analysis applies to the practice of A.'s own time.

(f) *The authenticity of* Poetics *12*

However, another defence of the Treatise and *Poet.* 12 seems to have been overlooked, the widespread tendency to elaborate the analysis with ever more terms, on the grounds that the work of a predecessor is 'too schematic'; this is the burden of Taplin's objections to *Poet.* 12, for example. These two analyses are much less complex than others that existed. Pollux IV 108 has a long list of quantitative parts of tragedy, displaying a sophisticated critical vocabulary; Byzantine sources show us that many of these terms fitted into more complex versions of the schema in *Poet.* Psellus' analysis improves on *Poet.* 12 by making of τὰ ἀπὸ σκηνῆς an autonomous part of tragedy; its inclusion under χορικόν is one of Taplin's objections to *Poet.* 12 (475). Psellus also adds ἐμμέλεια to the parts of the χορικόν, to designate very brief choral lyrics; cf. C's qualification here, which excludes these from the χορικόν, because the latter is needed to divide the episodes one from another — an unsatisfactory state of affairs. Browning shows (art. cit.) that in other parts of his treatise Psellus draws somehow on Aristoxenus, A.'s musical disciple, who is known to have written *On Tragic Poets* (fr. 113 − 6 Wehrli) and *On Dancing in Tragedy* (fr. 103 − 12 id.).

In his poem *On Tragic Poetry* Tzetzes, as is now evident, used a source close to Psellus' for some details. He also used the *Poetics*, but without naming A., to whom he is bitterly hostile elsewhere (*Prol.* XIaI 15ff. Koster: cf. sup.). But in the main he depended on a source whom he calls 'Euclides', of whom he is very critical; he reproaches him for such sins as the omission of ἐμμέλεια (v.61), another example of increasing elaboration. Euclides is not, by the way, the same as *Poet.* 12; he contradicts it over the parodos, calling this an ᾠδή not a λέξις, as Tzetzes explicitly remarks (v.39 with his schol., another place where knowledge of *Poet.* 12 is evident); likewise Euclides' absurd view that the chorus stood still to sing the stasimon (v.53f., cf. Schol. Eur. *Phoen.* 202, Hyp. Aesch. *Pers.* 7 — 10, Dale loc. cit.; Tzetzes had a fuller text of Euclides here than we possess).

By a stroke of fortune we need not rely on Tzetzes' testimony to this source, but can read an abridgement of it ourselves in Cramer's *Anecdota Paris.* I 19 from MS Parisinus 1773 (A.D. 1493), with variants from Florentine MSS Laur. 31.2 (saec. xv) and Conv. Soppr. 158 (saec. xiv in.) published by Vitelli, *Mus. ital. di ant. class.* I (1885) 2f. These show that Tzetzes did not invent it; Koster suspected (ad Tz. XXIc 39, 41) that he may have found it in scholia to Euripides fuller than we now possess, since he refers to Euclides for details found in the arguments to Euripides' plays (*Prol.* XIaI 152). Moreover, Par. 1773 prefaces the extract with the riddle of the sphinx, which occurs in the scholia to *Phoenissae* 50, while a more complete version of Euclides' definition of the stasimon and parodos is found in the scholia on 202 (where ἐξόδῳ is surely corrupt for εἰσόδῳ: *Phoen.* 202 is quoted by Hyp. Aesch. *Pers.* loc. cit.). But both there and in the extracts the writer on tragedy remains anonymous. Moreover this writer has no connexion with comedy except in Tzetzes' prose writings: as Koster argued, this is a fabrication. It is much more satisfying to be able to abuse named persons, rather than the anonymous scribes who had over many years diligently assembled and copied the introductory remarks to Aristophanes (v. sup. p.15f.).

Euclides' classification of tragedy also illustrates the growth of the industry. Tragedy is divided into ten parts (the missing one is presumably ἔξοδος): πρόλογος, ἄγγελος, ἐξάγγελος, πάροδος, ἐπιπάροδος, στάσιμος, ὑπ<ο>ρ<χη>ματικός, ἀμοιβαῖος, σκηνικός. But Tzetzes demands still more sophistication and brings in five more, ῥῆσις, κούρισμα, σάλπιγξ, σκοπός and χορός (121 — 45). These are from a ninefold analysis of tragedy at Schol. Dion. Thr. (Heliodorus) 451.33ff. Hilgard: πρόλογος, ῥῆσις, ἀμοιβή, ἄγγελος, σκηνικὴ ᾠδή, κούρισμα, σάλπιγξ, σκοπός, χορός, with interesting post-Aristotelian definitions; tragedy is defined as βίων καὶ λόγων ἡρωϊκῶν μίμησις ἔχουσα σεμνότητα μετ' ἐπιπλοκῆς τινος [ibid. 306.8 adds καὶ παθῶν after ἡρωϊκῶν, while ibid. 475.1 adds ἔμμετρος].

By contrast, *Poet.* 12 and the Tractatus are very basic and primitive — hence modern objections, and, I believe, ancient efforts at improvement. These occurred not only in tragedy, but in comedy also, e.g. the sophisticated analyses of the parabasis.

Likewise Psellus' (2ff.) list of qualitative parts of tragedy is more highly elaborate than A.'s, and Browning does not hesitate to label it 'presumably later' than the latter's (art. cit.). The complex quantitative division of comedy in Donatus is another example (*Comm. Terenti* p.27.2 Wessner = *CGF* p.69 Kaibel: omitted by Koster). This consists of πρόλογος, πρότασις, ἐπίτασις and κατα- στροφή, with the prologue further classified into συστατικός, ἐπιτιμητικός, δραματικός and μικτός. I have suggested that this tendency also affects the later analyses of humour, modelled on sections V—VI of the Treatise. Another parallel is the development in rhetorical theory of an elaborate system of 'figures of speech', beginning from *Rhet.* III, where A.'s analysis must have seemed very crude and incomplete to many among his epigoni: cf. Russell, *Longinus* pp.127ff. Thus I find the very simplicity and inadequacy of *Poet.* 12 and Tractatus XVII a strong argument for an early dating, to a time when the study was still in its infancy; and infants, by definition, tend to babble. Will the mewling of these twins, exposed on the harsh hillside of modern scholarship, condemn them to perish as bastards, or result in the recognition of their true parentage?

Above (p.60) I proposed that a quantitative analysis is needed in any Aristotelian work on comedy. Cf. Hubbard (ap. *ALC* 106 n.1), who sees that *Poet.* analyses tragedy according to the three categories, including quantity, that define an entity's essential nature. Thus *Poet.* 12 also is needed; although Hubbard considers that the repetition at its end is dreary and contains the non- aristotelian form εἴπαμεν (1452b26), 'it stands where it should stand, concluding the analysis of the nature of tragedy and preceding the consideration of its virtues, and though bald is not absurd in content.' In fact εἴπαμεν is not the sole reading attested: MS B has the correct εἴπομεν, and it is hazardous to put weight on a single vulgarising variant, despite Else 361 n.10. Else's additional objection, that *Poet.* 12 spoils the transition from Ch. 11 (definitive) to Ch. 13 (prescriptive), is weak, as such a transition is an excellent place for a section that combines both functions. Else further contends that 'the only thing divisible into separate parts is *a* tragedy', not tragedy in general, but it is an observed fact that helpful generalisations in quantitative terms *can* be made about corpora of poems: cf. on the *Homeric Hymns* at *Hermes* 109 (1981) 9—24, or recent work on Pindar.

Chapter XVIII: The iambic element in comedy

The rubric under which I write is itself controversial. Lane Cooper heads this Chapter '"Old", "New" and "Middle" Comedy', and comments (285):

'the allusion to the "New" comedy may place the source of this part of the Tractate after A.; and yet we know that Aristophanes produced comedies which anticipated the devices of Menander. Is it possible that A. invented all three terms . . . ? But this is mere conjecture.'

Fortunately we can do better than conjecture. I shall show first, that the language here is typical of A.; second, that the underlying idea is his also; third, that the tripartite division of comedy may not have originally included Menander; and fourth, that this chapter corresponds to the account of iambus expected in *Poetics* II, except that iambus itself could not be discussed as it is not mimetic. The comparative approach adopted is reminiscent of the end of *Poetics* I, and forms a conclusion well fitted to be that of *Poetics* II.

(a) Parallels in Aristotle

'Old' comedy is ἡ πλεονάζουσα τῷ γελοίῳ. Note *Metaph.* I 2.994b18 πλεονάζοντα τῷ λόγῳ. At first sight this is a very strange statement, as one would have thought that comedy, being dependent on the laughable to achieve its end, could not possess an excess of it. But this is precisely what the Greek says, and he says it again in *E.N.* IV 8, the familiar discussion of the buffoon, the boor and the wit. Excess is never far away in the *Ethics*, and here the buffoon overdoes his humour, the boor has none, and the wit preserves the mean. The phrasing is strikingly similar — οἱ τῷ γελοίῳ ὑπερβάλλοντες βωμολόχοι δοκοῦσιν εἶναι (1128a4ff.: 'those who *go to excess in humour* seem buffoons and vulgar fellows, eager to crack a joke at any cost . . . '). To illustrate, A. contrasts the old comedies, with their personal abuse, and recent ones, which use innuendo (cf. sup. on VII). I shall return to this below.

The 'new' comedy 'abandons this, and tends to be serious'. For προΐεσθαι cf. *Pol.* V 7.1307b4; cf. for the sense *Poet.* 5.1449b8 ἀφέμενος τῆς ἰαμβικῆς ἰδέας 'relinquishing the iambic form', of Crates who first introduced comedy with a plot to Athens, and

Rhet. III 1.1404a33 of tragedians relinquishing glosses (ἀφείκασιν). — σεμνός is one of A.'s favourite stylistic terms. 'Serious, stately, severe' all fail to render it. In *Rhet.* it is used of altered diction (III 2.1404b8, cf. 3.1406b3, *Poet.* 22.1458a21), speaking gravely about trivia (7.1408a13), and metres (8.1408b32ff.). Cf. also *Poet.* 4.1448b25, Demetrius 128. Someone will object that comedy can hardly be said to be σεμνόν; but it is not, it is only 'inclining towards' τὸ σεμνόν. — For ῥέπειν πρός τι cf. *Pol.* IV 7.1293b20, *E.N.* X 1.1172a31.

Most interesting of all is the same contrast between γελοῖον and σεμνόν at *Rhet.* III 3.1406b5, on 'frigidity' in metaphors. These are inappropriate, if they are either ridiculous (comic poets too use metaphors), or excessively stately and redolent of tragedy (εἰσὶ μεταφοραὶ ἀπρεπεῖς, αἱ μὲν διὰ τὸ γελοῖον — χρῶνται γὰρ καὶ οἱ κωμῳδοποιοὶ μεταφοραῖς — αἱ δὲ διὰ τὸ σεμνὸν ἄγαν καὶ τραγικόν). Thus we find in *Rhet.* the same scale of value as in *Tract.* XVIII, in a context where comedy is in A.'s mind. Note too the linking of σεμνόν with τραγικόν; a prominent feature of comedy's development in the fourth century is the influence of tragic patterns and models, as has often been remarked (cf. Satyrus, *Vit. Eur.* ap. *P.Oxy.* 1176, fr. 39 col. vii; Strabo I 18; Quint. X 1.69; Katsouris, *Tragic Patterns in Menander*). If *both* passages are by A., why should they not be put together to produce a hint that A. was well aware of this influence?

The contrast of γελοῖον and σεμνόν occurs again in the context of evolution, this time of tragedy itself, at *Poet.* 4.1449a19, ἐκ μικρῶν μύθων καὶ λέξεως γελοίας . . . ὀψὲ ἀπεσεμνύνθη ('tragedy, evolving from slight plots and *humorous* diction, took a long time to become *stately*'). To find something similar here of the development of comedy is extremely suggestive.

The Tractate's terms for 'old' and 'new' in describing the development of poetry are both current in A.:

Comedies:	παλαιαί	καιναί	*E.N.* IV 8.1128a22
Tragedians:	—	οἱ νέοι	*Poet.* 6.1450a25
Tragedians:	οἱ ἀρχαῖοι	οἱ νῦν	*Poet.* 6.1450b7
Tragedians:	οἱ παλαιοί	—	*Poet.* 14.1453b27
Comedy:	παλαιά	νέα	*Tract.* XVIII

(b) *The development of comedy in Aristotle*

Part of the proof that the underlying idea is Aristotelian has preceded; for the rest, cf. *E.N.* IV 8 on the old and recent comedies, where it is important that, although A. prefers the latter, he recognises some need for mockery (ἔδει δ' ἴσως καὶ σκώπτειν). The main objection to XVIII must be, not the classification of comedy into old and new, but the existence of a middle type: so e.g. Kaibel *Abh.* 57f., who contends that the twofold classification is also found in *Tract.* VII (comedy and abuse: cf. ad loc.). Certainly both poles are found there, as in *E.N.*; but there is no reason why, because two extremes exist, there can be no middle term. A. was good at middle terms, e.g. metaphors in good style between those too solemn and too absurd in *Rhet.* III 3. The absence of such a term in the discussion of comedy at *E.N.* IV 8 is not surprising, as it would have blurred the point A. is making.

The division must on the whole be chronological not typological; any individual comedy could be in either style or both, but the terms imply trends broadly operative through time (cf. Lane Cooper 285f.). It is fair to ask which the writer preferred: πλεονάζουσα conveys a note of disapprobation against the 'old' style, cf. VII; but if we compare *Rhet.* III 3 on metaphors, and also the reservation on σκώπτειν in *E.N.* IV 8, we can conclude that comedy ought not to be too solemn either. The writer prefers the middle term: after the discussion of γέλως at V—VI it would be illogical to give the prize to comedies that lacked it. Yet the middle term here is a *mixture* of the extremes, according to C, not qualitatively different like the wit from the buffoon. 'Middle' comedy is not devoid of buffoonery. Cf. the curious parallels at Tzetzes *Prol..* XIaII 58, ἡ κωμῳδία μεμιγμένον τοῖς σκώμμασιν εἶχε τὸν γέλωτα, and in Koster ad loc.: add Schol. Tz. *de diff. poet.* 113, which explicitly says that comic laughter is mixed with λοιδορία, while that of satyr-plays is unmixed.

(c) *The tripartition of comedy before Menander*

The tripartite division of comedy goes back at least to Hellenistic times (cf. Körte, *RE* XI (1921) 1256, Wehrli, *Motivstudien* 16—8), and originally omitted Menander (cf. Kaibel, *Abh.* 49ff., Cantarella *Aristofane* I 96f.). Kayser (42f.) adduces several late sources:

(i) *Prolegomenon* V Koster, and *Prolegomenon* XIb 49ff. Koster which is derived from it, have a primary bipartition of comedy into 'old' and 'new', and τὸ μέσον added as if an after-thought (V 2). 'Old' comedy itself is divided (ibid. 12ff.). In the oldest comedy, under Susarion, γέλως alone was all it offered (cf. πλεονάζουσα τῷ γελοίῳ). Cratinus made improvements, adding utility to entertainment (good Hellenistic terms these), but even he partook of the 'old style' (τῆς ἀρχαιότητος) and its lack of order (ἀταξία). Aristophanes achieved a new high level, and his *Plutus* had a verisimilitudinous plot and lacked choruses, a feature of the newer comedy (contrast XVI). At this juncture the excerpt ends. We see here C's point about τὸ γελοῖον, and A.'s about the importance of plot, but the terminology is post-Aristotelian.

(ii) Close to (i) is the *Life of Aristophanes*, XXVIII 2ff. Koster (cf. XXIXa 5ff., very similar): Aristophanes

πρῶτος δοκεῖ τὴν κωμῳδίαν ἔτι πλανωμένην τῇ **ἀρχαίᾳ** ἀγωγῇ
ἐπὶ τὸ χρησιμώτερον καὶ **σεμνότερον** μεταγαγεῖν, πικρότερον
καὶ αἰσχρότερον Κρατίνου καὶ Εὐπόλιδος βλασφημούντων ἢ
ἔδει. πρῶτος δὲ καὶ **τῆς νέας** κωμῳδίας τὸν τρόπον ἐπέδειξεν ἐν
τῷ Κωκάλῳ, ἐξ οὗ τὴν ἀρχὴν λαβόμενοι Μένανδρός τε καὶ
Φιλήμων ἐδραματούργησαν.

Aristophanes is accredited with putting an end to the 'old' style of production, and *in addition* showing the way to the New Comedy of Menander and Philemon in his *Cocalus*. These are separate events: if Aristophanes moves out of the 'old' style early in his career, and initiates the 'new' at the end of it, where is he during his prime, if not in the 'middle' style? Note too the direction of change in his work: 'towards the more serious', which is Aristotelian, and 'towards the more useful' which is not, but typically Hellenistic.

(iii) Diomedes, *Ars Gramm.* III 488.23 Keil (= XXIV 2 Koster) divides comedy into three periods, of which Old Comedy is again the midmost:

'Poetae *primi* comici fuerunt Susarion, Mullus et Magnes. hi *veteris* disciplinae iocularia quaedam minus scite ac venuste pronuntiabant ... *Secunda* aetate fuerunt Aristophanes, Eupolis et Cratinus, qui et principum vitia sectati acerbissimas comoedias composuerunt. *Tertia* aetas fuit Menandri, Diphili et Philemonis ... '

This omits our Middle Comedy altogether.

(iv) Tzetzes, in *Prolegomenon* XIaI 69ff. Koster, states that comedy began with direct abuse, a stage that ended during

Cratinus' career as a result of an (apocryphal) altercation with Alcibiades; the new style of veiled abuse was practised by Eupolis, Aristophanes etc., by the poets of Old Comedy in fact (cf. sup. p.206f.). The 'third' comedy, which attacked only slaves and foreigners in like fashion, is that of Menander and Philemon (103f.).

(v) The anonymous *Anecdoton Estense* II 5, from our MS M⁹, contains an account of poetry within an introduction to Theocritus. Although, unlike the rest of the MS, it is in the hand of G. Valla (A.D. 1430−99), its first editor Kayser (64ff.) perceived that it contained new material. It divides comedy into three, of which our Old Comedy is explicitly second, as in Diomedes:

τῆς κωμῳδίας ἡ μὲν πρώτη, ἥτις ἐμφανῶς πάντας ἔψεγε· κατῆρξε δὲ αὐτῆς Σουσαρίων· ἡ δὲ δευτέρα, ἧς ἦν ὁ ψόγος κατὰ πάντων, ἀλλὰ κεκρυμμένος. ἄριστοι δὲ ἐν αὐτῇ Κρατῖνος, Εὔπολις, Ἀριστοφάνης, Πλάτων. τῆς δὲ τρίτης ὁ ψόγος καὶ κεκρυμμένος ἦν καὶ κατὰ δούλων μόνον καὶ ξένων, ἀλλ' οὐκέτι πολιτῶν· διέπρεψαν ἐν αὐτῇ Μένανδρος καὶ Φιλήμων.

This important tract, omitted by Koster and his predecessors, shares a source with the next passage.

(vi) Tzetzes' Περὶ διαφορᾶς ποιητῶν (XXIa Koster: cf. here 80−7) has details omitted in the *Anecdoton*, and vice versa. The parallels with Tzetzes' writings are extensive, and his authorship of the *Anecdoton* beyond doubt (as proved by Kayser, loc. cit., cf. Wendel, *Ueberlieferung und Entstehung der Theokrit-Scholien* 9ff.).

(vii) The same tripartition of comedy into direct abuse, veiled abuse of citizens and veiled abuse of slaves and aliens only is found in the Scholia to Dionysius Thrax 19.15ff. Hilgard (= XVIIIa Koster: assigned to Melampus or Diomedes), with the difference that the three stages are called 'old', 'middle' and 'new', not 'first', 'second' and 'third' as in the four previous sources. Moreover this passage resembles *Prol.* V in treating Cratinus as less advanced than Aristophanes, and in referring to utility. After an account of comedy's rustic origins and Susarion, and of how the castigation of vices was a public benefit (ὠφέλουν κοινῇ τὴν πολιτείαν), the Scholiast tells how political restrictions were imposed, and led to indirect abuse and then to a total ban on the abuse of political figures. He sums up as follows:

διὸ καὶ τρεῖς διαφορὰς ἔδοξεν ἔχειν ἡ κωμῳδία· καὶ ἡ μὲν καλεῖται παλαιά, ἡ ἐξ ἀρχῆς φανερῶς ἐλέγχουσα, ἡ δὲ μέση ἡ

αἰνιγματωδῶς, ἡ δὲ νέα ἡ μηδ' ὅλως τοῦτο ποιοῦσα πλὴν ἐπὶ
δούλων ἢ ξένων. καὶ τῆς μὲν παλαιᾶς πολλοὶ γεγόνασιν,
ἐπίσημος δὲ Κρατῖνος . . . μετέσχον δέ τινος χρόνου τῆς
παλαιᾶς κωμῳδίας Εὔπολίς τε καὶ Ἀριστοφάνης. τῆς δὲ μέσης
καὶ αὐτῆς μὲν πολλοὶ γεγόνασιν, ἐπίσημος δέ Πλάτων τις, οὐχ ὁ
φιλόσοφος . . . τῆς δὲ νέας ὁμοίως πολλοὶ γεγόνασιν, ἐπίσημος
δὲ Μένανδρος.

The whole passage is closely followed in *Prol.* IV, transparently a
recasting of the same material, where the stages are called 'first',
'second' and 'third', but Aristophanes and Eupolis are assigned to
the 'first' and the inconvenient Susarion and Cratinus simply
omitted; Plato is assigned to the 'second', Menander to the 'third'.
A similar recasting of XVIIIa is found in Pseudo-Andronicus, alias
Palaeocappa, where Aristophanes, Eupolis and Cratinus are all
assigned to 'old', Plato to 'middle' and Menander to 'new'. The
subtle position of XVIIIa, that Cratinus is pure 'old' comedy, but
Aristophanes and Eupolis partook of it only for some time, is
crudely simplified in these two compilations, which show the
direction in which distortions occurred in the tradition: they seem *a
priori* less likely to have happened in the reverse direction, i.e.
towards making Aristophanes 'middle' comedy.

Given modern perspective, and the importance of Menander
and his contemporaries, it was inevitable that their comedy would
play a crucial part in any Hellenistic or later theory; the present
use of the tripartite division has a fair pedigree, e.g. in Platonius. It
may assist to tabulate the usages, according to whether Aristophanes belongs to 'Old' or 'Middle' comedy: the passages are in
Koster unless stated. I indicate their relations so far as they are
securely ascertained (see over).

The strength of the tradition giving Aristophanes this middle
position is notable (cf. Rostagni 136ff.). Dosi (621, 631) ascribed
the tripartition of comedy to Theophrastus, for six reasons: (i) the
doctrine is Peripatetic; (ii) A. could not have taken New Comedy
into account; (iii) Theophrastus' definition of comedy depends on
New Comedy; (iv) he is said to have taught Menander; (v) he liked
tripartitions; (vi) this tripartition is connected with the concept of
πλάσμα in some versions (e.g. *Prol.* V 25 Koster). I might add that
it is also connected with the Hellenistic notion of ὠφελία 'utility'
(*Prol.* V 17, Schol. Dion. Thr. XVIIIa 28, *Vita Aristoph.* XXVIII
3), and with the probably Theophrastean interest in verisimilitude
(*Prol.* V 25; cf. sup. p.50). (vi) is a valid proof that the tripartition
goes back to Hellenistic, post-Aristotelian scholarship, but not that

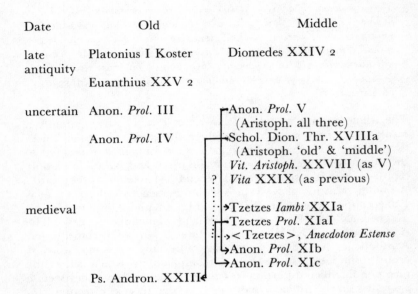

Date	Old	Middle
late antiquity	Platonius I Koster	Diomedes XXIV 2
	Euanthius XXV 2	
uncertain	Anon. *Prol.* III	Anon. *Prol.* V (Aristoph. all three)
	Anon. *Prol.* IV	Schol. Dion. Thr. XVIIIa (Aristoph. 'old' & 'middle')
		Vit. Aristoph. XXVIII (as V)
		Vita XXIX (as previous)
medieval		Tzetzes *Iambi* XXIa
		Tzetzes *Prol.* XIaI
		<Tzetzes>, *Anecdoton Estense*
		Anon. *Prol.* XIb
		Anon. *Prol.* XIc
	Ps. Andron. XXIII	

it originated there. The other arguments are very weak: (i) and (v) are as applicable to A. as to his follower, and (ii) rests on the *petitio principii* that A. knew no tripartition of comedy, which is precisely what Dosi is trying to show: Fuhrmann (64) commits the same error. 'Old' comedy is not necessarily Old Comedy.

There is one startling oddity about this Hellenistic tripartition. Where are the poets of Middle Comedy? Are Antiphanes, Eubulus, Alexis and Anaxandrides so unimportant that they can be omitted without trace? Ought they not to either merit a class of their own, as the modern division after Platonius allows, or be expressly included in the constellations of poets to either side of them? This surely underestimates the significance of Anaxandrides and his contemporaries, with whom A. for one was clearly familiar (e.g. *Rhet.* III 12.1413b26ff.). I think only one explanation for this yawning vacuum will carry conviction, which is that *the tripartite classification originated before Menandrian comedy existed*, i.e. no later than the 320s B.C.; this division was outdated by the rise of a new form of comedy; but, rather than call this a fourth type, the third type, 'new' comedy, was appropriated to cover Menander, leaving the poets of Middle Comedy in limbo. The Hellenistic phrasing in such versions as *Prol.* V shows that this occurred at that period; but the gap was felt, and to remedy it, while preserving the tripartition,

Aristophanes and his comrades were drawn into constituting 'old' comedy. That this too was a Hellenistic development is suggested by the language of *Prol.* III Koster (e.g. 9 οὐχ ὑποθέσεως ἀληθοῦς, 42 πλάσματος ποιητικοῦ, and 44 ποιητικὸν χαρακτῆρα; cf. on Theophrastus sup. p.50f., and [Longin.] *de Subl.* 15.8). To call Aristophanes 'old' is of course easier from this post-Menandrian perspective than from A.'s.

Such efforts to preserve a tripartite division at all costs are not unparalleled in the history of scholarship. Archaeologists will recall the effort made to impose tripartitions onto the different periods of the Aegean Bronze Age, and the contorsions ever since to maintain the system in the face of reassessments of the evidence.

If the tripartition did arise before Menander, there is only one place where it is likely to have evolved — the Peripatus, where the *Didascaliae* were being compiled. Precisely this tripartition — 'old' comedy down to Aristophanes, Aristophanes as 'middle' comedy, and his successors as 'new' comedy — is consistent with the Tractate's attention to Aristophanes in V—VI, and apparent approval of 'middle' comedy here. In fact this is the only way in which these sections of the Tractate can be reconciled as parts of the same work: that they are parts of the same work is argued on a structural basis sup. p.61 and overleaf. It is moreover congruent with the Aristotelian phrasing of XVIII, and contents of V. It is noteworthy that Aristophanes is seen as a mean by Platonius (II 14ff. Koster), but on a different scale of value, between the bitterness of Cratinus and the wit (χάρις) of Eupolis; for parallel views of Sophocles as a mean between Aeschylus and Euripides, cf. Dion. Hal. *Comp. Verb.* 24, Dio Chrys. *Or.* 52.15.

Else (188, 309f., cf. sup. p.205) thought that A. would view Old Comedy as a mere minor episode in the story of comedy's development, in fact a survival of iambus, and not really comedy at all. But if the Tractate is Aristotelian, Else has brought down the date too far — Aristophanes mixed old and new, and was very much admired (again I must refer the sceptic to *Poet.* 3.1448a25ff., where Homer, Sophocles and Aristophanes are given together). But it is not clear exactly where A. would have placed the dividing-lines. Presumably the latest plays of Aristophanes would, for him too, belong to 'new' comedy; conceivably he referred to decrees concerning τὸ ὀνομαστὶ κωμῳδεῖν as the boundary between 'old' and 'middle' comedy, although the evidence for these is dubious and contradictory (cf. Schol. Aristoph. *Ach.* 67, Maidment ap. *CQ* 29 (1935) 9ff., Brink, *Horace on Poetry* 317 and sup. p.207). The *Poetics* is no help here, as A. drew only a bipartite division within tragedy (on where he placed the division, cf. Denniston *CR* 43 (1939) 60, Lucas ad 1453b27; the problem seems unsolved).

(d) *The function of this section*

Lastly, this passage corresponds to the discussion of iambus expected by some in the lost *Poetics* II. It corresponds to it but does not represent it; for there was no account of iambus as a genre in its own right in the lost book. Iambus is not the comic equivalent of epic (that is burlesque like the *Margites*): it is not mimetic in A.'s use of the term, i.e. not poetry at all (v. sup. p.121ff. on *Poet.* 9.1451b11). It is taken account of in *Tract.* VII, but we do not expect a full-scale examination to parallel *Poet.* 23–5 on epic. Indeed, we are not promised one: 6.1449b21 promises only epic and comedy. There is the possibility that the end of *Poet.* 26 in MS B be restored περὶ δὲ [ἰάμβων . . . , sup. p.63; but even if a promise was made there to discuss iambus as well as comedy in the next book, the force of the argument that the treatment of a non-mimetic genre would be brief, or conveyed implicitly by means of contrast and comparison with comedy, is not diminished (verse iambus was classed as prose by Callimachus, fr. 112.9 with Pfeiffer ad loc., cf. Hor. *Serm.* II 6.17, and Philodemus thought Archilochus not mimetic, *Poem.* IV col. iv Gomperz). For A.'s work on Archilochus v. p.122.

The position of this account of the types of comedy, unparalleled in *Poetics* I, and its significance, are best explained if it is describing the decline of the iambic element in comedy, i.e. of the unmimetic part, direct abuse; comedy is seen as evolving towards its essential nature (cf. sup. p.204). The correspondence to *Poet.* 23–5 resides in the introduction of the non-dramatic genre depicting characters and actions of the equivalent moral level; asymmetry arises because Greek culture had as yet developed no genre of non-dramatic comic writing that did not describe real individuals, given that mime counts as dramatic. The correspondence to *Poet.* 26, the comparison of tragedy and epic, lies in the comparison implied here between types of comedy with a sharper or milder tang of the iambus, to the detriment of the former; not only do both passages compare and contrast, but in each the dramatic genre beats the non-dramatic. Thus XVIII makes an appropriate ending to the second book of the *Poetics*.

γέγραφα, ἀνεγνώκατε, ἔχετε, δικάζετε!

Bibliography

This bibliography comprises all works mentioned and editions used. Entries preceded by an asterisk are referred to in the text by the author's name only. Successive editions are denoted by superscript numerals. Abbreviations are given in brackets after the entry. Those for ancient authors and works follow Liddell-Scott-Jones, with some expansions: note A. for Aristotle in Part VI. *CAG* denotes the series *Commentaria in Aristotelem Graeca*: see BUSSE. Abbreviations for periodicals are those of *L'Année Philologique*.

Alfonsi, L. 'Sul Περὶ Ποιητῶν di Aristotele', *RFIC* 20 (1942) 193−200.

Allan, D.J. 'Some passages in Aristotle's *Poetics*', *CQ* 21 (1971) 81−92.

*Allen, T.W. *Homeri Opera V, Hymnos Cyclum Fragmenta Margiten Batrachomyomachiam Vitas continens*. Oxford 1912.

Allen, W.S. *Vox Graeca*.² Cambridge 1974.

Amundsen, L. 'Some remarks on Greek diminutives', *SO* XL (1965) 5−16.

Ardizzoni, A. ΠΟΙΗΜΑ. *Ricerche sulla teoria del linguaggio poetico nell'antichità. Μουσικαὶ διάλεκτοι* Suppl. 5 IV, Bari 1953.

Armstrong, A.H., ed. *The Cambridge History of later Greek and early Medieval Philosophy*. Cambridge 1967.

*Arndt, E. *De ridiculi doctrina rhetorica*. Diss. Bonn, 1904.

Arnim, H. von. *Stoicorum Veterum Fragmenta*. Leipzig 1903−24. (*SVF*)

Arnott, W.G. 'From Aristophanes to Menander', *Greece and Rome* 19 (1972) 65−80.

— Rev. of GUILLÉN, *CR* 29 (1979) 140−1.

*Atkins, J.W.H. *Literary Criticism in Antiquity*. Cambridge 1934.

*Austin, C. *Comicorum Graecorum Fragmenta in Papyris Reperta*. Berlin and New York 1973.

Barnes, J. 'Homonymy in Aristotle and Speusippus', *CQ* 21 (1971) 65−80.

Barnes, J. *Articles on Aristotle 4. Psychology and Aesthetics.* London 1979.

*Baumgart, H. *Handbuch der Poetik.* Stuttgart 1887.

Baumstark, A. *Aristoteles bei den Syrern von V—VIII Jahrhundert.* Leipzig 1900.

Bekker, I. *Anecdota Graeca.* Berlin, 1814—21. (The Antiatticist, Vol. I pp.75—116.)

— *Photii Bibliotheca.* Berlin 1824—5.

— *Aristotelis Opera. Ed. Academia Reg. Borusica,* Berlin 1831—70. (All citations from Aristotle use his chapters, pagination and line-numbering.)

Belfiore, E.S. *'Imitation' and Book X of Plato's* Republic. Diss. Univ. Calif. at Los Angeles; 1978.

— 'Aristotle's use of *praxis* in the *Poetics*', *TAPA* forthcoming (1984).

*Bergk, T. *Aristophanes. Comoediae.*[2] Leipzig 1861. (His text of the Tractate is at p.xliiif.)

— 'Kritische Beiträge zu den sogenannten Phokylides', *Philologus* 41 (1882) 577—601.

Bernays, J. 'Ergänzung zu Aristoteles *Poetik*', *RhM* VIII (1853) 561—96.

— *Grundzüge der verlorenen Abhandlung des Aristoteles über Wirkung der Tragödie.* Breslau 1857.

* — *Zwei Abhandlungen über die aristotelische Theorie des Drama.* Berlin 1880, repr. Darmstadt 1968.

Björk, G. *Das Alpha Impurum und die tragische Kunstsprache.* Uppsala 1950.

Bonitz, H. *Aristotelische Studien* I—V. Vienna 1862—7.

* — *Index Aristotelicus.* Berlin 1870. (Vol. V of *Aristotelis Opera,* editio Acad. Reg. Borusica: see BEKKER.)

Brancato, G. *La σύστασις nella Poetica di Aristotele.* Naples 1963.

Bremer, J.M. *Hamartia: tragic errors in the Poetics of Aristotle and Greek tragedy.* Amsterdam 1969.

Brink, C.O. *Horace on Poetry: Prolegomena to the Literary Epistles.* Cambridge 1963. (*Prol.*)

* — *Horace on Poetry: the 'Ars Poetica'.* Cambridge 1971.

— 'Philodemus, Περὶ Ποιημάτων, Book IV', *Maia* 24 (1972) 342—4.

Browning, R. 'A Byzantine Treatise on Tragedy', 67—81 in ΓΕΡΑΣ, *Studies presented to George Thomson,* Acta Universitatis Carolinae, Phil. et Hist. I, Graecolatina Pragensia II. Prague 1963.

Burnet, J. *The Ethics of Aristotle.* London 1900.

Busse, A. *Porphyrius. Isagoge, et in Aristotelis Categorias Commentarium.* *CAG* IV 1, Berlin 1887.
— *Ammonius. In Porphyrii Isagogen sive V voces. CAG* IV 3, Berlin 1891.
— *Ammonius. In Aristotelis Categorias Commentarius. CAG* IV 4, Berlin 1895.
— *Philoponi (olim Ammonii) in Aristotelis Categorias Commentarium. CAG* XIII 1, Berlin 1898.
— *Elias Philosophus. In Porphyrii Isagogen et Aristotelis Categorias Commentaria. CAG* XVIII 1, Berlin 1900.
— *Olympiodorus. Prolegomena et in Aristotelis Categorias Commentarium. CAG* XII 1, Berlin 1902.
— *David Philosophus. Prolegomena et in Porphyrii Isagogen Commentarium. CAG* XVIII 2, Berlin 1904.
*Butcher, S.H. *Aristotle's Theory of Poetry and Fine Art.*[4] London 1907. Repr. New York, 1951.
Butterworth, C.E. *Averroes' three short commentaries on Aristotle's 'Topics', 'Rhetoric' and 'Poetics'.* Albany 1977.
*Bywater, I. *Aristotle on the Art of Poetry.* Oxford 1909.
*Cantarella, R. *Aristofane. Le Commedie. I Prolegomena.* Milan 1949. (Citations in Apparatus Criticus.)
— *Scritti minori sul teatro greco.* Brescia 1970.
* — 'I "libri" della *Poetica* di Aristotele', *Rendiconti della Classe di scienze morali, storiche e filologiche dell'Accademia dei Lincei* 30 (1975) 289−97.
Cavalieri, P.F. de', with J. Lietzmann. *Specimina Codicum Graecorum Vaticanorum.* Bonn 1910.
Christ, W. von. *Aristotelis de Arte Poetica liber.* Leipzig 1878.
Cohn, L. 'Constantin Palaeokappa und Jacob Diassorinos', pp. 125−33 ap. *Philologische Abhandlungen M. Hertz zum 70 Geburtstag . . . dargebracht.* Berlin 1888.
— 'Eukleides (6)', P−W *RE* VI (1907) 1003.
Colonna, A. 'I prolegomeni ad Esiodo e la Vita Esiodea di Giovanni Tzetzes', *Boll. del Comitato per la preparazione dell'Edizione nazionale dei Classici greci e latini* 2 (1953) 27−39.
Consbruch, M. *Zu den Traktat περὶ κωμῳδίας.* Strasbourg 1889.
* — *Hephaestionis Enchiridion cum commentariis veteribus.* Leipzig 1906.
*Cooper, Lane. *An Aristotelian Theory of Comedy.* New York 1922, Oxford 1924.
*Cope, E.M. *The Rhetoric of Aristotle with a Commentary.* Revised by J.E. Sandys, Cambridge 1877. Repr. Hildesheim and New York 1970.
Cornford, F.M. *The Origin of Attic Comedy.* London 1914.

Cousin, J. *Études sur Quintilien I.* Paris 1936.

Couvreur, P. *Hermias, in Platonis Phaedrum Scholia.* Paris 1901. Repr. with index and afterword by C. Zintzen, Hildesheim and New York 1971.

*Cramer, J.A. *Anecdota Graeca e codd. Manuscriptis Bibliothecae Regiae Parisiensis.* Oxford 1839–41. Repr. Hildesheim 1967.

Cunningham, I.C. *Herodas. Mimiambi.* Oxford 1971.

Dahiyat, I.M. *Avicenna's Commentary on the 'Poetics' of Aristotle.* Leiden 1974.

*Dahlmann, H. 'Varro's Schrift "de poematibus" und die hellenistisch-römische Poetik', *Abh. d. Wiss. u. d. Lit. in Mainz, Geistes- u. Sozialwiss. Kl.* 3, Wiesbaden 1953.

Dale, A.M. *Collected Papers.* Cambridge 1969.

D'Alton, J.F. *Roman Literary Theory and Criticism.* London 1931.

Denniston, J.D. 'καθάπερ καί, ὥσπερ καί, οἷον καί', *CR* 43 (1929) 60.

Devreesse, R. *Bibliothèque Nationale, Catalogue des manuscrits grecs. Le fonds Coislin.* Paris 1945.

— *Introduction à l'étude des manuscrits grecs.* Paris 1954.

Dindorf, W. *Aristides.* Leipzig 1829.

* — *Aristophanis Comoediae. Tom. IV, Scholia graeca ex codicibus aucta et emendata.* Oxford 1838.

*Dobree, P.P. *Adversaria Critica.* Ed. J. Scholefeld, Cambridge 1831–3.

Dodge, B. *The Fihrist of al-Nadīm: a tenth-century survey of Muslim culture.* New York and London 1970.

*Dosi, Antonietta. 'Sulle trace della Poetica di Teofrasto', *Rendiconti dell'Instituto Lombardo,* Classe di Lettere, Scienze morali e storiche 94 (1960) 599–672.

Dover, K.J. *Aristophanes. Clouds.* Oxford 1968.

— *Aristophanic Comedy.* Berkeley and Los Angeles 1972.

Dübner, F. *Scholia Graeca in Aristophanem.* Paris 1842.

Duckworth, G.E. *The Nature of Roman Comedy.* Princeton 1952.

Düring, I. *Herodicus the Cratetan: a Study in the Anti-Platonic Tradition. Kunglinga Vitterhets Historie och Antikvitets Akademiens Handlingar,* Del. 51–2, Stockholm 1941.

* — *Aristotle in the Ancient Biographical Tradition.* Göteborg 1957.

— 'Ptolemy's *Vita Aristotelis* rediscovered', pp.264–9 in *Philomathes. Studies . . . in Memory of Philip Merlan.* The Hague 1971.

Edelstein, L., and Kidd, I.G. *Posidonius, I: the Fragments.* Cambridge 1972.

*Edmonds, J.M. *The Fragments of Attic Comedy.* Leiden 1957.

Eliot, T.S. *The Sacred Wood. Essays on Poetry and Criticism.*² London 1928.

*Else, G.F. *Aristotle's 'Poetics': the Argument.* Cambridge Mass. 1957.
— *The Origin and early Form of Greek Tragedy.* Martin Classical Lectures 20, Cambridge Mass. 1965.

Erbse, H. 'Beiträge zur Überlieferung der Iliasscholien', *Zetemata* 24 (1960) 17−77.
— *Scholia Graeca in Homeri* Iliadem. Berlin 1969−77.
— Rev. of *KOSTER, *Gnomon* L (1978) 4−9.

Fantuzzi, M. 'συμφωνία nel Tractatus Coislinianus', *LCM* 7 (1982) 24−5.

Feibleman, J.K. *In Praise of Comedy. A Study in its theory and practice.* London 1939.

Foerster, R. *Choricii Gazaei opera.* Leipzig 1929.

*Fortenbaugh, W.W. 'Aristotle's *Rhetoric* on emotions', pp.133−53 in *Articles on Aristotle 4*, ed. J. Barnes et al., q.v.
— *Aristotle on Emotion.* London 1975.
— 'Theophrast über komischen Charakter', *RhM* forthcoming.

Fragstein, A. von. *Die Diaeresis bei Aristoteles.* Amsterdam 1967.

Fraser, P.M. *Ptolemaic Alexandria.* Oxford 1972.

Fuhrmann, M. *Anaximenis Ars Rhetorica, quae vulgo fertur Aristotelis ad Alexandrum.* Leipzig 1966.
* — *Einführung in die antike Dichtungstheorie.* Darmstadt 1973.
— *Aristoteles: Poetik.* Munich 1976.

Gaisford, T. *Poetae minores Graeci.* Oxford 1814−20.

Gallavotti, C. *Aristotele. Poetica.* Milan 1974.

Glibert-Thirry, A. *Pseudo-Andronicus of Rhodes Περὶ Παθῶν.* Leiden 1977.

Glucker, J. 'Notes on the Byzantine treatise on tragedy', *Byzantion* 38 (1968) 267−72.

Goettling, C.G. *Theodosii Alexandrini Grammatica.* Leipzig 1822.

Golden, L. 'Catharsis', *TAPA* 93 (1962) 51−60.
— 'Mimesis and *katharsis*', *CP* 64 (1969) 145−53.
— '*Katharsis* as purification: an objection answered', *CQ* 23 (1973) 45−6.
— 'The purification theory of catharsis', *J. Aesthetics and Art Criticism* 31 (1973) 474−9.
— 'Is *Poetics* 1447b9−23 a digression?', *RhM* 122 (1979) 190−2.

Gomme, A.W. and Sandbach, F.H. *Menander: a Commentary.* Oxford 1973.

Gomperz, T. *Philodem und die aesthetischen Schriften der Herculanensischen Bibliothek. Sitzungsberichte der Wiener Akademie* 123, 1891.

Gosling, J.C.B. 'More Aristotelian Pleasures', *Proceedings of the Aristotelian Society* 74 (1973) 15−34.

Gow, A.S.F. *Theocritus.*[2] Cambridge 1952.

— *Machon. The Fragments.* Cambridge 1965.

Grant, Mary A. *Ancient theories of the Laughable: the Greek Rhetoricians and Cicero.* Univ. of Wisconsin Studies in Language and Literature 21, 1924.

*Grant, W.L. 'Cicero and the Tractatus Coislinianus', *AJP* 69 (1948) 80−6.

Gräser, A. 'Aristoteles' Schrift *Über die Philosophie*, und die zweifache Bedeutung der *causa finalis*', *Mus. Helv.* 29 (1972) 44−61.

Grilli, A. 'Una teoria di Dicearco sull'origine della commedia?', *RFIC* 40 (1962) 22−32.

Grimaldi, W.M.A. *Studies in the philosophy of Aristotle's Rhetoric.* *Hermes* Einzelschr. 25, Wiesbaden 1972.

Grosch, G. *De codice Coisliniano 120.* Jena 1886.

Grube, G.M.A. 'Theophrastus as a literary critic', *TAPA* 83 (1952) 172−83.

— *A Greek Critic: Demetrius on Style.* Toronto 1961. (*Demetrius*)

* — *The Greek and Roman Critics.* London 1965.

*Gudeman, A. *Aristoteles ΠΕΡΙ ΠΟΙΗΤΙΚΗΣ, mit exegetischem Kommentar.* Berlin and Leipzig 1934.

*Guillén, L.F. *Aristoteles y la Comedia media.* Madrid 1977.

Gurewich, M. *Comedy: the irrational Vision.* Ithaca N.Y., 1975.

Guthrie, W.K.C. *History of Greek Philosophy. VI Aristotle: an encounter.* Cambridge 1981. (*HGP*)

Halm, K.F. von. *Rhetores latini minores.* Leipzig 1863.

Hardie, W.F.R. *Aristotle's Ethical Theory.*[2] Oxford 1980.

Harlfinger, D. and Reinsch, D. 'Die Aristotelica des Parisinus Gr. 1741', *Philologus* 114 (1970) 28−50.

Haupt, S. 'Die zwei Bücher des Aristoteles περὶ ποιητικῆς τέχνης', *Philologus* 69 (1910) 252−63.

Hausrath, A. 'Philodemi περὶ ποιημάτων libri secundi quae videntur fragmenta', *Jahrbücher für cl. Philol.* Suppl.-band 17, 1890.

Hayduck, M. *Ioannis Philoponi in Aristotelis 'de Anima' libros Commentaria.* *CAG* XV, Berlin 1897.

*Heitz, E. *Die verlorenen Schriften des Aristoteles.* Leipzig 1865.

Hendrickson, G.L. 'The Peripatetic Mean of Style and the three stylistic characters', *AJP* 25 (1904) 124−46.

— 'The Origins and Meaning of the ancient Characters of Style', *AJP* 26 (1905) 249−70.

Henry, R. *Photius.* Paris 1959−77.

Heylbut, G. *Aspasii in Aristotelis Ethica Nicomachea Commentaria. CAG* XIX, Berlin 1889.

— *Eustratii et Michaelis et Anonyma in Aristotelis Ethica Nicomachea Commentaria. CAG* XX, Berlin 1892.

Hilgard, A. *Scholia in Dionysii Thracis Artem Grammaticam (Grammatici Graeci* III). Leipzig 1901.

*House, H. *Aristotle's Poetics: a course of eight lectures.* London 1956.

Householder, F.W. '*ΠΑΡΩΙΔΙΑ*', *CP* 39 (1944) 1–9.

Hubbard, M.E. See Russell, *ALC.*

Hunter, R. 'The Comic Chorus in the Fourth Century', *ZPE* 36 (1979) 23–38.

Immisch, O. 'Beiträge zur Chrestomathie des Proclus und zur Poetik des Altertums', 237–74 in *Festschrift T. Gomperz.* Vienna 1902.

Janko, R. 'The structure of the Homeric Hymns: a study in genre', *Hermes* 109 (1981) 9–24.

— 'A Fragment of Aristotle's *Poetics* from Porphyry, on synonymy', *CQ* 32 (1982) 323–6.

— '*αὐτὸς ἐκεῖνος*: a neglected idiom.' *CQ* 34 (1984).

Jensen, C. *Philodemus. Über die Gedichte fünftes Buch.* Berlin 1923.

Kaibel, G. 'Die Prolegomena *ΠΕΡΙ ΚΩΜΩΙΔΙΑΣ*', *Abh. der königlichen Gesellschaft der Wissenschaften zu Göttingen,* Phil.-Hist. Kl. N.F. II, no.4, Berlin 1898. (*Abh.*)

* — *Comicorum Graecorum Fragmenta I.* Berlin 1899. (*CGF*)

Kalbfleisch, K. *Simplicii in Aristotelis Categorias Commentarium. CAG* VIII, Berlin 1907.

*Kassel, R. *Aristotelis de Arte Poetica.*[2] Oxford 1966.

— *Der Text der aristotelischen Rhetorik. Prolegomena zu einer kritischen Ausgabe. Peripatoi* 3, Berlin 1971.

— 'Kritische und exegetische Kleinigkeiten', *RhM* 116 (1973) 97–112.

— *Aristotelis Ars Rhetorica.* Berlin 1976.

— *Dichtkunst und Versifikation bei den Griechen. Rheinisch-West-fälische Akademie der Wissenschaften,* Vorträge G250, Opladen 1980.

Katsouris, A.G. *Tragic Patterns in Menander.* Athens 1975.

*Kayser, J. *De veterum arte poetica quaestiones selectae.* Diss. Leipzig 1906.

Keesey, D. 'On some recent interpretations of catharsis', *CW* LXXII (1978–9) 193–205.

Keil, H. *Grammatici Latini I–VII.* Leipzig 1857–80.

Kennedy, G. *The Art of Persuasion in Greece.* London and Princeton 1963.

Kenny, A.J. *The Aristotelian Ethics.* Oxford 1978.

*Kock, T. *Comicorum Atticorum Fragmenta.* Leipzig 1880−8.

Köpke, E. *De Chamaeleontis Heracleotae vita librorumque reliquiis.* Berlin 1856.

Körte, A. 'Komödie', P−W *RE* XI (1921) 1207−75.

— 'Lynkeus (6)', P−W *RE* XIII (1926) 2472−3.

Koster, W.J.W. 'Ad novam editionem Aristophanis et Prolegomenorum de Comoedia', *Mnemosyne* VIII (1955) 19−24.

— 'Pseudo-Andronicus de variis poetarum generibus', *Mnemosyne* IX (1956) 319.

— *Autour d'un Manuscrit d'Aristophane écrit par Démétrius Triclinius.* Groningen and Jakarta 1957.

— *Scholia in Aristophanem.* Groningen 1960−.

* — *Scholia in Aristophanem. Pars I Fasc. IA. Prolegomena de Comoedia.* Groningen 1975.

— and D. Holwerda. 'De Eustathio, Tzetza, Moschopulo, Planude Aristophanis commentatoribus', *Mnemosyne* VIII (1955) 196−206.

Kroll, W. *Procli Diadochi in Platonis Rempublicam Commentarii.* Leipzig 1899−1901.

*Kühner, R., and Gerth, B. *Ausführliche Grammatik der griechischen Sprache.* Leipzig 1890−8.

Landfester, M. *Handlungsführung und Komik in den frühen Komödien des Aristophanes.* Berlin and New York 1977.

Landi, C. 'La chiusa della Poetica di Aristotele nel codice Riccardiano 46', *Riv. di Filol. e di Instr. classica* 3 (1925) 551−6.

Latte, K. 'Zur Zeitbestimmung der Antiatticista', *Hermes* 50 (1915) 373−94.

— *Kleine Schriften.* Munich 1968.

*Leeuwen, J. van. *Prolegomena ad Aristophanem.* Leiden 1908.

Lemerle, P. *Le premier Humanisme byzantin.* Paris 1971.

Lentz, A. *Herodiani Technici Reliquiae.* Leipzig 1867−70.

Lenz, L.H. 'Komik und Kritik in Aristophanes' "Wespen"', *Hermes* 108 (1980) 15−44.

Lesky, A. *Geschichte des griechischen Literatur.*[2] Bern 1963. Transl. C. de Heer and H. Willis, London 1966.

*Liddell, H.G., Scott, R. and Jones, H.S. *A Greek-English Lexicon.* With a supplement, Oxford 1968. (LSJ)

Lobel, E. 'A Crux in the Poetics', *CQ* 23 (1929) 76−9.

Lord, C. 'Tragedy without character: Poetics 6, 1450a24', *J. Aesthetics and Art Criticism* 28 (1969−70) 55−62.

Lossau, M. *Untersuchungen zur antiken Demosthenesexegese. Palingenesia* II, Bad Homburg 1964.

*Lucas, D.W. *The Poetics of Aristotle.* Oxford 1968.

Lucas, F.L. *Tragedy: Serious Drama in relation to Aristotle's Poetics.*[2] London 1967.

McCall, M.H. (Jr.). *Ancient Rhetorical Theories of Simile and Comparison.* Cambridge Mass. 1969.

McKeon, R. *Introduction to Aristotle.*[2] Chicago 1973.

McLeish, K. *The Theatre of Aristophanes.* London 1980.

*McMahon, A.P. 'On the Second Book of Aristotle's *Poetics* and the source of Theophrastus' Definition of Tragedy', *HSCP* 28 (1917) 1−46.

— 'Seven questions on Aristotelian Definitions of Tragedy and Comedy', *HSCP* 40 (1929) 97−198.

Maidment, K.J. 'The later comic chorus', *CQ* 29 (1935) 1-24.

Mau, J., Mutschmann, H. and Janáček, K. *Sexti Empirici Opera.* Leipzig 1958−62.

Mayer, A. *Theophrasti ΠΕΡΙ ΛΕΞΕΩΣ Fragmenta.* Leipzig 1910.

*Meineke, A. *Fragmenta Comicorum Graecorum.* Berlin 1839−57. (*FCG*)

Meiser, C. *Boetii commentarii in librum Aristotelis ΠΕΡΙ ΕΡΜΗΝΕΙΑΣ.* Leipzig 1877−80.

Mette, H.J. *Parateresis. Untersuchungen zur Sprachtheorie des Krates von Pergamon.* Halle 1952.

Minio-Paluello, L. *Aristoteles Latinus XXXIII. De Arte Poetica: translatio Guillelmi de Moerbeka.*[1] Bruges and Paris 1953. Second edition, Brussels and Paris 1968.

Mittelhaus, K. *De Plutarchi praeceptis gerendae reipublicae.* Berlin 1911.

Moles, J. 'Notes on Aristotle, *Poetics* 13 and 14', *CQ* 29 (1979) 77−94.

*Montmollin, D. de. *La Poétique d'Aristote.* Neuchâtel 1951.

Moraux, P. *Les Listes anciennes des ouvrages d'Aristote.* Louvain 1951.

— *Der Aristotelismus bei den Griechen, von Andronikos bis Alexander von Aphrodisias.* Peripatoi 5, Berlin 1973.

— 'La Critique d'authenticité chez les commentateurs grecs d'Aristote', 265−88 in *Mélanges Mansel* I, Ankara 1974.

Müller, B.A. *De Asclepiade Myrleano.* Leipzig 1903.

Müller, C.W. 'Die neuplatonischen Aristoteleskommentatoren über die Ursachen der Pseudepigraphie', *RhM* 112 (1969) 120−6.

Nardelli, M.L. 'La Catarsi poetica nel P. Herc. 1581', *Cronache Ercolanese* 8 (1978) 96−103.

Nauck, A. *Iamblichus. Vita Pythagorica.* Leipzig 1884.

— *Porphyrii Opuscula.* Leipzig 1886.

Neobarius, C. *Εἰς τὴν Ἀριστοτέλους ῥητορικὴν ὑπόμνημα ἀνώνυμον. Nunc primum in lucem editur.* Paris 1539.

Newiger, H.-J. (ed.) *Aristophanes und die alte Komödie*. Darmstadt 1975.
— Rev. of *KOSTER, *Byzantinischer Zeitschrift* 72 (1979) 334 — 46.
Ničev, A. *L'Énigme de la catharsis tragique chez Aristote*. Sofia 1970.
— 'Olympiodore et la catharsis tragique d'Aristote', 641 — 59 ap. *Studi in onore di A. Ardizzoni*, Rome 1978.
Nickau, K. 'Epeisodion und Episode', *Mus. Helv.* 23 (1966) 155 — 71.
Norden, E. *Die antike Kunstprosa*. Leipzig 1898, repr. Stuttgart 1958.
Öllacher, H. 'Griechische literarische Papyri aus der Papyrussammlung Erzherzog Rainer in Wien', *Études de Papyrologie* IV, Cairo 1937.
Owen, G.E.L. 'Aristotelian Pleasures', *Proceedings of the Aristotelian Society* 72 (1971 — 2) 135 — 52.
Pack, R.A. 'Errors as subjects of comic mirth', *CP* 33 (1938) 405 — 10.
Page, D.L. *Aeschyli septem quae supersunt Tragoediae*. Oxford 1972.
— *Literary Papyri: Poetry (Select Papyri* vol. 3). Cambridge Mass. and London 1941.
— *Poetae Melici Graeci*. Oxford 1962. (*PMG*)
Pauly, A. and Wissowa, G. (edd.). *Real-Encyclopädie der classischen Altertumswissenschaft*. Stuttgart 1894 — . (P — W, *RE*)
Pertusi, A. *Scholia vetera in Hesiodi Opera et Dies*. Milan 1955.
Peters, F.E. *Aristoteles Arabus*. Leiden 1968.
Pfeiffer, R. *Callimachus*. Oxford 1949 — 53.
— *History of Classical Scholarship: from the beginnings to the Hellenistic Age*. Oxford 1968.
Pickard-Cambridge, A.W. *Dithyramb, Tragedy and Comedy*. Oxford 1927. Revised ed. by Webster, T.B.L., Oxford 1962.
*Plebe, A. *La teoria del comico da Aristotele a Plutarco*. Turin 1952.
Plezia, M. 'De Ptolemaeo pinacographo', *Eos* 58 (1975) 37 — 41.
Prescott, H.W. 'The Comedy of Errors', *CP* 24 (1929) 32 — 41.
Quandt, K. 'Some Puns in Aristotle', *TAPA* 111 (1981) 179 — 96.
Rabe, H. *Anonymi et Stephani in Aristotelis Artem Rhetoricam Commentaria. CAG* XXI 2, Berlin 1896.
— *Prolegomenon Sylloge (Rhetores Graeci* 14). Leipzig 1931.
Radermacher, L. and Usener, H. *Dionysii Halicarnasei Opuscula*. Leipzig 1899 — 1904.
Rau, P. *Paratragodia. Untersuchungen zu einer komischen Form des Aristophanes*. Munich 1967.
Reale, G. *Aristotele: Trattato sul Cosmo per Alessandro*. Naples 1974.
Redfield, J.M. *Nature and Culture in the Iliad*. Chicago 1975.

Regenbogen, O. 'Theophrastos', P—W *RE* Suppl. VII (1939) 1354—1562.

Reich, H. *Der Mimus.* Berlin 1903. Repr. Hildesheim 1974.

Reynolds, L.D. and Wilson, N.G. *Scribes and Scholars.* Oxford 1968.

Richardson, N.J. 'Literary criticism in the exegetical scholia to the *Iliad*', *CQ* 30 (1980) 265—87.

Riginos, Alice Swift. *Platonica: the Anecdotes concerning the Life and Writings of Plato. Columbia Studies in the Classical Tradition* 3, Leiden 1976.

Rispoli, G.M. 'Filodemo sulla musica', *Cronache Ercolanese* 4 (1974) 57—87.

*Roberts, W. Rhys. *Demetrius on Style.* Cambridge 1902.

— *Longinus on the Sublime.*[2] Cambridge 1907.

Rose, V. *De Aristotelis librorum ordine et auctoritate commentio.* Berlin 1854.

* — *Aristoteles Pseudepigraphus.*[3] Leipzig 1863.

— *Aristotelis qui ferebantur librorum fragmenta.* Leipzig 1886.

Rosenthal, F. 'From Arabic Books and MSS: V', *J. American Oriental Society* 75 (1955) 14—23.

— *Humor in Early Islam.* Leiden 1956.

Ross, W.D. *Aristotelis Fragmenta Selecta.* Oxford 1955.

— *Aristotelis Ars Rhetorica.* Oxford 1959.

— with Smith, J.A. *Aristoteles. Works.* Oxford 1908—52.

*Rostagni, A. 'Aristotele ed aristotelismo nella estetica antica', *Studi it. di Filol. cl.* N.S. II (1922) 1—147.

— 'Il dialogo aristotelico ΠΕΡΙ ΠΟΙΗΤΩΝ', *Riv. di Filol. e di Instr. classica* LIV (1926) 433—70, LV (1927) 145—73.

— *Orazio. Arte Poetica.* Turin 1930.

— *Aristotele. La Poetica: introduzione, testo e commento.* Turin 1934.

— *Scritti minori.* Turin 1955—6.

Russell, D.A. *Longinus. On the Sublime.* Oxford 1964.

* — *Criticism in Antiquity.* London 1981.

— with Winterbottom, M. (edd.). *Ancient Literary Criticism. The principal texts in new translations.* Oxford 1972. (*ALC*)

*Rutherford, W.G. *A Chapter in the History of Annotation, being Scholia Aristophanica vol. III.* London 1905.

Saïd, Suzanne. *La Faute tragique.* Paris 1978.

*Salingar, L. *Shakespeare and the Traditions of Comedy.* Cambridge 1974.

Sandys, J.E. *Aristotle's Constitution of Athens.*[2] London 1912. Repr. New York 1971.

Schenkeveld, D.M. *Studies in Demetrius 'On Style'.* Amsterdam 1964.

Schofield, M. 'Aristotle on the Imagination', pp.103 – 32 in *Articles on Aristotle 4*, ed. J. Barnes et al., q.v.

Schütrumpf, E. *Die Bedeutung des Wortes ēthos in der Poetik des Aristoteles. Zetemata* 40, Munich 1970.

Schwartz, E. *Scholia in Euripidem.* Berlin 1887 – 91.

Severyns, A. *Recherches sur la Chrestomathie de Proclos.* Paris 1938 – 63.

Sheppard, Anne D.R. *Studies on the 5th. and 6th. Essays of Proclus' Commentary on the Republic. Hypomnemata* 61, Göttingen 1980.

Sifakis, G.M. 'Aristotle *EN*4.2.1123a19 – 24 and the Comic Chorus in the Fourth Century', *AJP* 92 (1971) 410 – 32.

— *Parabasis and Animal Choruses.* London 1971.

Silk, M.S. *Interaction in Poetic Imagery.* Cambridge 1974.

*Smith, K.K. 'Aristotle's "Lost Chapter on Comedy"', *Classical Weekly* 21 (1928) 145 – 61.

Snell, B. (ed.). *Griechische Papyri der Hamburger Staats- und Universitäts-Bibliothek.* Hamburg 1954.

Solmsen, F. *Die Entwicklung der aristotelischen Logik und Rhetorik. Neue philologische Untersuchungen* 4, Berlin 1929.

— 'The Origins and Methods of Aristotle's *Poetics*', *CQ* 29 (1935) 192 – 201.

Sorabji, R. *Necessity, Cause and Blame.* London 1980.

*Spengel, L. *Rhetores Graeci.* Leipzig 1853 – 6.

Stabryła, S. 'Problemy teorii genologicznej Diomedesa', *Meander* 31 (1976) 445 – 61.

Stanford, W.B. *Enemies of Poetry.* London 1980.

Starkie, W.J.M. *Aristophanes' 'Acharnians'.* London 1909.

— 'An Aristotelian analysis of "the Comic"', *Hermathena* 42 (1920) 26 – 51.

Stefani, A. de. *Etymologicum Gudianum.* Leipzig 1909 – 20.

Steinschneider, M. *Die arabischen Übersetzungen aus dem Griechischen. Centralblatt für Bibliothekwesen*, Beiheft 12, Leipzig 1893. Repr. Graz 1960.

*Stephanus, H. *Thesaurus Graecae Linguae.* Paris 1831 – 65.

Stinton, T.C.W. '*Hamartia* in Aristotle and Greek tragedy', *CQ* 25 (1975) 221 – 54.

Strecker, C. *De Lycophrone, Euphronio, Eratosthene comicorum interpretibus.* Diss. Greifswald 1884.

Sudhaus, S. *Philodemi Volumina Rhetorica.* Leipzig 1892 – 6.

Süss, W. 'Zur Komposition der altattischen Komödie', *RhM* 63 (1908) 12 – 38.

Swabey, M.C. *Comic Laughter: a Philosophical Survey.* New Haven 1961.

Syme, R. 'Fraud and Imposture', 3—17 in *Pseudepigrapha I, Entretiens sur l'Antiquité classique* XVIII, Fondation Hardt 1971.

Taillardat, J. *Les Images d'Aristophane. Études de langue et de style.* Paris 1962.

Taplin, O. '*XOPOY* and the structure of post-classical tragedy', *LCM* 1 (1976) 47—50.

* — *The Stagecraft of Aeschylus.* Oxford 1977.

— *Greek Tragedy in Action.* London 1978.

Tarán, L. *Anonymous Commentary on Aristotle's 'de Interpretatione'. Beitr. zur kl. Philol.* 95, Meisenheim am Glan 1978.

— 'Speusippus and Aristotle on Homonymy and Synonymy', *Hermes* 106 (1978) 73—99.

* — *Speusippus of Athens. Philosophia Antiqua* XXXIX, Leiden 1981.

Thilo, G. and Hagen, H. *Servii grammatici qui feruntur in Vergilii carmina commentaria.* Leipzig 1878—1902.

Threatte, L. *The Grammar of Attic Inscriptions. I Phonology.* Berlin 1980.

*Tierney, M. 'Aristotle and Menander', *Proceedings of the Royal Irish Academy* XLIII (1936) 24—54.

*Tkatsch, J. *Die arabische Übersetzungen der Poetik des Aristoteles und die Grundlage der Kritik des griechischen Textes.* Vienna 1928—32.

Treadgold, W.T. *The Nature of the* Bibliotheca *of Photius.* Dumbarton Oaks, Washington D.C. 1980.

Trendelenburg, A. *Grammaticorum graecorum de arte tragica iudiciorum reliquiae.* Diss. Bonn 1867.

Usener, H. *Kleine Schriften.* Leipzig and Berlin 1912—3.

Ussher, R.G. 'Old Comedy and "Character", some comments', *Greece and Rome* 24 (1977) 70—9.

— *Aristophanes. Greece and Rome, New Surveys in the Classics* 13, Oxford 1979.

Vahlen, J. 'Zu Aristoteles' Poetik', *RhM* 28 (1873) 183—5.

— *Aristoteles. De Arte Poetica liber.*[3] Leipzig 1885.

— *Opuscula Academica* I—II. Leipzig 1907—8.

— *Gesammelte philologische Schriften* I. Leipzig and Berlin 1911.

— *Beiträge zu Aristoteles' Poetik.* Leipzig 1914. Repr. Hildesheim 1965.

Valk, M. van der. *Eustathii Archiepiscopi Thessalonicensis Commentarii ad Homeri Iliadem pertinentes.* Leiden 1971—.

Verdenius, W.J. *Mimesis.* Leiden 1962.

Vicaire, P. *Platon, critique littéraire. Études et commentaires* 34, Paris 1960.
— *Recherches sur les mots désignant la poésie et le poète dans l'œuvre de Platon. Publ. de la Fac. des Lettres et Sciences humaines de l'Univ. de Montpellier* 22, Paris 1964.
Vickers, B. *Towards Greek Tragedy.* London 1973.
Vitelli, G. 'Spicilegio Fiorentino', *Mus. ital. di ant. class.* I (1885) 2—12.
Waldock, A.J.A. *Sophocles the Dramatist.* Cambridge 1951.
Wallies, M. *Ammonii in Aristotelis Analyticorum Priorum librum I Commentarius. CAG* IV 6, Berlin 1899.
— *Ioannis Philoponi in Aristotelis Analytica Priora Commentaria. CAG* XIII 2, Berlin 1905.
Wallis, J. *Claudii Ptolemaei Harmonicorum libri tres.* Oxford 1682.
Wallis, R.T. *Neoplatonism.* London 1972.
Walzer, R. 'Zur Traditionsgeschichte der aristotelischen Poetik', *Studi ital. di Filol. cl.* 11 (1934) 5—14.
— *Greek into Arabic: Essays on Islamic Philosophy.* Oxford 1962.
Webster, T.B.L. *Studies in later Greek Comedy.*[2] Manchester 1970.
Wehrli, F. *Motivstudien zur griechischen Komödie.* Zürich 1936.
* — *Die Schule des Aristoteles.*[2] Basel 1967—9.
*Wendel, C. *Scholia in Theocritum vetera.* Leipzig 1914.
— *Überlieferung und Entstehung der Theokrit-Scholien.* Berlin 1920.
— 'Tzetzes', P—W *RE* Suppl. VIIA (1948) 1959—2010.
Wendling, E. 'Chamaileon', P—W *RE* III (1899) 2103.
Wessner, P. *Aeli Donati quod fertur commentum Terenti.* Leipzig 1902.
West, M.L. 'Tryphon "de tropis II"', *CQ* 15 (1965) 230—48.
Westerink, L.G. *Olympiodorus: commentary on the first Alcibiades of Plato.* Amsterdam 1956.
— 'Elias on the *Prior Analytics*', *Mnemosyne* 14 (1961) 126—39.
— *Plato: Anonymous Prolegomena to Platonic Philosophy.* Amsterdam 1962.
— 'Quotations from Attic Comedy in Olympiodorus', *Mnemosyne* 9 (1966) 175—6.
— *Olympiodorus: commentary on the Gorgias of Plato.* Leiden 1970.
— *The Greek Commentaries on Plato's 'Phaedo'. I: Olympiodorus.* Amsterdam 1976.
— *Texts and Studies in Neoplatonism and Byzantine Literature: collected papers.* Amsterdam 1980.
Westphal, R. *Scriptores metrici graeci. I: Hephaestionis De metris Enchiridion et De poemate libellus, cum scholiis.* Leipzig 1866.
Whitman, C.H. *Aristophanes and the Comic Hero.* Cambridge Mass. 1964. (*ACH*)

Wilamowitz-Möllendorff, U. von. *Aeschyli Tragoediae*. Berlin 1914.

Wilkinson, L.P. 'Philodemus and Poetry', *Greece and Rome* 2 (1932 — 3) 144 — 51.

Wilson, N.G. 'A Chapter in the History of Scholia', *CQ* 17 (1967) 244 — 56.

— 'Two Notes on Byzantine Scholarship: I The Vienna Dioscorides and the History of Scholia', *GRBS* 12 (1971) 557 — 8.

— Review of ZUNTZ, *CR* 27 (1977) 271.

— *Scholars of Byzantium*. London 1983.

— and Reynolds, L.D.: see REYNOLDS.

*Wimmer, F. *Theophrasti Eresii Opera quae supersunt omnia. III: Fragmenta*. Leipzig 1862.

Wouters, A. *The Grammatical Papyri of Greco-Roman Egypt*. Brussels 1979.

Ziegler, K. 'Tragödie', P — W *RE* Suppl. VI (1937) 1899 — 2075.

Zieliński, T. *Die Gliederung der altattischen Komödie*. Leipzig 1885.

Zimmermann, F.W. *Al-Farabi's commentary and short treatise on Aristotle's De Interpretatione*. London 1981.

Zuntz, G. *Die Aristophanes-Scholien der Papyri*. Berlin 1975.

Index of Passages cited

An asterisk prefixed to the entry indicates that textual problems are discussed or the meaning of the passage substantially reinterpreted. Inverted commas around an author's name indicate that the ascription is doubtful, square brackets that it is false. Obeli indicate a corrupt title.

Index of Greek

This index contains (a) all main words in the text of the Treatise: these are followed by a reference in brackets to the section and sub-section of the text, in Roman numerals; (b) other Aristotelian, grammatical, literary-critical and rhetorical terms: these are preceded by an asterisk. The numbers refer to pages. Words found in the text of the Treatise and discussed in the commentary on the relevant passage have the reference to the Treatise in bold type.

General Index

I have taken the opportunity to indicate the meanings of less familiar ancient grammatical, rhetorical and literary-critical terms.